TEACHING THE BIBLE

SBL

Society of Biblical Literature

Resources for Biblical Study

Susan Ackerman,
Hebrew Bible/Old Testament Editor

J. Ross Wagner,
New Testament Editor

Number 49

TEACHING THE BIBLE
Practical Strategies for Classroom Instruction

TEACHING THE BIBLE

Practical Strategies for Classroom Instruction

Edited by

Mark Roncace and Patrick Gray

Society of Biblical Literature
Atlanta

TEACHING THE BIBLE

Library of Congress Cataloging-in-Publication Data

Teaching the Bible : practical strategies for classroom instruction / edited by Mark Roncace and Patrick Gray.
    p. cm. — (Resources for biblical study ; no. 49)
    Includes index.
  ISBN-13: 978-1-58983-171-1 (paper binding : alk. paper)
    1. Bible. O.T.—Study and teaching. 2. Bible. N.T.—Study and teaching. I. Gray, Patrick, 1970– II. Roncace, Mark. III. Series.
  BS1193.T43 2005
  220'.071—dc22   2005010892

Contents

WRITINGS

PART 3: NEW TESTAMENT

THE GOSPELS AND ACTS

INDICES

Introduction

What one learns, it is no secret, depends in no small part upon where one learns it. This principle applies at many different levels—geographic, cultural, political, and institutional. Location, as they say, is everything. Or almost everything. The focus of this volume is upon one particular location: the classroom. To be sure, the classroom is not the only locus for learning, nor is it always the most conducive. Most of the teacher and student preparation for a successful educational event, moreover, takes place outside the classroom. The traditional classroom setting nevertheless retains a tremendous capacity for enhancing or impeding student progress and enthusiasm in practically every field of study, and not simply by virtue of its ubiquity. Notwithstanding the promises (or threats?) made by proponents of "distance learning" and other alternatives, the classroom—whether it is in a college, seminary, church, or synagogue—is here to stay for the foreseeable future.

The purpose of this volume is to make available to those who teach biblical studies a wide range of effective classroom strategies for approaching specific topics in the field. Books on pedagogy have proliferated dramatically in recent years. These books fall, more or less, into one of two categories: those that focus on theory and those that focus on practice. Excellent teaching clearly requires a sound pedagogical philosophy. One resource that deserves special mention in this regard—and not simply because it happens to have the same title as the present volume—is Fernando F. Segovia and Mary Ann Tolbert, eds., *Teaching the Bible: The Discourses and Politics of Biblical Pedagogy* (Maryknoll, N.Y.: Orbis, 1998). This excellent collection of essays addresses a variety of postmodernist and postcolonial pedagogies in the teaching of the Bible.

Sooner or later, however, theory must take the form of concrete practices or else it becomes like the proverbial tree falling in the forest—it effectively makes not a sound because no one is there to hear it. In this regard we highly recommend the resources made available by the Wabash Center for Teaching and Learning in Theology and Religion (http://www.wabashcenter.wabash.edu). Although it does not deal exclusively with biblical studies, the Wabash Center website contains a wealth of information, including a guide to Internet resources and a list of recommended books on pedagogy. The Wabash Center's quarterly journal (*Teaching Theology and Religion*), especially its "Notes from the Classroom" section, features discussion of specific teaching strategies together with theoretical reflection of the first order. Strategies for teaching biblical studies are indeed plentiful but they are scattered among numerous books, journal articles, websites, and religion departments. This compilation brings together the collective pedagogical wisdom of dozens of innovative teachers from around the world, and we are grateful to them for sharing their "secrets" with the rest of us.

Nearly every work on pedagogy places a high premium on active learning. The transfer model of education—the notion that the teacher is the "sage on the stage" who possesses all wisdom which is transferred, mainly by lecture, into the knowledge base of the students—is going largely by the wayside. In this model, students passively take notes as the teacher tells them the information that they need to know; students then reproduce a body of knowledge on exams. By default, this is how many teachers begin their careers, in part because most graduate programs in biblical studies make little or no place for sustained reflection on pedagogical issues. For someone with an advanced degree, learning to lecture is relatively easy. But research consistently shows that even the best lecturers have a limited capacity to engage the attention of students, to improve retention of material, and to cultivate critical thinking skills. To facilitate student progress, the "sage on the stage" must, at least on occasion, act as the "guide on the side," empowering students as junior partners in a collaborative educational enterprise.

Once one is armed with effective teaching techniques, there remains the task of implementing them in specific biblical studies courses. "How do I adapt generic learning activities to fit the content I teach?" asks Maryellen Weimer (*Learner-Centered Teaching: Five Key Changes to Practice* [San Francisco: Jossey-Bass, 2002)], 70). This is easier said than done. Weimer believes that

> [W]e greatly underestimate the complexity of the process involved in taking a generic active learning strategy and adapting it so that it fits the content, learning needs of students, instructor style, and instructional setting in which it will be used. The process is rarely addressed in active learning material or workshops. The focus there is on building a collection of techniques, an important objective, but real teaching skill shows itself in the management of that technique repertoire.

Simply knowing where to start is difficult for many teachers. We hope that this collection of strategies will be of assistance in adapting generic strategies to fit the specific content of courses on the Bible.

We have turned to our colleagues to gather creative ideas for enabling students to acquire new information, practice new skills, and reorganize or build upon what they already know. For all of the collegiality in our field, in our classrooms we remain isolated. We walk in and—perhaps in the name of academic freedom—close the door behind us; classrooms are sacred spaces that no one else invades. Except for the occasional obligatory peer review, we rarely see how other teachers conduct their classes. There is no foolproof method for becoming a stimulating instructor, nor is there any rigid formula for identifying effective classroom practices. But at most institutions a consensus emerges as to which teachers engage their students and which ones do not. We may not be able to define "good teaching," but we know it when we see it. No other resource (to our knowledge) makes available such a wide range of strategies for approaching specific subjects in the field of biblical studies.

The present volume is an eclectic compendium. Each "entry" assumes a critical, academic approach to the Bible, but entries come from a variety of methodological, theological, and ideological perspectives. They vary in length and in sophistication. Some entries are best suited for an introductory class, others perhaps for an upper-level university or seminary course. Many entries draw on resources already available on the Internet by telling readers where they can find the relevant information and materials to use in presentations. The entries, however, do not presume a high level of technological expertise or high-tech classrooms. While most entries outline specific activities or assignments for a single class session, a few provide a more general introduction to a certain set of practices or approaches for those who may not have special expertise or previous exposure (e.g, the incorporation of archaeology, "the Bible and Film" courses, and the like).

Some of the entries spell out a classroom activity in more detail than others—that is, some entries explicitly utilize active learning techniques while other entries may outline a particularly creative way to present a text or topic. Those who prefer lecture or some other teacher-oriented format can easily take the active learning entries and incorporate them into their presentations, and those who prefer a student-oriented format can quite easily transform an entry detailing an innovative presentation into an activity or exercise. Many of the entries feature good discussion questions, which are the key to framing productive active learning exercises. Readers can decide the format—small-group work, plenary discussions, test questions, paper prompts—in which those questions are best employed in their particular educational context.

In a volume this diverse it is only natural that readers will likely find something objectionable. Indeed, some may disagree sharply with the historical, ethical, or theological content of one piece or take issue with the execution of another. As much as possible we have tried to avoid discriminating on the basis of theological or scholarly content, at least where respectable scholars can legitimately disagree on a given question. Had we approached the project with too many filters in place—for example, inclined to favor only those strategies that take a strictly historical approach or those attending to the social location of the interpreter—we would have prematurely excluded valuable resources or foreclosed certain worthwhile discussions.

Accordingly, we have striven not necessarily to present a collection of strategies that any and all teachers would, or even could, employ in the classroom. (The vast majority, however, do fall into this category.) Rather, we aimed at presenting "reports from the front," so to speak, without attempting to be exhaustive. Sometimes good teaching takes risks or meets resistance. Part of the value of this collection, we believe, is that it will generate conversation, even—or perhaps especially—when one takes issue with the content or the manner of presentation. The contributors' ideas, to be sure, have stimulated our own thinking. In fact, we have already successfully implemented a number of their strategies into our own classrooms. Furthermore, we have occasionally put different contributors into contact so that they might learn from one another as well. In this and in other ways, we have conceived of this volume from the outset as a collaborative enterprise.

Each entry, therefore, represents a highly compressed form of practical scholarship. While the entries do not directly respond to one another, they do create a dialogue of sorts as there are multiple entries on similar texts or topics. This volume has been written by the guild of biblical scholars for the guild. The 273 entries have been written by 93 different professors who have taught in a wide range of educational contexts—small colleges, major state universities, and seminaries.

Although our objective was not to reflect the status quo or to present a perfectly representative sample of academic biblical studies instruction, we suspect that this collection provides something like a snapshot of the discipline in this first decade of the twenty-first century from a number of different angles. For example, the collection of entries is uneven; some biblical texts have many more entries than others. Apparently, Numbers, Obadiah, and 2 Peter appear less frequently on course syllabi than Genesis, Job, and 1 Corinthians, hence teachers have many more creative ideas regarding the latter than the former. Likewise, there are more entries devoted to Gen 22 (four) than to the entire book of Isaiah (three). Perhaps this reflects a natural proclivity toward narrative, or toward theologically challenging texts, or toward texts with numerous intertexts—artistic renderings, for example. Or maybe it reveals a deep interest in the character of "father Abraham," or a debt to Kierkegaard, or a Christian fascination with child-sacrifice as somehow salvific. But whatever the reason in this specific instance, the general unevenness of the entries indicates where we spend our teaching energies, which, of course, says a great deal about the current state of the biblical studies classroom.

What else did we discover about our field in the process of soliciting material from colleagues who teach at several dozen different institutions? Among other things, the collection of entries shows that the rising generation of teacher-scholars is more likely than previous generations to draw on popular culture in formulating effective teaching strategies. In addition, a small but growing number of teachers are beginning to engage the interpretive traditions of Islam as a way of bringing together the three Abrahamic faiths in constructive conversation. Last of all, despite the inroads made by Jewish scholars and scholarship, it remains far more common to find teachers referring to Christian exegetical traditions as a resource for understanding the biblical text. Some of these trends are due in part to demographic realities or curricular constraints (e.g., Jewish scholars comprise a minority of the professorate; the academic calendar does not allow sufficient class time for equal or adequate coverage of all parts of the Bible; etc.). Some are perhaps the legacy of a jaded past while others may hold out great promise for the future. By highlighting these trends, our hope is that this compilation will serve as a valuable resource for further reflection and collaboration on these and other pedagogical issues relating to the teaching of the Bible.

Finally, a few thoughts on how to use the book. The entries are divided into three sections. Part One contains a number of strategies for introducing general skills and concepts in biblical studies courses. Parts Two and Three are devoted to the Hebrew Bible/Old Testament and the New Testament. The organization of the entries in these sections roughly follows the canonical order of the Hebrew Bible and the New Testament. (Note: For the Hebrew Bible, the order of texts corresponds to that found in Bibles printed in Hebrew, not to the order of the NRSV or other editions which follow the order of the Protestant or Catholic Old Testament.) The layout of the volume makes it easy to consult all the entries on a given text or topic. One may choose to read through large sections at one time as preparation for a course or unit on a specific subject or section of the canon. The volume may also serve primarily as a reference tool, a resource to which one turns daily in preparing for class. Cross references at the end of several entries direct the reader to other entries that treat similar topics or pursue similar strategies, when such links are not already evident from the arrangement of each sub-section. (Note: Entries by the same author are not cross-referenced, as each author's entries are located on the list of contributors.) An index of biblical references is also included, as well as indices devoted to music, art, film, and literature, for those who wish to incorporate certain kinds of materials into their lesson plans. All abbreviations of ancient and modern sources conform to the lists in *The SBL Handbook of Style* (ed. P. H. Alexander et al.; Peabody, Mass. : Hendrickson, 1999).

List of Contributors

David Barnhart (206)—Fairview United Methodist Church, Centre, Alabama

Michael Barram (26, 61, 64, 117, 189, 190)—Saint Mary's College of California, Moraga, California

Roland Boer (97)—Centre for Studies in Religion and Theology, Monash University, Australia

Karla G. Bohmbach (65, 156, 161, 214)—Susquehanna University, Selinsgrove, Pennsylvania

Ryan Byrne (77)—Rhodes College, Memphis, Tennessee

John Byron (218, 231, 264)—Ashland Theological Seminary, Ashland, Ohio

William Sanger Campbell (209, 265)—The College of St. Scholastica, Duluth, Minnesota

Greg Carey (170, 195, 216, 232)—Lancaster Theological Seminary, Lancaster, Pennsylvania

J. Bradley Chance (74, 153)—William Jewell College, Liberty, Missouri

Emily R. Cheney (48, 171, 176, 178, 225, 241, 247)—Athens, Georgia

L. Juliana M. Claassens (114, 153)—Baptist Theological Seminary at Richmond, Richmond, Virginia; University of Stellenbosch, South Africa

Ron Clark (108, 256)—Cascade College, Portland, Oregon

Jaime Clark-Soles (4, 12, 31, 167, 183, 188)—Perkins School of Theology, Southern Methodist University, Dallas, Texas

L. Stephanie Cobb (247, 272)—Hofstra University, Hempstead, New York

Michael R. Cosby (42, 76, 96, 121, 137, 145)—Messiah College, Grantham, Pennsylvania

Amy C. Cottrill (146)—Emory University, Atlanta, Georgia

Kenneth L. Cukrowski (196, 219, 236, 238, 239, 240)—Abilene Christian University, Abilene, Texas

Nicola Denzey (16, 27, 28, 197, 261)—Bowdoin College, Brunswick, Maine

David A. deSilva (250)—Ashland Theological Seminary, Ashland, Ohio

Ira Brent Driggers (36, 203)—Pfeiffer University, Misenheimer, North Carolina

C. D. Elledge (181)—Gustavus Adolphus College, Saint Peter, Minnesota

Julia Lambert Fogg (1, 244, 262)—California Lutheran University, Thousand Oaks, California

Mary F. Foskett (17)—Wake Forest University, Winston-Salem, North Carolina

Julie Galambush (41, 70)—The College of William and Mary, Williamsburg, Virginia

Daniel E. Goodman (2, 169, 175)—Gardner-Webb University School of Divinity, Boiling Springs, North Carolina

Sandie Gravett (58, 95, 215)—Appalachian State University, Boone, North Carolina

Patrick Gray (3, 19, 172, 179, 204, 220)—Rhodes College, Memphis, Tennessee

Leonard Greenspoon (86, 87, 88, 89)—Creighton University, Omaha, Nebraska

F. V. Greifenhagen (9, 22, 40, 45, 47, 55, 66, 67, 69, 91, 138, 159)—Luther College at the University of Regina, Regina, Saskatchewan, Canada

Roy L. Heller (5, 107)—Perkins School of Theology, Southern Methodist University, Dallas, Texas

T. Perry Hildreth (84)—Palm Beach Atlantic University, West Palm Beach, Florida

Mary E. Hinkle (224)—Luther Seminary, St. Paul, Minnesota

Susanne Hofstra (68)—The American School of Classical Studies at Athens, Athens, Greece

Lynn R. Huber (252, 260)—Elon University, Elon, North Carolina

Susan E. Hylen (198)—Vanderbilt University, Nashville, Tennessee

Glenna S. Jackson (43, 191, 194)—Otterbein College, Westerville, Ohio

Rolf Jacobson (102, 106, 124, 126)—Luther Seminary, St. Paul, Minnesota

Nyasha Junior (144)—Princeton Theological Seminary, Princeton, New Jersey

John Kaltner (56)—Rhodes College, Memphis, Tennessee

Kyle Keefer (38, 53, 143, 210, 258)—Eckerd College, St. Petersburg, Florida

Brad E. Kelle (14, 80, 92, 105, 109)—Point Loma Nazarene University, San Diego, California

Nicole Kelley (201, 207)—Florida State University, Tallahassee, Florida

Sara Koenig (23, 132, 150)—Seattle Pacific University, Seattle, Washington

John R. Levison (104, 119, 157, 186, 205)—Seattle Pacific University, Seattle, Washington

Karoline Lewis (20, 174)—Emory University, Atlanta, Georgia

Tod Linafelt (44, 78)—Georgetown University, Washington, DC

Francisco Lozada Jr. (10)—University of the Incarnate Word, San Antonio, Texas

William L. Lyons (82)—Florida A&M University, Tallahassee, Florida

Carleen Mandolfo (208)—Colby College, Waterville, Maine

Thomas W. Martin (165, 184, 226, 257)—Susquehanna University, Selinsgrove, Pennsylvania

Mark McEntire (110, 125)—Belmont University, Nashville, Tennessee

Heather A. McKay (37, 81)—Edge Hill College of Higher Education, Ormskirk, United Kingdom

Bernadette McNary-Zak (162, 163)—Rhodes College, Memphis, Tennessee

James K. Mead (59, 127)—Northwestern College, Orange City, Iowa

Megan Bishop Moore (93, 120)—Decatur, Georgia

Guy D. Nave Jr. (83, 192, 200, 246, 267, 273)—Luther College, Decorah, Iowa

Roger Newell (57, 199, 259)—George Fox University, Newberg, Oregon

Michael Philip Penn (29, 30, 266)—Mount Holyoke College, South Hadley, Massachusetts

Todd Penner (50)—Austin College, Sherman, Texas

Donald C. Polaski (15, 46, 79, 116, 134, 150)—The College of William & Mary, Williamsburg, Virginia

Sandra Hack Polaski (193)—Baptist Theological Seminary at Richmond, Richmond, Virginia

Anathea Portier-Young (147)—Duke University Divinity School, Durham, North Carolina

Philip A. Quanbeck II (212, 234, 235, 263)—Augsburg College, Minneapolis, Minnesota

Raymond H. Reimer (227)—Associated Mennonite Biblical Seminary, Elkhart, Indiana; North American Baptist Seminary, Sioux Falls, South Dakota

David Rhoads (25)—Lutheran School of Theology at Chicago, Chicago, Illinois

Nicolae Roddy (62, 85, 99, 101)—Creighton University, Omaha, Nebraska

Mark Roncace (7, 71, 73, 75, 90, 112, 131, 139, 141, 151, 152, 254)—Wingate University, Wingate, North Carolina

Timothy J. Sandoval (136, 158)—Chicago Theological Seminary, Chicago, Illinois

Stanley P. Saunders (265)—Columbia Theological Seminary, Decatur, Georgia

Joseph F. Scrivner (39, 123)—Samford University, Birmingham, Alabama

Carolyn J. Sharp (6)—Yale Divinity School, New Haven, Connecticut

Scott Shauf (32, 230, 268)—Bluefield College, Bluefield, Virginia

Christine Shepardson (18, 180)—University of Tennessee, Knoxville, Tennessee

Mary E. Shields (34, 51)—Trinity Lutheran Seminary, Columbus, Ohio

Ronald A. Simkins (33, 49, 52, 54, 60, 63, 94, 100)—Creighton University, Omaha, Nebraska

Russell B. Sisson (269)—Union College, Barbourville, Kentucky

Matthew L. Skinner (182, 187, 270)—Luther Seminary, Saint Paul, Minnesota

Elna K. Solvang (21, 72, 128, 142)—Concordia College, Moorhead, Minnesota

F. Scott Spencer (98, 166)—Baptist Theological Seminary at Richmond, Richmond, Virginia

Jeffrey L. Staley (173, 177, 222, 255)—Seattle University, Seattle, Washington

Thomas D. Stegman (228, 233, 237, 243)—Weston Jesuit School of Theology, Cambridge, Massachusetts

Gregory Stevenson (221, 229)—Rochester College, Rochester Hills, Michigan

Johanna Stiebert (113, 114, 148)—University of Tennessee, Knoxville, Tennessee

D. Matthew Stith (122, 133, 155)—Community Presbyterian Church, West Fargo, North Dakota

Brent A. Strawn (8, 11, 24, 103, 111, 129, 130, 140, 160)—Emory University, Atlanta, Georgia

Gail P. C. Streete (135)—Rhodes College, Memphis, Tennessee

Marianne Meye Thompson (169, 253)—Fuller Theological Seminary, Pasadena, California

Richard Walsh (164, 185, 223)—Methodist College, Fayetteville, North Carolina

John B. Weaver (213, 217)—Emory University, Atlanta, Georgia

Audrey West (211, 242, 245, 271)—Lutheran School of Theology at Chicago, Chicago, Illinois

Bryan Whitfield (35, 220)—Mercer University, Macon, Georgia

B. Diane Wudel (202, 249)—Wake Forest University Divinity School, Winston-Salem, North Carolina

Frank M. Yamada (13, 118, 149)—Seabury Theological Seminary, Evanston, Illinois

PART 1
PROLEGOMENA

Hermeneutics

1. VISUAL EXEGESIS: AN INTRODUCTION TO BIBLICAL INTERPRETATION

College students have some familiarity with interpreting written texts from high school English classes. But after years of watching TV, movies, and music videos, most college students are more comfortable with visual media than written texts. Before even opening a Bible, I introduce interpretation using a visual text, such as a political poster from a different country or historical era. As students focus on the visual cues, they make decisions about what the poster "means" using the same basic tools they will use when reading a written text (social, historical, and cultural context, language, symbols, colors, tone, genre, form and structure, their own knowledge and experience, and conversation with other interpreters). The role of the instructor in this exercise is to name the tools, to help students reflect on the interpretive process, and to show students how they construct an interpretive argument to make sense of the evidence they see.

For the visual text, I suggest a poster of political propaganda unfamiliar to the students. I use a photo of a Sandinista freedom fighter in a white shirt, who stands feeding a baby at her breast, carries an automatic rifle over her shoulder, and smiles broadly at the viewer. It is important to choose a poster with a concrete historical context (to illustrate the point that the historical context matters for constructing meaning), and with visual elements that are polyvalent (the color white may symbolize different things in different cultures), or even discordant (holding a baby and a rifle). The polyvalence and discord push students to make decisions about how they are weighing the visual details in their interpretation.

There are three steps to this exercise. First, I divide the class into groups of four and ask each group to interpret the poster. I ask, "What is happening in this text?" Their goal is to determine the most coherent interpretation (they can vote on which group wins at the end). Each group must come to consensus on their interpretation, state their interpretation

3

in one or two sentences, and list the evidence that supports their interpretation. In essence, each group is formulating a thesis and outlining a simple argument. (I remind them of this exercise when they write their first paper.)

Second, each group presents its interpretation and evidence to the class. After the presentations, I open discussion with a few questions for the groups. What piece of evidence was most important for your group's interpretation? Does your interpretation change when you hear how another group weighed the evidence or noted a detail you missed? In the presentations, and in the discussion that follows, the class experiences a multi-faceted process of interpretation. The students learn to articulate their ideas and gain insights from conversation with other interpreters. They brainstorm together. They ask questions and discover that people of other experiences, backgrounds, and cultures have different ways of seeing. They hear the way other students' expertise and insights affect meaning. (For example, the poster I use has a phrase in Spanish. Any group with members who speak Spanish has access to an additional interpretive clue.) Finally, students see that multiple, coherent interpretations of the same text can coexist peacefully.

The third step is to reflect on the exercise. We begin by naming the tools needed to interpret the visual text. What did we need to know to interpret this poster? The answers will include: Spanish (language), the situation in Nicaragua in the 1970s (historical context), what kind of poster this is (genre), if the woman is happy (emotion/tone), what white means (symbols), why she has a baby and a gun (social setting), the role of the photographer (author), what the poster was used for (intended audience), and the like. We also discuss the different perspectives involved in determining the poster's meaning. For example, the author of the poster has one set of intentions, socio-historical contexts, and cultural influences, while the interpreter may have other intentions, socio-historical contexts, and cultural influences. Moreover, the poster itself has its own integrity, independent of author and interpreter.

The last reflection question is: What process did you follow to develop your interpretations? Although every process is different, generally students move from observing (seeing), to finding patterns in their observations (seeing what you see), to articulating the interpretation that makes sense of the observations (saying what you see). When students understand interpretation as a process of analysis, culminating in an argument that organizes their observations, they are ready to begin writing an exegetical paper.

Julia Lambert Fogg

2. *GUERNICA* AND THE ART OF BIBLICAL HERMENEUTICS

Most undergraduate students consider hermeneutics—once they learn what the term means—in archaeological terms: the meaning that the biblical writer intended for the text must be uncovered and dug out of that text. Less familiar to most students are approaches to hermeneutics that understand meaning not as "author-centered" but as "text-centered" or even "reader-centered." This exercise helps raise that issue and demonstrates the value of text-centered and reader-centered hermeneutics.

Distribute or display a copy of Picasso's famous painting, *Guernica*. (If distributing, use 11x14 or even 11x17 paper; Picasso's mural was over 20 feet wide, and a bigger image for the students to look at helps them see the details of the painting better and appreciate the scope of Picasso's vision.) Do not tell class members anything about who painted it or when it was painted. Ask the students to look at the picture and express what they believe the painting is about (Note: Most students have not seen the painting before, and its cubist style evokes quick reactions). Write down on the board all the words or impressions students speak as they look at the picture. The board will quickly be covered with terms like "violence," "destruction," "chaos," "anguish," and similar interpretations.

Once the students have finished "reading" the painting, tell them the story of Guernica: On April 27, 1937, in the midst of the Spanish Civil War, Hitler's airplanes, with the cooperation of Spanish dictator Francisco Franco, carpet-bombed the civilian village of Guernica. For more than three hours, German bombers dropped one hundred thousand pounds of explosives on the village. The village burned for three days, over 70 percent of the town was destroyed, and one-third of the population was killed or wounded. Guernica had served as a testing ground for the new Nazi strategy of carpet-bombing a civilian population in order to demoralize resistance. Picasso painted the mural in three weeks after learning of the devastation in Spain. It was first exhibited in the Spanish Pavilion at the World's Fair in Paris in 1937 and quickly became one of the most moving depictions of the horrors of war ever put to canvas. A reproduction of *Guernica* now hangs outside the entrance to the United Nations Security Council. (Ironically, when Colin Powell appeared at the Security Council on January 27, 2003, to argue the case for war against Iraq, the *Guernica* reproduction was covered by a huge blue curtain.) The image and additional background is available online (http:// www.spanisharts.com/reinasofia/picasso/e_guernica.htm; http://www. pbs. org/ treasuresoftheworld/a_nav/guernica_nav/main_guerfrm.html; http:// www.faculty.de.gcsu.edu/~rviau/guernica.html).

The point of the exercise, of course, is that the painting really is about violence, destruction, chaos, and anguish—just as the students had articulated. How is it significant that the students understood the meaning of the text without knowing anything about the artist, the artist's time, or the artist's intentions? At the very least, it suggests that "meaning" resides not solely in authorial intention but in the text (independently of the author) or even in the encounter between a reader and a text (again, independently of the author's intention). That realization makes for a nice transition into semester-long discussions about the limitations of historical criticism and the hermeneutical promise of literary, contextual, and reader-centered reading strategies.

Daniel E. Goodman

3. INTERPRETATION AND INTERROGATION

Beginning students hear the phrase "biblical interpretation" and frequently assume that it refers to the act of translating the text from one language to another. It is easy enough to correct this misunderstanding. It is more difficult to convey precisely what we mean when we speak of interpreting the Bible. Many students tacitly assume that "interpretation" simply refers to the standard mode in which to read when the text is obscure or its surface meaning is too fantastic or bizarre to be accepted. This exercise has two aims. One is to demonstrate the ways in which we are always making interpretive decisions, even when we are not conscious of it. The other is to demystify the process of interpretation by redescribing it as the practice of posing questions to a text and seeking appropriate ways to answer them.

I distribute a paragraph to the class and ask students to generate a list of questions they would need to answer in order to make sense of it. The paragraph is Song of Solomon 3:1–5 ("By night on my bed I sought him whom my soul loves..."), slightly edited so as to remove one or two telltale signs that it is a biblical text. They do not know the source, and I ask that they say nothing if they happen to know what it is. They sometimes need help getting started, but soon they get the hang of it. At this stage, no question is out of bounds, so students do not feel too shy to contribute to the discussion.

The basic journalist's questions usually come out first (Who? What? Where? When? Why?). Who wrote it? When? To whom? Why? There is an almost endless series of variations on these basic questions: Is the author male or female? Am I the intended recipient of this message, or is it meant for someone else? Is this an autobiographical report of actual events? Is it a report of a dream or a fantasy? In what language was it originally written? How was this message received? Does the "you" in v. 5 ("I implore you") refer to any reader or to a specific person? Can I get the phone number of the speaker? How do you feel when you read this? Would the speaker be embarrassed by this message being read publicly as we are doing? There is no need at this stage to try to answer any of the questions raised. In each case the follow-up question "What difference does it make?" should be asked. For example, students might regard the paragraph as a touching excerpt from a woman's diary, but if the speaker is a man, their response might be quite different on both an emotional and intellectual level.

Once the brainstorming has gone on for some time, I reveal that the paragraph is taken from the Bible. Now that you know it is from the Bible, I ask, does this give you everything you need to make sense of the passage? Well, no, not exactly. In fact, it complicates matters even further in some ways. Why is *this* in the Bible? *Should* it be in the Bible? It resembles erotic literature, so it must be allegorical, right? If it is from the Song of Solomon, is Solomon really the author? Why would a king write this? Why would a man write this? Or is "Solomon" adopting a feminine persona for some literary purpose? If the latter, what might that purpose be?

Since this is the Bible, perhaps it would be appropriate to ask, "How should I live my life in light of what this text says?" After all, one of the functions of sacred texts is to provide guidance on how to live. But why is it that this question occurs to few, if any, readers, either before or after learning that it comes from the Bible? Consciously or unconsciously, this question has in fact occurred to the reader and has already been answered in the negative. Every reader of every text is constantly asking and immediately answering questions at a subconscious level about the proper way to read any text. Most readers assume, without ever articulating the assumption to themselves, that any biblical text with a romantic flavor is not meant to titillate or to be used as a "how to" guide. As they read, most students will assume certain tentative answers to many of the questions raised above. It is difficult to make sense of a text if everything about it remains up in the air. The habit of asking and answering questions to make sense of a text is part and parcel of the act of interpretation. It is only when something is not clear on account of faulty assumptions on the part of the reader, that we stop and think about the fact that we have been interpreting all along.

I use this exercise to introduce a presentation on pre-modern and modern approaches to the interpretation of the Bible. Interpretation involves the framing of appropriate questions about a text and then figuring our how to answer them. While I acknowledge that the dichotomy between "modern" and "pre-modern" is a somewhat artificial one, I use the opening exercise to make the point that these two general types of approaches can be distinguished according to (1) the kinds of questions deemed appropriate for making sense of a text and (2) the ways of answering them that are deemed valid. The various types of criticism practiced by scholars (source, redaction, structuralist, form, et al.) pose different kinds of questions to the texts under examination and use different methods for answering them. I usually follow this exercise with a paper assignment in which students are given another short passage and asked to generate questions to help make sense of it. The heart of the assignment is to explain why, of all the possible questions one could pose to a text, the student's questions are especially important ones to answer.

Patrick Gray

4. POETRY AND EXEGESIS

One of the hallmarks of an academic approach to biblical interpretation is to treat the Bible "just like any other text." It can be helpful, therefore, to begin with one of these "other texts." In this task, poetry can be used to great effect in the classroom. Almost any poem would work, but I use the Thomas Hardy poem "Channel Firing," discussed in a famous essay by New Critic Cleanth Brooks ("In Search of the New Criticism," *The American Scholar* 53 [1984]: 41–53). The poem can easily be found on the Internet.

When we examine an excerpt in class, students almost always raise the most important issues relevant to the exegetical process: lexical questions, rhetorical features, character, syntax, meter, historical and literary allusion, how the part relates to the whole, issues of authorial intent, the use of metaphor, and more. Because they are not emotionally attached to the poem in the way that they are attached to Scripture, students feel free to brainstorm. They realize that the text at hand is only part of a whole; in order to understand one portion of the poem, they need the whole poem. Some words (e.g., "glebe") are not familiar and so a lexicon must be consulted. Other words are familiar, but fail to form a coherent point outside of their context. They deduce that it is a poem because of the form, rhyme, and meter. They wonder who the narrator of the poem is and how the narrator relates to the author. They suggest that one might make more sense of this poem if one were to examine other writings by the same author. They wonder about the socio-historical context of the poem (e.g., where and when did the phrase "mad as hatters" arise, and how can we use that information to date the poem?). Phrases such as "red war yet redder" lead to a discussion of metaphor, how it functions, and how it is to be valued, especially when compared with more "historical" language. They notice how punctuation affects the flow of the text.

I then hand out a copy of the whole poem for further observation, and answer students' questions using information provided in the Brooks article. For example, Brooks explains that the poem depicts gunnery practice in the English Channel. He gives the history behind the "mad as hatters" phrase. He identifies the church in the poem as Stinsford Church on the basis of information provided by Hardy's second wife, Florence. He indicates that Parson Thirdly appears as a character in a Hardy novel. He notes the date of the poem and wonders if part of Hardy's goal was to prophesy World War One, and so on. As one might imagine, these observations quickly lead students to consider the biblical materials in an analogous way. Subsequent discussion may focus on the ways in which it is appropriate or inappropriate to approach the Bible just as one would approach any other writing.

Jamie Clark-Soles

5. RED RIDING HOOD AND THE BIBLE

When students first arrive in a class on the Bible, often they fall into one of two camps. Either they already know what the text says (and, therefore, what it means) or they are fully prepared for me to tell them, straightforwardly, what the text says (and, therefore, what it means). Encouraging students to become active readers and engage the text is a most difficult task. This exercise, which I use in the second class session of the semester, addresses this problem.

I explain that doing textual interpretation (whether "good" or "bad" interpretation) is directly tied to the questions we ask when we read texts. The better the questions, the better the interpretation we are able to produce. We are not always conscious of the questions that we are asking of a text; in fact, most of the questions that we ask of and about texts are done without our even being aware. I tell the students that I will pass out a text with which almost all of them will be very familiar, but that they should not confuse familiarity with understanding. In fact, familiarity is very often the primary hindrance to gaining an understanding of a text. I then pass out a complete copy of Red Riding Hood. (An English translation of the Grimm version is available at http://www.fln.vcu.edu/grimm/redridinghood.html.) I ask the students to take about ten minutes and read through the story and to note the places at which questions arise in their minds as they read.

While they are reading, I draw two vertical lines, dividing the board into roughly three equal parts. After they are finished, if the class is large, I ask them to get together with two or three other people to discuss their questions and to choose one or two that seem like "good questions." I then solicit the groups for their inquiries and I write them in one of the three columns on the board.

The questions generally fall into one of three types:

1. "Historical questions" (in the left column)—questions about authorship, original audience, original purpose of red hats, original attitudes about wolves, original purpose of the story as a whole, "source" questions (since the Grimm version has an appendix with an alternate ending), and so forth. I note that these questions see the text like a window through which additional information is sought.

2. "Structural questions" (in the center column)—questions about plot, characterization, word meanings, and the like. Consistently, students will ask mostly structural questions, such as "What is the role of 'eating' and how does it tie the story together?" or "What, according to the text, was Red Riding Hood's failure? Disobedience? Curiosity? Naïveté?" I note that these questions see the text like a painting or movie and attempt to make sense of it as a work of art.

3. "Hermeneutical questions" (in the right column)—questions about what the story reveals or teaches about life: the nature of evil, the move from innocence to experience, the valuation of gender roles, the nature of sexuality, and so forth. I note that these questions see the text like a mirror or like a lens and attempt to view reality in terms of the text.

After all the questions are written on the board, I start pointing out how the questions within the center column (Structural Questions) often relate to one another: one question will presuppose others; one question will negate others. I then point out how questions in the other two columns (Historical and Hermeneutical Questions) often depend upon the more foundational questions in the center column. Next, I provide them with some of the historical background of the development of the Red Riding Hood story, available on the website mentioned above. I note how the historical information can, likewise, affect what answers might be given to the questions in the central column.

Finally, I reflect with them on some of the hermeneutical questions that were raised and point out how, often, these questions also affect the answers that might be given for the questions in the central column. In this way, the students are accustomed, when they begin actively reading the Bible, to recognize the different types of questions that different people ask, and to acknowledge the way that different questions may be related and may work with (or against) one another. By this they may, perhaps, be better prepared to hear and respect questions that are not their own. (For a similar exercise introducing exegesis, see §198.)

Roy L. Heller

6. TEACHING HERMENEUTICS THROUGH CREATIVE COMMUNAL PRAXIS

Teaching hermeneutics well requires that one invite students to reflect on a number of complex issues, among them textual determinacy and indeterminacy, authorial intention, criteria for discerning intertextual resonances, the role of reader agency in the construction of meaning, and the pressures and constraints generated by reading communities and interpretive cultures. One danger of any class on hermeneutics is that students may become bogged down in abstract discussions of complicated literary theories. To avoid this, I have students engage in a creative hands-on exercise designed to help them identify their own reading strategies and honor the diverse hermeneutical strategies of others within the intentional "reading community" of our divinity school classroom.

First, students prepare by responding to provocative prompts that ask them to fill in the blanks about ways in which they read. This serves as a catalyst for their thinking about interpretation. The prompts I provide usually include some variation of the following: "I am a credulous reader because _____. I am a skeptical reader because _____. A Scripture text that makes me joyful is _____. A Scripture text that frightens me is _____. Rightminded reading as a process involves _____. Illegitimate readings are those readings that _____. When I read Scripture, I try never to forget _____. When I read Scripture, I try to let go of _____. Reading the Bible matters because _____."

Next, each student creates a text on a single sheet of paper that represents what he or she finds to be at stake in the reading of Scripture. I encourage students to use color, varied fonts, art, handwriting, Hebrew or Greek or other languages, graphics, collage or pastiche techniques—whatever creative ways they find helpful to articulate their own reading strategies and their understanding of the importance of interpreting the Bible. They turn in enough copies of their sheets for all in the class, and I have the sheets bound at a copy shop into professional-looking "books" that represent both the utterances and the hermeneutical strategies of our classroom community. My own participation has entailed designing the front and back covers to reflect my own hermeneutical commitments and my hopes for the class; but one could also invite students to work collaboratively to design the covers. (Laminating the covers and providing bound copies for all students has cost me from about $40 to $70 each time, for class sizes of approximately twenty students. I incur the cost because I choose to make the books as attractive and durable as possible, as a way of honoring my students' contributions. But one could simply staple the sheets for a cost-free version.)

When I distribute the books, we have a class session in which students describe to the group what they were getting at in the words and images provided on the sheet, and others respond. Because I schedule this exercise near the end of the semester, considerable trust and rapport have been established in the classroom, so my students have been willing to be extraordinarily open about what is at stake for them in their reading strategies and their encounters with Scripture. The resulting discussions have been engaging and passionate, providing fascinating glimpses into the diverse temperaments of readers, their processes of negotiating the demands, risks, and affirmations of particular reading communities, and their keen reflections on why the interpretation of Scripture matters for their vocations and for the church.

The hermeneutical "book" that a class makes comprises a multivocal witness to encounters with the sacred. Juxtapositions within these books are often striking. Playful, humorous observations about the demands of reading and writing about Scripture are followed by raw confessions of despair concerning the misogyny and violence in some biblical texts. High-gloss graphics involving concentric circles and dynamic arrow-vectors of meaning yield to grainy photocopied images from Byzantine art and definitions from an old liturgical dictionary. One student's sheet was composed of sayings cut from popular magazines intermingled with her own responses as a reader of the Bible, this complicated dialogue between believer and culture represented in strips that were shaped into a star with "God" handwritten at the center. Another student superimposed a map of New Haven on torn pieces of paper that had been distressed to look like ancient scroll fragments with meaningful phrases from Scripture on each one, thus "mapping" her contemporary social context onto the biblical text and her impressionistic view of ancient history.

The excitement students feel about this creative assignment has been palpable. Many observe that they have never been asked to bring their creativity into a biblical studies classroom. It has been both moving and pedagogically edifying to see how deeply attentive students can be to one another in the discussions as each struggles to articulate how the hermeneutics of a lifetime of reading Scripture has taken shape.

This exercise could be modified in a number of ways to further particular curricular or pedagogical aims. Students could be asked to reflect on a single hermeneutical method or a specific ethical issue. They might focus their attention on one text or tradition (e.g., the motif of Exodus throughout the Bible), or on relationships between the Old and New Testaments. Or they could be asked to add their own voices to a pre-designed interdisciplinary conversation (perhaps joining Søren Kierkegaard and Jon Levenson on Gen 22). There are many possibilities for creative variation, so the assignment can easily be tailored to the needs of a particular class.

Carolyn J. Sharp

7. READING INKBLOTS

In order to help students to begin thinking about the complex process of interpretation, I have them play the game Thinkblot. The objective of this board game from Mattel is to see what objects players can spot in a (largely) random splattering of inkblots on a page. (Samples can be viewed at www.thinkblot.com.) The game is much like looking at the clouds and trying to see what objects one can identify. While Thinkblot could be purchased very cheaply, teachers could also make their own inkblots on individual sheets of paper to give to small groups or could draw random shapes on the board and have the whole class look at the same blots.

I break the class into small groups and give each group a different page of inkblots. I give them a few minutes to write down as many images as they see in the inkblots on their page. After time is called, each person in the group reads their list to the other group members, explaining how and where they see each image (e.g., "Here I see a fish. These are the fins" or "Here I see a person swimming. This is her head and here is her arm"). If students can convince the other group members to see what they saw, and if no one else in the group saw that image, the student earns two points for their creative and convincing reading. If someone else observed the same image in the same inkblot, the player earns one point. If players cannot convince a majority of the other players, they receive no points.

After finishing, I ask each group to compose a list which explains how playing this game is analogous to reading texts, which, after all, are also composed of dark ink spots on a white page. In the plenary discussion that ensues, I try to draw out the following related points:

1. There is more than one way to interpret a text, just as there is more than one way to interpret an inkblot. People will see the exact same inkblot in very different ways, just as readers will understand the exact same text in very different ways.

2. One's interpretations depend on those parts of the inkblots on which one focuses and how one sees the different parts of the inkblots as related to one another (e.g., one could see a circle as an eye which is part of a face, while others may only see the circle as a baseball, not seeing it as a part of a larger image). Similarly, any reading of a text depends on the part or aspect of the text on which one focuses and how one relates it to the surrounding texts (i.e., its context).

3. One's personality (opinions, background, knowledge, prejudices, etc.) influence interpretation. Imagine a circle with a "handle" attached. If you are an athlete, you may see a tennis racket; if you are a chef, you may see a spoon; if you are a musician, you may see a banjo. Likewise, readers bring their own experiences, preferences, and predispositions to the reading of texts. Those in power, for example, read differently from those who are disenfranchised.

4. Interpretation involves conversation. Just as students must discuss among themselves the different ways to see the inkblots, so readers of the Bible converse about different possible ways to read the text. The whole scholarly enterprise, I explain, is essentially about participating in this conversation in which we show one another what we see in the texts.

5. Such conversation helps one to see the text or image in a variety of ways. There are multiple levels of meaning to texts and multiple approaches to take (historical, sociological, literary, etc.). In discussing with their partners, students will likely have had that stimulating moment when they said, "Oh, I see what you are saying. I never saw it that way" or "Wow, I never would have seen that." It is this capacity to see new things in familiar texts that makes biblical interpretation so fascinating. Furthermore, imaginative interpreters generate the most engaging readings (those earning two points), often by studying the image more carefully than others.

6. The conversation, however, is not a free-for-all. Rather, the cogency of one's interpretation depends on how well it is explained. Interpreters must be able adequately to demonstrate and defend their reading. Here I raise the "it's all relative" question. Can interpretations be wrong? The game, I think, is particularly good at illustrating the complexities of this question. It is difficult to say that honest, well-meaning interpretations are "wrong." But yet, if one produces a peculiar reading of an inkblot, and cannot get anyone else to understand how they arrived at their reading, one can say that the reading is a bit of a stretch, if not totally unconvincing (hence earning no points). So it would seem that, while it is all interpretation, it is not all equally legitimate interpretation. Here I usually draw a circle with a curved line coming out of the top and observe that this could be seen as an apple or a bomb, but it is hard to see how it could be a kangaroo.

7. The blots are just blots until someone interprets them. Likewise, a text derives meaning only from the interaction between it and a reader. The text or blots will not speak for themselves; someone must read them in order to produce meaning.

Mark Roncace

8. ANCIENT TEXTS AND ARTIFACTS

In the course of a lecture on interpretive method I casually put up on the screen a picture of a Lamaštu plaque which highlights this demon as well as her antithesis, the protective demon Pazuzu (see O. Keel, *The Symbolism of the Biblical World: Ancient Near Eastern Iconography and the Book of Psalms* [trans. T. J. Hallett; repr., Winona Lake: Eisenbrauns, 1997], figs. 91–92). At this point in the lecture I am usually speaking (facetiously) of how easy it is to understand the Bible now given recent archaeological discoveries, developments in interpretive method, translation theory, and the like, and how the culture of the biblical subjects was probably not vastly different from ours. Their art and literature, religious experience, and the like—I continue (tongue-in-cheek)—would be immediately transparent to us. The students usually realize the dissonance between what I am saying and the odd imagery on the plaque displayed on the screen. The plaque underscores yet again just how deep (and ugly) Lessing's big, ugly ditch really is. This piece—just one of many that could be used to make the point—is a harsh reminder that the biblical world is not contemporary but its exact opposite: ancient, foreign, different. Simply because a student can read the Bible in English translation does not mean that they can understand the culture behind these texts. The familiarity of the English Bible is offset markedly by the unfamiliarity of the Lamaštu plaque.

But showing this object has yet another important use. The plaque also provides an opportunity to talk about the importance of art and artifactual evidence vis-à-vis textual evidence, their interrelationship, and their occasional interconnection. There are, in fact, a number of incantations against Lamaštu that describe her (see B. R. Foster, *Before the Muses: An Anthology of Akkadian Literature* [2nd ed.; 2 vols.; Potomac: CDL Press, 1996]); the plaques provide pictures. Happily, there is some correspondence between the textual and artistic depictions, which is not always the case when dealing with textual and artistic evidence. The texts help to explain some of the imagery in the art pieces (e.g., why there are protective figures present, why there is sometimes the depiction of a sick individual, etc.), but the art pieces also help to explain parts of the textual material (e.g., who would have said such an incantation, etc.). In the texts, Lamaštu is described in various ways by means of different metaphors; in the pictures, the metaphors are, literally, "fleshed out." So, the exercise not only demonstrates the vast differences between the ancient world and today, it also gives students a sense of at least two major tools (image and text) by which to begin to build ditch-bridges. Wise students (and teachers!) will use more than one tool and build more than one bridge. (For a similar exercise, see §159.)

Brent A. Strawn

9. THE SOCIAL LOCATION OF THE READER

The social location of the interpreter is increasingly recognized as having a determinative effect on biblical interpretation. The following exercise is meant to facilitate student understanding of this dynamic; it also enables students to define their own social locations.

I ask the students to read in advance Jonathan Magonet's "How a Donkey Reads the Bible—On Interpretation" (in *A Rabbi's Bible* [London: SCM, 1991]). I begin the class by asking, "If you were a donkey, what would you look for in reading the Bible?" The discussion is focused on the ways in which the reader's particular perspective and presuppositions affect what the reader finds in the Bible, that who is reading the text is as important as what is being read. Various examples can be solicited from the essay as well as from the students.

To help students begin to articulate their own social location, the following inventory is distributed. It is closely based on an inventory first developed by Dianne Bergant. Students are requested to answer each question in as much detail as possible:

Your social location will influence the way you read or interpret the biblical text. Our heritage predisposes our judgments, calls forth our values, and shapes the way we perceive reality. Our presuppositions are never fully self-conscious. We are not always aware of all the ways in which our heritage may promote our well-being and enhance our lives, or may frustrate our potential and confine our activities. It is usually in situations where we feel restricted that we begin to question the appropriateness, even the justice, first of the situation and then of its underlying presuppositions. This explains why those who are relegated to a marginal or "invisible" position within a society are sometimes better critics of that society than those who are privileged and satisfied. This

P
R
O
L
E
G
O
M
E
N
A

latter group frequently takes privilege for granted and does not question its appropriateness. Becoming aware of our social location can help us to discover some of our presuppositions.

Gender. (1) How does your gender identification relate with that of the dominant culture? the same? or different? Is this problematic? (2) Is your gender location an advantage? or a disadvantage?

Culture/Ethnicity. (1) Are you a member of the dominant culture? Is this an advantage? a disadvantage? (2) Are you bicultural? Do you consider this an advantage? a disadvantage? What is your preferred culture? (3) Is your cultural location an advantage? a disadvantage?

Race. (1) Are you a member of the dominant race? a marginal race? an oppressed race? (2) Is your racial identity an advantage? a disadvantage?

Class. (1) Into which economic class were you born? Are you in the same class today? (2) Have you ever belonged to an "invisible" class (e.g., displaced, chronically un- or underemployed, disabled, etc.)? (3) Has your education improved your class standing? (4) Is your class location an advantage? a disadvantage?

Religion. (1) Were you raised in a religious tradition? What did that tradition teach you about the interpretation of the Bible? (2) Are you presently participating in a religious tradition? How does that tradition make use of the Bible? (3) Are you a member of the dominant religious group? of a religious minority? (4) Is your religious location an advantage? a disadvantage?

Typically, white middle-class students have the greatest difficulty in seeing the difference that social location can make. They want desperately to believe that in Western society everyone is equal and that the relative advantages and disadvantages of gender, class, and race are more problems of perception than anything else, usually the problem of the person who feels at a disadvantage. This, of course, allows for the disadvantaged victim to be blamed while allowing those who are privileged to continue denying that they are in fact privileged. To counter these misperceptions, it is useful to bring in statistics, for example, detailing relative employment and salary levels or incarceration rates of different genders, races, and classes. Some of this discussion can take place more fruitfully, and in a less intimidating manner, if conducted as an online discussion.

The social location inventories can be operative at later points in the course. I often ask students to incorporate them into papers in which they are analyzing and interpreting a specific biblical text or theme. (For other exercises related to social location, see §§50, 51.)

F. V. Greifenhagen

10. SOCIAL LOCATION AND BIBLICAL INTERPRETATION

One of the exercises I use in my biblical studies courses to help students understand the discipline from a cultural studies (intercultural criticism) standpoint is the social location paper. Each semester I require that students write at least two papers. The first paper focuses on one or more identity factors, such as race/ethnicity, gender, class, religious affiliation, sexual orientation, motherhood, fatherhood, body (e.g., eating disorders), physical disability, diasporic identity, and geographical location, to name a few that might define their identity or identities. The aim of this first paper is not to concentrate on how one's identity or identities influence how biblical texts are read, but rather to engage the reader of the biblical text. One of the principles of intercultural criticism is that not only the text (both diachronically as well as synchronically) should undergo serious engagement, but also the reader who comes to the text must go through a critical engagement.

In the past, the results of such an exercise have been quite rewarding. At first, students remark that the exercise appears quite easy, but after attempting to write a paper on their social location they begin to realize that the assignment is much more challenging because most students have never been asked the question. Most of their identity or identities have been constructed by difference alone. In other words, their identity or identities are defined by how others (e.g., media) define who they are. The assignment is also very helpful for the instructor to get to know the students. During the semester when any critical close reading of the text is done during class, the instructor understands why a student is perhaps taking a feminist approach to the portrayal of women in Luke or why another reads the character of Ruth from a bicultural perspective. The close reading of texts and the conversations that follow in class are much more enriching when difference and plurality are embraced.

The second paper is related to the first. The assignment calls on students to write a paper (informed, for example, by the results of historical criticism and literary criticism) on a particular biblical text. (Almost any text would work. A few that seem to work well include Gen 9:18–10:7; Susanna; Mark 7:24–30; John 4.) However, the paper also needs to be informed by the student's defined social location, which they wrote about in the beginning of the semester. The aim here is to help students realize that social location surely plays a role in the interpretation of texts. By the end of the semester, students begin to understand this principle of intercultural criticism and are much more aware of how the interpretative exercise of biblical texts (and other texts for that matter) is constructed. In this paper, students must also consider how their interpretation might serve to benefit (or not benefit) others. Intercultural criticism is also an approach that calls for the interpretation of texts to be engaged. Not only is the text to be engaged, but readers and their interpretations must also be scrutinized in order to achieve the overall objective of the social location paper.

In learning to read biblical texts critically, the social location paper enables students not only to learn to read the world behind the text or the world in the text but also the world in front of the text, namely, the world of the flesh-and-blood reader This exercise is a step in helping students understand that their social location plays a role, consciously or unconsciously, in the interpretative process, and that the search for truth or meaning is not done independently of one's social location. (For other exercises related to social location, see §§50, 51.)

Francisco Lozada Jr.

11. GENRE: INTERPRETATION, RECOGNITION, CREATION

Responsible biblical interpretation requires an adequate appreciation of genre. But it is not always easy to teach new students about how to interpret different genres, let alone cultivate in them the appropriate skills necessary for competent genre-recognition. I introduce the topic of genre by showing two different snippets of poetry. The first is a quite serious poem about "not refusing to do the good that I can do"; the second is a humorous piece that recounts a worker's ode to how to get out of doing much work on the job, especially if the day happens to be Friday. I first encountered these pieces at a previous place of employment where they were posted next to each other, the second above the first. I immediately found the juxtaposition somewhat jarring, especially for a new worker like myself. That is, which poem should I believe and (perhaps) enact? Ought I "not refuse to do the good that I can do" or should I seek to get out of as much work as possible, especially on Fridays?

I show a picture of the two poems *in situ* and pose these questions to the students who subsequently begin to answer by analyzing the presentation of the poems. The first is rather austere, with the lines arranged stichometrically with just a simple black-line border. The second, placed above the first, is larger, with different typefaces, many punctuation marks, and a border that is made up of humorous cartoon figures who are obviously frustrated workers on the job. These are just a few of the things that the students pick up on to make a determination as to which poem is "serious" and to be enacted by the workers and which is purely humorous. Some of the other factors influencing interpretation include items such as the content and rhythm of the poem, their relative sizes (which is larger?) and positioning (which is on top?), aesthetic consideration (which is most engaging?), as well as the social context in which the pieces were posted (in the kitchenette/break room).

The exercise highlights several things simultaneously: First, even if two compositions are of the same literary genre (poem), this does not mean that they have the same function or that they are susceptible to the same interpretation. Not all genres are created equal, that is, even when they are the selfsame genre. Second, genres can have more than one function and belong to more than one type (at least according to function), even simultaneously. These and other items help students see that readers help to create or construct genre on the basis of what they already know as well as on the basis of preexisting genre-clues. The perduring problem, of course, is that some of the genre-clues used in the exercise are typically absent from the biblical text. For example, there are no cartoons scribbled in the margins of the Bible (at least not in most modern versions, though one might perhaps compare illuminated manuscripts) that indicate when a passage is to be taken more lightly than another. (Even this observation helps students read more carefully, wondering what they might be missing or entertaining other readings than the simple and straightforward one.) Still more problematic is the fact that even when genre-clues are present in a text many Bible readers simply lack the literary or cultural competence to recognize them as such, particularly beginning students who are unfamiliar with "the strange new world of the Bible" (Karl Barth) and the very ancient contexts from which it comes. Hence the need for the study of genres, specifically ancient ones, in the first place.

Brent A. Strawn

12. SIMONE WEIL AND BIBLICAL STUDIES COURSES

Many first-year seminary students find the introductory New Testament course challenging because it is the first time they have been asked to study the Bible critically. At times they feel that their professors are making the reading and interpretation of the New Testament far more complex than necessary. Some of them come to the class with the idea that, since they have been doing so since childhood, they know all there is to know about reading the Bible. In particular, the arduous task of critical exegesis can seem overwhelming and not entirely relevant to their perceived short-term goals: "I don't want to be a scholar; I just want to be a pastor."

To help students reflect upon this issue, I have them read at the beginning of the course Simone Weil's "Reflections on the Right Use of School Studies with a View to the Love of God" (in *Waiting for God* [New York: Putnam, 1951], 105–16). Weil writes that "the development of the faculty of attention forms the real object and almost the sole interest of studies" (105). She contends that all scholarly efforts must be directed toward the long view. It may not be obvious how the subject one is currently studying will bear fruit, but it will certainly do so. One may not be especially gifted in a particular subject. No matter; effort and attention are the point. Weil argues that slow, methodical, faithful attention to one's studies finally develops the capacity for prayer: "The key to a Christian conception of studies is the realization that prayer consists of attention" (105).

It is especially important for students to understand this as they slowly and painstakingly learn the task of biblical exegesis, which is nothing more than the practice of focused attention and effort applied to particular texts. After the student has mastered the various exegetical steps—setting the passage into its literary context, employing the concordance, investigating ancient social customs, and the like—students must then move to the difficult task of integrating the results to produce a cogent interpretation. They must then attempt to convey their insights in an articulate, concise fashion, so that the reader can join them in their discovery.

Attentiveness of the type described by Weil is a crucial habit for budding exegetes to cultivate. Patient waiting is the opposite of "muscular" attention which frenetically attempts to hunt down the truth. Only students who have taken the time to live with a text arrive at a substantive interpretation. Those who try to cram all the steps of exegesis and composition into a brief period will fail. Weil writes, "In every school exercise there is a special way of waiting upon truth, setting our hearts upon it, yet not allowing ourselves to go out in search of it. There is a way of giving our attention to the data of a problem in geometry without trying to find the solution or to the words of a Latin or Greek text without trying to arrive at the meaning" (113). For pastors-in-training, moreover, it is helpful to remember that, according to Weil, the development of this kind of patient attention finally leads to the love of one's neighbor (114–15).

Rightly undertaken, the exegetical task has the potential to make the exegete not only a smarter person, but also a better person, and that is why Weil can call academic work the pearl of great price. With this in mind, I ask the students on the first day to reply in writing to these two questions: What do you hope to get out of this course? How do you plan to make this happen? In this way, by clarifying the means and ends of the course at the outset, it is possible to avoid some of the frustrations along the way for both student and teacher.

Jaime Clark-Soles

P
R
O
L
E
G
O
M
E
N
A

Methodologies

13. TEACHING BIBLICAL
INTERPRETATION METHODOLOGIES

When we read the biblical text, we are not always conscious of the inter-pretative assumptions we make as readers. Reading and interpreting comes naturally. Interpretative methodologies help us to see the kinds of questions we ask of texts in a structured and critical way. In order to help students better understand what is going on when we interpret texts, I have them write reports on different methods for approaching the bibli-cal texts (source, form, literary criticism, etc.). In class, I then walk the students through an exercise that helps them to foreground their assump-tions about how they interpret texts.

Students come to class with their one-page reports on different forms of biblical criticism. In this assignment, I ask students to summa-rize a methodology, focusing on the question of where "meaning happens" in this form of criticism. Does meaning occur in the history behind the text, in the text itself, or in the realm of the reader? There are many good textbooks on biblical methodologies (e.g., S. McKenzie and S. Haynes, eds., *To Each Its Own Meaning: An Introduction to Biblical Criti-cisms and Their Application* [rev. ed.; Louisville: Westminster/John Knox, 1999]). The students, who are put in groups of six, choose one of six assigned chapters for their summary. They then distribute their sum-maries to each person in their group.

In class, I begin the interpretative exercise by having the students look at unidentified texts in their small groups. I make sure to select texts that are interesting and short enough to read. I also choose texts that vary in form, style, and content. Songs with words, poems, novel excerpts, journal entries, and even comic strips work well for this exer-cise. (I often use, among other texts, the lyrics from XTC's "Dear God" and an excerpt from Frederick Buechner's *Wishful Thinking: A Seeker's ABC* [rev. ed.; San Francisco: Harper San Francisco, 1993] on the use of grape juice in communion.) Each group of students works on two texts.

It is fine for more than one group to be working on the same text. I ask them to respond to two questions: "What is the meaning or meanings of this text?" and "What does one need to know to be able to interpret this text?" To clarify this last question, I suggest to them the following scenario: "In the year 3104, archaeologists unearth these texts from an ancient site. What would they need to know to interpret these texts?" After the small-group discussion, I have the groups read the texts aloud to the whole class and report back on the questions. I fill in some of the details (authorship, literary context, historical factors) of the different selections, and we discuss how this information helps, hinders, or complicates their interpretation.

After our discussion of the texts, I ask the students to report back to the larger class on the different forms of biblical criticism, comparing their observations about "where meaning resides" with the questions that emerged from previous discussion of the different texts. We then chart out where the different methodologies are located in relation to the history behind the text, the text itself, and the realm of the reader—the same exercise that we did in response to the question, "What does one need to know to interpret this text?" This part of the exercise helps the students to connect biblical methodologies with their own interpretive questions and reflections.

I end with an example of how these questions of meaning affect the interpretation of a specific text (e.g., Gen 1 and 2). It is important to remember that the point of the exercise is not to suggest that one method is more correct than another. The goal is to foreground assumptions of biblical interpretation in a critical and structured way.

Frank M. Yamada

14. CRITICAL METHODS: HISTORICAL CRITICISM

To introduce the critical method of classic historical criticism (particularly to undergraduates who are not familiar even with such traditional approaches to the biblical literature), I present the class with a "make-believe archaeological find." This "find" actually consists of a letter that my wife received from a friend several years ago. After removing some items that are historically explicit (e.g., the year in the date formula), I invite the students to read the letter as if they had just discovered it without an accompanying context. This exercise can be done either in small groups or with the class as a whole, depending on the size of the group. The portion of the letter that I use reads as follows:

July 31

Dear Dee,

Hi! How are you? Everything here is going well. We have some exciting news to share! In January, we are going to have a baby! So far,
everything is going well. We have been working on the nursery and it is
almost complete; just a little painting left to do. We are decorating it in
classic Winnie the Pooh.

Anyway, has it been hot down your way? I'm sure it has because it's
been hot up here. Today, however, we're getting some much needed rain.

I'll let you go for now. Tell Brad hi for me!

Once the students have read the letter, I ask them to identify what
types of historical questions they want to ask about the letter in general
and what kinds of historical information they want to acquire in order to
understand the letter's origins, references, writer, recipient, and so forth.
The responses typically hit quite quickly upon the most obvious items:
"What year should accompany 'July 31'?" "Where is 'here' and who are
'we'?" "What is 'classic Winnie the Pooh'?" "Where is 'down your way'?"
and "Who is 'Brad'?"

From this starting point, the teacher can move into a discussion of the
basics of the historical approach to biblical texts, highlighting the ways in
which it is similar to the exercise just completed on the make-believe
archaeological find. It may be useful in this regard to have the class (or
the groups) move to examine a particular biblical text that lends itself to
historical analysis and calls forth some of the same questions of identification, location, and cultural references as the letter (e.g., the cryptic
oracle against Damascus and its rulers in Amos 1:3–5).

In addition to providing a springboard for discussing the basics of historical criticism, however, this exercise can move the class toward
recognition of some of the larger issues connected with the historical
approach. For example, by contrasting this letter with another type of literature (e.g., a piece of poetry), the teacher can highlight how some texts
lend themselves to historical analysis while others do not. The nagging
question in biblical studies, of course, is how to tell the difference! Addi-
tionally, the exercise can highlight some of the inherent difficulties in a
historical approach to texts by noting that even though we are from essentially the same time period (the letter was written in 1998) and culture (i.e.,
most of us know who Winnie the Pooh is), we were still unable to identify
firmly the locations, dates, or addressees. How much more might that be
the case with much earlier literature from ancient Israel or early Christianity? These surplus benefits of the exercise may help the teacher transition
to, but also show the interconnections among, the different critical

approaches to a wide variety of biblical texts. (For similar exercises, see §§220, 221.)

Brad E. Kelle

15. TOM LEHRER AND HISTORICAL CRITICISM

While most of our students have already had courses in history, thinking like historians is frequently foreign to them. This is especially pronounced when the Bible is put into the mix. My goal in presenting historical criticism is to help students understand that historical criticism reads the Bible for a particular reason: the construction of historical knowledge. As such, historical criticism obeys a certain set of rules and procedures.

In this exercise, I use the Tom Lehrer song "National Brotherhood Week" to disclose the importance of historical criticism and the ways it can proceed. (Any speech, song, or text which contains historical references or requires historical knowledge that students lack would serve the same purpose.) Lehrer's song satirizes an initiative by the National Conference of Christians and Jews which called for Americans to celebrate a week advancing racial and other forms of reconciliation. (Lehrer: "This year, on the first day of the week, Malcolm X was killed, which gives you an idea of how effective the whole thing is.") I use the live recording of Lehrer's performance, *That Was the Year That Was*, made in San Francisco in July 1965.

While I could make similar points using only the written lyrics, I believe in this case hearing the actual performance makes a difference: the students get to hear the response of the original, intended audience. And, even more basic, when I play the recording, students can readily tell that it is intended to be humorous, if for no other reason than the audience laughs. But the class does not understand many of Lehrer's jokes. His association of Frank Fontaine and Jerry Lewis with "Make Fun of the Handicapped Week" gets a huge laugh on the recording, but, at best, students recognize Jerry Lewis as a figure linked to fighting multiple sclerosis, so the joke makes little sense. The largest laugh line in the song, "Lena Horne and Sheriff Clark are dancing cheek to cheek," is likewise baffling. After the song, I provide an explanation for some of this material, such as Frank Fontaine's role on the *Jackie Gleason Show* and Sheriff Clark's role in the events in Selma.

The exercise makes three main points that I bring out in discussion afterwards. First, the students need a certain amount of historical context to get Lehrer's jokes; they likewise need a certain amount of historical context to get the Bible's "jokes," as it were. Second, the Lehrer "text" is easily datable and is datable to a period about which we have a copious amount of information. Thus it is easy to do the historical work necessary to understand the "text." Here the Bible presents difficulties, as it is not always clear when texts should be dated. But the demands of historical analysis show why historical critics attempt to eliminate, often in highly speculative ways, the texts' ambiguous relationship to historical context.

Third, as a work of satire, Lehrer's song could be read in two different ways. One could see Lehrer as claiming that attempts at any kind of reconciliation are doomed, given that groups of people will always hate each other. Or one could understand Lehrer to be poking fun at what he sees as a particularly naïve and ineffective way of pursuing reconciliation (his introduction indicates this is probably the correct interpretation). I tell the class that if they want to resolve this issue, they could simply call Lehrer (a retired math professor) on the phone. The Bible, however, also includes satire (as in the prophetic literature) but we have no access to Isaiah to determine the possible meanings of his remarks. Thus we are forced even more to read the texts carefully and attempt to place them in historical context. But even the most careful reading cannot assure us of uncovering the author's meaning. Nor is the supposed author's meaning always the goal as we read.

Donald C. Polaski

16. WORKING WITH PRIMARY SOURCE DOCUMENTS

Although most of us, as professional educators, are used to working with a variety of primary sources to reconstruct the complexities of the ancient past, our students may not yet be aware of the different types and genres of documents which comprise an anthology like the Bible, and have very little sense of how to work critically with this range of sources.

To begin to raise student awareness of different types of historical sources, it can be helpful in one of the first class meetings to give students a variety of types of primary source documents and objects. Choosing sources that are not drawn from the established canon of the Hebrew Bible or the New Testament—while sharing the same genre as those sources—is useful for getting students to think of the Bible as a collection of types of documents rather than monumentally, as "revealed" and "infallible" (and thus, by extension, inappropriate to consider from scholarly perspectives). The collection of primary source types can and should be varied, depending on what the instructor is able to gather; you might include a letter, a diary entry, a third-person historical narrative, a hymn or war song, and a king list. These should be photocopied and handed out on separate sheets to each student or group. I like to add to these some sort of object, like an ancient coin (a reproduction will do!), a potsherd, or another type of archaeological find.

Students are then divided into groups and asked to read and evaluate each object. They are to draw up a list that ranks the documents in order of their "usefulness" for uncovering the past. Each group is asked to present their ranking before the whole class and to justify it. Students should be encouraged to challenge each other on their choices, and to explore why the rankings are often different from group to group. If one type of document or source is consistently identified as the "most important," such as the third-person historical narrative, the instructor might at that point begin to talk, for instance, about the problems inherent in the construction of historical narrative. Similarly, if something like poetry is deemed the least likely to uncover the past, then the instructor might suggest ways to read poetry as part of a historical matrix. Overall, the point is to encourage critical analysis and contextualization: What sorts of interpretive problems are endemic to each type of document? Under what sets of conditions and with what assumptions do we approach each source? What sort of information do we need about each object before we can begin to evaluate its usefulness for reconstructing the past?

Of course, there is no "correct" answer for which document is the "most important," but the point is to encourage students to think about genres and to begin to apply elementary hermeneutical principles. This exercise works well to increase awareness of the types of documents involved in a composite anthology like the Bible and to facilitate discussion concerning the interpretive difficulties when dealing with various types of ancient documents.

Nicola Denzey

17. HISTORICAL MEMORY AND BIBLICAL NARRATIVE

It is not uncommon for beginning students in biblical studies, both those with explicit religious commitments and those without, to trip over their often unarticulated assumptions that meaning is fixed and that religious narrative must be factually precise and proximate to historical events in order to be received by religious communities as either true or significant. For many students, this happens when they are first introduced to the literary history of biblical texts. The notion that biblical texts evolved long after the events to which they refer suggests to some students or causes them to infer that historical criticism invalidates religious narrative.

To help beginning students identify and examine their assumptions concerning chronological proximity, meaning, and historical memory, I assign a mock journal exercise as a short homework assignment. I have found it very useful in stimulating student conversation, interaction, and collective reflection. The assignment is as follows:

Please answer the following two questions in order, giving no more than one single-spaced page to each. Be sure to take at least a full hour break before moving from question #1 to question #2. Bring the completed assignment to our next class session. Be prepared to discuss your assignment in a small group.

1. Think back to either (a) your first day of high school (if you are a first- or second-year student) or (b) your first day of college (if you are a third-or fourth-year student).Try to recall the thoughts, feelings, concerns, hopes, and preoccupations that were foremost on your mind at the end of that important day. Re-creating as best you can your experience of that day, compose a journal entry about that day as if you were writing it on that very first evening of your high school or college experience.

Take at least an hour break before continuing on to question #2.

2. Now think about the same day you wrote about in question #1 again, only this time reflect on your experience of that day from your current perspective. Rather than trying to re-create how you felt at the close of your first day in high school or college, compose a journal entry about that experience that recounts how you now view and understand that day and its events.

When students return to class with their completed assignments, I ask them to discuss the following questions in small groups: What differences and what similarities do you see in your two journal entries? How do you account for the differences? Which account do you consider "more true" and why? What do the two entries suggest about the relationship between chronological proximity, meaning, and historical memory?

Following plenary reflection on the exercise, I ask students to talk aloud about how their reflections might affect the way in which they view biblical narrative and the relationships between the history of the composition of biblical texts, memory, and religious meaning.

Mary F. Foskett

18. SOURCE CRITICISM AND EYE-WITNESS ACCOUNTS

Anyone who introduces source criticism in relation to someone's Scripture is likely to meet at least some level of resistance from some of their students. The following exercise is one that I use early in the semester of my "Introduction to the New Testament" class, but it could easily be used in any course that discusses source criticism or textual transmission. This exercise requires a modicum of courage, as it begins by inexplicably acting in unusual ways in front of your class, but I find that by the end of the exercise the explanation has become very clear and the students have learned something valuable in the process.

Although I am usually precisely on time for my class, for this exercise I intentionally arrive several minutes late. This is so that the class will be settled down, and ready for class to begin the moment I enter. When I arrive, I perform—without saying a word about it—a skit for them, the details of which can vary widely, but the purpose of which is to get their attention with things written, spoken, and performed. I usually include the following, among other things: greeting the class; dropping books or papers on the floor; writing Syriac on the board; writing English on the board with a small misspelling ("Febuary" works well for this, as does switching an "m" with an "n"); and pretending to trip on something. I try to make the skit long enough to catch everyone's attention but short enough that they have a chance of remembering it, all the while allowing them to think that I am just trying to get class started as usual. I then ask them to get out a piece of paper and write down everything that I just said, did, and wrote from the time I walked into the room, giving as much detail as they can.

After they have had time to write, I erase the board (this is important, since it then leaves the written text open for debate), and ask the class orally to reconstruct what happened. I also choose a few volunteers to read their descriptions aloud. I sometimes do this in small groups first, and sometimes start out as a whole class, but in either case I get the students to try to sort out the differences in their descriptions. What sentences did I actually say? What words did I use? Did I trip before I wrote on the board, or after? It is good to give them enough time to talk about several different aspects of what happened.

The next stage in the exercise is to begin to talk with the students about what criteria they find themselves using in order to determine which descriptions are more accurate than others. Through this discussion, the students often come up themselves with many of the criteria that scholars use in comparing different manuscripts of the same text, and different textual descriptions of the same event. They will usually validate the majority recollection over the minority. They will recognize that it is more likely that multiple people copied the same spelling error because it really was on the board, than that these student scribes just happened to make the same mistake themselves. With conversation, they will realize that a student's claim that I, as someone from New England, greeted them as "y'all" is more likely to be the student putting my sentence into his or her own vocabulary than an accurate rendition of my own sentence. Finally, when I ask for volunteers to come up to the board and recreate the Syriac words I had written, they all agree that it is very difficult for scribes to reconstruct accurately a text in a script that is not their own.

From this discussion, it is easy to make a transition to discussing textual transmission, scribal errors, oral accounts, and eye-witness accuracy in relation to the texts about Jesus. What criteria helped us choose the most "accurate" description? What happens when eye-witness accounts disagree? Was the transmission of the writing more consistent than that of the spoken sentences? My hope is that in the process they will be willing to question the history of the words and stories in the New Testament texts in ways that they may have been unwilling to do without going through the exercise. Of course, this will not suddenly change a student's belief about the inerrancy of the biblical texts, but I have found that the exercise does allow for more willing discussion of source criticism and textual transmission than they might otherwise be able to have. So take courage through the first few minutes—it will be worthwhile, and the students will remember the lesson far longer than your performed mishaps! (For a similar exercise, see §46.)

Christine Shepardson

19. INTRODUCING TEXTUAL CRITICISM

Textual criticism is tedious work but someone has to do it. Because of the specialized skills it requires, very few students will pursue it as a vocation. Before we interpret the Bible, however, we must first establish the text, and many students will have little idea of what is involved in the transmission of the text from its original composition down to the present day. This exercise "dramatizes" the process of transmission as a way of introducing students to textual criticism and the peculiar problems its practitioners have to solve.

Before I lecture on the aims and methods of textual criticism, I have the class play the child's game of "telephone" in which one person whispers a message to the person in the next seat, who whispers it to the next person, and so on until the message has been whispered to the last person in the queue. The original message changes, sometimes significantly, by the time it reaches the end of the line. When it reaches the end, I have each student write down what they think was the original message. Some will already have guessed it, but I do not announce that the game is meant to illustrate certain dynamics of the copying process. Once the game is complete, I draw a comparison between "telephone" and the scribal process of copying manuscripts. Discussion revolves around the reasons for any distortions of the message or, depending on how much it has been altered, the reasons it did not change more than it did. Due to the human element, the discussion is never the same because the outcome is always, if only slightly, different, even when I start with the same message.

The "message" I like to use is from a song written by Mick Jagger and Keith Richards of the Rolling Stones: "You can't always get what you want. But if you try sometime, you might just find, you get what you need." (Other possible messages may include snippets from the Declaration of Independence, the preamble to the U. S. Constitution, the Gettysburg Address, John 3:16, or a quotation from Confucius, Shakespeare, or Emerson.) This message is long, but not unreasonably so. It is also familiar, but not so familiar that every link in the human chain will be able to reproduce it verbatim whether or not they hear it clearly. Its familiarity moreover simulates the influence of oral tradition on the process of textual transmission.

Rarely do students have trouble coming up with excellent observations on what took place between the beginning of the game and the end. It is nevertheless a good idea for teachers to be prepared ahead of time with their own reasons. This will help later in using examples from "telephone" to explain the detective work textual critics must do to arrive at the original text. The most basic factor for variations between the "autograph" (the original message) and the final "manuscript" is a dictation error; one or more persons simply hears it the wrong way. The speed at which the message is transmitted may either exacerbate or ameliorate the problem. Individual words may be left out (haplography) or the order of the words may get reversed. Foreign students may not realize when they have missed key prepositions, conjunctions, or verb inflections. Some

may try to smooth out the slightly awkward syntax. Others may unconsciously adjust the message so that it harmonizes with the song as they
remember hearing it previously. (In the original recording, there are
slight variations in how the line is phrased.) Sometimes a word or two
will be added accidentally. The nature of the larger "text" from which the
excerpt is taken might further influence the care with which one person
passes it on to the next.

No analogy is perfect, and this one is no exception. Once the students
learn the basic methods by which scholars attempt to reconstruct the
original text, the differences between "telephone" and scribal practices
leading to variant readings will become evident. In pointing out the ways
in which the analogy is an imperfect one, they become better able to put
themselves in the place of the scribe and thus more cognizant of what can
happen to the manuscript during copying. Each student in the chain is in
effect a copyist. The consequences of mistakes on their part are not very
great. When the message is regarded as the Word of God, however, one
can see that it is a game with high stakes indeed.

Patrick Gray

20. TEXTUAL CRITICISM

To introduce the topic of text criticism, I use a small-group exercise that
can be accessed on the Internet (www.earlham.edu/~seidti/iam/exer-
cise.html). The site provides four different "manuscripts" of paragraph
length recounting the event of a master class led by the famous violinist,
Pinchas Zukerman. Each manuscript is either a copy of the original text
(which the site also provides) or a copy of one of the copies. The site
includes its own set of instructions for the activity that I adapt, depending on the purpose of the exercise or the nature of the class I am teaching.
I divide the students into four groups with each group responsible for
deciphering a manuscript and creating a "translation" without the aid of
the "original" text. The manuscripts resemble both in type and form
ancient Greek manuscripts by using all capital letters, no spaces between
words, and no punctuation. If the classroom permits, I will sometimes
darken the room and provide each group with some kind of lighting to
"create the mood."

As a text-critical exercise, it is a "hands-on" way for the students to
experience the conditions under which the copying of manuscripts
occurred and the reasons for and nature of the scribal errors that tran-
spired. In our group discussion, we compare each of the manuscripts and

note the assumptions and mistakes of the copyists by comparing them to the original text. The students are usually able to arrive at most of the common scribal errors on their own and occasionally suggest some humorous ones as well. Since all four groups have a copy of each manuscript, they are able to see quite clearly the possibility of variants. To introduce the process of adjudicating manuscripts, I ask each group to assess the reliability of its manuscript and to include criteria in support of its conclusions. The depth of this discussion will vary considerably depending on the level of the class and whether or not the students have taken Greek.

While this exercise is primarily intended to illustrate the issues surrounding text criticism in New Testament studies, I have also used it to introduce more general topics such as how the Bible came to be and Bible translation(s). At a basic level, the students begin to understand the complicated processes that produce the Bibles they are able to purchase. This exercise can generate introductory lectures on both the formation of the Bible as well as the text transmission histories specific to each testament. I also use this exercise to foster the critical reading of chapter delineation, versification, headings, and titles. I typically have the students turn to Luke 10:29–37 and tell me the title of the story provided by their Bibles. We then have a discussion of the title, why it works, the interpretive assumptions that led to this title, and what the meaning of "good" is according to the story. I take suggestions for different titles and ask how these titles might change the focus and meaning of the story.

This exercise can also be used as a foray into the issue of Bible translation or a discussion that compares Bible versions and editions. Here I ask the students what it was like to "translate" their manuscript. What kinds of decisions did they have to make? What assumptions were at work in their decision-making? Usually, the students will talk about having to make a choice based on what they *thought* the story was about or what they *assumed* the text was saying. They note that their ability to translate the text was also dependent on the knowledge they brought to the text (e.g., did they have any familiarity with Pinchas Zukerman or have a musical background?). This leads to a conversation about translation as interpretation and what it means to make such an equation.

By recreating a visual picture of what an early manuscript would have looked like, this activity achieves several possible goals. First, it fosters a beginning appreciation for the text the students have in front of them at a most fundamental level. Second, it "creates the distance," so to speak, between the Bible and the students sometimes necessary to propose the issues frequently addressed in introductory Bible classes. Third, for classroom situations in which there is significant diversity in Bible knowledge it "levels the playing field" by creating an environment in which all of the students have little experience.

Karoline Lewis

21. TEXT CRITICISM AND TRANSLATIONS

To help students realize that there is no "original" version of the Bible and appreciate the manuscripts that stand behind the English translation on which they rely, I do a brief exercise in class in which I put on an overhead the Masoretic text of 2 Sam 13:21. Students obviously cannot read the Hebrew but this helps them glimpse the role translation plays in what they read. Then I put up the Greek (LXX) version of the same verse. Students are often pleased to be able to recognize the name "David" in the line.

Next I show them an overhead that has the Hebrew on one line and the Greek version retroverted into Hebrew written directly underneath the MT version. Students get a bit more interested because even though they do not read a word of Hebrew they can see that LXX line is longer than the MT. I then show them the English translations of the two lines. We talk about the difference in meaning between the two lines and about how one might decide which represents the more "original" or oldest form of the passage (e.g., something dropped out when it was copied; something was added for explanation; the shorter reading might be the more original because things generally expand over time; etc.). Those who want to delve into the technical details of text criticism at this point may consult P. Kyle McCarter Jr., *Textual Criticism: Recovering the Text of the Hebrew Bible* (Philadelphia: Fortress, 1986), 26–43, 72–75.

Then I show them a picture of the fragment of this verse from the Dead Sea Scrolls. They are impressed with how tiny it is, and when I reveal the Hebrew from the DSS fragment and add it to the overhead comparing the Hebrew from the MT with the Hebrew version of the Septuagint, students immediately recognize the match between the DSS piece and the LXX version. We then check to see how the NRSV has translated this verse. Students not only discover that the NRSV has adopted the LXX reading but I am able to provide them with a quick lesson in how to read the footnote explanation.

This exercise has not produced any aspiring text critics, but it does pique curiosity about the biblical languages and helps students be more aware of the ongoing attention to understanding and translating the biblical text. Throughout the semester students will often inquire about the meaning of a word or phrase in Hebrew and draw their classmates' attention to information they spot and find interesting in the footnotes. (For similar exercises, see §§93, 207.)

Elna K. Solvang

22. TEXT CRITICISM WITH DAVID AND GOLIATH

In this exercise, students are given a copy of an English translation of the LXX version of 1 Sam 17 (Zondervan has republished the Greek and English LXX previously published by Samuel Bagster & Sons in London). Either in groups during class or as homework, they are to compare the LXX version to the 1 Sam 17 in their Bibles (based on the MT). It quickly becomes apparent that the LXX version is "missing" significant portions of the chapter (vv. 12–31, 50, 55–58). In class, students are asked to speculate on the reasons for these discrepancies.

Generally, the options can be narrowed down to two: (1) The LXX has abridged the story as found in the MT, or (2) the MT has expanded upon or supplemented the story as found in the LXX. Either option has possible explanations. For example, the LXX may have abridged the story for literary or ideological purposes, much as Chronicles radically abridges parts of Genesis through Kings. Or, the MT may have supplemented the story with material from another source or expanded the story in order to make it fit a pattern of negative contrasts between David and Saul. (On the various options, see A. G. Auld and C. Y. S. Ho, "The Making of David and Goliath," *JSOT* 56 [1992]: 19–39.)

This exercise allows the instructor to introduce the MT and the LXX as two of the major text-types behind English translations of the Hebrew Bible. It also shows that textual criticism does not only deal with small differences of detail within single verses but also with larger differences between what appear to be different editions of various books of the Hebrew Bible. Furthermore, these different editions may display their own unique theology or ideology.

If time and interest allow, a similar comparative exercise can be constructed around Job 2:9–10. In this case, it is the LXX that puts more words in the mouth of Job's wife and thus presents a significantly longer text than the MT. Again, discussion can focus on possible reasons for this textual difference.

F. V. Greifenhagen

23. COLORFUL SEMIOTICS

Undergraduate students who are not able to work with the primary biblical languages, especially those who have never learned a foreign language, often express concern that too much is lost in translation. Some of that concern is warranted; as the grandson of Ben Sira notes, certain words, phrases, and ideas are difficult to render perfectly from Hebrew, Aramaic, or Greek. A related concern for students is the question of multiple Bible versions. Which is the best? Which is the most accurate? These concerns become more worrisome as students realize that any given word may be translated in a number of ways, and there are a number of potential linguistic choices that a translator may make. To use the technical language of semiotics, any given signifier has a range of signification. In translation, therefore, any given text has a range of potential meanings. Students betray a certain naïveté when they assume that all questions about meaning could be answered if they could only read the original language and translate it themselves. (Having them read the prologue of Sirach helps to correct this misconception.) Students need to understand that there are interpretive decisions made in any act of translation.

On other hand, it is important for students to understand that translation is not done arbitrarily or capriciously. Although all translation is interpretation, there are also limits and constraints to interpretive possibilities of a text. Even though a text may have a number of different potential meanings, there are also boundaries for those possibilities. In other words, there is more than one way to render a translation, but there are not unlimited ways to translate (cf. B. Blount, *Cultural Interpretation* [Minneapolis: Fortress, 1995], and P. Ricoeur, *Interpretation Theory* [Fort Worth: Texas Christian University Press, 1976]).

As a simple exercise to help students understand possibilities and constraints in linguistic choices, I ask them to identify colors. In a given class period, I wear a sweater that is a heathered aqua (any subtle color would work), and ask them to identify the color as precisely and creatively as possible. The responses vary: blue, green, sage, gray-green, ocean, and so forth. The more responses the students give, the more they recognize that there are multiple interpretive possibilities. It is rewarding to see students recognize the freedom to choose between varying possibilities. Often, a student will respond with frustration, "You could say anything!" At that point, I ask them to identify constraints. One cannot say that an aqua sweater is orange, black, or brown.

This exercise will work with any visual that has subtle, variegated colors. An engaging alternative could be investigating the colors found in clothing catalogues and paint chips. J. Crew and Ralph Lauren Home, for instance, both have color names that range from the sublime to the ridiculous. First, present students with the color names, such as "Bright Papaya," "Lapis," "Ivy," or "Rain.". Then ask students to identify which colors the names represent. Next, show them the colors in the catalogue or paint chip and ask them to invent their own names. Finally, and perhaps most importantly, ask them to identify which names should not be used. When does the interpreter's word choice enlighten a concept? When does it get in the way? Why use "Bright Papaya," for instance, when "yellow" will do? By the end of the exercise, students should be aware that there is both freedom and constraints when it comes to translation and interpretation.

Sara Koenig

24. POETRY AND HISTORY

In a lecture covering various interpretive methodologies, I often segue from historical approaches to literary ones by means of a poem. Almost any poem will do, but I have tended to use a poem of my own, which means that it will be a far cry from the best of poems, but will also contain a number of elements that I have intentionally put in so as to maximize the learning experience (read: stack the deck!). It is easy for students in biblical studies to be overwhelmed by historical approaches and historical data and to get the impression that it is history that rules the interpretive roost. Teachers know otherwise: that the historical-critical paradigm, while still operative, maybe even dominant, does not occupy the place it enjoyed fifty years ago. Other approaches now share the stage with equal, if not more, importance. This exercise is designed to demonstrate not only *that* this is true, but *why* it is true, even necessary.

Putting a piece of poetry up at this particular point in the lecture highlights two points: (1) that there is more to interpretation than just history (i.e., poetry is a different genre with different rules than historiography proper); and, (2) *at the same time*, even poetry can be interpreted historically. Given the placement of the exercise, coming right after a treatment of historical approaches, I find it helpful to start with the second point. I do so by asking the students to analyze the poem historically: Who was the writer, where was it written, when was it written, what other historical data can be culled from the poem, and so forth. There are clues, typically, by which to get at some or most of these questions (especially if the poem is my own and I've intentionally—or unintentionally—left some). And yet, after some discussion, the class soon gets to the point where they have uncovered a certain amount of data about the poem, but much of the poem's subject matter—what it is really and ultimately about—has not been touched. That is, even when the historical information has been carefully investigated by means of the poem itself, the question of the poem's meaning(s)—something that is not coterminous simply with the poem's historical circumstances or the earlier facts discussed by the students—remains. The students have identified certain things about the poet and the poem, but have not yet adequately addressed other, equally important aspects, especially when the genre is poetry: items such as what is said, how it is said, imagery, metaphor, and the creation of a certain density of lived experience that characterizes poetic speech (see C. Wiman, "Fugitive Pieces," *Poetry* 182/3 [June 2003]: 155). Poetry, ultimately, is less about specific informational content than about the creation of an experience in the reader.

This leads directly to the first of my two points, and I usually facilitate this by simply asking the students, after the historical exercise, "Yes, good, but what does the poem *mean*? What is it *about*?" They quickly see that, at least with poetry, the rules of the game have shifted and that historical analysis only goes so far in the hermeneutical question of the interpretation of poetry. This helps them begin to shift into a different mode of interpretation and see how it is distinct from (even while it can be related to) predominantly historical approaches.

Although this exercise may be used in a lecture on interpretive methods, it should work just as well as an introduction to biblical poetry in general or the Psalms in particular.

Brent A. Strawn

25. THE NARRATIVE ANALYSIS OF EPISODES

Based on the assumptions of narrative criticism, this series of exercises enables students to analyze narrative episodes as stories, apart from the question of their historicity. The focus of analysis includes characters, places, events, and values in the story world. You may have students switch their partners or small-group members with different exercises in order to maintain interest, avoid repetition, and enable them to learn more from each other. The exercises may be used with any biblical narrative.

Careful Reading. This exercise is designed to lead students to read an episode carefully. Invite each member of the class to form pairs.

Step One: (a) Both persons in each pair read and study the episode silently for a few minutes as a means to recall it word for word as best they can. (b) Both close books, then one person recounts to the other what they read as faithfully as possible. Be sure to tell the one recounting to seek to tell the story as they can recall it word for word. Be sure to make it clear that the one listening is not to follow along in the Bible while the other recounts the episode. (c) Both now look at the episode and see what details were omitted, added, or changed in the telling.

Step Two: (a) Both reread/re-study the episode silently. (b) Both close books, and the other person recounts the episode as faithfully as possible. (c) Both check to see what details were omitted, added, or changed in the telling.

Step Three: Both partners should now go line by line asking questions about the passage (without trying to answer them), based on what they noticed in steps one and two.

Return to Plenary: (a) Ask the students as a whole to note some things they changed, added, or omitted when they were going through the memory exercise. Then suggest why they may have done so—often because it represents what they do not like or do not understand or wish were different about the episode. (b) Then have the whole class engage in naming their questions in a rapid, scattershot fashion. Do not try to answer any or let students answer them. The purpose is to open the episode up to examination rather than closing options down. A good question is better than a pat answer.

Point of View and Character. The purpose of this exercise is to enable students to identify with various characters and to see the insights and problems that come with changing point of view. The exercise shows how the narrator has the overarching point of view and encompasses other points of view within a larger framework.

Step One: (a) Have each person in the small group choose a different character in the episode and reread the story from that character's point of view. In other words, change the pronouns to the first person for the character you have chosen and then read the episode as if you were that character. (b) Take a few minutes to study silently the episode with the pronouns changed. Do not try to do this exercise by recall. Rather, simply prepare to read it. Be sure to prepare to read the episode with the attitudes and emotions you might imagine of your character in this situation (excitement for someone healed, anger for someone offended, and so on). (c) Then have each person in turn read the episode from the point of view of the character they have chosen. Be sure to tell those listening not to follow along in the Bible but simply to listen intently to the story.

Step Two: When reading is completed, address the following questions in the small groups: What did you learn of the character's point of view? About the character's relation to others? Did you identify with the character? What emotions were involved? What parts of the episode are not realistically recounted by this character? Additional questions may include: What drives or motivates the character? What does this episode reveal about the character? Does the character change? What are the beliefs and values of the character? Is this character illuminated by comparison or contrast with other characters? How does this episode fit into the role of this character in the whole gospel?

Return to plenary: Ask students to reflect on what they learned from this exercise.

Stage it! The purpose of this exercise is to expand the imagination so as to be specific about the setting of the episode—climate, landscape, villages, cities, houses, synagogues, clothes, customs, laws, cultural assumptions, and so on.

Step One: Imagine you were responsible for producing a brief film or video of this episode. What questions would you need to have answered in order to produce a faithful version of this story?

Step Two: Choose several questions and try to answer them. In each case, ask how the element of the setting relates to the characters, problems, conflicts, and events that may be present in the episode.

Return to plenary: Seek to answer some of the pressing questions they may have. Clarify what difference the setting makes to the episode as a whole.

Analysis of Conflicts. This exercise enables students to analyze the plot of an episode that involves conflict.

Step One: Identify the conflicts in this episode. These include conflict within a person (inner conflict); between people; with nature; with society or authorities; and with supernatural beings.

Step Two: Trace the progress of the conflict. What is the source of the conflict? Who initiates it? How does it escalate? Is it resolved? How? Is anything left unresolved? Does the resolution lead to further conflict? With what words would you characterize the nature of the conflict?

Step Three: Assess the conflict. State in one sentence what is at stake in the conflict. Identify the beliefs and values of each party in the conflict.

Return to plenary: Be sure to see what questions they have. Ask several different groups to state what they thought was at stake in the episode and how the group made that determination.

Standards of Judgment. This is an exercise designed to enable students to see the beliefs and values in an episode. Standards of judgment are those norms (beliefs, attitudes, values, model actions) that are implicit or explicit in the narrative by which the readers are led to evaluate the characters. This exercise may be done in groups from two to four in size.

Step One: Note on what bases the standards of judgment are identified. Are the standards suggested by the narrator's words? By the words and actions of reliable characters? By God's words? By quotation from

P
R
O
L
E
G
O
M
E
N
A

Scripture? By negative words or actions of unreliable characters (showing what not to do or believe)?

Step Two: Based on the analysis of step one, identify and list the implicit and explicit standards in the episode.

Step Three: Evaluate the characters in the episode by the standards of judgment you identified in step two. What other standards of judgment, drawn from the whole gospel, are relevant for evaluating these characters?

Return to plenary: Ask who are the good and bad characters in the episode and how they know that based on the standards of judgment. If they have done work in the whole of that particular gospel, pose the following question: How do the standards in this episode fit into the larger (usually dualistic) standards of the whole gospel in which the episode is found?

(Other such exercises may be found in D. Rhoads, J. Dewey, and D. Michie, *Mark as Story: An Introduction to the Narrative of a Gospel* [2nd ed.; Minneapolis: Fortress, 1999)], 151–59). (For an exercise using narrative criticism, see §212.)

David Rhoads

Approaches and Resources

26. INTRODUCING THE "INTRODUCTION TO BIBLICAL LITERATURE" COURSE

Because many students, if given a choice, would opt for a root canal operation instead of showing up for the first day of a required class on the Bible, it is crucial to get the course off on the right foot. On the first day, although most of our time is spent on introductions and going over the syllabus, I try to frame the class as an opportunity to become equipped as an interpreter of and participant in culture, society, and the arts. I suggest that whether or not students have any religious interest in biblical literature, an understanding of literature, film, music, religious conflicts, and current electoral politics virtually requires some basic knowledge of the Bible. In this way, I suggest that the course is fundamental to their overall liberal arts training and I encourage them to keep an eye out for biblical themes beyond the classroom.

For the second day of the class, students are to read several short passages from the Sermon on the Mount (e.g., Matt 5:1–12, 17–20, 27–30, 38–48; 6:19–7:12), as well as Gen 1–2. I have them read the New Testament passages not to subsume the Hebrew Bible under some kind of christological interpretation, but rather to pique their interest in the course as a whole. Most students are intrigued enough with the figure of Jesus to be interested in what he reportedly said. I offer them a few thought-provoking passages to consider right away (e.g., sayings on God and mammon, lust and adultery, "an eye for an eye"). As a class, we discuss what the students noticed as they read Jesus' comments. This is a great way to find out something about the students in the class—where they are coming from intellectually, culturally, and religiously. In particular, we identify what we do not understand. We note, for example, what Jesus actually presupposes about first-century Jewish religion and society (e.g., scribes, kingdom of heaven, law, prophets, righteousness, hell, tax collectors). Doing this helps the students see an immediate rationale for learning more about ancient Jewish experience, history, and religion.

At this point, we begin to look at the creation and "fall" narratives. Initially, I show the students Michelangelo's *Creation of Adam* (see the Web Gallery of Art: http://www.wga.hu/frames-e.html?/html/m/michelan/3sistina/1genesis/6adam/index.html). I ask students to analyze the painting in light of what they have read in Genesis. They notice an uncircumcised, belly-button bearing, Caucasian man limply reaching out for a white-haired male surrounded by an odd entourage. We talk about the painting and what it suggests about Michelangelo's view of God and his use of Gen 1–2, which leads into a discussion of perspective and social location. One colleague suggested that I ask about the facial expression on the apparently female figure next to God. Is God embracing her? Strangling her? Who is she? Students become very engaged in conversation and good-natured debate at this point. They realize that they are not in a catechetical course, and that it just might be fun to learn something about the Bible. In short, they are ready to come back for the next class meeting. (For other introductory exercises, see §§119, 156.)

Michael Barram

27. INTRODUCTORY EXERCISE: BONE, STONE, BIBLE, FLAG

This exercise is designed for the first class meeting in a variety of religious studies classes (including biblical studies). This exercise works well with Christian students who must consider the way in which they consider the Bible to be sacred, and for a mixture of Christian and non-Christian students, who must develop early on a way to discuss both similar and diverse perspectives.

Students are presented with a human bone, a stone, a Bible, and an American flag placed on a table at the front of the room. If these objects themselves can not be procured, it is sufficient simply to write the words, well spaced, across the blackboard at the front of the room. Students, however, must be able to see all the objects, and to know what they are (e.g., a human bone, and not an animal bone; a Bible and not just a book). Students are then asked, "Which one of these objects is sacred?" and then encouraged to justify their answer. The wording ("Which one is sacred?") is important, because the exercise plays with objectivity, subjectivity, and relativity. Students might be inclined to say, for instance, "I think that the Bible is sacred," to which the instructor (or a classmate) might respond, "But what about the American flag? Don't we as Americans treat it like a sacred object, because we don't deface it or allow it to touch the ground?" Students often are tempted to say that while the Bible is "sacred sacred," the flag is "secular sacred," to which one may counter, "... but isn't 'secular' the opposite of 'sacred'?" Questions may be raised, then, about what it means to live in a secular society, what we mean by "sacred," if the sacred can be manifest in different forms, and *what* part of *which* object is sacred, and why (e.g., are the pages on which the Bible is written sacred too? The binding? If the cover were removed, would the cover be sacred? Can the sacred be desecrated? Is burning the Bible equal to burning the flag? Why is burning a body different? If the bone, stone, and flag are desecrated by throwing them on the ground, does this mean the earth is not sacred? What about the stone—under what circumstances does it become a sacred object? If it is sacred to one society and not to another, what does that say about a category of "objective sacrality"?

There is, needless to say, no "right" answer to the question of "which one of these objects is sacred," but students are encouraged to listen and respond to one another, and to consider and respect the perspectives of others. Overall, it works well to stimulate thought and discussion, and to give both instructor and student a sense of the range of student perspectives with regard to faith. (For other introductory exercises, see §§119, 156.)

Nicola Denzey

28. INTRODUCTORY SITE VISIT:
FINDING SCRIPTURE IN STONE

The primary goal of a biblical studies course is to teach students various ways of working thoughtfully and critically with the written text of the Bible. This is important, necessary, and central to our work as textual scholars. Nevertheless, it can be important in some pedagogical contexts to remind students of the way in which the Bible operates in Christian community primarily non-textually, yet in vibrant and significant ways. For this reason, it can be helpful to organize a site visit. Because of the accessibility of churches in virtually every community in North America, it is easy to arrange to take students for a visit even during assigned class time. Synagogues, unfortunately, are more difficult to find, but make for wonderful site visits since relatively few students taking biblical studies courses in North America have ever visited a synagogue. If time permits, it can be especially illuminating for students to visit two very different denominations—such as a Catholic church and a store-front-type evangelical church—or a synagogue and a church, and to compare the ways in which the Bible is used and is symbolically present in each of those spaces.

The goal of the site visit is simple: for students to discover and think about ways in which the Bible is present in the physical space of a church or synagogue. By this, I do not mean only the actual Bibles placed in the pew; I mean the way in which the Bible—its stories, themes, and symbols are present within the space. What elements in the distinctive architecture of a church or synagogue present or represent Scripture (e.g., as symbol, as written text, as biblical injunction)? Students might notice that a church has stained glass windows, and that those windows select particular themes or stories; there may be a typological connection between themes from the Old Testament and the New Testament present in the windows' iconography. They might notice the symbol for the Gospel of John, the eagle, around the pulpit. They might notice a crucifix and the way in which it visually interprets the gospel passion narratives. They might notice, in a Protestant church, the preference for plain crosses over crucifixes; this, too, can become a "talking point." They might wonder why, in a Catholic church, the stations of the cross are moments from the passion narratives arranged a particular way in physical space. Entering a synagogue, students might note the *mezuzah* and perhaps even know what piece of Scripture it contains; they might ask about the relationship between the physical dimensions of the sanctuary and the dimensions or layout of the Jerusalem Temple. They might ask about the *Aron-ha-Kodesh*, the Ark of the Sanctuary, and note the difference between the Torah as a sacred object and the Hebrew Bible as a sacred book.

A part of the visit may concern how or when a Bible is read in the physical space of a church or synagogue. Is all of it read, or just certain parts? Can people just pick up the Bible and read it in a church, or does that have to be done only at certain times, or in certain ways, or in certain areas of the church? How is the way that the Bible is read in a church different from the way it is read in a college classroom? It can be helpful to make up in advance a student worksheet asking students to report on what they notice, but bear in mind that such worksheets can sometimes inhibit the discussion of ideas.

It is best to organize this site visit at the beginning of a biblical studies course. Christian students can benefit from viewing their sacred space from an academic perspective, and non-Christian students can better appreciate that, for many, the Bible is at the very center of a living tradition. To help encourage this bridge-building, I often ask students to work in pairs during the site visit and to look together, question together, and share their knowledge. This also helps to build relationships in the class, which will start the course with students feeling that they know each other better and thus feel more comfortable participating in class discussions.

Nicola Denzey

29. THE COUNTERFACTUAL ESSAY

It is often difficult for students to appreciate why scholars spend so much time debating seemingly trivial questions such as in what decade was a given source written or how might two documents relate to each other. As a way to illustrate why issues such as the Documentary Hypothesis or the Synoptic Problem are important, I ask my students to choose one of the most prominent hypotheses in the critical study of the Bible and then tell me what the implications would be if the majority of scholars were actually wrong. The point is to think backward. Exploring what would happen if one of these central theories were wrong helps students understand why these hypotheses might be important in the first place. Such an exercise also forces students to examine how different topics in biblical studies relate to each other. For example, if the theory of Marcan priority were incorrect, how might this affect our understanding of the historical Jesus? I use this as a paper topic, but with some adjustment it could also function as the basis for in-class discussion or even an examination question in a class at any level.

The question I distribute is as follows: What If We're Wrong? As we have frequently noted in class, modern scholars do not have a time machine. Our conclusions about the sources we read are almost always probabilistic, albeit some hypotheses are more probable than others and not all arguments are equally strong. What would happen, however, if one of the field's base assumptions were wrong? For this essay, choose one of the most popular hypotheses regarding the origins of our gospel sources and examine what would be the impact of it being incorrect. Good candidates would include: Mark was not the source of later Synoptic Gospels but rather Matthew (or Luke); Q is a figment of the modern scholarly imagination; John had read all of the Synoptic Gospels before writing his gospel; the longer ending of Mark is actually the earliest; Thomas had read the Synoptic Gospels before writing his gospel; Matthew and Luke read the *Protoevangelium of James* previous to writing their infancy narratives; or John is actually the earliest of the gospels. For purposes of this paper, do not argue that such a drastic change in scholarly consensus is likely to occur; just assume that it has (in a sentence or two simply state, e.g., that John is earliest, or Q is dead). The rest of your paper needs to concentrate on the impact of this "discovery" on our understanding of the New Testament and early Christianity. In discussing the impact of this change, you should give examples of how it would affect the interpretation of specific passages as well as a more general shift in how we view first-century Christianity.

Michael Philip Penn

30. TAKING A STAND

This exercise is physical as well as intellectual and seems particularly good for early morning or late afternoon classes; it gets the blood, as well as the conversation, flowing. Although applicable to a range of issues, I most often make students "take a stand" when we study a text regarding community structure or ethical norms. Examples of texts that I use for "taking a stand" range from ancient Near East legal collections (e.g., the Code of Hammurabi, much of Deuteronomy, etc.) to early church orders (e.g., parts of 1 Timothy). Before class I choose half a dozen or so of the most controversial passages from the text. I begin class by designating one wall of the classroom "agree" and the opposite wall "disagree." I tell students to pretend that they are a member of the community to which this text is addressed, that is, they are part of a seventh-century B.C.E. Israelite community or a late first-century house church. We then all get up out of our seats and stand in the middle of the room. I read the first of the passages that I have chosen and ask students, from the perspective of their newly acquired persona, whether they think the regulation they just heard would be a good idea for their ancient community. Students walk to the appropriate wall; no fence-sitting is allowed. Once everyone has moved to one side of the classroom or the other, I ask students why they are standing where they are. I then invite those from the other side to reply to some of these points. This often results in a very engaging debate about the potential motivations of an ancient text and why it might have formulated a given regulation the way that it did. As soon as the conversation is becoming less productive, we simply reset with everyone returning to the middle and proceed to the next passage.

This exercise runs the danger of being reductionistic. Students could leave class feeling that it is not only possible but even easy to imagine what ancient folks thought; they might believe that every text has an agenda clearly discernable to twenty-first-century eyes. I feel that an explicit debriefing regarding these issues is the best way to avoid such problems. Despite these potential drawbacks, when appropriately framed, "taking a stand" often results in quieter students contributing to class conversations, allows one an entry-way into discussing a difficult document, and helps a class examine possible rationales and ramifications of ancient prescriptive texts.

Michael Philip Penn

31. SHORT STORIES AS EXEGETICAL TOOLS

Short stories can be excellent tools for teaching exegesis. Students are usually surprised to find such material on their New Testament syllabus, some happily, others not. To convince the reluctant that reading short stories will aid their New Testament studies, I make three points. First, reading and understanding a well-crafted short story requires a close reading of the text. Flannery O'Connor stories make this point particularly well. Reading O'Connor trains one to look beyond the surface meaning of things, to expect complexity, to account for symbolic language, images, and characters, and to read not merely for information but for transformation. There is no New Testament text which will not repay the reader who brings these sensibilities to the reading of it. The story is often told of Brevard Childs, Professor of Old Testament at Yale Divinity School, who, when asked how to become a better exegete, he responded: "Become a deeper person." Reading and appropriating good literature helps to do just that.

Second, reading good short stories can make students better writers (and preachers). I stress the fact that short story writers, unlike their novelist counterparts, must achieve maximum rhetorical effect with a minimum of words—not at all a bad goal for any writer (or preacher). To write forcefully and concisely are worthy goals.

Third, and most important, reading good short stories keeps the imagination active. Many students give up reading fiction during seminary for lack of time, and their studies suffer for it. Imagination is one ingredient essential to all serious intellectual inquiry. The same points may be made about poetry as well.

There are numerous anthologies of short stories with religious themes: *A Celestial Omnibus: Short Fiction on Faith* (ed. J. P. Maney and T. Hazuka; Boston: Beacon, 1997); *God: Stories* (ed. C. M. Curtis; Boston: Houghton Mifflin, 1998); and the multi-volume series *Listening for God: Contemporary Literature and the Life of Faith* (ed. P. J. Carlson and P. S. Hawkins; Minneapolis: Augsburg-Fortress, 1994–2000). I also recommend William H. Willimon's *Reading with Deeper Eyes: The Love of*

P
R
O
L
E
G
O
M
E
N
A

Literature and the Life of Faith (Nashville: Upper Room, 1998). Each of its ten chapters is related to particular pieces of literature. While it is short on short stories, assigning Willimon's three-page introduction might help students see the value of such reading.

For poetry, consult the following: *Chapters Into Verse: Poetry in English Inspired by the Bible, Vol. II: Gospels to Revelation* (ed. R. Atwan and L. Wieder; Oxford: Oxford University Press, 1993); Vassar Miller, *If I Had Wheels or Love: Collected Poems of Vassar Miller* (Dallas: Southern Methodist University Press, 1991); Kilian McDonnell, *Swift, Lord, You are Not* (Collegeville: Saint John's University Press, 2003); and Lisel Mueller, *Alive Together: New and Selected Poems* (Baton Rouge: Louisiana State University Press, 1996).

Particular stories or poems I have used with good effect include:

1. Fyodor Dostoevsky, "Rebellion" and "The Legend of the Grand Inquisitor," in *The Brothers Karamazov* (trans. R. Pevear and L. Volokhonsky; San Francisco: North Point, 1990). It is arguably the best material ever written dealing with theodicy, the nature and burden of truth, the constant desire of human beings to confuse freedom and slavery (cf. Galatians), love versus paternalism, the role of clergy, satanic motivations (temptation in the wilderness; Peter at Caesarea Philippi), and the paradoxical power of the cross (Jesus never speaks to the Inquisitor; he only kisses him).

2. Frederick Buechner, "The Two Battles," in *The Magnificent Defeat* (San Francisco: HarperSanFrancisco, 1966), 36–43. Useful for Ephesians.

3. Flannery O'Connor, "Parker's Back," in Curtis, *God: Stories*, 167–85. Useful in connection with "conversion" themes.

4. Flannery O'Connor, "Revelation," in Carlson and Hawkins, *Listening for God*, 15–36. Especially good for use with Luke's theme of the Great Reversal.

5. Brendan Gill, "The Knife," in Curtis, *God: Stories*, 78–82. Especially good for a discussion of miracles.

6. Zora Neale Hurston, "Sweat," in Maney and Hazuka, *A Celestial Omnibus*, 139–49. Useful for texts concerned with evil and God's justice.

7. Anne Lamott, "Why I Make Sam Go To Church," in *Traveling Mercies: Some Thoughts on Faith* (New York: Pantheon, 1999), 99–105.

8. James Baldwin, "Sonny's Blues," in *The Oxford Book of American Short Stories* (ed. J. C. Oates; Oxford: Oxford University Press, 1992), 409–39. Especially good with the parable of the Prodigal Son.

9. W. B. Yeats, "The Second Coming." Widely available on the Internet and in anthologies. Useful with the Book of Revelation.

10. William Hoffman, "The Question of Rain," in Curtis, *God: Stories*, 95–107. Great for helping students think about (a) their role as pastors and (b) the purpose, power, or place of prayer.

11. Peggy Payne, "The Pure in Heart," in Curtis, *God: Stories*, 222–35. Good with the Sermon on the Mount.

12. Alice Walker, "The Welcome Table," in Carlson and Hawkins, *Listening for God*, 110–113. Especially good when studying Matthew's parable of the wedding banquet or its Lukan parallel.

13. Amy Tan, "Fish Cheeks," in *The Bedford Reader* (ed. X. J. Kennedy, D. M. Kennedy, and J. E. Aaron; 6th ed.; Boston: Bedford, 1997), 54–56. Useful for consideration of assimilation, boundaries, identity, and alienation within a host culture.

14. Ursula LeGuin, "The Ones Who Walk Away from Omelas," in *The Short Story: 50 Masterpieces* (ed. E. C. Wynn; New York: St. Martin's, 1983), 702–8. A stunning story that fits many themes, particularly those connected with atonement and social justice.

15. James Weldon Johnson, "The Creation." Widely available on the Internet and in anthologies. Good with the Prologue to John, the Christ Hymn of Colossians, or any "Cosmic Christ" texts.

16. Reynolds Price, "A Chain of Love," in *The Names and Faces of Heroes* (New York: Atheneum, 1963). This story fits well with almost any New Testament text. Its major themes include death, family relationships, and the mystery of Christian rites and rituals as practiced by different denominations.

17. Frederick Buechner, "The End is Life," in *The Magnificent Defeat*, 74–81. Good for use with the resurrection narratives.

18. Lisel Mueller, "Hope" and "The Exhibit," in *Alive Together*, 103, 169. Useful with apocalyptic texts and others whose theme is hope.

19. Shirley Jackson, "The Lottery." Widely available on the Internet and in anthologies. Useful in reading Matthew or Paul especially when addressing the potential for accepted traditions to cause harm rather than edify.

20. Susan Glaspell, "A Jury of Her Peers." Available on the Internet. Read with the Gospel of John to stress the power of irony; things are not always as they appear.

Jaime Clark-Soles

32. PALESTINIAN GEOGRAPHY

A basic knowledge of Palestinian geography is extremely helpful for students in following the storyline of the New Testament gospels. But I also often find that if one simply goes over the geography in class or even has a simple quiz where one identifies or locates place names, retention levels are fairly low. What I have found works better is to have students not only learn place names, but to be able actually to generate the map. This may sound like a daunting task, but if one is willing to live with a bit of simplification, it is really quite easy.

A crude but useful map of Palestine consists of a vertical line on the left, and to the right a small oval at the top, from which a vertical line comes down to a larger oval at the bottom. If you cannot stand the crudeness, you could make the left line slant outward slightly towards the bottom, but I find that the simpler the map the better it works. Obviously, to the left of the left line is the Mediterranean Sea. The small (top) oval is the Sea of Galilee, the larger (bottom) oval is the Dead Sea, and the connecting line is the Jordan River. In between the two lines lies the land of Israel. I then label the three major regions of Israel in New Testament times (Galilee, Samaria, and Judea). I do not include precise borders, simply the fact that Galilee is at the top, Samaria in the middle, and Judea at the bottom. I generally include only Jerusalem, Bethlehem, Nazareth, and Capernaum, but naturally other areas such as Caesarea Philippi, Jericho, Bethany, or the Decapolis could also be included, according to need.

Having introduced the simple map and shown them how to draw it, I then give a quiz at a later date that consists simply of a blank piece of paper upon which students must draw the map and place the appropriate labels. One can either provide them with a list of place names or require them to memorize the place names themselves. A compromise might work best—for example, require them to memorize the regions and bodies of water but provide them with a list of the cities/towns. In any case, I find that the requirement of having to generate the basic features of the map dramatically increases the retention level of geographical knowledge. I also find that once students are taught to draw the map, they do not mind having to do so at all—they rather appreciate and actually sometimes become enthusiastic about being able to draw the map. They tend to feel like they really "know something" about the Bible that they did not know before.

This way of teaching Palestinian geography could of course be easily adapted for the Old Testament/Hebrew Bible. The map stays the same; only the place names need to be changed.

Scott Shauf

33. ARCHAEOLOGY OF THE BIBLE

Archaeological and material remains can transform the students' understanding of the Bible. Archaeological excavations have uncovered many of the key places mentioned in the Bible, and the material remains from these excavations can put flesh and blood on the bones of the narrative. Archaeology can aid the teaching of the Bible by providing visual images of the original setting, supplementing and complementing the biblical narratives, and offering alternative perspectives to those of the biblical texts.

The easiest way to incorporate archaeology into a course is by selectively supplementing class lectures or discussions through a visual presentation of archaeological remains. Several options are possible. Many good slide sets of the archaeology of the Bible are available commercially, but I prefer to create my own digital slides with a scanner and PowerPoint. With an inexpensive scanner, I can create slides from any image or diagram from any book or archaeological magazine. As I research broadly for my teaching and scholarship, I come across numerous images that would be relevant to the content of my courses. I simply scan the image, save it on my computer in a meaningful way (such as in a directory entitled "Jerusalem images"), and in little time, I can build a substantial image library to use in my courses. PowerPoint provides a convenient way to use the images in class. I select the relevant images for the particular class, and load each image on a separate PowerPoint slide. Then, at the appropriate point in class, I use PowerPoint to display the images. An alternative to scanning images is to use digital images already published on the web. Holy Land Photos (http://holylandphotos.org), for example, provides numerous images of biblical sites that can be downloaded for use in presentations. The images include brief descriptions to facilitate their use in teaching the Bible.

Another means of incorporating archaeology into teaching of the Bible is by using the Virtual World Project, which provides teachers and students the opportunity to explore interactively the archaeological remains of biblical sites. The Virtual World Project is a publicly accessible, web-based project (http://moses.creighton.edu/vr), consisting of a series of interactive, virtual tours of archaeological sites (presently including sites in Israel, Turkey, and Greece). The tours are constructed from a series of 360–degree, virtual reality images that are linked together to cover an entire site. Navigation through the site is linked to interactive, detailed maps of the site so that the viewers can orient themselves within the site and jump to any other location. The virtual tours are supplemented with textual descriptions of the site and its features, appropriate samples of ancient texts, and bibliographies for further research. The project is continually growing, with new sites and text added regularly.

The Virtual World Project offers numerous pedagogical uses for aiding in the teaching of the Bible. As a lecture supplement, the interactive images presented in the virtual tours will help make concrete what is often abstract and bring to life what is remote and dead. In discussing Jesus' ministry, for example, I lead the students on a tour of Capernaum, Bethsaida, or Chorazin. The students can "stand" in the synagogue of Capernaum, then "go outside" to the traditional house of Peter. I show the students the theater in Sepphoris and discuss the background of Jesus' use of the term "hypocrite." In discussing the ministry of Paul, I illustrate the large Roman urban centers in which he ministered by touring the sites of Corinth or Ephesus. When I teach the stories in Samuel and Kings, I illustrate the Kingdom of Solomon by exploring the sites of Megiddo, Hazor, and Gezer. The students can "pass through" the so-called Solomonic gates at each site, noting the similarities and differences, and get a sense for the modest scale of the kingdom. I also "take" the students to the site of Dan and explore the temple first built by Jeroboam I. At the gate of Dan, the students explore the prominent role of "standing stones," which are condemned by the prophets, and compare their use at Bethsaida, a non-Israelite site in this period, and in the temple at Arad, an officially sanctioned temple in Judah. In different contexts, I lead the students on a tour of the Essene community at Qumran, and illustrate their concern for ritual purity by "walking around" the many *mikvoth* (pools for purification baths) at the site, and point out the caves in which the Dead Sea Scrolls were discovered.

The advantage of the Virtual World Project over a simple Power-Point presentation is that it can be utilized in many student-centered activities. The students can be assigned themes (using the project index) or sites in the project to explore and read before class as a supplementary textbook. I assign the students to explore the site of Lachish, for example, before we discuss Hezekiah's reform (2 Kings 18–20) in class. Students can also be assigned individual or group research reports that make use of the Virtual World Project. For example, the students can be assigned to give a report on "high places." By exploring the Virtual World Project, the student will discover a number of high places in their archaeological contexts. They will be able to note where such high places are located, their distinctive features, and differences between the various high places. Similarly, the students can use the project to explore town planning, domestic life, economy, fortifications, administration and public life, sacred spaces, and many other features of the material world of the Bible. As the project continues to grow, so also will the many uses for which it can serve teaching and learning of the Bible.

Ronald A. Simkins

34. AN APPROACH TO A "BIBLE AND FILM" COURSE

A film is essentially a cultural statement or an interpretation of cultural signifiers. As such it is an inherently ideological form. Most students, however, watch (especially "religious") films totally uncritically, never questioning the view of reality that the film portrays. My primary goals in the summer intensive course, "Bible and Film," are (1) to teach students that, while films often display the world in convincing and immediate terms, they nevertheless represent particular cultural and worldviews; (2) to enable students to "read" films for those views; and (3) to critique the film and its presentation in light of the biblical text itself.

To accomplish this task, I begin by asking the students to read an essay or two introducing them to the process of "reading" a film (I usually assign the introduction and conclusion of Joel W. Martin and Conrad E. Ostwalt Jr., eds., *Screening the Sacred: Religion, Myth, and Ideology in Popular American Film* [Boulder: Westview, 1995]). We also discuss the fact that films are not neutral. When we read films in the class, we will look for *how* they mean as well as *what* they mean.

On the first day of class we watch the 1922 version of *Salome*, comparing and contrasting it with the biblical text, and then discussing what cultural messages are being given. We then break to watch *The Ten Commandments* (1956), for which I provide the following guided questions: (1) How accurately does this film depict the text? (2) How does that depiction develop into a cultural statement (be specific—refer to specific scenes and/or lines and characters)? (3) Do you endorse this use of the Bible? Why or why not?

On the second day we discuss their secondary readings and apply what we discuss to *The Ten Commandments*. The class continues with "Jesus on Film." I have normally used *Jesus of Montreal* (1989) for this class for a number of reasons. It is actually a story within a story, with the characters' personal lives mirroring the Passion play they have been hired to perform, so students have several levels from which to read and comment on the film. Second, it is a controversial rendering of Jesus, so students can readily see how cultural ideas and concepts play into the way the film is structured. Third, it seems to bring students to a new level of being able to read films.

On the fourth day we discuss *Blade Runner* (1982). In preparation for viewing the film, I ask the students to read Genesis 1–3, and then look for themes from the biblical text in the film itself. In addition, they come to class having written a one- or two-page reflection covering the following questions: (1) What is/are the major social, political, and/or cultural issue(s) being addressed in the film? Give evidence for your assessment. (2) How does this film use biblical themes or citations to discuss these issues? Be specific, again referring to specific scenes, lines of dialogue, characters, etc. (3) Do you endorse these uses of biblical themes? Why or why not?

The students invariably come to class with strong opinions about the film. In addition, they all see different things in the film. While I have a list of issues and questions prepared in case students have missed much of the biblical and religious depths of the film, I usually do not have to use it; between all the students in the class, the direct and subtle allusions to Gen 1–3, Roy's morphing from Lucifer into a Christ figure, the focus on eyes as the mirror of the soul, the recurring theme of how creator relates to creation (including the issue of creatures trying to take over the creator's role), and the overarching issues of what it means to be human, are all raised. I show clips illustrating some of the themes as time permits. If there are students in the class who did not "get" the film when they watched it on their own, by the end of class, they have come to an appreciation of what the film does. In addition, I do not specify whether they watch the Director's Cut or the market version (with narration and a "happy ending"). This makes for some lively conversation on what difference the various cuts make for the meaning of the film as a whole, and for its biblical and theological messages. There is always a debate as to what the "true" message of this use of biblical themes is (e.g., is this a Christian or anti-Christian view?). The discussion of the figure of Roy as a possible Christ figure prepares students particularly well for the final film, which is always a "secular" film with a Christ figure in it. I usually choose *Babette's Feast*, which most of the students have not seen, but which is rich in biblical and theological symbolism.

For the final paper, I ask students to choose either a Jesus film or a film using a Christ figure and write a paper using a set of guided questions. They are to discuss both how that film correlates (or not) with the gospels or other theological representations of Christ, including references to camera angles, framing, dialogue, and the like, all of which we have discussed during the week. If a student chooses a Jesus film, they are to use the following guidelines: (1) Choose a secondary character (e.g., Peter or Mary) or group of people (e.g., Romans, priests) in the gospels and describe how the gospels portray them. (2) After viewing the Jesus movie, write an essay describing the similarities and differences between the gospels' depiction and the movie, and explain what cultural point is made by that treatment. (3) In a final section of the paper, deal with the following questions: How does this film portray Jesus? What is the central focus of Jesus' life in this film? Explain what cultural point is made by this film's treatment of Jesus. (This set of questions comes from a 1998 article by Paul V. M. Flesher and Robert Torry in a "Spotlight on Teaching" section of the AAR/SBL News.) If students choose a Christ-figure film, they are to use these guidelines instead: (1) Identify the Christ figure and any biblical references in the film. (2) Write an essay describing the depiction of the Christ figure in the film, as well as any references or allusions to the biblical text. Discuss in detail the particular slant the film takes—that is, which aspect(s) of Christ are emphasized. (3) Explain what cultural point is made by this film's use of a Christ figure, and show how that point is made.

I regularly have comments come to me in the year or two after the class that the students never watch films the same way again. Some also tell me that they now see biblical and religious themes in almost all of the films they watch. Many have gone on to do a "Bible and Film" or "Religion and Film" series in their internships or first call churches. Every once in a while I hear from a student with a suggestion for the next "Bible and Film" class I teach—either a suggestion for a film to use in the class or a possible paper topic. The ongoing conversations, long after the class has ended, show me how transformative a course such as this can be. (For exercises using movies, see §§44, 96, 177, 208, 209.)

Mary E. Shields

35. CANON FORMATION

When I introduce the concept of canon, I first ask students to write down three of the most significant movies they have seen. I distinguish "most significant" from "favorite" but do not define "significant." The definition of the term is part of their own work. Then I ask students to work in pairs to select, by consensus, four movies from their six. Then I ask them to work with another pair, forming a group of four, to select five movies, then finally to form a group of eight to select six movies. At that point there are three groups (given that my enrollment is usually 20–25). Each group writes its list on the board.

Then I ask the students to reflect on their group process and to write down answers to these questions: (1) How did they reach consensus, if they did, or what prevented it? What factors helped and what factors hindered their ability to reach agreement? (2) What were the criteria for selection that emerged in the process? Were these criteria explicit, that is, did they verbalize the criteria during the selection? Or were the criteria implicit?

In the ensuing plenary discussion, students will often notice that similar choices on individual or small-group lists make the decision process faster, as does group homogeneity. Conversely, they realize that differences of race, gender, and geographical background often multiply the number of movie choices and make consensus harder to reach. They note as well the role of personality and willingness to compromise on the part of group members.

A few groups develop explicit criteria. (I once had students who insisted that all movies on their list must represent major advances in the art of special effects!) Most students, however, list more implicit criteria than explicit ones. One class, for example, decided that their implicit criteria included movies with the themes of good and evil, with striking images and strong cinematography, with emotional appeal and Academy recognition, and those with "big," epic stories. Other students have suggested additional implicit criteria: movies that you want to see again, that require interpretation, that are transformative, that evoke a diversity of response, and those in which you identify with the characters.

This activity generates a rich matrix of analogies for exploring the canonization process. The model underscores that decisions about canon were the result of a process of conversations by "real" people. These conversations required discussion, common experiences, compromise, and reflection across time and space. Since many students desire to reach a consensus (which the instructor has requested), this activity does not foreground power dynamics in the selection process. I have found that some group discussions will begin to explore the politics of exclusion without additional prompts. For others, the instructor may decide to intervene at some point and impose certain constraints on the selections. This activity leads students to engage in some heated debate, and few of them are reluctant to bring their perspectives to the table.

An alternative approach, using the same format, is to ask which six books students would bring if they knew that they would be stranded on a desert island for a significant period of time. (For another exercise on canon, see §264.)

Bryan Whitfield

36. VISUAL ART AS A TEACHING TOOL

The presentation of visual art in introductory Bible courses carries three pedagogical advantages. First, it reaches the "visual learners" in our midst—those who retain visual information more easily than oral/aural information. In every class I teach there are students who remember a particular Bible story primarily because they have seen it artistically depicted. A student's recollection of God's rejection of Saul, for instance, might stem from Francis Cleyn's depiction of Saul tearing Samuel's robe. Nor is this particular painting the only thing they remember. The same student may also remember the larger significance of the scene, including Samuel's theological explanation of the torn robe (1 Sam 15:28–29), simply because she has had the story presented to her visually. For the visual learner, a painting creates the cognitive space in which a teacher's lecture can take root.

Second, the presentation of visual art offers students (regardless of their particular learning styles) a refreshing change from traditional teaching formats. Even the most dynamic lecturer will fail to engage all the students all the time. When lecturing on a more intricate historical narrative like 2 Kings, for example, the presentation of art depicting the miracles of Elisha or the death of Jezebel can trigger an instant (and quite visible) refocusing among students. Stopping briefly to observe the details of a painting may be all a teacher needs to refill the collective gas tank of the class.

How exactly does one integrate visual art into a lecture? Though the answer to this question depends upon one's particular goals as a teacher, I have found the presentation of art most effective when it introduces a new section of material rather than when it reviews a section already covered. This order takes better advantage of the class' newfound focus by using the artwork as a kind of "teaching moment": Gustave Doré's dark representations of Jezebel's death catch the eye, allowing the teacher to retell the larger story that stands behind them. Thus the lecture becomes a way to help students better understand what they are seeing.

Third, the presentation of visual art can assist a teacher in explaining the details of a specific biblical passage. Whether in lecture format or small-group discussion, artwork allows students to apply what they have learned—often to the point of triggering lively discussion. When faced with Michelangelo's depiction of Adam, Eve, and the serpent, for example, students will automatically recognize Michelangelo's liberal use of artistic license: Adam is not passively receiving the fruit from Eve (Gen 3:6) but is actually reaching over her to grab the fruit himself! Particularly for students prone to relieve Adam from all "blame," this painting affords the teacher an opportunity to explain the complexity of the passage and the collective blame it implies. That Adam apparently stands by Eve during the entire conversation with the serpent often goes unnoticed. In this way Michelangelo, despite misrepresenting a specific detail of the story, offers a wonderfully accurate depiction of collective guilt as depicted in Genesis 3.

Although the presentation of visual art does not require computer technology, access to programs such as PowerPoint and related accessories (projector and screen) ensures a more efficient presentation, enabling an entire class to view one or more works at the same time. Resources for finding biblical art are readily available on the Internet. The most comprehensive and best-documented site that I have found is part of the "Text This Week" site (http://www.textweek.com/art/art.htm), which allows users to search artwork according to biblical book. The Web Gallery of Art (http://gallery.euroweb.hu/search.html) has a comparable index but is not limited to biblical art. (For exercises using visual art, see §§58, 183, 260.)

Ira Brent Driggers

37. THE EDUCATIVE POWER OF THE RHETORIC OF BIBLICAL STORIES

P
R
O
L
E
G
O
M
E
N
A

Here I present an outline for a session based on three biblical passages that try to effect a process of maturation in the listeners or readers: the Parable of the Trees in Judg 9, the Song of the Vineyard in Isa 5:1–7, and the story of the Good Samaritan in Luke 10:29–37.

We begin with Judg 9:8–15, a simpler passage that helps students understand more fully the rhetorical expertise of biblical writers. Open the session by asking the students to recall an occasion when a new person tried to join in a group at their school and how the other children made fun of them by pretending to take them into the group, while really setting them up to get into trouble or to appear foolish before the teachers. Or ask them to recall when something similar happened to them. Give five minutes to discuss the topic in small groups and take feedback along the following lines: As well as being new, what other characteristics did the "fall guy/gal" have (less wise, younger, from another culture, etc.)?

Now read aloud to them Judg 9:8–15. The verses are told in the manner of a hard-hitting teacher passing on a cautionary tale. Then pose the following questions: What characteristics are allocated to the "trees" by this story? (Childlike, childish, expecting too much while offering little or nothing in return, ending up at the mercy of an unscrupulous "ruler.") What do you think readers of the story are meant to learn from it? (To be sure they know what exactly they are asking for and just how much it could cost both the giver and themselves.) Give the students a few minutes in their small groups to pull together their conclusions.

The second passage, from Isaiah, is an extremely complex piece of poetry that works best when declaimed aloud by an experienced monologue performer who can change voice, tone, and also the register of spoken English to indicate the different speakers and to highlight the contrasting perspectives portrayed through the poem. As we listen we realize that we, the listeners, are being differently constructed by each change in the "voice" of the speaker in the different sections of the poem. We note that although we begin as casual listeners we become less so as the poem progresses and finish as the targets of savage criticism of our lives and characters. First, ask the students to recall an occasion when a teacher outsmarted them into agreeing that they had been wrong or unwilling to carry out work properly or to follow through on something they had agreed to do. Give five minutes to discuss the question in their groups and take feedback along the following lines: How did the teacher get hold of your attention? (By praising your skills or enthusiasm, etc.) How were you conned into listening and then realizing that you had not lived up to your word? (By the teacher referring to the better behavior of people you admire who portray those skills/qualities, etc.)

Now read aloud to them Isa 5:1–7, the Song of the Vineyard. Verses 1–2 are spoken by a woman lover, in a suggestive, mocking-yet-loving voice with the implied sexual innuendo of a wedding song to beguile the reader into listening. In vv. 3–5 there is a change of voice (and tone) to a rather angry vintner (the beloved of the poem). In v. 6 the voice begins to thunder its angry revenge on the vineyard in words that give away the lover's identity. In v. 7 the voice changes to the similarly sharp but explanatory voice of the prophet who explains just who is talking now and also why he is so angry. After the reading, pose these questions: What characteristics are allocated to the "men of Judah" by this story? (They are selfish, idle, self-seeking, expecting too much while offering little or nothing in return, ending up irritating their Lord.) What do you think readers of the story are meant to learn from it? (To keep their side of the covenant agreement with the Lord.)

Finally, understanding the power and effectiveness of the nuances lurking within the story of the Good Samaritan will similarly be easier after working with the two Old Testament stories. First, ask the students to recall an occasion when a teacher maneuvered them into doing something quite exciting yet also challenging that they had not really wanted to sign up for, yet found themselves agreeing to do. Give them five minutes to discuss this and take feedback along the following lines: How did the teacher get hold of your attention? (By apparently addressing something you had asked about or were interested in.) How were you persuaded into changing your ways? (By realizing that you had been behaving like the unpleasant people in the story and not at all like the exemplary character.)

Now read aloud to them the story of the Good Samaritan (Luke 10:29–37), but before you do so you must portray the racial contempt and scorn felt for Samaritans by the Jews of that time. Then ask: What characteristics are allocated to Jesus' listeners by this story? (They are selfish, racist, self-seeking, expecting to be the "goodies" in the story, not the "baddies.") What do you think readers/listeners of the story are meant to learn from it? (That in the eyes of Jesus all people are to be valued equally and to do less is to be unworthy of his respect.)

Heather A. McKay

38. THE BIBLE, SLAVERY, AND AMERICAN CULTURE

One section of my course examining the ways in which the Bible has affected American culture focuses on civil rights and race. The Bible has significantly influenced discourse about race relations in the U.S. and served as a focal point in debates between pro-slavery proponents and abolitionists in the middle of the nineteenth century. By looking at biblical texts, along with some writings from that era, students can explore how the Bible has been and can be used to address ethical issues.

I give the students the following set of texts to read before class: Gen 9:25–27; Exod 20:17; 21:1–27; Lev 19:20–22; 25:44–53; Deut 15:12–18; 21:10–14; 23:15–16; 24:7; 1 Cor 7:20–31; Gal 3:27–28; Eph 6:5–9; 1 Tim 6:1–6; Phlm 4–22; 1 Pet 2:16–25. I also assign them two readings from mid-nineteenth-century rabbis: M. J. Raphall, "The Bible View of Slavery" (http://www.jewish-history.com/raphall.html); and D. Einhorn, "Anti-Slavery Answer to Dr. Raphall by Dr. David Einhorn" (http://www.jewish-history.com/einhorn.html). Both of these pieces originally appeared in Jewish newspapers.

In class, I first ask students which side—abolitionists or pro-slavery— would seem to have the easier argument to make, based solely on the biblical texts. The students usually recognize that the bulk of the texts assume the existence of slavery and provide little, if any, reason to denounce it. We then discuss how abolitionists who wanted to argue from the Bible might make their case. Not only would the abolitionists need to find other texts, they would also need to develop interpretive strategies that went beyond literal exegesis. Often students will refer to the Exodus story or to Jesus' ministry toward the poor and outcast. Both of these examples certainly pertain to the slavery issue, but not as directly as the texts I have assigned. I encourage the students to see how the hermeneutical stance of using my list of biblical texts differs sharply from the stance of using the Exodus story.

Turning to the historical documents, the documents demonstrate concretely two differing hermeneutical practices. In Raphall's sermon, he rests his case primarily on the literal sense. Since the Bible nowhere denounces slavery, it cannot be considered a sinful institution. One of the most interesting sections involves his support of the Fugitive Slave Law, based on an exegesis of Deut 23:16. On the other hand, Einhorn asks not whether the Bible explicitly condemns slavery but whether it is a moral evil. His response leans heavily upon the Exodus narrative, and he asks how Jews who thank God daily for their deliverance from Egypt could possibly support enslavement of other humans. He therefore takes a more holistic and narrative approach to the question and the evidence. Because both rabbis closely read a variety of texts from the Hebrew Bible and the New Testament, they are excellent case studies.

To conclude the discussion, I ask the students to think about other examples of groups or individuals who make ethical stands on contemporary issues based on the Bible. Reading the slavery texts and these two sermons provides a lens for understanding the hermeneutics that lie behind such positions.

Kyle Keefer

PROLEGOMENA

PART 2
HEBREW BIBLE

TORAH

39. GENESIS 1 AND ANCIENT COSMOLOGY

A basic objective of an introductory course on the Bible is that students understand the historical distance between the time of the Bible and the present. Because the Bible's influence is omnipresent in Western culture, some effort at distancing is necessary for proper historical interpretation. One's historical interpretation of the ancient biblical text should have contextual credibility. Teachers can accomplish one aspect of this objective by demonstrating the ancient cosmology of the biblical writers. This can be done very effectively in the first days of class by leading students in the drawing of Gen 1.

If students are told to draw what is described in Gen 1, many will create drawings that reflect their modern scientific understanding. Students often draw the earth as a planet with the sun and moon as separate celestial bodies outside the earth's sphere. Their tendency to impose what they know on the text can nevertheless be used effectively. In a homework assignment I require students to read Gen 1:1–31 and draw as best they can what is described in the text. The students can portray the days in various boxes on their paper. Artistic skill is not important. In the next class meeting, I lead the students in an inductive reading of the text, drawing on the board step by step what is described in each creation day. A chalkboard or a dry erase board allows me to create images that can be erased or adjusted as the narrative develops. This is very helpful for representing water as it is described in the text. In fact, one can begin the drawing by representing the presence of water all over the board and then erase areas and aspects of the water to correspond to the textual description as it unfolds, particularly in 1:1–19.

The crucial component of this exercise is the explanation and translation of the Hebrew word *raqiya'*. This word occurs nine times in Gen 1 (vv. 6, 7 [thrice], 8, 14, 15, 17, 20). It is important that students understand this word does not connote their modern conceptions of the earth's atmosphere. In Genesis the *raqiya'* is a solid surface that has water above it and water below it (see also Gen 7:11; 2 Kgs 7:2, 19; Ps 104:3, 13). The term is best rendered "dome" (NRSV) or "vault." Considering what we know about ancient Near Eastern cosmology, the distance between those ancient conceptions and modern scientific knowledge, and the assumptions of many beginning students, the alternate translation "expanse" is unhelpfully ambiguous (see NJPS, NIV, NAS). When read uncritically, "expanse" can be interpreted as referring to modern scientific conceptions of atmosphere and outer space. Leading students in the drawing of Gen 1 should dispel such notions. After the drawing is complete, I explain to students how the ancient cosmology makes sense of observed reality when viewed with the naked eye. There does appear to be water above and beneath the earth's surface. The sun, moon, and stars do appear to be "lights" *in* the dome (Gen 1:14–17). Such a view is consistent with what one would expect when interpreting an ancient text historically.

The ancient cosmology of Gen 1 is very different from what we now know. The realization of this fact enables students to consider the historical distance between our world and the world of the biblical authors.

Joseph F. Scrivner

40. GENESIS 1:1–3: TRANSLATION AND INTERPRETATION

This exercise introduces students to the effect of translation on interpretation. I provide students with a number of different biblical translations of Gen 1:1–3. (If students bring their own Bibles to class, there may already be a good number of different translations in the class.) Each verse is read slowly from one translation; students with different translations are asked to note any differences.

Two main translation differences are highlighted. First, it is noted whether v. 1 is translated as a complete or absolute statement (e.g., NIV: "In the beginning, God created the heavens and the earth") or as a relative temporal clause (e.g., NRSV: "In the beginning, when God began to create the heavens and the earth ... "). Both translations are possible but the first supports the traditional notion of creation *ex nihilo,* while the second suggests creation out of something pre-existing such as the chaotic *tohu* and *bohu* mentioned in v. 2. The second rendering can possibly lead to a consideration of the original context of this text amongst ancient Near Eastern myths of creation (e.g., *Enuma Elish*) whereby pre-existing chaos is defeated and ordered. Other biblical texts allude to this method of creation, for example, where the primordial monsters of chaos, Leviathan or Rahab, appear. The second possibility can also lead to a consideration of how the grammatical ambiguity in the text allowed for creative interpretations finding Wisdom or the Logos at the beginning of creation (Prov 8:22-27; John 1). Useful information on this stream of interpretation can be found in James L. Kugel, *Traditions of the Bible* (Cambridge: Harvard University Press, 1998).

Second, it is noted whether v. 2 contains the translation "spirit of God," "wind from God," or "mighty wind," all rendering the same Hebrew phrase *ruach Elohim*. Students discuss which rendering they prefer and why. It soon becomes apparent that the first possibility is especially attractive to those who would see a Christian trinitarian interpretation in this verse while Jewish translations prefer the second or third possibility.

The exercise is summed up by the observation that translation is not disinterested; that is, that the particular choices made by the translator are sometimes driven by the translator's ideological concerns. A consideration of the various ideologies behind available Bible translations can follow this discussion of Gen 1:1–3. (For a similar exercise, see §88.)

F. V. Greifenhagen

41. INTRODUCING THE DOCUMENTARY HYPOTHESIS USING GENESIS 1–2

I often find that students are resistant to (or even arrive in my class armed against) the idea that the Bible is "a cut-and-paste job," that is, a combination of literary sources. I get less resistance if I let the students discover this possibility on their own. The following exercise can be done in two parts, with students working in small groups and reporting on their conclusions after each part, or as a homework assignment including both parts. The worksheet I distribute contains the following questions:

1. Read Gen 1, taking notes on the following aspects of the text: (a) Name used for the deity; (b) Order in which things are created; (c) Way in which humans are created; (d) Tone/Mood of text (Awe-inspiring? Entertaining? Wondrous? Playful? Gloomy?).

2. Now take notes on Gen 2:4–25: (a) Name used for the deity; (b) Order in which things are created; (c) Way in which humans are created; (d) Tone/Mood of text (Awe-inspiring? Entertaining? Wondrous? Playful? Gloomy?).

As students discuss their conclusions they begin to speak about differences between "the first story" and "the second story." This lays the groundwork for a discussion of Israel's sacred traditions (plural), which were preserved in the text.

One final note: Students who are using the NIV will be puzzled by other students' claim that creation happens "in a different order" in the two accounts. The NIV eliminates the differences in the order of creation by translating some imperfect verbs in the pluperfect: thus, God had already planted a garden and created the animals before forming the "adam." The NIV provides a great opportunity for a discussion of translations and their role in interpreting a text. The NIV translators chose to change verb tenses in order to "correct" a discrepancy in the text. Was this a good decision, since it makes for a less confusing text, or not? (For related exercises, see §§82-84.)

Julie Galambush

42. TWO CREATION STORIES?: DRAWING THE ISRAELITE COSMOS

Most of my students are unaware of the differences between the two creation stories in Gen 1–2, and some feel very threatened when they first see these divergences. Consequently, out of concern for their sanity, I do not use Genesis to introduce them to the concept of a biblical book being composed of materials from different time periods. I deal with this issue earlier when studying Proverbs—whose different sections are obvious to students. They are less threatened when they see the various collections in a Wisdom writing.

When we get to Genesis, I give the following brief writing assignment: "Contrast the first creation account in 1:1–2:3 with the second account in 2:4–25. Explain how they differ in (1) the names they use for God, (2) the order in which God creates things (be specific in your listing), (3) the way in which God creates, (4) the portrait of God presented in each, and (5) the style of writing used to tell each creation story." This assignment brings them to class already in a state of bewilderment, and I capitalize on this condition. I begin by discussing what they saw in the two stories, and then I let them work with me in constructing a picture of an ancient Israelite concept of the cosmos.

I ask them to tell me what was created day by day in the account of Gen 1. As they look at the text and tell me what happened each day, I draw that stage of the cosmos on the board. To begin the drawing, I ask them what was there in the beginning according to 1:1–2. When they tell me "a dark, watery chaos," I draw wavy lines on the board, representing the formless, watery beginning. Then I ask them what happened on Day 1. As they tell me that God separated the light from the darkness, forming day and night, I ask them if I should draw the sun yet. This lets them tell me with some curiosity in their voice that "No, that doesn't come until Day 4—after vegetation is growing." When I ask about Day 2, however, there is more to draw. As the students tell me about the creation of the dome to separate the waters above from the waters below, I draw what looks like an inverted bowl over the wavy lines that represent the watery chaos. Then I add wavy lines for water above the dome. By this time the drawing is beginning to look sufficiently strange that students are quite attentive.

In response to what students tell me about Day 3, I draw some dry land in the midst of the water and add line drawings of vegetation. For Day 4 I draw representations of the sun, moon, and stars inside the dome. For Day 5 I add bird figures in the air and fish figures in the sea. Finally, for Day 6 I add line drawings of a cow-like animal and a human.

Thus, as we progress through the creation days, students see the Israelite view of the cosmos begin to take shape before their eyes. Accomplishing the task in this way helps students see the logic of the narrative—a logic that differs substantially from their own. Suddenly they begin to realize that reading the text with a twenty-first-century view of the universe in mind simply does not work. At this point I use an overhead projector or a document camera to show them a more professional looking drawing of the ancient Israelite view of the cosmos and tell them to memorize it for the test.

Of course, some students are disturbed by what they see; but the point is that they see it for themselves. When I discuss with them the dangers of subjecting modern science to this ancient Israelite narrative, they begin to see my point. And when I discuss with them the dangers of interpreting the Genesis creation stories through the lens of modern science, they begin to gain a very different perspective on debates about teaching Creationism in public schools. Consistently, my students leave this class period in an agitated state of discussion. Every year I hear stories about the debates that follow the class as students continue their discussions over meals and in their dorm rooms. It is stressful for some, but the end result is that most find it liberating. They realize that if they read Genesis as ancient Near Eastern literature, they can live more peacefully with the discoveries of modern science.

Michael R. Cosby

43. TEACHING THE CREATION STORIES IN GENESIS

There are a variety of ways to approach the creation stories in Genesis. First, ask students to bring to class two or three creation stories from children's books. Examples include Julius Lester and Joe Cepeda, *What a Truly Cool World* (New York: Scholastic, 1999); Julius Lester, *When the Beginning Began: Stories about God, the Creatures, and Us* (San Diego: Silver Whistle, 1999); Eric J. Sundquist, *The Hammers of Creation: Folk Culture in Modern African-American Fiction* (Athens: University of Georgia Press, 1992); and C. Shana Greger, *Cry of the Benu Bird: An Egyptian Creation Story* (Boston: Houghton Mifflin, 1996).

As a large group, discuss briefly the traditional mythology of the creation stories found in Genesis. For example, what are some modern mythologies that arise from these ancient stories? Examples might include the prescriptive or descriptive interpretations of gender relations in regard to the "rib" or "apple" stories or the pronouncement in Gen 3:16 ("... yet your desire shall be for your husband, and he shall rule over you"), the relationship between humanity and the earth in relation to Gen 1:26 ("... and let them have dominion over the fish of the sea, and over the birds of the air, and over the cattle ... "), and even the number of ribs that humankind has—many assume that women have one more rib than men!

Second, in small groups, ask one student to read aloud while the others listen as though in an oral culture where one person is the storyteller and all others are listeners (i.e., pretend that no one is literate). The assignment is as follows: (1) Read Genesis 1:1–2:4a from a non-traditional text, such as Mary Phil Korsak, *At the Start: Genesis Made New* (New York: Doubleday, 1993). (2) Close the text and rehearse what was just read within each group. (3) Make a list of events, using terminology from the text itself (e.g., the names of God, the human being, etc.). (4) Open the text and check the list to be sure that nothing was added or assumed from traditional "knowledge" of the story.

As you walk around the room and listen in on the small-group conversations, you will undoubtedly hear "facts" about the story listed that are not actually there. This provides the opportunity to discuss the tendency to impose what we think we know about a text onto the story that is really there. It also presents a chance to discuss the potential dangers of biblical illiteracy. The same exercise can be performed with Gen 2:4b-3:24.

Next, ask students to compare the lists from the two stories—the biblical version and the non-traditional one—and ask the following questions (you may want to have some students put their lists on the chalkboard from which everyone can work): What are the similarities? What are the differences? What is, if any, the relationship between the two? Which story was learned as a child—the first, the second, or a combination? Which one do you think came first? Why? Is there mention of the term "sin"? Is there mention of the phrase "original sin"? (Read the definition of Original Sin from a Jewish encyclopedia and discuss the differences in the use of the stories in Genesis between Jews and Christians.)

Third, set up the classroom with various pieces of artwork depicting the stories in Gen 1–3. I include Michelangelo's *The Creation of Adam* and *The Creation of Eve*, Blake's *Elohim Creating Adam,* and scenes from creation stories from other cultures. For music, I use Haydn's *The Creation,* Martinu's *The Epic of Gilgamesh,* and *Missa Luba: An African Mass.* The possibilities are endless.

Draw attention to the artwork and music that provides the setting and discuss the genre of creation stories and their importance in religious and cultural traditions from around the world. The selections from children's creation stories fit in well with this discussion. Pointing to art from different parts of the world, discuss the elements of one's culture that are present in the artist's interpretation of the story. For example, is God really an old man as Michelangelo portrays the creation scenes? Look at African art and discuss the origin of humankind; if humanity began in Africa, as scientists argue, what might have been the color of "Adam's" and "Eve's" skin? Is the Benu Bird in the Egyptian creation story any more "fantastic" than the creation stories in Genesis?

These exercises can help students discover the beauty of numerous sources and vehicles for describing the relationships among people, between humanity and the divine, and between humanity and earth. Students discover and appreciate a wide range of religious literature and develop a sense of participation in the wider scope of human history.

Glenna S. Jackson

44. THE HUMAN CONDITION IN GENESIS 2–3 AND IN *BLADE RUNNER*

For all their supposed jadedness, undergraduates today still, in my experience, have a strong desire to think and to talk about "existential" questions, about the possibilities and limitations of the human condition. The Garden of Eden story is a fine place to begin such discussion in a biblical studies course, and I have found it fruitful to put the biblical story in conversation with the science fiction movie *Blade Runner*.

Blade Runner (1982), directed by Ridley Scott, did rather poorly at the box office. Coming in the wake of the bright and hopeful *Star Wars,* the darker and more ambiguous vision of *Blade Runner* seemed to puzzle audiences at the time. But in the decade after its theatrical release the movie gained a strong cult following and eventually started being referred to as a modern classic of science fiction, a status solidified by the release in 1992 of the far superior director's cut which differed in small but significant ways from the theatrical release (cf. S. Bukatman, *Blade Runner* [London: British Film Institute, 1997]). And it became clear that the movie's more dystopic vision of the (near) future was very influential in later sci-fi, especially in what became known as "cyber-punk." Outside of its subsequent cultural influence, the movie is interesting in several respects, including its foregrounding of several themes that are associated with the sort of "postmodernism" that came to the fore in the 1980s: a future constructed from the detritus of the past, the blurring of the lines between images and reality, and the constructed nature of the self. It also features a number of memorable lines: Roy (a replicant, or synthetic human) to the eye-maker Chu, "If only you could see what I've seen with your eyes"; the character Gaff to Deckard about his replicant lover Rachael, "It's too bad she won't live—but then, who does?"

This last line by Gaff, which is in fact the final line spoken in the movie, represents well one of those existential questions that *Blade Runner* shares with the Garden of Eden story, namely, human mortality. Like virtually all sci-fi novels or movies that feature androids or synthetic beings such as the replicants in *Blade Runner*, the primary question being negotiated is "What does it mean to be human?" Any answer to this question must take account of human mortality, of an endpoint to any human life, which as much as it is resisted, repressed, or raged against, has always proven inevitable. Both *Blade Runner* and the Garden of Eden story reflect explicitly on this defining limitation of our existence, and both also tie this fact of mortality to the equally existential issue of "knowledge." How do we know that we are human? Indeed, how do we know the reality of the world around us? (This is the classic philosophical question of epistemology, and it seems clear that it is no accident that the protagonist's name in *Blade Runner*, Deckard, is a pun on Descartes, especially given that the philosopher's famous dictum, "I think, therefore I am," is quoted in the movie.)

In Gen 2–3 the relation between these two themes of mortality and knowledge is represented by the two trees in the garden: the tree of life and the tree of the knowledge of good and evil. The story seems to be set up so that humans could eat of either tree and remain essentially "human." That is, what initially separates humans from the gods is the twofold limitation of mortality and lack of knowledge. Having gained the latter by eating of the fruit of the tree of knowledge of good and evil (which can be taken both as gaining knowledge of the world as it really is and as gaining the capacity, and necessity, to function as moral decision-making creatures), the humans are expelled from the garden so that they cannot eat of the former and thereby become gods rather than humans. In *Blade Runner* the relation of these two themes drives the plot, in that a group of replicants have discovered what they really are, synthetic as opposed to natural creatures, and that they are in fact mortal (with inbuilt termination dates). The plot follows the replicants as, pursued by Deckard, they try to reach their maker Tyrell in order to demand immortality. When Roy, the last surviving replicant, finally confronts Tyrell (in a wonderfully climactic scene that echoes not only the Bible but *Paradise Lost* and *Frankenstein*) he learns that such immortality is technologically impossible; there simply was no way to make the replicants that did not include mortality. Throughout the movie the question is up for grabs as to whether these synthetic beings are to be considered genuinely human or not. Had Roy gained the immortality he desired, along with the knowledge he has recently acquired, it seems clear that the answer would have been no, Roy is not human, since mortality is a defining feature of the human condition; but by remaining mortal, and in fact accepting that mortality, Roy has also become human.

So, both *Blade Runner* and the garden story offer a chance to reflect on these two defining conditions of human existence: knowledge and mortality. Despite our resistance to full knowledge of good and evil—who does not want to protect a small child from the horrors of the world?—to be a mature human being means to look squarely on what is both good and bad in the world and to claim one's own moral agency. And despite our perhaps more strenuous resistance to our mortality, to lack such mortality would render one unrecognizable as a human being.

Tod Linafelt

45. CAIN AND ABEL: INTERCANONICAL, MIDRASHIC, AND ARTISTIC COMPARISON

The story of Cain and Abel can be studied from a variety of angles. One way is to compare the biblical account with the one in the Qur'an. While students are generally aware that Christians and Jews share the Hebrew Bible, they may not know that Muslims in their holy scripture also read many of the scriptural stories familiar to Jews and Christians. In this exercise, students compare the story of Cain and Abel in Gen 4:1–16 with the similar story in the Qur'an (5:27–32).

I usually have students work in groups in which they read both versions of the story and then draw up lists of similarities and differences. Then the significance of these observations is discussed in a classroom plenary. Items that should be noted include the following: (1) In the Qur'anic account the brothers are not named nor are their occupations or the nature of their respective offerings described. These details appear in the biblical account and open up a host of interpretive possibilities as to why God rejected the offering of one brother and not the other. In contrast, the Qur'anic account focuses on the brothers as examples of righteousness and unrighteousness without concern for distracting details. (2) In the biblical account, no dialogue between the brothers is recorded (the short phrase, "Let us go out to the field," in 4:8 appears in the versions but not in the MT), but God talks to Cain both before and after the murder. In the Qur'an, an extensive conversation between the two brothers takes place before the murder. In both cases, the conversations function to explain the situation theologically. (3) In the Qur'anic account, the murderer is full of regret at having to be taught by a raven how to bury the corpse of his brother. In the biblical account, the murderer is condemned to a life of wandering but upon appeal to God is granted a protective sign. In either case, it is interesting to ask whether the text gives any indication that the murderous brother repented of his sin. (4) The Qur'anic account ends with an explicit moral lesson about the relative value of preserving life over taking life. While this is absent in the biblical account, a parallel version is found in the Mishnah (*Sanhedrin* 4.5). The exercise shows the common springs of the three Western monotheisms; the differences are employed to illuminate mutually each telling of the story.

A second approach is to divide students into groups to plan how they would script the story of Cain and Abel to be enacted in a play or movie. Attention is drawn by the instructor to various "gaps" in the text—places where the text lacks explicit details that are necessary for an enactment. An important gap is found in Gen 4:8, which does not relate what happened in the field before the murder nor exactly how Cain killed his brother. Students are asked to imagine what the brothers may have said to each other and how the murder took place.

They are then introduced to midrashic interpretations that fill a gap in the text by putting words into Cain's and Abel's mouths, and to artistic representations that portray a variety of ways in which Cain may have murdered Abel. The midrashic texts are available from different sources, such as James L. Kugel's *Traditions of the Bible* (Cambridge: Harvard University Press, 1998), Nehama Leibowitz's *Studies in Bereshit (Genesis)* (3rd ed.; Jerusalem: World Zionist Organization, 1976), or in an English translation of *Bereshit Rabbah*.

Artistic representations of Cain's murder of Abel can easily be found in artistic image databases on the Internet. A simple image search using Google will turn up many interesting depictions of the murder. Artistic representations can also, of course, be found in various books and magazines. For example, Bill Moyers' *Genesis: A Living Conversation* (New York: Doubleday, 1996) contains reproductions of *Cain Kills Abel, God Banishes Cain*, an eleventh-century ivory from France, Francisco de Goya's *Cain and Abel* (ca. 1817–20), Max Band's *Am I My Brother's Keeper?* (1948), and Perle Hessing's *Cane and Abel* (1985).

This second approach introduces students to the idea of "gaps" as openings for interpretation, to the rich resources of midrash, and to the visual imagining of biblical texts in art.

F. V. Greifenhagen

46. THE FLOOD AS JIGSAW PUZZLE: INTRODUCING SOURCE CRITICISM

I use the flood narrative to explain the principles behind source criticism. I begin class discussion by asking leading questions which focus students' attention on the various contradictions within the text: the number of animals taken aboard, the length of the flood, the reason for the flood. After this general discussion, I hand a different piece of the flood narrative (always entirely P or J) to each student. (I base my division on A. F. Campbell and M. A. O'Brien, *Sources of the Pentateuch: Texts, Introductions, Annotations* [Minneapolis: Fortress, 1993].) These pieces vary in size from half-verses to short paragraphs; most have some salient feature which allows them to be grouped with other snippets. By using a copy of the chapters of Genesis in word-processing format, I am able to remove all verse numbers. I then instruct the students to assemble from these pieces a coherent, non-contradictory narrative, with the added proviso that they will probably come up with two parallel narratives (while this short-circuits the "discovery" of the sources, it also helps prevent simple reconstruction of the biblical narrative). The students invariably argue about what should be included and what should not, "trading" students and their snippets to the other group.

When the groups are fairly satisfied, I "check" the work to see whether we have generated P and J. In most cases, what emerges in the process looks like them, especially if I have provided some coaching along the way. Using this work, I am able to line out some salient differences between J and P. More importantly, in my view, I am able to show the students how source criticism assumes coherence as a necessary attribute of texts. This is, of course, not beyond question, and I find it important to help students learn that methods have their own sets of assumptions about language. In addition, the very physicality of the process in this exercise helps demonstrate source criticism's reliance on written, as opposed to oral, texts.

At other times, either before or after this exercise, I have had students try to assemble a coherent narrative out of all the fragments. If done before the sources are isolated, this exercise shows the contradictions in the story as well as the way modern readers insist on coherence. If done after the sources are isolated, this exercise emphasizes the role of the redactor and raises the issue of the redactor's competence (how could the redactor have let so many problems remain?) and the question of the "vanishing redactor" (if redactors did their work perfectly, we would not be aware of underlying sources). (For another exercise on source criticism, see §18.)

Donald C. Polaski

47. THE THREE WORLDS OF THE BIBLE: THE TOWER OF BABEL

This exercise is a way of introducing the distinction between the historical, literary, and contemporary worlds of the Bible as a helpful way of sorting out and validating different approaches to the biblical text. It is based on the approach of C. J. Hauer and W. A. Young in *An Introduction to the Bible: A Journey Into Three Worlds* (Englewood Cliffs: Prentice Hall, 1986).

It begins with a reading of Gen 11:1–9, followed by brainstorming on any and all possible questions that can be asked of this text. The questions are then sorted into the three categories: (1) Questions that seek to understand the world *behind* the text: the historical world from which the text emerged and which it may reflect. Possible questions in this category might include: When was this text written and to whom was it originally addressed? What kind of culture and society is reflected in the text? (2) Questions that seek to understand the world *in* the text: the literary world of the story itself. Possible questions in this category might include: Who are the main characters and how are they described? What is the narrative complication and how is it resolved? (3) Questions that seek to understand the world *in front* of the text: the world created by the interaction of the contemporary concerns of the reader with the text. Possible questions in this category might include: Does the situation in the text relate in any way to contemporary situations or concerns? How is this text used in the synagogue or church?

What follows is a sampling of observations from each of the three categories:

The Historical World. (1) The tower motif, in connection with the mention of Shinar and Babel, seems to be a reference to the ziggurats of ancient Mesopotamia, which were seen as joining heaven and earth; archaeological remains of these towers have been found and they are also mentioned in ancient Near Eastern documents (e.g., in the Babylonian creation epic *Enuma Elish*). (2) Verse 3 suggests that the original audience of this story was familiar with stone and mortar as building materials, whereas the builders of ziggurats used bricks and bitumen (a cultural difference). (3) The Sumerian Epic of *Enmerker* contains a description of the confusion of languages due to the rivalry between two gods. (4) The pun on the name "Babel" suggests that the story is meant as a satire on the elevated Babylonian culture; what they call a "gate of God" is actually a cause of confusion. (5) Which Babylon is meant? the Babylonian empire of ca. 1800–1700 B.C.E.? or the Babylonian empire of the sixth century B.C.E. which destroyed Jerusalem and sent the Israelites into exile? If the latter, then the story tells the Israelites that the mighty Babylon that dispersed and exiled them will itself be dispersed and scattered (cf. also Isa 14:12-20; Jer 51, 53). (6) God's words "Come, let us" (v. 7; see also Gen 1:26) seem to reflect the ancient idea of God as a king with a divine court, later transformed into the angels of heaven.

The Literary World. (1) Note the two-fold structure: vv. 1–4 = the human challenge; vv. 5–9 = God's response; or a chiastic structure: a (vv. 1–2), b (vv. 2-4), c (v. 5, a transition), b' (vv. 6–7), and a' (vv. 8–9). (2) Note the repeated phrase: "Come, let us" in vv. 3- 4 mirrors "Come, let us" in v. 7. (3) The gathering in one place in vv. 1–4 is the opposite of the scattering in vv. 5–9. (4) Note the balance of human pride and divine justice. (5) Note the irony: God needs to "come down" to see this tower, which is obviously not that high! (6) Note the double meaning of the name "Babel" (= "gate of God" and "to mix-up/confuse"). (7) The story represents the genre of etiology, a story told to explain why things are the way they are (why do people speak different languages?). (8) Literary context and intertextual connections within the book of Genesis abound: "Look…" (v. 6) echoes Gen 3:22, suggesting that human attempts to transgress limits and become divine are problematic (cf. Gen 3:5); the scattering in vv. 8–9 echoes God's command to spread and fill the earth (Gen 1:28; 9:7) and suggests that the problem is humanity's refusal to heed this command; Gen 10 offers a different story of the spread of humanity; Gen 10:8–10 links Nimrod with Shinar and Babel.

H
E
B
R
E
W

B
I
B
L
E

(9) This story, together with Gen 4:17 and 10:11–13, suggests a negative attitude towards cities.

The Contemporary World. (1) This story raises the question of the reason for the diversity of cultures and languages in the world, and whether this is a good or bad situation. (2) It raises the question of the driving force behind human technological achievements. (3) The idea of one original universal language connects with the search of linguists for a universal linguistics (e.g., N. Chomsky's generative grammar). (4) The story could be read as a critique of the self-exaltation of oppressive imperial powers. (5) For Christians, the story is theologically resolved in the account of Pentecost in Acts 2.

F. V. Greifenhagen

48. GENESIS 1–11 AS MYTH

Many students have difficulty understanding the ways in which the accounts in Gen 1–11 are myths. By discussing the terms "myth" and "history," students can understand that the opening chapters of the Bible are not primarily historical records. They will begin to see how these texts attempt to explain the role of the divine in the earliest beginnings of the Israelites and are not primarily interested in recording historical or scientific facts.

Prior to class, have the students research several definitions of the terms "myth" and "history" (from the Internet or from a list of sources provided for them). This reading makes it possible to discuss and critique the definitions and to begin to formulate academic definitions. Also assign students to read Gen 1:1–11:9 and write down the purpose of each account in these chapters. (The purpose, naturally, is the subject of much debate. Students may make their own educated guesses or report on what different scholars have suggested as the purpose.)

In class, after discussing their definitions of "myth" and "history," ask for non-biblical examples of myth (e.g., Julius Caesar's unusual birth) and history (e.g., a book about the American Revolution). Usually a discussion of legend and other genres emerges so that examples can begin to be placed on a myth-history continuum on the blackboard. Then discuss the purpose of each story in Gen 1:1–11:9 and how each account leans more towards myth, pointing out that myth can contain historical elements. What does each myth emphasize about the relation of humanity to the divine? What are the implications of labeling this section of the Bible as myth? How might one respond to the view that myths are, by definition, not true? How might the historical situation of the Priestly writer have influenced the editing of Gen 1–11?

The articles and bibliographies under the entry for "Myth and Mythology" in the *ABD* (4:946–965) provide a helpful resource. The articles (by R. A. Oden Jr. and F. Graf) are accessible to advanced under-graduates, but the instructor may select appropriate items from the bibliography for the purposes of this exercise.

Emily R. Cheney

49. TRADITIONAL TALES (GEN 12:10–20; 20:1–8; 26:6–11)

The ancestor stories in Genesis are made up of traditional tales that are told according to "fixed-forms." These are typical tales composed of traditional elements, which any particular storyteller may elaborate and vary within limits determined by skill and audience rapport. Some of the various fixed-forms found in Genesis are: birth of an ancestor to a barren mother; encounter with the future betrothed at a well; the ancestor pretends that his wife is his sister; rivalry between a barren, favored wife and a fertile co-wife or concubine; danger in the desert and discovery of a well; treaty between the ancestor and a local king; and the testament of a dying ancestor. This exercise uses fixed-forms to lead students through a reading of Genesis.

Fixed-forms are culturally determined; the stories have a fixed form because they describe typical features of the culture. For example, the "encounter with the future betrothed at a well" became a traditional fixed-form because wells were one of the few places in the ancient Near East where men and women would meet. Both men and women would go to wells because the water they provided was essential to life. Thus, when a person told a story about a man meeting his future wife, the well was a natural setting.

Because fixed-forms are culturally determined, what is interesting for interpretation is not how one story is similar to another, but rather how each story is different. The differences in the story result from the partic-ular message that the author is communicating, for the author will give each story of a fixed-form unique details depending on the context in which the story is told. For example, Genesis contains three stories in which "the ancestor pretends that his wife is his sister" before a foreign king. Each story is told differently concerning the relationship of the king to the ancestor's wife. This "difference" is the result of the meaning of the particular story in its context.

HEBREW BIBLE

I begin class with a brief presentation of Genesis and the character of traditional tales. In order to illustrate the dynamics of such tales, I use the three wife-sister stories (Gen 12:10–20; 20:1–8; 26:6–11) as the subject of a collaborative group exercise. I divide the students into groups and ask them to reread the three wife-sister stories (the students would have been assigned to read large portions of Genesis, including these stories, in preparation for the class). After the students have had sufficient time to read the stories, I hand out to each group an assignment sheet asking them to do the following: (1) Identify and list all the features of the three stories that are similar. (2) In three separate columns, list the distinguishing features of each story. (3) From the list of similarities, describe in a paragraph the "fixed-form" of the story. (4) Identify the social and cultural values embedded in this "fixed-form"— in other words, what kind of culture would tell such stories? (5) From the list of distinguishing features, explain how each feature fits the literary context of the story.

If time permits, I select four of the groups to write one of their "lists" (of similarities and distinguishing features) on the blackboard, and then supplement those lists with suggestions from other groups. After the groups finish their assignments, I discuss their results of the third and fourth tasks with the whole class. The students easily recognize the skeleton of the stories and present this as the fixed-form. It is often sufficient to have one or two groups read their paragraph of the "fixed-form." More interesting are the values that the students associate with the fixed-form; values related to gender roles and social status are readily identified. The significance of the distinguishing features of the stories is more difficult for the students to grasp, and thus results in a more engaging discussion. The students note the different status of the wife in each story, among other differences. I lead the students to recognize how the wife's status shapes the story. For example, in Gen 12 the childless Sarai is given to the Pharaoh as a wife. In this context, Sarai's barrenness is an obstacle to the fulfillment of God's promise of descendants to Abram, and so the story implies that Abram gives her in exchange for the wedding gifts from Pharaoh. However, in the stories preceding Gen 20, God promises Sarah a child. Thus, when Abraham gives her to Abimelech as a wife, the narrator emphasizes that Abimelech does not have sexual relations with her. The new context of the story raises concern over the paternity of the child that Sarah will bear in Gen 21. Finally, in Gen 26, Isaac simply tells Abimelech that Rebekah is his sister; he does not give her to the king in marriage. Because she is the mother of two sons, Rebekah's status in the house is secure.

Ronald A. Simkins

50. READING HAGAR

Students are often unaware of the complex role social location and historical context play in reading a biblical text. Students are wont to take their own readings of a narrative for "the" reading, failing to perceive any gap between their world and the ones that came before. This assignment is set up to engage precisely this issue as it relates to a particular biblical narrative and its "after-lives." It is designed to engage a student's own interpretation of the Hagar narrative in Genesis and then to examine their interpretation against others, ancient and modern. One of the important features of the assignment is that it uses not only non-canonical interpretations, but deliberately includes a selection from the New Testament as well. This latter move is critically important in terms of making the task more complex and revealing for students, as their reading is now "read against" another text (Paul in Galatians) that (in many cases) they also accept as authoritative. That their reading will very likely not reflect Paul's reading often proves to be a point of contention but also an occasion for reflection on the nature of the interpretive process.

In the first part, students should come to class having read Hagar's story (Gen 16:1–16; 21:9–21) as well as the interpretations of Paul (Gal 4:21–5:1) and Philo (*On the Preliminary Studies* 20–24). The student should offer their own interpretation of the Hagar narrative in Genesis, focusing on the meaning of the story within the context of the surrounding narrative. Why is this story included? What does the writer of Genesis mean to communicate about God and about Abraham and the promise? Students may want to refer to commentaries in the library or other reference works in this part of the assignment (but should be careful to formulate their own perspective). Students should then look at Paul's interpretation of the Hagar story. What is allegorical interpretation? Discuss his interpretation in light of Galatians. In what way does Paul use this "reading" of the Hagar story to bolster his overall argument? Does Paul manipulate the meaning of the text to serve his own ends? Does his reading address the "original" meaning of the text? Is Paul's interpretation "correct"? Why or why not?

The second part of the exercise focuses on modern interpreters. Have students read P. Trible, "Hagar: The Desolation of Rejection" (in *Texts of Terror: Literary-Feminist Readings of Biblical Narratives* [Philadelphia: Fortress, 1984], 9–35); J. A. Hackett, "Rehabilitating Hagar: Fragments of an Epic Pattern" (in *Gender and Difference in Ancient Israel* [ed. P. L. Day; Minneapolis: Fortress, 1989], 12–27); and D. S. Williams, *Sisters in the Wilderness: The Challenge of Womanist God-Talk* [Maryknoll, N.Y.: Orbis, 1993], 15–59). What is the common thread in these three views of the Hagar story? Are there any differences? Whose reading do you find to be

H
E
B
R
E
W

B
I
B
L
E

the most persuasive? Are these readings different from your own? From Paul's? How can one assess the legitimacy and validity of a particular interpretation of the Bible?

Individual instructors may determine how to cover the material (whether in a writing assignment or in discussion). The overall point of the exercise is a hermeneutical one. I have substituted different readings on occasion, especially the ones related to modern interpreters. Moreover, at times I have added a component that includes Reformation interpretations of the Hagar story (from Calvin and Luther), creating a further point of engagement in the interpretive trajectory. The possibilities are varied and extensive. (For other exercises on women in biblical texts, see §§55, 153, 191, 226, 242, 267.)

Todd Penner

51. THE IMPORTANCE OF SOCIAL LOCATION: A STUDY GUIDE ON SARAH AND HAGAR

To help students recognize how one's social location influences interpretation, I use the following study guide on Gen 16 and 21, the story of Hagar and Sarah. (The guide was developed by Patrick D. Miller Jr., and Katharine Doob Sakenfeld [Princeton Theological Seminary], and adapted and expanded by Carolyn Pressler [United Theological Seminary].) The required outside readings are Walter Brueggemann, *Genesis* (Atlanta: John Knox, 1982), 150–53, 182–85, and two articles on Gen 16 and 21 from Jewish feminist and womanist perspectives respectively— Sharon Pace Jeansonne, *Women of Genesis* (Minneapolis: Fortress, 1990), 18–21, 27–29, 43–52; and Renita J. Weems, *Just a Sister Away: A Womanist Vision of Women's Relationships in the Bible* (San Diego: LuraMedia, 1988), 1–19. I ask the students to work with the first two questions of the study guide before reading the assigned articles.

The study guide is as follows:

1. Carefully read and reread the stories in Gen 16 and 21 concerning Hagar and Sarah, giving attention to small details. Traditional interpretation of these stories focuses on the theme of promise-fulfillment and etiology of the nations surrounding Israel. Consider how these chapters contribute to these themes with the ancestral narratives.

2. More recent analysis focuses on these stories as they are intertwined with problems of ethnic prejudice and class distinctions. How would you describe the characters of Abraham, Sarah, and Hagar in each narrative? Is it possible to identify "perpetrators" and "victims"?

3. What tensions and points of complementarity do you find between the more traditional promise-fulfillment or etiological interpretations of the text and the more recent feminist and womanist interpretations? What role does God play in these narratives?

4. Different biblical scholars interpret these texts very differently, in part because of their social and religious contexts (i.e., their race, class, nationality, gender, and faith tradition). Look carefully at the commentaries of Brueggemann (a male, Euro-American, UCC scholar), Jeansonne (a female, Euro-American, Jewish feminist scholar), and Weems (a female, African American, Protestant womanist scholar). How does their race, gender, education level, and denomination affect their interpretations of Abraham, Hagar, Sarah, and Ishmael? Begin to reflect on the way in which *your* context affects your interpretation of these two passages.

All three times I have used this study guide I have been amazed at the conversations which result. Most students are astounded that there could be such divergent interpretations of one text. They are usually resistant to at least one of the interpretations. Sometimes that resistance is due to their own discomfort with that racial/ethnic group. At other times the resistance is due to what they always thought that passage said.

After working through the questions, most express surprise at Brueggemann's dismissive comments about Hagar and Sarah, as well as his focus on Ishmael in a text which only tangentially deals with him. This surprise opens up the opportunity to talk about the lenses through which we read. I stress that I normally find Brueggemann's work to be very helpful, but that he was reading the text through the lens of traditional biblical scholarship which focuses almost exclusively on the patriarchal line and the theme of promise and fulfillment. When one focuses on a particular way of reading a text, one can miss other aspects. This conversation often leads to a discussion of the importance of reading a variety of views on a given text, on reading even commentaries (or people whose work is generally outstanding) critically, and becoming aware that we do not read in a vacuum. No reading is completely unbiased. Even when we try our best to read "objectively," our own personal backgrounds, knowledge, and experiences play a big part in how each of us interprets scripture. I can usually see the "aha!" moments as they happen for students in the conversation. I challenge them to write down some of the factors that influence their own interpretation and to be aware of those as they do the rest of their written work in the quarter. The fruits of this discussion are visible in their written work throughout the remainder of the two quarters. (For other exercises related to social location, see §§9, 10.)

Mary E. Shields

52. KINSHIP IN GENESIS 16 AND 21 AND NUMBERS 27 AND 36

Kinship refers to the social and cultural patterns we place on the biological features of procreation. Kinship deals with four fundamental areas of human life: selection of marriage partners, marriage bond, the family of procreation, and the extended family. The kinship system is distinct for each cultural group, and our views of marriage and the family do not correspond to the views of the ancient Israelites. It is thus important for our students to understand how their views of marriage and the family differ from the Israelite kinship system if they are to understand the many biblical references to the family.

An obstacle that students face in understanding the kinship system of ancient Israel is that they are unfamiliar with their own kinship system. Kinship systems are cultural assumptions and practices that are rarely legislated or otherwise codified, and students have rarely reflected on their own kinship system. They often assume that their views and practices regarding marriage and the family are natural, whereas those practices attested in the Bible are "primitive," or "backwards," or just simply "weird." What the students need to understand is that all kinship systems are socially constructed according to socially embraced values and purposes. I thus begin class by having the students individually answer the following questionnaire: (1) Whom can you marry? (2) Why will you get married? (3) What is required before marriage may take place? When can you get married? (4) What is the relationship between marriage and children? (5) What is the status (expectations) of the husband? Of the wife? (6) Where will you live? (7) To whom does family property belong? (8) Who will inherit family property? (9) How is family property divided after divorce? (10) What constitutes adultery? The questions are spread out across a sheet of paper with sufficient space for a brief answer and notes. I tell the students that this exercise will not be handed in or graded, but that I will ask them to share their answers with the class. The students can answer the questionnaire in ten minutes.

After all the students have completed the questionnaire, I engage the entire class in a discussion of their answers. Because the students' answers to the questionnaire will differ from how an ancient Israelite would answer the questions, this exercise becomes an opportunity for the students to understand their own kinship system and a context for discussing the Israelite kinship system. I work through the questions one at a time, eliciting and comparing students' answers, and then contrasting their understanding with how an ancient Israelite might answer the question. Typically, the students answer the questions quickly with brief comments, apparently with no need to reflect upon what seems natural. Once we begin to discuss their answers, however, the students slowly realize that their kinship system is more complicated and more constructed than they originally thought. For example, the students often answer the first question with a simple, "whomever I want." They generally see this question within a legal context: They are allowed to marry anyone who is old enough and not a close relative. In response to their simple answers, I raise cultural and pragmatic issues that complicate their understanding of marriage and the family. Gradually, the students recognize that their choice of marriage partners, to use the example above, can be limited by ethnic, religious, or socioeconomic considerations.

When I turn to the Israelite kinship system, I emphasize what is distinctive about Israelite marriage and family. For example, endogamy is the means for creating a lineage, but exogamy is used for creating alliances. Monogamy is the ideal, but polygyny and concubinage are practiced for political and inheritance reasons. Sons receive inheritance, a share of the paternal estate, when they leave home to start their own lineages. (For an excellent introduction to Israelite kinship, see N. Steinberg, *Kinship and Marriage in Genesis: A Household Economics Perspective* [Minneapolis: Fortress, 1993], esp. 5–34.)

As we discuss the students' answers to each question, I repeatedly challenge them to explain their views or practices: What values or purposes do these views or practices serve? In reference to the first question, for instance, why might you limit potential spouses to those who share your same faith tradition? Through discussion, the students learn that their own views of marriage and the family are not so natural after all. Similarly, when I contrast the students' views to the Israelite kinship system, I ask the students to identify the values implicit in the system or to explain what purposes such a system might serve. Why would the Israelites prefer to marry kin from their clan? Having examined their own kinship system, the students are generally able to draw some reasonable conclusions about Israelite kinship.

For the remainder of the class period, I turn the students' attention to one or two biblical stories in which kinship issues play a prominent role. I divide the class into groups and give each group a list of questions that lead the group to interpret the stories in the context of Israelite kinship. Many biblical stories could be used in this context, but two that I have used successfully are as follows:

The Story of Abram, Sarai, and Hagar (Gen 16 and 21): Why does Sarai offer Abram her slave-girl for a wife? What does she hope to accomplish? Why does Hagar "look with contempt" on Sarai after she becomes pregnant? Is she justified in doing this? Why does Sarai blame

Abram for Hagar's actions? What has Abram done? Why does Sarai need Abram's permission to deal with Hagar's contempt? Why does Sarah want Abraham to send Ishmael away? What is the motivation for her demand? Why is Abraham reluctant to follow Sarah's demand? Going beyond the text, how does this social world pit woman against woman? What is Abram's role in this conflict?

The Story of the Daughters of Zelophehad (Num 27 and 36): Why do the daughters want to inherit their father's property? What is their concern? Why should daughters inherit before relatives that are more distant? Why does the daughters' inheritance of land pose a problem? What concerns are raised by the kinsmen? Why must the daughters marry kinsmen if they want to inherit property? How do the daughters' and the kinsmen's view of the family differ?

As the groups work through interpreting stories, I answer questions and redirect their efforts as necessary. After the groups have had sufficient time to discuss the questions and thereby form a basic interpretation of the stories, I conclude this exercise with a brief class discussion of kinship in the stories, trying to draw out insights from each group.

Ronald A. Simkins

53. SODOM AND GOMORRAH: AN EXEGETICAL EXERCISE

This is a discussion-based exercise for small groups that provides an overview of the concerns of Gen 18–19. One student reads the following script in this present form. It is important that the reader stop at each question mark to allow the other members to respond because the script is designed to have a narrative flow. If discussion wanes, the leader can prod the fellow group members but should primarily be a facilitator rather than a discussant:

The words "Sodom and Gomorrah" have connotations that echo throughout history. They show up in the New Testament on Jesus' lips and in a multitude of rabbinic writings in Judaism. You likely have heard of these cities, even if you haven't read this story. As you know, the term "sodomy" (used to describe various sexual acts usually deemed to be deviant) comes from this city.

Before discussing the destruction of these cities, it is important to consider the conversation between Abraham and God that precedes the destruction. The narrative begins with an interior monologue of God in which he deliberates about how much to reveal to Abraham. Read Gen 18:16–21. What are God's reasons for telling Abraham about his impending actions? What would be the benefit to either God or Abraham of this conversation? One persistent question in Genesis relates to God's foreknowledge. For instance, many readers have wondered whether God did or did not know what Adam and Eve were going to do in Gen 2–3. How far does God's foreknowledge extend here? In vv. 20–21, God explains the situation by talking about an outcry that has come to him. From where does this outcry from? Is it reliable?

Now read vv. 22–33, the conversation between God and Abraham. What are Abraham's motivations for "bargaining" with God? Do the verses show a concern for people in general, Lot's family, or perhaps Abraham himself? Why does he finally stop at ten people?

After God and Abraham end their conversation, the dramatic narrative of chapter 19 begins. Read vv. 1–7. Now characterize the dramatic players—Lot, the angels, the men of Sodom. For each of these three, discuss their motivations, their desires, and whether you would count them as righteous or wicked.

By the time we get to vv. 8–11, the nature of the conflict has changed. Read these verses. Lot's gambit is, most would agree, disgusting. David Gunn and Danna Fewell argue that Lot shows himself to be even less righteous than the men of Sodom. Do you agree? The chief legacy of this passage, however, has not been a castigation of Lot but rather of the Sodomites and homosexuality. Does this passage condemn gays? What would be the textual evidence for condemnation? If it is not about homosexuality, what is it denouncing?

Another person who is seen as a negative exemplar in this story is Lot's wife. Like many women in the Bible, she has no name. Lot, however reluctantly, leaves the city with his wife and daughters. (By the way, what happened to the sons-in-law?) His wife, though, does not make it far. Read vv. 15–26. Does this seem a harsh punishment for curious rubbernecking? What is the reason for Lot's wife getting turned into a pillar of salt?

We now turn to the end of the story, where righteousness and incest become intertwined. What sort of moral judgment do either you or the text make about the daughters' (unnamed again) having sex with their father? They claim to have no other choice than to sleep with their father. They have been marginalized throughout the narrative and now take strong initiative. Should their action be taken as admirable? Does the text see it this way? Read Gen 9:20–27. Both of these texts deal with children, drunkenness, and a parent's nakedness. What do either or both of these passages imply about the relationship between children and their parents' sexuality?

Finally, we return to God and Abraham. Read Gen 19:27–29. What do we learn about either of these characters in the aftermath of Sodom and Gomorrah? What sort of conclusion is this? (In this script, I draw heavily from D. Gunn and D. Fewell, *Gender, Power, and Promise* [Nashville: Abingdon, 1993], 56–67.)

Kyle Keefer

54. HOSPITALITY IN GENESIS 18:1-15 AND 19:1-11

The social world of the ancient Israelites is embedded in the biblical texts. In order for our students to understand the biblical texts in the social context of ancient Israel, it is necessary for the students to understand how their social world differs from the social world of the Bible. Hospitality is a widely practiced custom with which many of our students are familiar. What they generally do not understand is the purpose of hospitality and the obligations entailed in hospitality. The Bible contains many examples of hospitality, so it is important that our students understand the role that hospitality played in the social world of ancient Israel.

I approach the topic of hospitality inductively by examining with the students the stories of Abraham in Gen 18:1–15 and Lot in Gen 19:1–11. At the center of both stories is the act of hospitality. Dividing the students into groups, I ask the groups to identify the similarities and differences of the practice of hospitality in the two stories. After the groups have completed their lists, they report their results to the class, and I record them on the blackboard, creating an inclusive list from all the groups. From this information, I guide the students in creating a model of hospitality. The students quickly include the similarities in both stories in the model: Hospitality is offered by the host; the guests are considered worthy recipients; the guests make no demands on the host; the host offers food and rest; the guests do not repay the hospitality, though they may offer something to the host. The students find the differences between the two stories, mostly additional elements in the Lot story, more difficult to include in the model. That Lot protects his guests from the unruly men of the city seems appropriate to hospitality, but that he offers his daughters to the mob instead of his guests does not seem appropriate. Students also raise questions about the motives of the men of the city in the context of hospitality.

The differences in the stories provide the opportunity to discuss the purpose of hospitality: Why does a guest seek hospitality? Why does a host offer hospitality? Students are able to discern that a guest might seek hospitality for protection in a foreign environment, but they are less successful in recognizing why a host would offer hospitality. I explain to the students the two primary purposes of hospitality: (1) to transform strangers, who might be dangerous, into guests and thus allies; and (2) to display one's honor through generosity toward and protection of others. Once the students understand the importance of honor in hospitality, they are better able to understand the differences in the story of Lot. I use some of the following questions to guide their thinking: What is Lot's relationship to the men of Sodom? As an "outsider," how might Lot's offer of hospitality affect the honor of the men of Sodom? How might the mob's actions affect Lot's honor? In terms of honor, why would Lot offer his daughters to the mob instead of his guests?

The result of this discussion is that the students construct a model of hospitality that they are able to use to interpret other biblical narratives in which hospitality plays a prominent role (such as the story of Jael in Judg 4, the story of the Levite and his concubine in Judg 19, and the story of the Shunammite woman in 2 Kgs 8).

Ronald A. Simkins

55. LOT'S WIFE: BRINGING MINOR BIBLICAL CHARACTERS OUT OF THE SHADOWS

Many characters in the Bible only play minor roles or appear only in passing. This is particularly true of female characters. One of my students recently remarked, upon completing an outline of Genesis, "Where are the women?" The following presents one way to bring minor characters out of the shadows, in this case, Lot's wife.

Students are asked to volunteer to take on the roles of the characters: the angels, Lot, the townspeople of Sodom, Lot's daughters and sons-in-law, and Lot's wife. Genesis 19:1–24 is read aloud and the characters act out their roles. After the enactment, the students who played the various characters are interviewed by their other classmates as to their experience of the event. "What did it feel like to be Lot?" "What went through your mind as a citizen of Sodom?" "Why did you refuse to heed Lot's warning as one of his sons-in-law?" "What is it like to be a daughter of a man who offers you to the city mob?" The last person to be interviewed is the student who volunteered to be Lot's wife—"What was it like to be Lot's wife? To leave your home? Why did you look back?" The instructor should make sure that the portraits of Lot's wife that emerge include sympathetic ones.

Finally, several poems on Lot's wife are read aloud and discussed. The collection edited by David Curzon (*Modern Poems on the Bible: An Anthology* [Philadelphia: Jewish Publication Society, 1993]) contains two riveting poems, both entitled "Lot's Wife"—one by Anna Akhmatova and the other by James Simmons. Both poems give Lot's wife a voice but read the biblical account differently. Akhmatova's poem is a lament for the death of a woman who is too easily dismissed as insignificant, while Simmons' poem regards the salt as a metaphor for grief. The class discussion often connects with the way that the sufferings of women are routinely trivialized and absent from the annals of history. Or the discussion might focus on the experience of women forced to march away from their homes or the plight of those immigrants who may fear to look back at their former lives and yet feel the compulsion to do so. At times the discussion brings up personal experiences of transition in the lives of the students. In the end, not only is Lot's wife brought out of the shadows, but she becomes a living character with which the students can identify.

Other poems on Lot's wife can be found with a simple search on the Internet, including Rosin Cowman's "Lot's Wife" and Norman Doidge's "Pillar of Salt." These poetic treatments provide an opportunity to introduce the notion of contemporary midrash as a way of reading, interpreting, and interacting with the biblical text. (For other exercises on women in biblical texts, see §§50, 153, 191, 226, 242, 267.)

F. V. Greifenhagen

56. ABRAHAM AND HIS SON: USING THE QUR'AN IN THE BIBLICAL STUDIES CLASSROOM

A strategy commonly employed when teaching the Bible is to expose students to non-biblical sources that are somehow related to the course content, such as the *Enuma Elish* or the Code of Hammurabi. Another biblically affiliated work that is rarely used for comparative study in the classroom is the Qur'an. Jews and Christians are often quite surprised when they discover that the Qur'an has much in common with the Bible. Many central biblical figures appear in the pages of the Qur'an with great frequency. This material can be a valuable resource for instructors seeking to challenge their students' perceptions of these Bible characters and the communities that read stories about them. Studying how the Qur'an presents a familiar biblical story can raise a host of interesting and important questions about canonicity, historicity, and the relationships among the world's religions. Such comparative study is particularly effective when it enables Jewish and Christian readers to discover aspects of the Bible that they had not noticed before and therefore come to think about their text in a new way. Another potential benefit of such an approach is

that it can introduce students to central elements of Muslim faith
help them realize that the distance between Islam and the other monoistic faiths is not as great as they have assumed.

An example of how this might be done can be seen in the story of
Abraham's near sacrifice of his son Isaac, which is related in Gen 22. The
Islamic version of this episode is found in Qur'an 37:100–112. The Qur'an
passage shares the same basic plot with the Genesis narrative; however,
the two accounts also vary in some significant ways. I have students
respond to the following questions in preparation for class discussion:

1. How do the literary contexts of the two passages differ? Ask the
class to read the material in Genesis and the Qur'an immediately following Abraham's near sacrifice of his son. While the Genesis version
continues with the story of Abraham's life, the Qur'an account shifts
gears and considers the prophetic careers of Moses, Elijah, Lot, and
others. All of these stories emphasize the prophet's fidelity to the divine
will, which leads to a blessing that each receives. This pattern suggests
that the Abraham of the Qur'an is setting an example that the subsequent
prophets will follow. This gets at the heart of a key difference between
the Bible and the Qur'an. While the former text opts for a more or less
chronological telling of the events, the Qur'an arranges its material
according to a different order, often grouping together passages with a
common theme. In this case the theme being stressed is the prophets'
complete commitment to carrying out God's will, and Abraham is held
up as the paradigmatic example of such obedience.

2. Which of the two versions is a better story? Students invariably
prefer the Genesis telling of the tale to its Qur'an counterpart. The biblical
narrative flows more smoothly, and it does not seem as choppy as the
Islamic text. The biblical text contains many details that help to make it a
compelling story, most of which are absent from the Qur'an. Here, too,
the different agendas of the two texts become clear. The Qur'an is more
concerned with making a specific point than with recounting history or
telling a good story. Here, the key point is Abraham's obedience to God's
will, even to the point of being ready to kill his own offspring. Only the
narrative elements that are necessary to teach that lesson are included.

3. What is the most significant difference between the versions?
Students often call attention to the fact that while Abraham's son is identified as Isaac in Genesis he remains unnamed in the Islamic text. This is
an important difference, and for centuries Muslim commentators have
debated the boy's identity. In the early period, Muslim victim
scholars favored the view that Isaac was the intended sacrifice, but eventually there was a shift to seeing Ishmael as the how
dominant view among Muslims today. So
the son? What does this difference tell

functions in the Judeo-Christian and Islamic traditions? In the Bible, episode is intimately linked to the theme of God's choice of Isaac over Ishmael. Isaac is the child of the covenant while his brother is the son not chosen who disappears from the story, cut off from the family and forced to lead a nomadic existence. This is not the case in the Qur'an, where the sons of Abraham do not give rise to an ethnic or religious divide. Both Isaac and Ishmael are recognized as links in a chain of prophets that extends from Abraham through Jesus to Muhammad. The brothers are esteemed equally in the Qur'an. Neither is the sole heir of God's blessing as Isaac is in Genesis. There is no suggestion in the Qur'an of a special people set apart to enjoy a unique relationship with Allah. Abraham's son is not named in the Qur'an because his identity is irrelevant. Both Ishmael and Isaac are models of faith, and either could play the same role in the story. The key thing is that Abraham was prepared to sacrifice a son, which one does not matter.

4. Does the Qur'an provide any information not found in Genesis? Even though the name of the son is not present in the Qur'an, other details about him—details absent from the biblical record—are included. The most important detail is the mention that at the time of the near sacrifice he was "old enough to work with his father." The Arabic term for this concept (sa'ya) can refer to someone who is physically active, but it can also describe someone who is able to act according to his or her own judgment or discretion. In other words, he has reached the age of reason. Interestingly, this is the very quality he exhibits when Abraham asks him for his opinion about the troubling dream. The son immediately surrenders himself to the will of God as he tells his father to do what he has been commanded. Abraham follows his son's lead and the text goes on to say that they both submitted. The important point here is that by interpreting his father's dream as a command from God Abraham's son took the initial leap of faith that allowed both of them to respond in complete submission (in Arabic, *islam*).

5. Does the Qur'an text enable us to think about the Genesis version in a new way? Classroom discussions of Gen 22 tend to focus on Abraham's way? reread the chapter, but the Qur'an's condensed account encourages us to testing of the Genesis story through the son's eyes. Is the biblical version a way? The father and son? Does Isaac bring Abraham to faith in any just as in the questions can be answered affirmatively when we note that, ham in Gen 22, the only verbal exchange between Isaac and Abraham in Gen 22 who does the form of a question and answer. Only this time it is will be sacrificing. After Isaac asks him where the animal is that lamb for a burnt ham responds, "God himself will provide the only line of dialogue my son" (Gen 22:7–8). This is not small talk. In the chapter, Isaac's words indicate that he is

distinguish the voice of cultural expectations from the authentic voice of God. My goal in this exercise is to help students explore alternatives to simply extracting moral lessons from the text. By giving attention to ancient context, Hebrew midrash, and contemporary Jewish and Christian theology, I want students to consider more deeply how the text continues to prompt reflection on current issues as well as a deepening contemplation of God's nature and intentions.

Roger Newell

58. GENESIS 22: ARTISTS' RENDERINGS

Using works of art certainly breaks no new real pedagogical ground for the creative teacher. Sometimes, however, the simplest learning techniques yield fruitful results through their very obviousness. The intensity of the Akedah—Abraham's binding of Isaac—comes through with greater power when you see faces, study the positions of bodies, and experience the details visually as opposed merely to hearing a familiar tale.

I like to use a combination of images from different periods. Some of the most evocative include Rembrandt's *The Sacrifice of Abraham* (and yes, we ponder the title as well as the painting), Caravaggio's *The Sacrifice of Isaac* (both versions), Salvador Dali's *The Sacrifice of Isaac*, Marc Chagall's *The Sacrifice of Isaac* (*Abraham and Isaac en route* is also helpful), Karoly Ferenczy's *Isaac's Sacrifice* (*Sacrifice of Abraham*), Laurent de La Hire's *Abraham Sacrificing Isaac*, Alfred Hallet's *Abraham Sacrificing Isaac*, and Cigoli's *The Sacrifice of Isaac*.

When looking at the pictures, we start by thinking about how artists communicate biblical content. In the moment presented, do we see Isaac bound? Placed on wood? Does his father hold a knife? How is God's voice represented? Is a ram nearby? I like to get students thinking about how much room for variation an interpreter has in telling a story by discussing where any responsibility to convey details begins and ends. We consider things such as color, shadow, and symbol as modes of expressing content, mood, and fleshing out the narrative. In this phase of the exercise, students become aware of the sparse quality of biblical narrative. How much the narrator does not tell—particularly about the inner lives of characters—comes into focus and students develop greater sensitivity to the construction of a story and for the perspective from which it is told.

From this point, engaging the emotions of the characters enters in as we explore their positions, expressions, and the ways in which they interact with one another. Students routinely ponder if Abraham comes across as zealous, anxious, resigned, or weary, and what his state of mind means to his relationship with God. They also seriously analyze how Isaac reacts to the situation—is he surprised by his father, obedient, fearful? And what happens to their relationship as a result of this incident? What stake does Isaac have in this God, and does his near death affect his feelings about the deity?

God's request of Abraham also becomes more real when students look at the paintings. No one can imagine sacrificing a child or being sacrificed by a parent. When I first used this exercise, Susan Smith's 1994 murder of her two sons by drowning them in a lake came to mind for many; more recently Andrea Yates' 2001 drowning of her five children enters the conversation. The horror of these actions stands in sharp contrast to the lauding of Abraham for a faith willing to kill his son at God's command. Students struggle with why God makes such a demand and why Abraham follows without question. For students with religious commitments to this text, they wonder what exactly this story models for a contemporary reader.

In smaller classes, this exercise can work effectively when everyone contributes. More often, however, I divide students into smaller groups and project each image for a few minutes so that each group can discuss them separately. I then can lead the class through the above points with my order while always allowing space for the unexpected insights that come.

Sandie Gravett

59. THE NEAR SACRIFICE OF ISAAC

The story of the near sacrifice of Isaac can be approached from so many different angles that it becomes difficult to know just what approach to take. Depending on how the ancestral narratives fit into the course's organization of material, Gen 22:1–19 offers a manageable portion of scripture in a discrete literary unit. Hence, classes may pause and explore questions about God's character and actions as well as Abraham's faith and obedience.

I expect the students to have read most of the Abraham cycle of stories (Gen 12-25) in preparation for the class, encouraging them to formulate questions about the biblical narrator's depiction of God and

Abraham. In the class session itself, I use several media and various levels of student involvement.

1. Students volunteer to do a "dramatic reading" of the text. There is no practice required for this; I simply provide scripts with highlighted parts for the narrator and all the characters quoted in the story. After this reading, we discuss how we hear others tell the story differently from the way we read it to ourselves. Students usually sense how clearly the relative amounts of narration and dialogue stand out when hearing the text read in this way. They also begin to grasp the amount of attention the biblical author is giving to some characters (Abraham) as opposed to others (Isaac, the servants, and Sarah by her complete absence!) and what function this (in)attention has for the story.

2. Shifting focus to the compelling theological and human dimensions of the story, I show them pictures of a sculpture by George Segal, *In Memory of May 4, 1970—Abraham and Isaac,* originally commissioned as a memorial for the student deaths at Kent State during the Vietnam era. The sculpture currently sits on the campus of Princeton University (photographs available online: http://www.burr.kent.edu/archives/may4/closure/closure2.html). We reflect on the portrayal of the scene of Isaac's binding and relate this to the Jewish interpretation of the Holocaust as Akedah ("binding"). Students think about the interaction of art and biblical interpretation, as well as the way contemporary experience shapes our reading of the story.

3. We return to a close reading of the text, emphasizing aspects of literary structure, plot, narration, dialogue, characterization, setting, and so forth. Prompted by questions related to these matters, students work on these questions individually and then in groups. They begin to notice what literary scholars have often emphasized, namely, that the central portion of the narrative (vv. 9–11) slows down the action to an excruciating pace, with seven key verbs for Abraham's preparations to sacrifice Isaac. This pace stands in stark contrast to the jump of three days between vv. 3 and 4. One of the most challenging aspects of interpreting Gen 22 is the temptation to move too quickly to New Testament connections with Jesus' death, since many Christian students have heard sermons that do as much. I do not completely discourage this kind of intertextuality, but I urge students first to consider connections within the Hebrew Bible itself (e.g., the mention of Moriah in 2 Chr 3:1), and only then to look for linguistic parallels in places like Rom 8:32.

4. We conclude the session listening to a vocal piece by Michael Card, "God Will Provide the Lamb" (on his 1994 *Legacy* CD), asking how the lyrics and music capture the story line and its pathos. Card's moving melody changes in tempo in much the same way that the Gen 22 narrative speeds up or slows down. The refrain that originally is sung in the

HEBREW BIBLE

future tense—"God will provide a lamb"—concludes by shifting to past tense—"God has provided a lamb"—evoking the sorts of New Testament connections mentioned above. We discuss how all of these interpretations are expressions of the meanings of this classic story.

James K. Mead

60. LIMITED GOOD IN GENESIS 23

The Israelites practiced different social customs, embraced different values, and perceived the world differently from our students. In order for our students to understand the biblical texts in the social context of ancient Israel, it is necessary for the students to understand how their social world differs from the social world of the Bible. Although our students might recognize that many resources in our world, such as oil, fresh water, and topsoil, are limited, largely they share the assumption of a limitless world. Upon graduation, they expect to get jobs that will include annual pay raises and an increase in their standard of living. They expect innovations and discoveries in science and health. The world presents our students with endless horizons. This assumption about the world contrasts dramatically with the worldview of peasants who live and act as if all the goods of the world were limited. Indeed, in order for our students to understand the peasant behavior of the people of the Bible, they must recognize how their worldview differs from that of the ancient Israelites.

I introduce the assumption of limited good early in the course because it underlies many social values (such as honor and shame) and practices (such as hospitality and patronage). I begin my discussion of limited good by eliciting from the students the many ways in which they view the world as unlimited. Students quickly recognize this assumption, which they uncritically hold. I then introduce them to the assumption of a limited good (cf. the classic treatment of G. M. Foster, "Peasant Society and the Image of Limited Good," *American Anthropologist* 67 [1965]: 293-315). According to the peasant view of the world, all the good things in life exist in fixed quantities and in short supply, and their distribution is largely outside the peasant's control. Thus, in terms of economy, there is no connection between work and wealth. Work is about subsistence, not producing capital. Emotions and attitudes like friendship and love are also limited. Health is limited so that the loss of semen and blood is regarded as a loss of life and vitality. Limited good also applies to honor. The only way for a man to gain honor is to take it from another man, and thus peasant societies are characterized by the competition for honor.

Following this brief introduction of limited good, I ask the students to reflect on the implications of this worldview on behavior: "If your world was limited in this way, how would you treat your possessions? Conduct business? Relate to your peers?" Students generally note the defensive posture that would emerge from such a worldview. After a few minutes of discussion, I suggest three implications of limited good for understanding economic transactions in ancient Israel. First, a man takes a defensive position to maintain his honor against claims that he is exploiting the fellow members of his community. As a result, all economic transactions are made public so that all may see and judge that the parties have acted according to honor. Second, the honorable man will maintain his given status, neither gaining at the expense of others nor losing to others. Third, all gain is attributed to outsiders. Because outsiders do not belong to the community, one does not need to deal honorably with them, and therefore they may be exploited. Gain may also be attributed to newly found treasure (which does not belong to anyone) or to God (who has an abundant supply of resources). The critical factor is the need to ensure that gain did not come from fellow members of the community.

Finally, I divide the class into groups and ask each group to apply the model of limited good that we have constructed in class toward an interpretation of Gen 23, the story of Abraham's purchase of a cave to bury Sarah. I give them the following questions to consider in their interpretation: Why is the negotiation for purchasing the cave carried out publicly? Is Abraham treated as an insider or outsider to the community? Why does Ephron offer to give the field to Abraham at no cost? Why does Abraham refuse to accept the field as a free gift? What might have been the consequences if Abraham had accepted the field for free? Why did the price finally go from "free" to 400 shekels of silver? What is the effect of this price increase on the community's perception of the transaction?

When the groups have sufficiently discussed the story, I randomly choose one group to answer each question for the entire class. After each group answers its question, I survey the other groups to see whether they agree or disagree with the answer, and then use their responses to generate further discussion of the question and the story for the entire class.

Ronald A. Simkins

61. JACOB: SAINT OR SINNER?

In my introductory Bible course, I regularly stage a debate between students when we study the story of Jacob (Gen 27:1–36:8). Although "saint" and "sinner" are essentially anachronistic categories, I find that framing the issue in this overly simplistic way actually helps students to read, analyze, and problematize the biblical narrative through a fun and engaging activity. I do not attempt to specify what I mean by the terms; I let the students determine how they will understand the categories as the exercise develops. Initially, I divide students into small groups; half of the groups are assigned to argue that Jacob is a "saint" and the other groups will argue that he is a "sinner." The groups have 20–30 minutes to prepare for the debate. Their task during this time is to search for and discuss any biblical texts that might support their side of the argument; moreover, students are encouraged to consider and prepare for the kinds of texts and arguments the other side will use in the debate. After the groups have prepared, they are combined into two debate teams (ideally, facing each other). Each team chooses a person who will make a one-minute opening argument. Then each member of the debate team is encouraged to participate. I usually do not require that teams alternate speaking; anyone can make a point. One danger is that a handful of strong or extroverted students may dominate the debate. To offset this tendency, I often restrict speakers to two or three "speeches." (Students who have exhausted their time are still allowed to assist teammates.) When the debate has run its course, the groups briefly reconvene and then make one final statement. Throughout the activity, the emphasis is upon textual evidence. Arguments must be rooted in the text. Students may be surprised to find how "rounded" and human a character Jacob is. Evidence is ample on both sides of the debate. Questions about the nature of God, morality, family, and faith may well come into play. In the process, students are challenged to read the text more carefully, and they seem to gain a lasting sense that biblical characters and the God they worship merit careful consideration and reflection. (For similar exercises, see §§65, 95, 112.)

Michael Barram

62. SOME STRIKING TEXTUAL PARALLELS IN GENESIS 34 AND 2 SAMUEL 13

The purpose of this exercise is (1) to motivate students toward close and careful reading of the biblical text and (2) to equip them to participate in informed speculation about the nature of the Deuteronomistic History and the editorial processes involved in the Hebrew Bible's formation.

Assign students the task of reading Gen 34 and 2 Sam 13. (If class time is limited, the assignment may be completed in advance.) Have the students work together in small groups, working collectively to find as many correspondences in language and motif as possible between the two stories.

The correspondences between both accounts are as follows: A daughter (Dinah/Tamar) of Jacob-Israel/Israel's king is subjected to the physical advances of a prince (Shechem/Amnon), who "seizes her and lays with her by force" (Gen 34), or "forces her and lays with her" (2 Sam 13 NRSV; in Hebrew, same verbs only reversed). One of the princes (Shechem) seizes the woman and falls in love with her; the other (Amnon) assaults his victim and loathes her (another corresponding reversal). Note: Although the verbs suggest that force was used, the nature of Shechem's advances in Gen 34 is somewhat unclear in that the terms used here are elsewhere distinguished from actual rape (see Deut 22:23-24). In the case of Amnon, however, the matter is less ambiguous. In each account the act is described as a "foolish thing in Israel," and says that "such a thing is not done," and that the act is a cause of "disgrace" (unfortunately, the uniformity of the Hebrew text is often obscured by the translation). The fathers of both women appear to be angered by the acts, yet they take no direct action; instead, revenge is plotted by the women's brothers, who orchestrate a deception in which the perpetrator is rendered vulnerable (Shechem, pain/Amnon, drunkeness), facilitating the murder of the offending prince. In both cases (and this is the toughest one for students to find), the avenging brothers stand to gain far more than mere satisfaction of just recompense (the sons of Jacob, an entire city/Absalom, succession to the throne).

Spur discussion by asking the following questions, some of which of course are ultimately unanswerable: What might account for the striking degree of textual and literary similarity between these two narratives (e.g., single authorship, a striking case of emulation [if so, which is older?], mere coincidence, etc.)? Is there enough similarity to suppose that both stories were in fact composed by the same author? Which of these two events appears to be more anchored in history than the other? What do you suppose the author(s) might be saying about the nature of Israel's leadership? What might be some theological implications for presenting Israel's leadership in this way?

By wrestling with these questions, students will have an opportunity further to develop their critical thinking skills both in comparing texts and thinking historically. They may decide, for example, that the degree of similarity between the stories is high enough to warrant single authorship and that, logically, the author therefore had to have lived after the time of David (at the very least). Although perhaps unsurprising to some, it has been the experience of this writer that occasionally students will decide upon single authorship, yet fail to grasp the implication that both stories would then have to have been produced during roughly the same period in time! Instructors will find this exercise even more rewarding if students have had some prior exposure to the Documentary Hypothesis. Depending on the instructor's academic bent, one might argue, like Richard Friedman, that J overflows the Pentateuch and was composed sometime during the time of Solomon. Others may find here an opportunity to reject the notion of the Yahwist altogether and posit that both stories represent an exilic (or even post-exilic) prophetic critique of national leadership thematically retrojected into Israel's past. Finally, students and instructors with theological concerns may want to focus on the critical portrayal of Israelite leadership as the biblical writers' way of affirming the sovereignty of God by stressing the inherent deficiencies of human institutions.

Nicolae Roddy

63. HONOR AND SHAME IN GENESIS 34 AND 1 SAMUEL 25

In the United States, honor and shame are largely regarded as a matter of private virtue. The honorable man or woman is good, moral, honest, and virtuous. Shame is equivalent to guilt. In the world of the Bible, honor and shame are connected to public reputation (often more so than private virtue) and sexuality. They are the fundamental values of the people in the Bible. Our students need to be able to distinguish between their vague conceptions of honor and shame and the social values that shaped the lives of the ancient Israelites.

I begin class with a brief lecture on the primary characteristics of honor and shame for the ancient Israelites. I emphasize that honor is a person's public claim to worth combined with the public acknowledgement of that worth. Shame, as a positive value, is a person's concern for reputation. Although honor and shame concern both men and women, a man's public demeanor is characterized by honor whereas a woman's is characterized by shame. A man publicly seeks to demonstrate that he is worthy of a good reputation but a woman in public guards herself out of concern to avoid a bad reputation. In the quest of honor, men compete with one another. Indeed, every encounter between social equals, who are not kin, is a challenge of honor. In order to maintain one's honor, a challenged man must respond to the challenge in a comparable way. The man who does not respond adequately to a challenge loses honor to his challenger. If the man's response is out of proportion to the challenge, he risks escalating the conflict. The competition for honor is played out only among social equals. A man of high social status gains nothing by challenging someone of low social status—his honor is already greater than the one whom he challenges. Similarly, a man of low social status cannot challenge a man of high status—his challenge is ineffective because he lacks the public honor to support his challenge. But among social equals, the social prestige of individual members of society is ranked through the gain and loss of honor (cf. the essays in D. Gilmore, ed., *Honor and Shame and the Unity of the Mediterranean* [Washington, D.C.: American Anthropological Association, 1987]).

In the remainder of the class period, the students inductively explore the dynamics of honor and shame by examining two biblical stories: the story of Dinah (Gen 34) and the story of David and Nabal (1 Sam 25). I help the students to appropriate this material by leading the class through an examination of the first story, the story of Dinah. I begin by noting how the common characterization of the story as the "rape of Dinah" is perhaps incorrect. Whereas the students' Bibles read that Shechem "seized her [Dinah] and lay with her by force," a literal translation of the Hebrew states, "he took her and lay with her, and humbled her." I ask the students to consider what this translation might mean in the context of honor and shame. We then look at other aspects of the story that argue against a "rape" interpretation: Shechem wants to marry Dinah, Dinah is found in Shechem's house, and her brothers accuse Shechem of treating her as a "whore." This discussion adequately problematizes the story: If the story is not about the rape of Dinah and her brothers' vengeance for that rape, what is it about?

Having set up the story for discussion, I guide the students carefully through the narrative, directing them to consider the following questions: Why is Dinah alone in the countryside? How does sexual intercourse with Shechem "humble" Dinah? How have Shechem's actions challenged the honor of Jacob and her brothers? Why does Hamor intercede on Shechem's behalf? How should Shechem's offer of marriage be interpreted in the context of challenges and responses? Why does Shechem offer such a large bride price? Why do the brothers act deceitfully in their negotiations with Shechem? Why do the brothers insist on circumcision? Why does Jacob rebuke his sons for their actions against Shechem? How do the brothers justify their actions?

After the class has worked through Gen 34, the students are sufficiently familiar with honor and shame to attempt an interpretation on their own. I divide the class into groups and ask each group to interpret 1 Sam 25, the story of David and Nabal, in the context of honor and shame. But this story needs some set-up before the students can adequately tackle it. I note first that David in this context is on the run from the pursuit of Saul. David had been a member of the court of Saul, but he left the court and fled when it appeared that Saul was determined to kill him. As an outlaw on the run, David attracted to himself a large band of fellow outlaws who served him. Second, I clarify that Nabal is a made-up name assigned to the man in this story. Nabal means "fool," and he is called Nabal because in this story the narrator interprets his actions to be foolish. I remind the students that they do not need to accept the narrator's judgment of his actions. Finally, this story is set in a larger context of stories that attempt to exonerate David of any wrongdoing in his dealings with Saul and in his rise to the kingship over Israel. The passage is thus heavily biased. David can literally "do no wrong." I then give each group the following set of questions to guide their interpretation of the story: Did Nabal interpret David's request as a positive or negative challenge? Does Nabal's interpretation of the challenge have any validity? Describe Nabal's response: Does he accept the challenge? Is he unable to meet the challenge? Does he reject the challenge? What is the meaning of Nabal's response: "Who is David? Who is the son of Jesse?" What does Nabal imply about David when he states: "There are many servants today who are breaking away from their masters"? Why does David respond to Nabal by gathering his men to kill Nabal and his household? What is the effect of Abigail's actions on David and on Nabal?

After the groups have had sufficient time to interpret the story, I lead a discussion of the story for the entire class. I randomly ask the groups to share their answers to some of the questions, and I focus on the interpretive issues that groups wrestle with most.

Ronald A. Simkins

64. GENESIS AND *THE RED TENT*

One of the primary objectives in my introductory course on the Bible is that students will develop increasing skill and insight as readers of primary texts. I choose not to use a textbook for the course since students may be tempted to focus on the secondary analysis and neglect the primary text. The lack of a textbook, however, requires that students be introduced to contextual and hermeneutical issues through other means. In addition to lectures and discussion, I have found that reading Anita

Diamant's popular novel, *The Red Tent* (New York: Picador, 1997), in concert with the biblical text can be very effective in helping students explore such contextual and interpretive issues.

The Red Tent is an entertaining story detailing the life, loves, and tragedies of Dinah, Jacob's daughter by Leah (Gen 30:21). In the biblical account (Gen 34), Dinah is raped by Prince Shechem, who then falls in love with her and arranges for himself and every male in his city to be circumcised in order that he might marry Jacob's daughter. While Shechem and his compatriots are healing from their wounds, Simeon and Levi, two of Dinah's brothers, murder them. Dinah never speaks, and readers never hear from her again.

The premise of *The Red Tent* is that the biblical story suppresses the actual events involving Dinah and the Shechemite slaughter. In the novel, Dinah and Shechem are lovers; there is no rape. The murder of Shechem's male inhabitants is an unprovoked slaughter. Presumably, Diamant's version of the story is at least partially inspired by several factors in the biblical text. For example, the Bible does not explain why Dinah "went out to visit the women of the region" (Gen 34:1 NRSV). Immediately after the rape, readers are informed that Shechem's "soul was drawn to Dinah," and that "he loved the girl and spoke tenderly to her" (Gen 34:3). Indeed, Dinah remained in Shechem's house until Simeon and Levi laid waste to the city. Such sketchy details—and the brevity of the entire biblical account—may inspire curiosity in discerning readers. At the very least, they may wonder what Dinah would say about these events if she were able to speak. In *The Red Tent*, Diamant gives Dinah a voice, allowing her to narrate her own story from beginning to end. The resulting story often parallels the account of Jacob and his sons in Gen 25–50, though it differs significantly in both major and minor details.

In my course, students read through Genesis during the first three weeks of the semester. They begin reading *The Red Tent* as soon as we encounter the biblical story of Dinah, and they complete the book within about three weeks. From the very beginning, I explain that we are reading the novel to become more skilled and observant readers of the biblical text. I ask them to make particular note of places where the plot or other narrative details differ between the two accounts, and to consider carefully why Diamant may have altered the biblical text as she did. In doing this, students learn inductively to read more closely, to analyze fissures and gaps in a text, and to consider perspective, social location, and related hermeneutical issues. As students begin to see and focus on what is and what is not stated in the biblical text, they increasingly appreciate how the Bible privileges some, especially male, perspectives and stories.

Though a few students have found it challenging to read a novel that occasionally turns the biblical account on its head, most students have enjoyed the book and have become better readers, and more interested in the biblical story itself. In particular, female students often feel empowered by Diamant's "rereading" and become noticeably more interested in class discussions. Male students, too, inevitably learn new things through the process of reading and discussion. In short, reading and discussing *The Red Tent* provides opportunities to introduce students to feminist and other marginalized perspectives apart from extensive theoretical background and debates. Moreover, students appreciate how the novel encourages them to imagine biblical figures as well-rounded and developed characters not unlike themselves. Following this exercise, students seem equipped to read further biblical texts with new eyes, new questions, and new interest. In that sense, *The Red Tent* has been an effective pedagogical tool.

Michael Barram

65. DEBATING JOSEPH'S CHARACTER

Many students are habituated towards seeing only one, fixed meaning to the text. To introduce them to the complicated interplay of different, even rival, meanings within a single text-narrative, early on in the semester of the survey course on Hebrew Bible I facilitate a classroom debate on the character of Joseph. More specifically, I ask them to debate the question: Is Joseph an admirable character or not?

To prepare for the class, students are asked to read ahead of time Gen 37, 39–50. While they are told we will have a class debate, and what the debate question will be, they are not told which side of the debate they will take. To prepare effectively, they must thus read the text for both sides of the question. When they walk into class that day, they simply draw a "pro" or "con" slip out of a hat. The class then divides itself into the two groups—the "pro" side and the "con" side. Together, we briefly review effective debate strategies (e.g., begin with your strongest arguments, cite specific biblical texts for support, consider how you will refute the arguments presented by the other side). I then give the groups about 20–30 minutes to marshal their evidence and prepare for the debate. During this time, each group also decides on a spokesperson (or two). Each group is also encouraged to choose at least one official note-taker, so that in the midst of all their discussion, no important points are lost.

For the debate itself, each side first takes turns presenting its case, being as complete and thorough as possible. About 5–7 minutes suffices for each group. After this first exchange, each side is given the further opportunity (3-5 minutes) of refuting what the other side has said, as well as adding further points to their case. Each time, it is the spokesperson who takes the lead in making the case. However, when finished, he or she is able to consult with the other group members and bring forward any additional points. At the end of all these exchanges, I normally open up the conversation to all the students.

Near the end, I give my judgment on which side presented the more convincing case. Alternatively, I have occasionally brought in an outside judge responsible for giving the verdict. This is quite effective, since students are less suspicious of a potential bias on the part of this outsider; moreover, they become especially invested in presenting a quality debate for this guest. In the ten or so years I have been doing this exercise, both sides have "won" about an equal number of times. The judgment considers both the quantity and the quality of student arguments, as well as how effectively they were presented.

Even though most students initially want to be on the "pro" side because they think it will be easier to debate, the "con" side often comes up with the more effective arguments. Some of this is due to that side working harder to call up effective arguments, but some of it is due, of course, to the fact that the text lends itself quite readily to open-ended readings of the Joseph character—as both admirable and non-admirable. Not only does this exercise introduce students to the complexity of meanings in the biblical texts, they also discover how much fun can be had in reading and discussing the Bible. It also helps that we are dealing with a story that is familiar to many of them. Even if they have scarcely ever read the Bible, they know the story, if only through the musical *Joseph and the Amazing Technicolor Dreamcoat.* (Indeed, part of what this exercise effects is a deconstruction of that musical.) (For similar exercises, see §§61, 111.)

Karla G. Bohmbach

66. EXODUS FROM EGYPT:
UNIVERSAL STORY OF FREEDOM?

The story of the exodus from Egypt is popularly pictured as a paradigmatic story of the passage from slavery and oppression to freedom. As such it has inspired and has been applied to freedom struggles in many parts of the world. In this exercise, students are prodded to consider other interpretations of the Exodus story, interpretations that read the text carefully and often find in it either a story of freedom for some at the cost of others or no modern notion of freedom at all.

This exercise involves using the "jigsaw" process, a method of getting students to engage with a number of reading assignments without the usual complaints that the readings are too many, too long, and too difficult to understand. The process works by having each individual student read only a portion of the required reading and then teach what has been read to classmates assigned different readings. Essentially, each student reads only one piece of the jigsaw puzzle; in groups, the students work together to put the whole jigsaw puzzle together.

In this particular exercise, each student is assigned one of the following texts: George V. Pixley, "A Latin American Perspective: The Option for the Poor in the Old Testament," who interprets the exodus as a universal paradigm of liberation, but only in the earliest layer of the story; Naim Stifan Ateek, "A Palestinian Perspective: The Bible and Liberation," who interprets the exodus from the perspective of the Canaanites displaced by the freed Israelites and concludes that for the Canaanites (and by extension today's Palestinians) the exodus is not liberating; Robert Allan Warrior, "A Native American Perspective: Canaanites, Cowboys, and Indians," who, like Ateek, takes the perspective of the displaced Canaanites, comparing them to the native peoples displaced by the arrival of the Europeans, and likewise concludes that for native peoples the exodus is not therefore a story of liberation; or Jon D. Levenson, "Exodus and Liberation," who critiques liberation interpretations of the exodus story for anachronistically reading modern notions of freedom back into the text, and for universalizing the story by erasing its emphasis on God's particular relationship with a particular people. (The first three articles can be found reprinted in S. Scholz, ed., *Biblical Studies Alternatively* [Upper Saddle River, N.J.: Prentice Hall, 2003]. The fourth can be found in J. Levenson, *The Hebrew Bible, the Old Testament and Historical Criticism* [Louisville: Westminster/John Knox, 1993]. Since the Levenson text is rather lengthy, one might substitute his "Liberation Theology and the Exodus," in *Jews, Christians and the Theology of the Hebrew Scriptures* [ed. A. O. Bellis and J. S. Kaminisky; Atlanta: SBL, 2000].)

In the following class, students are divided into groups of four, such that each group has at least one person who has read the first reading, one who has read the second reading, and so on. Each student in turn presents the main ideas and thesis of his or her reading to the rest of the group in no more than five minutes; the other students take notes. After the presentations are done, the group discusses whether or not the exodus story is a story of liberation, and for whom, by comparing and contrasting the information and perspectives of the different articles. A general classroom plenary with the instructor summarizes the discussion.

The point of this exercise is to illustrate that the same biblical text can be read and used by various groups for various, sometimes opposing, purposes, and that the biblical text is not neutral but a powerful tool for diverse purposes. The social location of the interpreter is also highlighted as an important influence on interpretation (Pixley works in Nicaragua, Ateek is Palestinian, Warrior is a native American, and Levenson is Jewish).

F. V. Greifenhagen

67. ISRAELITE AND/OR EGYPTIAN? ETHNIC IDENTITY IN EXODUS

As students read the exodus story, or perhaps in preparing them for reading Exodus, the instructor can call attention to a repeated theme that becomes quite explicit in the plague narrative: "that the Lord makes a distinction between Egypt and Israel" (11:7; see also 8:23; 9:4; 33:16). In fact, much of Exodus can be read as the story of how Israel established an identity separate from that of Egypt. Such a differential identity is ethnic in nature in that it focuses on the cultural boundaries (language, diet, religion, kinship, etc.) that separate *us* from *them*, rather than on cultural commonalities. That is, in the story of Exodus, the people of Israel are urged to differentiate themselves from the Egyptians, thus raising the possibility that they (and/or the addressees of the story) considered themselves as Egyptian.

Ethnic identity is often ambiguous because it needs to be asserted by focusing on difference in the midst of commonality. One way to introduce this ambiguity is to go back to the beginning of Exodus and the portrayal of the midwives in 1:15–21. Translations generally describe the midwives in v. 15 as "Hebrew midwives." Translating thus, however, obscures the ambiguity of the expression in Hebrew: "midwives of the Hebrews." Is the genitive construction here adjectival or objective? Are the midwives Hebrews or are they Egyptians serving as midwives to or for the Hebrews? Jewish commentators noticed the ambiguity and disagreed about which way to resolve it. Nehama Leibowitz, in *Studies in Bereshit (Genesis)* (3rd ed.; Jerusalem: World Zionist Organization, 1976), presents commentators that insist the midwives are Hebrew (as also the impression given by most modern English translations) and others that insist they are Egyptian. The latter option is also presented in Josephus and Philo. Students find it interesting to discuss the various options presented by these commentators on the identity of the midwives.

If the ethnic identity of the midwives is ambiguous, how much more the ethnicity of Moses. Although he is given a proper Hebrew lineage (2:1–2), Moses is raised as an Egyptian (2:5–10), given an Egyptian name (2:10), and recognized as an Egyptian (2:19). While the biblical story is intent on presenting him originally and ultimately as a Hebrew or Israelite, students can be asked to note that Moses needs to be persuaded to identify with the Israelites (Exodus 3–4) and always seems somewhat at odds with them. At the last, of course, Moses is not allowed to enter the Promised Land with the people whom he has so faithfully led (Deut 34).

This discussion of ethnic identity can fruitfully lead to a reading of Randall Bailey's "'Is That Any Name for a Nice Hebrew Boy?' Exodus 2:1–10: The De-Africanization of an Israelite Hero" (in *The Recovery of Black Presence: An Interdisciplinary Exploration* [ed. R. C. Bailey and J. Grant; Nashville: Abingdon, 1995], 25–36). Another discussion that issues out of this topic is the experience of students who are bi- or multicultural and the pressures they encounter to identify with one main culture (see, for example, Mitzi Uehara-Carter, "On Being Blackanese," at http://www.webcom.com/intvoice/mitzi.html). (For exercises on similar topics, see §§154, 158.)

F. V. Greifenhagen

68. ISRAELITE OR EGYPTIAN?

As a means of getting students to examine their assumptions about early Hebrew society, the class is initially offered a short quiz in the style of a fashion magazine "What's my style?" poll. Their answers may reveal that, although the tendency of modern Christians and Jews is to identify with the Israelites, their own worldview and experience may have more in common with that of a highly complex, stratified society such as ancient Egypt than that of the Israelite nomadic herding groups featured so prominently in the Genesis and Exodus narratives.

I pose the following questions (in a handout or via PowerPoint):

1. The nation I'm part of could accurately be described as: (a) a global superpower; or (b) a tribe.

2. In my future career, important job skills will include: (a) reading and writing; or (b) shearing sheep.

3. Common occupations in my community include: (a) accountant, architect, brewer, chef, civil engineer, entertainer, fisherman, gardener, laundry owner, painter, physician, priest, sailor, administrative assistant, shipbuilder, soldier, and tailor; or (b) prostitute and shepherd.

4. I live: (a) in a house in this big town on a major river. We have indoor plumbing; or (b) in a tent, like most of the people I know. We wander around in the hills a lot.

5. Ultimately I owe my allegiance to: (a) this guy who runs my nation-state. I've never met him in person, but I see his picture all the time. He seems like a caring, religious, family-oriented guy, but he knows when to get tough with our nation's enemies, and I like that; or (b) Grandpa.

6. My leader: (a) is presently engaged in a massive military campaign against those dastardly people near the Fertile Crescent; or (b) is not.

Afterwards, the instructor can elicit discussion of evidence in the texts for the structure of Hebrew society, and students can discuss how differences between modern American society and viewpoints might affect their understanding of the ancient text and its meaning.

Susanne Hofstra

69. EXODUS 1:1–5: EXPLAINING VARIATION IN SMALL DETAILS

This exercise introduces students to textual variants and the importance of such variants in establishing the particular ideologies or worldviews of different versions of the same text. It is based on Andrew E. Steinmann's "Jacob's Family Goes to Egypt: Varying Portraits of Unity and Disunity in the Textual Traditions of Exodus 1:1–5" (available in the online journal *TC: A Journal of Biblical Textual Criticism*, Vol. 2, 1997 [http://rosetta.rel-tech.org/TC/vol02/vol02.html]).

Students are given a one-page handout of the text of Exod 1:1–5, in both the original language and English translation, as it appears in the MT, the Samaritan Pentateuch, the LXX, and 4QExod[b]. Steinmann includes the original language texts; the instructor will need to add the appropriate English translations as follows:

MT: "1 And these are the names of the sons of Israel who came to Egypt with Jacob. Each man came with his family. 2 Reuben, Simeon, Levi and Judah; 3 Issachar, Zebulun and Benjamin. 4 Dan and Naphtali; Gad and Asher. 5 And all the persons who came from the loins of Jacob were seventy persons. And Joseph was in Egypt."

Samaritan Pentateuch: "1 And these are the names of the sons of Israel who came to Egypt with Jacob. Each man came with his family. 2 Reuben and Simeon and Levi and Judah 3 and Issachar and Zebulun and Benjamin. 4 Dan and Naphtali; Gad and Asher. 5 And all the persons who came from the loins of Jacob were seventy persons. And Joseph was in Egypt."

4QExod[b] (as reconstructed by F. M. Cross): "1[These are the names of the sons of Israel who came to Egypt] with Jacob their father. Each man [came with his family. 2 Reuben, Simeon, Levi <and > Judah;] 3 Issachar, Zebulun, Joseph and Benja[min]. 4 Dan and Naphtali; Gad and Asher. 5 And all the persons <from Jacob> were seventy-five persons."

LXX: "1 These are the names of the sons of Israel who came to Egypt with Jacob their father. Each came with his family. 2 Reuben, Simeon, Levi, Judah, 3 Issachar, Zebulun and Benjamin. 4 Dan and Naphtali; Gad and Asher. 5 And Joseph was in Egypt. And all the persons who came from Jacob were seventy-five."

In groups, the students compare and contrast the various textual traditions and (1) construct a list of variants; (2) discuss whether these variants might be accidental or deliberate; and (3) try to establish which textual traditions might be first and which ones derivative. Their results are shared and discussed in a classroom plenary. The instructor can draw on Steinmann's article both for a discussion of all the possible variants, and for a possible reason for them. Since this exercise focuses on variants that are not easily attributable to copying mistakes, the instructor can focus on the concept of "multiple editions" of ancient biblical texts, and the ideological perspectives that might be embedded in such variants. (For other exercises on textual criticism, see §§19–21.)

F.V. Greifenhagen

70. THE HISTORICITY OF THE EXODUS: WHAT'S AT STAKE?

Most of my students are very reluctant to question the historicity of the exodus narrative. On the contrary, what they want from me is a scholarly validation that it really did happen. In order to defuse their intense "yes or no" expectations from the outset, I sometimes put them through the following exercise prior to discussing the evidence (and lack of evidence) supporting the biblical version of the exodus from Egypt.

I tell the students that I want them to think for a few minutes about exactly what it would mean to claim that the exodus story was "true." Specifically, just how much of it would have to be true in order for them to consider the narrative true? I then ask them to take a piece of paper and put a vertical line down the middle with "true" on one side and "not true" on the other side. I then ask a series of questions, and they are to decide whether they would consider the exodus narrative "true" or "not true" under the following circumstances:

1. If there had never been a historical people called "Israel" in antiquity, would you say that the exodus narrative was true?

2. If there had been a people called Israel, but they had not been freed from slavery in Egypt, would you say that the narrative was true?

3. If it should turn out that Israel had existed, and had been freed from slavery in Egypt, but they did not receive the Ten Commandments, would you say that the narrative was true?

4. If Israel had in fact been freed and had received the Ten Commandments, but it turned out that the tablets were written on tablets of clay, not stone, would you say that the narrative was true?

5. If Israel had been freed from slavery, had received the Ten Commandments on tablets of stone, but it turned out that Moses made them up, rather than receiving them from God, would the story be true?

6. If it should turn out that Israel was freed from slavery, did receive the Ten Commandments, written on tablets of stone, and that the commandments had *come* from God but had not actually been "written by the finger of God," would you say that the narrative was true?

7. And finally, what if it should turn out that God does not have fingers?

The students, of course, tend to be of the opinion that God does not have literal fingers, and that the image is metaphorical. But they will have made quite diverse decisions about just how much of the narrative must be literally true in order for it to "count" as true. The exercise does not help anyone decide how much of the exodus narrative is true. It does, however, help students realize that questions about whether or not the Bible is "true" are more complicated than they may seem.

Julie Galambush

71. MULTIPLE PERSPECTIVES ON EXODUS 15

When one considers an issue or question from multiple perspectives, a certain degree of complexity and ambiguity often emerges. It is important for students to recognize this, and the Song of Moses in Exod 15 affords such an opportunity.

After discussing the contents of Exod 1–14, I read aloud the Song (Exod 15:1–18). We then consider the image of the Lord in the Song as an all-powerful warrior who violently destroys his enemies (vv. 3-12); yet the Lord is also described as a loving God (v. 13). This tension between the images of God reveals the point of view of the Song. Only from an Israelite perspective could the killing of the Egyptians be considered a gracious act of love and liberation. Then I ask students to write the "Song of the Egyptians." I ask them to imagine Moses and the people of Israel standing on one side of the sea singing triumphantly, and to place themselves on the other side of the waters, perhaps as a brother or sister or child of one of the Egyptians who drowned in the sea. Students then write one verse expressing their sentiments about the events of that day from their Egyptian perspective. What would they be thinking and feeling? What would they say to the deity that they worshipped? Who or what would they question? Or would they only grieve? After a few minutes, the students read their verses, and in so doing the class collectively produces the "Song of the Egyptians." Quite simply, the goal of the exercise is for them to realize, to use the cliché, that "there are two sides to every story"—in this case, one from each side of the Red Sea.

In Exod 15 the Israelites are on the winning side, but this is not always the case. Later in their history the Israelites will be defeated (722 and 586 B.C.E.), and they too will struggle to come to terms with their destruction, as is seen, for instance, in the book of Lamentations. Thus, the Bible recognizes the importance of expressing one's grief, as the "Song of the Egyptians" does. So as students read their verse of the Song I explain that their thoughts and feelings echo those of the Israelites when they occupy the losing side. While many students express great lamentation over their tragic loss, others blame themselves (or the Egyptians generally) for the disaster, interpreting the destruction of the Egyptian army as divine punishment for some sin. Here I note that this is also a prevalent biblical explanation for evil (cf. 2 Kgs 17). Still others express frustration, anger, and disappointment at their deity for not helping them. This too is part of the biblical tradition (Lamentations, Job, Habakkuk, lament Psalms). Finally, given the biblical Song's focus on God's indomitable power, some students say that their Egyptian deity was too weak and was conquered by the Lord. While this is a completely legitimate and understandable sentiment, it is striking that there is no testimony in the Hebrew Bible of the Lord's strength proving inferior to that of another deity. This can lead to a discussion of the notion of divine sovereignty.

It is not difficult to tie the discussion to contemporary issues. Some in the Muslim world sang triumphantly as the towers fell in New York on September 11, 2001, while Americans grieved. Similarly, some in the U.S. cheered as the dead bodies of Saddam Hussein's sons were displayed, while some in the Muslim world mourned. It is all a matter of perspective.

Mark Roncace

72. ACTING OUT EXODUS 19–20

Movies such as *The Prince of Egypt* and *The Ten Commandments* focus on the heroic role of Moses in delivering the people from slavery and in receiving the commandments. No attention is given to the making of the covenant, and the commandments appear to be handed down in a vacuum. It is this cinematic representation of Moses—the hero alone on the mountain receiving tablets of stone from God—that students substitute for what is written in Exod 19–20, missing the assent the community makes to the covenant with God and God's address to the community as a whole. Consequently, they view the commandments as disembodied laws descending from on high rather than the framework for a community in covenant relationship with God and in right relationship with each other.

In an attempt to create an alternative visual representation of the events and to do a close reading of the text, we act out these chapters in class. Our script is the text of Exod 19:1–20:21. The chapters divide neatly into four scenes: Exod 19:1–9a, 9b–15, 16–25, and 20:1–21. The characters are God, Moses, the people, and a narrator. It is not hard to get students to volunteer to play God and Moses or read the narrator's part. The rest of the class also participates, speaking as "the people." "God" and "Moses" position themselves "on the mountain" or "with the people." Often "God" will climb up on a table, sit on a tall stool, or stand at the front of the room. "Moses" has to run back and forth between "God" and "the people." The narrator guides the action by reading the text and the characters follow the instructions in the text. As director I halt the action at the end of each "scene" and invite questions and observations from students on that scene.

The first scene (Exod 19:1–9a) allows students to focus on the covenant that is to be established, to recognize its conditional nature, and to hear its purpose that the people live as a "priestly kingdom and a holy nation." Typically the first comment after this scene is read is a question: "To what covenant is God referring?" (Exod 19:5). They recognize it is not the Ancestral Covenant because of the "if" clause. That draws attention to the way these verses anticipate the commands in chapter 20, but, more importantly, links those commands back to the covenant-making narrative. The reference to the deliverance from Egypt (19:4) provides an opportunity to contrast the character of the "holy nation" that is to be established through the covenant with the character of the Hebrews' former life in service to Pharaoh. The covenant can be seen as shaping an alternative society to the one the Hebrews experienced in Egypt. The movement of "Moses" between "God" and "the people" in this scene allows students to recognize Moses' role as a mediator while also recognizing that the people speak for themselves.

The second scene (19:9b-15) introduces students to a theophany and prompts discussion about the boundaries between "clean" and "unclean" and between "holy" and "unholy" that are key to understanding this passage. While the third scene (19:16–25) is also a theophany, breaking at v. 15 allows the class to focus on how the people are to prepare for God's appearance. Typically "Moses" has barely finished reading the line before students blurt out the question, "Why does God say to 'not go near a woman'?"

The "narrator" has most of the third scene (19:16–25) in which the visual and sound effects accompanying the presence of God on the mountain are described. By this point students are generally fully engaged in the drama so that often one or more of them spontaneously provides a soundtrack to accompany the narration. This scene rarely prompts much discussion but halting at v. 25 allows "Moses" to head down the mountain to the people.

In the final scene (20:1–21), students recognize that "Moses" is not in the mediator role as "God" addresses "the people." Because the commandments are spoken by "God" students can hear that the commands are introduced with a reminder of God's gracious deliverance of the people "out of the land of Egypt, out of the house of slavery" (20:2). With "Moses" among "the people," the commandments are more clearly heard as addressed to all the people. Hearing the words of "God," rather than viewing the image of words carved in stone, prompts students' curiosity about the details and reasons for the commands that are presented in this passage. They also realize that there are no numbers assigned to each commandment and, among those who are familiar with the commandments from catechetical instruction, there is often the discovery that there are different patterns for numbering the commandments. Since "the people" address "Moses" in response to what they have heard in this final scene, there is opportunity to return to considering Moses' role as mediator and to discuss the connection between the commandments and the Covenant Code that follows.

When we have completed the four scenes in Exod 19–20, students always ask where the scenes in the movies come from. I gladly point them to Exod 32-34, but we do not look at those chapters in class nor do I assign them for reading. Most students who participate in this collective reading of Exod 19–20 are able to retain the chapters' description of the Sinai Covenant and the giving of the commandments for their work throughout the semester. It also often prompts them to raise questions about other cinematic depictions of biblical texts. (For similar exercises involving role-play, see §§90, 142, 161, 199, 203, 241, 246, 265.)

Elna K. Solvang

73. THE FOURTH COMMANDMENT AND ETIOLOGIES

I use the fourth commandment to introduce and discuss etiologies. This commandment—remember the Sabbath day and keep it holy—contains a rationale explaining why one is not to work on the seventh day: because the Lord rested on the seventh day (Exod 20:8–11). First I define an etiology as an explanation for the origin of something—for example, a tradition or the name of a certain place. The Hebrew Bible, of course, contains a variety of etiologies which can be mentioned specifically at this point. I then remind students (pointing to our earlier discussion of the creation stories) that no one was there videotaping the creation of the world; it is not as if God literally rested, which formed the Israelite basis for resting. Rather, a tradition developed in ancient Israel of resting on the seventh day, and in order to explain this tradition, they told the story of God resting on the seventh day. It is surprising how difficult a concept this can be for students.

In order to help them grasp the idea, I have students create their own etiology explaining the origin of a tradition on campus. I usually solicit from the class possible topics, framed as questions. Just as the ancient Israelites would have answered the question, "Why do we rest on the Sabbath?" the class must compose a story explaining, for example, Why do we not get Labor Day off? Why is there a statue of Mr. Stegal in the center of campus? Why are freshman obligated to take an orientation class? Why don't we have a football team? I typically break students into small groups and each composes its own etiology. I encourage groups to be as imaginative as possible. The etiologies that the groups generate need not be particularly long, just as the one for the fourth commandment is quite concise. Incidentally, the Labor Day example works particularly well at our institution since, as in the fourth commandment, it involves an official day of rest.

Each group then shares its explanation with the class and we analyze the nature of the various etiologies. Some are social (we do not have

Labor Day off because the administration does not want us having a three-day weekend this early in the semester), economic (it is not practical to take a Monday off since it would extend the semester by a day), or ideological (the administration does not believe in resting). Some etiologies may fall into other categories or be a combination of several, but rarely do students think in theological terms. This, of course, can be contrasted with the Israelite way of thinking. I conclude the discussion by pointing out the theological profundity of the Israelite explanation for the Sabbath day. The Israelites rested because God rested, not because it was deemed to be socially or economically valuable or because they needed a day to play games. The Israelites accounted for their practices in terms of God's activity (or inactivity, in this case), which demonstrates a different way of thinking about the world.

Mark Roncace

74. THE DEVELOPMENT OF ISRAELITE LAW

The Hebrew Bible in its canonical form leaves the impression on the reader that the Torah emerged in the life of Israel in two major phases: (1) at Sinai (in Exodus through Numbers); and (2) on the east side of Jordan, a generation later (in Deuteronomy). The Torah was, therefore, complete and intact prior to Israel's entering Canaan to begin the conquest/settlement. Critical reconstructions of the development of Israel's Torah shatter this literary presentation. It is, of course, this literary presentation itself that makes many student readers resistant to the idea of the gradual emergence of discrete codes (e.g., the Covenant Code and Deuteronomic Code) that were, only later, woven literarily into the current portrayal. The goal of this exercise is to offer students evidence that careful reading of the laws themselves offers evidence of development.

I begin with a hypothetical scenario. Imagine that 3,000 years from now, long after the United States has disappeared from the stage of history, a historian found a complete copy of the Constitution as one document, free of footnotes or any historical introduction. All that the historian had was the text itself. Her first assumption might be that the document was woven of seamless cloth, that it was written or had emerged, essentially, at one time. However, upon careful reading she would find clues in the document itself that it had, in fact, gradually emerged over time. There are many such clues and cues in the text itself, but I focus on one. I present on an overhead or PowerPoint side by side the following "laws" regarding the selection of U. S. Senators.

The senate of the United States shall be composed of two Senators from each State, *chosen by the Legislature* thereof, for six years; and each Senator shall have one vote.	The senate of the United States shall be composed of two Senators from each State, *elected by the people* thereof, for six years; and each Senator shall have one vote.

Students can easily recognize that the Constitution presents two methods of selecting Senators. In the one instance, they are chosen by state legislatures; in the other they are elected by the people. There exists, within the text itself, evidence of development, for it would be difficult to put into practice both methods of selection at the same time. (The discrepancy is a result of the Seventeenth Amendment, ratified in 1913.)

I then divide students into three groups and ask them to find guidance in the Torah on the following issues. Group One is assigned the question, "Where may Israelites offer sacrifice?" They are directed to Exod 20:24 and Deut 12:13–14. Group Two is assigned the question, "How are slave owners to treat male and female slaves? Are they to treat them differently or the same?" They read Exod 21:2–11 and Deut 15:12–17. Group Three is assigned the question, "What are the options of the father and the male seducer if an unmarried woman is seduced?" They consider Exod 22:16–17 and Deut 22:28–29. The groups do their research and report back to the class.

Consensus consistently emerges that these laws that deal with the same issue do not prescribe the same behavior. Group One notes that Exodus assumes numerous sites for altars, while Deuteronomy prescribes sacrifice in only one place. Group Two observes that Exodus prescribes different treatment for men and women slaves, while Deuteronomy specifically states that women are to be treated the same. Group Three observes that the father's and seducer's options are much more limited in Deuteronomy: the seducer must marry the woman and cannot divorce her, while in Exodus the fate of the daughter is left up to the father. Most students recognize that, like the example from the Constitution, the respective laws in the two biblical books would be difficult to follow precisely at the same time. Recognition of differences in the laws lays a foundation (1) to discuss the existence of discrete law codes (in this instance, the Covenant Code and Deuteronomic Code) and (2) to proceed with the examination of other evidence that the law codes of Israel developed over time, in response to changing social situations.

J. Bradley Chance

75. THE RELEVANCE OF THE LAWS

The goal of this exercise is to reflect on the appropriation of biblical texts, specifically the Jewish laws, by religious communities today. We begin with the familiar Ten Commandments in Exodus 20. I point out that everyone (unless one is an Orthodox Jew) regularly and unashamedly breaks one of the ten, namely, the fourth commandment to keep the Sabbath holy. This observation helps to de-familiarize the text, an important step when considering how to appropriate the laws. After noting that none of the first four commandments are laws in the United States, I ask which of the final six are laws today. While murder, stealing, and bearing false witness are illegal, dishonoring one's parents and coveting are not. That leaves adultery; here the correct answer will depend on one's state of residence. An "extramarital affair" is illegal in the District of Columbia and in twenty other states; it is a felony in five states. (Students are also interested to learn that fornication, along with adultery, is a misdemeanor in North Carolina—where I teach—as well as a few other states.) The point, simply, is that only three or four of the Ten Commandments are laws in our society. We follow some of the laws, but not all of them. At this juncture, I ask students to compose a "Decalogue" for our contemporary culture. They produce laws that deal with important issues not addressed by the biblical text—drug abuse, rape, child abuse, environmental laws, and the like. This further distances the biblical laws and challenges the notion that they can be applied wholesale to our society.

To develop this idea further, I read the following humorous letter written to conservative radio talk-show host Dr. Laura Schlesinger. The letter is widely available on the Internet in different versions. It is important to introduce the letter by explaining that Dr. Laura does not condone homosexuality, and she cites the biblical text as her main support:

Dear Dr. Laura,

Thank you for doing so much to educate people regarding God's law. I have learned a great deal from you, and I try to share that knowledge with as many people as I can. When someone tries to defend the homosexual lifestyle, for example, I simply remind him that Lev 18:22 clearly states it to be an abomination. End of debate. I do need some advice from you, however, regarding some of the specific laws and how to best follow them.

When I burn a bull on the altar as a sacrifice, I know it creates a pleasing odor for the Lord (Lev 1:9). The problem is my neighbors. They claim the odor is not pleasing to them. How should I deal with this?

I would like to sell my daughter into slavery, as it suggests in Exod 21:7. In this day and age, what do you think would be a fair price for her?

I know that I am allowed no contact with a woman while she is in her period of menstrual uncleanliness (Lev 15:19–24). The problem is, how do I tell? I have tried asking, but most women take offense.

Leviticus 25:44 states that I may buy slaves from the nations that are around us. A friend of mine claims that this applies to Mexicans, but not Canadians. Can you clarify?

I have a neighbor who insists on working on the Sabbath. Exodus 35:2 clearly states he should be put to death. Am I morally obligated to kill him myself?

A friend of mine feels that even though eating shellfish is an abomination (Lev 11:10), it is a lesser abomination than homosexuality. I don't agree. Can you settle this?

Most of my male friends get their hair trimmed, including the hair around their temples, even though this is expressly forbidden by Lev 19:27. How should I deal with this?

I know from Lev 11:6–8 that touching the skin of a dead pig makes me unclean, but may I still play football if I wear gloves?

My uncle has a farm. He violates Lev 19:19 by planting two different crops in the same field, as does his wife by wearing garments made of two different kinds of thread (cotton/polyester blend). He also tends to curse and blaspheme a lot. Is it really necessary that we go to all the trouble of getting the whole town together to stone them (Lev 24:10–16)? Couldn't we just burn them to death at a private family affair like we do with people who sleep with their in-laws (Lev 20:14)?

I know you have studied these things extensively, so I am confident you can help. Thank you again for reminding us that God's word is eternal and unchanging.

As long as students understand the tongue-in-cheek nature of the letter, it nicely demonstrates the difficulties and complexities of appropriating biblical law—that is, people pick and choose. Lest some students think that the challenges arise only with the Jewish law, I hasten to add that the same type of letter could be written about New Testament commands (Jesus' teachings on divorce; 1 Timothy on women not braiding hair or wearing jewelry; etc.).

In the ensuing discussion, I write the words "biblical law" on the board and then draw a big circle which encompasses nearly both words (leaving the "w" out of the circle) and a little circle around only one or two of the letters. I suggest that appropriation of biblical texts is a circle-drawing activity in which believing communities determine which of the laws are still relevant for today. But it is important to recognize—particularly for the big circle-drawers—that virtually no one thinks that all of the biblical injunctions apply to today without any exceptions whatsoever. Determining how big to draw the circle is a tricky matter.

Mark Roncace

76. "DOES TITHING MAKE ANY SENSE?": EXPLORING THE RELEVANCE OF LAW CODES

Most of my students have never read through the law codes in the Hebrew Bible, so they have little idea of the content of most of the laws. Nevertheless, they have dogmatic views on a few laws that their home-town ministers have emphasized in sermons. To ask why they choose to keep some but ignore most of the rest is a waste of time. I need something much more concrete and less theoretical to get them thinking.

Most students who come from religious backgrounds have heard ser-mons about tithing. In my tradition this normally involves an admonition to give ten percent of your income to the local church to use for all of its many expenses. Tithing typically means writing a check and putting it into an offering plate. Consequently, my students tend to view tithing in these terms and have no notion of what tithing involved for the Israelites. As a means of getting at issues of interpreting ancient agricultural cus-toms and determining their relevance, or lack thereof, for modern faith communities, I have students analyze Deut 14:22–28. My question is simple: "For what things was the tithe to be used?" When they actually read the text, however, they are shocked at what they see, and our dis-cussions of tithing are usually lively.

I often hear comments such as "No way! You're supposed to have a major party with it!" They are particularly intrigued with the command-ment in 14:25–26: "With the money secure in hand, go to the place that the Lord your God will choose; spend the money for whatever you wish—oxen, sheep, wine, strong drink, or whatever you desire. And you shall eat there in the presence of the Lord your God, you and your house-hold rejoicing together." My follow-up question helps them to see another of the vast differences between us and ancient Israel: "How does the collection and use of the tithe in Deut 14:22–28 compare with what you have been taught about tithing in your own faith community?" Their responses are animated and revealing.

In light of the fact that most of my students do not keep the vast majority of biblical laws, I ask, "Do you believe that the law codes in the Hebrew Bible should function as rules for today for those who live in faith communities, or should we view them primarily as cultural artifacts—as windows into ancient Mediterranean cultures? Or both? Why?" After listening to mostly confused assertions, I ask, "Do you believe that we should follow some biblical laws but not others? If so, how do you decide which to follow and which to ignore?" I give them a few examples of laws surrounding Deut. 14:22-28, such as burning entire cities of apostates, executing those who commit adultery, keeping kosher food laws, and remission of debt every seven years.

This exercise helps develop critical thinking skills as students reflect on their own use and abuse of Scripture. In a subsequent session, the instructor may turn to alternative approaches to the appropriation of biblical material in moral, ethical, and legal decision-making. (For another exercise on tithing, see §123.)

Michael R. Cosby

77. "DECODING" LAWS STILL ON THE BOOKS OF MOSES

In nearly every docket year of the Supreme Court, there is at least one case reflecting a push-button religious issue that connects to biblical law, however indirectly. I ask students to make a list of current social and legal debates that involve religious perspectives. Then I ask them to trace the biblical underpinnings of the religious positions. With a little research, most students can figure out that perhaps objections to gay marriage have something to do with how people are reading the Holiness Code in Leviticus. Or perhaps public debate over the death penalty intersects with the Covenant Code's "life for life" language. Exercises like this help illustrate how relevant biblical law may be for some of the more prominent social issues of the present. This may prompt some classroom discussion of what Israelite law attempted to do, how it functioned, and whether its prescriptions are culturally relative.

Although scholars continue to use the term *code* out of habit, there are no codes of laws *per se* in the Hebrew Bible. A code of laws is prescriptive, which means its function and intent are serious: it enjoins citizens to behave in a given way with constabulary power to enforce its commands. The legal material in the Hebrew Bible is mostly descriptive, which essentially means that there is a mixture of laws that may resemble jurisprudence "on the ground" (law as it is actually practiced), but it also seems to include unenforceable, idealistic, and anachronistic laws. Biblical laws represent academic collections of legal language, paradigms, and idioms rather than functional codes.

I ask students to consider what a law was intended to do, on one hand, and what it may actually accomplish, on the other. The laws a society adopts to prohibit certain behavior may inform not only what people are actually doing but also what those in power fear people might be doing. Societies adopt laws in an effort to establish communal order, but that is not always the effect of laws. Some laws are functional. Others are symbolic or idealistic. Still others are ignored. To flesh out these points, I give students examples of laws that the police rarely if ever enforce because they reflect anachronistic cultural or moral sensibilities. For example, it is illegal in Memphis for a woman to drive an automobile unless a man walks ahead of it with a red flag to warn approaching motorists. In Wilbur, Washington, one may not legally ride an ugly horse. A Kansan may not catch fish barehanded. In these instances, we see that laws also function as relics. The efficacy of a law is only as great as the power or interest of the court to enforce it.

It is always useful to provide some sense of context for the Israelite legal material. Martha Roth's volume *Law Collections from Mesopotamia and Asia Minor* (2nd ed.; Writings from the Ancient World 6; Atlanta: Scholars Press, 1997) has good translations of Mesopotamian legal collections. One parallel between Israelite and Babylonian texts is the device of *lex talionis,* or the law of retaliation. "You may take life for life, eye for eye, tooth for tooth," states Exod 21:23, while Hammurabi also mentions life for life and tooth for tooth. It is helpful to ask students what they make of this parallelism and how they might account for it from a cross-cultural perspective. This is a possible example of values that two cultures held in common, but it may also reflect the academic compilation of legal language. Even today people often quote this language of retaliation for their own purposes, but there is an obscure legal practice at work beneath the idiom. In the ancient Near East, there was little to no distinction between criminal and civil law. In extreme cases, the state might act to punish a criminal, but in most instances what we would consider criminal offenses were resolved through personal lawsuits. Plaintiffs sued defendants who knocked their teeth out for monetary compensation, the family of a murder victim might (under some conditions) sue the murderer for compensation, and so on. In modern civil law (e.g., small claims court), it is difficult for the court to compel a defendant to pay the plaintiff to whom he has lost a lawsuit. Near Eastern law provided leverage to the plaintiff in the form of optional retaliation; if the defendant refused to pay, then the plaintiff could demand that the same injury be visited upon the defendant. This option of retaliation is called the "fullest extent of the law" and it would have been applicable to many acts that the Hebrew Bible regards as capital offenses. It is no coincidence that the Covenant and Deuteronomic Codes emphasize torts (personal injuries and damaged/stolen property). Personal lawsuits drove the legal system in ancient Israel.

Framing the ancient legal system in this way tends to produce pretty strong reactions. I ask students to imagine a legal system in which crimes were largely resolved through personal lawsuits rather than prosecution. Would it be more or less efficient? Some students recoil at the notion that a person's body parts or life could be assigned a monetary value so arbitrarily. This strikes many as particularly alien and unsophisticated. Most major airlines provide their Accidental Death and Dismemberment compensation policies on their websites. I like to print these out to show students the arbitrary values that airlines have assigned to a passenger's thumb, leg below the knee, or leg above the knee. These values are usually given as percentages of the maximum assumed liability for a passenger's life, which many airlines value at $25,000. This brand of clinical valuation for compensatory claims might have struck the authors of the Covenant Code as particularly efficient.

Ryan Byrne

78. WHY LEVITICUS IS THE MOST IMPORTANT BOOK IN THE BIBLE

Whether or not it is actually true that Leviticus is the most important book in the Bible—and I have to admit that I think a good case could be made in the affirmative—it is both instructive and somewhat fun to make the claim to an undergraduate class on biblical literature.

In my "Introduction to Biblical Literature" course I will typically schedule two days on Leviticus. One day will be concerned with a general overview of the book and will then focus on the sacrifices in the opening chapters; the second day will focus on the "body issues" found in chapters 12–21, including the dietary regulations, skin diseases, bodily emissions, and sexual prohibitions. Typically, for the second day I will ask the students to do a close reading, in addition to reading through ten or so chapters not-so-closely, of the sexual prohibitions in chapter 18 before coming to class, in which they are asked to outline the passage and try to discern the underlying logic or logics for the various prohibitions.

But in the class session before we begin Leviticus, having read through Genesis and Exodus by this point, I usually announce that next time we will be considering the most important book in the Bible. (It is also fun to claim that while Christians often think John 3:16 is the most important verse in the Bible, that distinction belongs to Lev 3:16: "All fat is the Lord's.") Even if some of the students think I am putting them on, the announcement helps to focus their attention a bit on a book that nearly all of them tend to describe as boring ("all those laws"), irrelevant ("leprosy?"), or even offensive ("those poor animals!").

I then make the case for the importance of Leviticus in a couple of ways. Especially for Christian students, one needs to understand the background of ancient Israelite and Judean atonement theory and practice in order to begin to get at the early church's thinking on the atoning death of Jesus. But I also try to relate the book to contemporary societal issues in two ways.

First, in relation to animal sacrifice, I ask students how many have ever killed an animal themselves (leaving out fish, birds, bugs, and limiting it to mammals). Given that my students tend to come from upper-middle class, non-rural settings, inevitably very few have. I then ask how many eat meat, and the large majority of them do. This opens up a discussion—often one of the best of the semester—about the ethics of animal slaughter. We tend to think in the first instance that the sacrifice of animals in a religious context is primitive, even offensive, and yet we in the United States live in a society that slaughters several billion animals every year (and as I tell my students, I do not know how many animals would have been slaughtered in ancient Israel and Judah, but in its entire history it would not have been this many). Does the fact that this massive slaughter takes place outside of any religious or indeed, for the most part, any moral context whatsoever make it more or less ethically problematic? Obvious but important contrasts can be made between the relatively infrequent, hands-on slaughter of valuable animals in a religious (and inherently moral) context in ancient Israel and the massive but repressed (and relatively contextless) slaughter of animals in contemporary America. Suddenly Leviticus does not seem so primitive.

Secondly, in relation to the rituals associated with what goes into and comes out of one's body, I ask the students to think about what rituals they have or that society endorses with regard to such things. A little Mary Douglas-like talk about the maintenance of borders and the danger of border crossings, taken literally in relation the body, tends to open up productive discussion of analogous contemporary rituals both of eating and of bodily emissions. Again, although our rituals tend to be non-religious in nature ("wash your fruit before eating it," or "don't have unprotected sex") they are not always so different from those in Leviticus. Students begin to see that they do not have to be willing to adopt the specific practices in the book in order to take seriously its willingness to think through, again in a religious and moral context, the implications of having a body, with all the attendant pleasures and dangers such a body entails.

Tod Linafelt

79. HOLINESS AS AN UNKNOWN CULTURE

Students often find Leviticus stultifying or mystifying (on occasions, both). I admit this up front, but claim that Leviticus is not difficult, and is actually very interesting, if we can understand its basic assumptions (the basic assumption I will address is holiness, but I do not yet mention that). As an example of a text that relies upon our understanding of its basic assumptions, I play Michael Reno Harrell's "Southern Suggestions" (2002, on his *Southern Son* album) while also posting the lyrics on a screen. Harrell is a country/folk songwriter from Charlotte, North Carolina. (The lyrics to this song are, unfortunately, not posted on any website, so the only way to use this particular song is to purchase the CD, available at michaelreno.com. Teachers may be able to think of other, more readily available songs that require specific cultural knowledge that some or all of the students will not have.) The song, in humorous fashion, describes a variety of markers of southern culture, such as fried green tomatoes, using painted tractor tires as planters, NASCAR, and the effect clear fingernail polish has on chigger bites. Interestingly, given Leviticus's emphasis on kosher regulations for food, the song contains numerous references to what may or may not be eaten. The song's refrain is: "These aren't rules; it's just some things that we've figured out/To make livin' easy when you're livin' here in the South," providing a nice parallel to Leviticus, which is, in fact, a set of rules.

This song has worked well in classes I have taught in Virginia. Some students immediately "get it." This semester I had a student blurt out, "This is all so true!" But others do not "get it," especially those from urban, northern settings, such as the student this semester who had to be told what chiggers were (he knew about them, but had a different name for them). This exercise has the students discover how cultural knowledge works. Those who grew up in certain places easily understand the references. They have insider knowledge, they "know the rules," or they at least perceive the assumptions behind the rules. My point is that holiness in ancient Israel (which involves food, like many of the "Southern Suggestions"), places us on the "outside" of a culture filled with rules and assumptions which we at best dimly perceive. I draw these rules and assumptions, all dealing with the priestly emphasis on order, from Mary Douglas' *Purity and Danger: An Analysis of Concepts of Pollution and Taboo* (New York: Praeger, 1966). The lecture which follows serves to expose those assumptions to make Leviticus's "suggestions" understandable.

Donald C. Polaski

80. REMEMBERING DEUTERONOMY

The book of Deuteronomy occupies a key place in an introduction to both the opening books of the Old Testament and the larger story that unfolds throughout the whole of the primary history of Genesis through Kings. At the same time, however, Deuteronomy has much that sets it apart from its canonical neighbors. One such feature is the book's emphasis on remembering. The story's own setting is that of a farewell address by Moses directed to a new generation that has not had the benefit of being directly involved in the "mighty acts" that God did for their ancestors in the past. Thus, early on Deuteronomy stresses the importance of memory and the dangers of forgetfulness: "Keep these words that I am commanding you today in your heart. Recite them to your children and talk about them when you are at home and when you are away, when you lie down and when you rise" (Deut 6:6–7 NRSV).

In order to emphasize this theme of Deuteronomy as representative of the book's overall theological voice, I show the prologue scene of the movie adaptation of J. R. R. Tolkien's *The Lord of the Rings: The Fellowship of the Ring* (approximately seven minutes long). The scene mostly consists of narration over suggestive pictures. In terms of content, the scene describes the background events that led to the current situation at the beginning of the movie. This background includes the origin of the rings, their subsequent loss, and, most significantly, the long interval in which the ring of power, as well as the story of its origin and significance, was lost from memory. All of this content provides the background for the dramatic opening scenes of the movie in which the ring of power makes it reappearance and begins to drive the plot.

Two aspects of the film clip are useful for moving the class toward Deuteronomy. First, the way the movie and the book portray the past for their main characters is similar. In the movie, the prologue tells the story of a strange, primordial world that saw the forging of the rings, the battle of Mordor, and so on. Thus when the movie begins, the characters are implicitly shown to be connected to those ancient, seemingly foreign, events in ways that they must come to realize more fully. Likewise for Deuteronomy, the actions that God did for the ancestors of those in Moses' audience are described in Deut 1–4 as distant, seemingly foreign, events. Nonetheless, the book continually tries to link the present audience with those events: "Not with our ancestors did the Lord make this covenant, but with us, who are all of us here alive today" (Deut 5:3 NRSV).

Secondly, I emphasize the issues of memory and the forgetfulness of later generations. I ask the class to comment on the role of memory and forgetfulness as they see it portrayed in the prologue of the movie. In this regard, they usually highlight a crucial line of the narration: "The world is changed.... Much that once was is lost, for none now live who remember it.... And some things that should not have been forgotten were lost." These words indicate that the primary problem that initially drives the story's plot is the lack of remembrance by later generations and the dangers inherent in their forgetfulness. From here I can move to the primary theme of remembrance for a new generation within the rhetoric of Deuteronomy. Through the lens of *The Lord of the Rings,* the class can explore both Deuteronomy's positive appeals for remembrance and negative warnings concerning forgetfulness, particularly as they are captured in some of the key verbs of the book: "keep," "do," "observe."

Brad E. Kelle

81. LEARNING ABOUT THE LAWS OF KASHRUT AND KOSHER FOOD

The following exercise studies the Laws of Kashrut from Lev 11; 17:10–16; and Deut 14:3-21. It identifies those meals, as represented by pictures of food glued onto paper plates, that might politely be offered to a Jewish person who obeyed the laws of Kashrut. Because it is a "hands-on" activity dealing with "real life" applications, the exercise is much more effective than a lecture on the same topic.

One needs the following resources: a range of photographs of meals, drinks, snacks, and party foods glued onto paper plates; copies of the relevant biblical texts; copies of the *Good News Bible,* with illustration relating to Lev 11; handout (see below) giving details of kosher rules, foods considered to be *parev,* and the use of carrageenan in foods as a substitute for gelatin; and charts for recording group decisions and rationales.

Participants are divided into groups of three and given a set of twenty possible meals that confront them with the need to apply the rules in such a way that the proffering of the plate to an Orthodox Jew will not cause that person any moral reason to refuse it. They will be given the different sets of information listed above and asked to eliminate the plates that are not kosher. In the next step, participants exchange their selection of plates with another group and see if they agree, discussing any discrepancies or difficulties in the larger group of six and recording their findings. Finally, the whole class will name the agreed kosher plates.

The handout should have several sections, the first of which is entitled "Kosher and Non-kosher Meat, Fish, and Poultry." It should include the following information:

Meat: Lev 11 gives the key features of mammals accepted as kosher, namely: they chew the cud (ruminants) and have a cloven hoof. Cows, sheep, goats, and reindeer are kosher; pigs, horses, and camels are not.

Preparing meat: The Torah forbids the eating of the blood of an animal, hence blood sausages such as black pudding are not kosher. The two methods of extracting blood from meat are salting and broiling.

Poultry: There are more than twenty forbidden species of fowl. Acceptable and commonly eaten kosher fowl are: chicken, turkey, duck, and goose.

Fish: To be counted kosher, fish must have fins and scales. All shellfish are prohibited. (Fish should not be eaten with meat according to some authorities.)

The second section of the handout is entitled "Separating Meat and Milk in Kosher Eating" and includes the following information:

Eating and, hence, cooking meat (or meat products, such as gelatin) and milk (or any milk products) together in any form is forbidden. To make certain that this rule is observed, the prohibition is extended to forbid the eating of meat and dairy products at the same meal or preparing them in the same utensils. Furthermore, one must wait up to six hours after eating meat products before any dairy products may be eaten. However, meat may be eaten following dairy products with the one exception of hard cheese (six months old or more), which also requires a six-hour interval.

The section of the handout on "*Parev* Foods: Able to be Eaten with Either Milk or Meat Meals" should include the following information: Fruit and vegetables, including grains and nuts, because they contain neither milk nor meat, may be eaten with either meat or milk and are known as *parev* or *parve*. Eggs from kosher poultry are also *parev*.

The section of the handout on "Other Common Animal Products and Their Alternatives" should include the following information: Rennet (for hardening cheeses) and gelatin (for jellies and glazes) have animal origins. Rennet is from an enzyme in the stomachs of cows and pigs, and gelatin is from animal bones. Thus they can be considered meat products, although some Jews regard them as purified chemicals and no longer "animal products." A gelatinous substance, carrageenan, is extracted from seaweed, and hence is kosher.

The chart to be distributed to each group should have five columns. The one on the far left should simply be numbered one through twenty for each of the twenty plates; the second column is labeled "Kosher or non-Kosher," the third "reasons for decision," the fourth "most helpful sources," and the fifth "least helpful sources."

Heather A. McKay

82. TEACHING THE DOCUMENTARY HYPOTHESIS TO SKEPTICAL STUDENTS

One of the perennially difficult topics to teach in an introductory Bible course is the Documentary Hypothesis. Beginning with the very early chapters of Genesis, the student must confront what has become a scholarly convention, that is, Moses did not write the Pentateuch. Despite passages where Moses is directed to write something down (Exod 17:14; Deut 32:22), and despite early Jewish and Christian tradition which claims Mosaic authorship, the books of the Pentateuch remain anonymous. Student reaction to this "radical concept" is predictably varied, ranging from sincere confusion to pointed resistance. "How could anyone claim that the Bible is merely a compilation of sources?" "What about divine inspiration?"

Rather than consuming an inordinate amount of class time addressing a myriad of questions, I have found an approach that allows even the most skeptical of students to begin to consider the merits of the theory. I divide my presentation of the Documentary Hypothesis into two subcategories: "Actual Biblical Sources" and "Theoretical Biblical Sources."

1. "Actual Biblical Sources" are those sources that are specifically mentioned in the Bible (e.g., The Book of the Wars of the Lord, Num 21:14; The Book of the Annals of the Kings of Israel, 1 Kgs 16:27; The Book of Jashar, Josh 10:13; 2 Sam 1:18; The Book of the Annals of Solomon, 1 Kgs 11:41). Once the students discover that the Bible itself refers to multiple extrabiblical sources by way of what may be called an "ancient footnote format," they are generally more willing to consider the possibility of multiple authorial imprints on the text as well. (In especially resistant contexts, I have students read several of the passages listed above and discuss in class the unifying motifs underlying the different passages.) These are sources which, although they have not survived, were certainly available to the ancient Israelites when the Pentateuch was being written and provided additional material that was not repeated in the Bible. (At this point it is helpful to remind the students that New Testament authors as well relied upon sources. Witness the Gospel of Luke which begins by acknowledging sources to which the author is indebted [Luke 1:1–4].)

2. Once I establish the possibility of the use of sources in biblical composition by using the text itself, I proceed to the second subcategory, "Theoretical Biblical Sources." These are sources that have been reconstructed by scholars in order to reflect different literary traditions in the Bible and to account for many biblical difficulties, including: duplication or repetition of biblical stories (two creation stories, two flood stories, Abraham's claim that Sarah was his sister [Gen 12:10–16;

HEBREW BIBLE

20:1–7], etc.); multiple names used to refer to God; two lists of the Decalogue (Exod 20; Deut 5); differing vocabulary and literary styles in the
Pentateuch, and so on.

Since this is not a semester-long class on the Pentateuch, I then
move quickly through the primary literary characteristics of each of the
four sources. For example, when studying the earliest chapters of Genesis, Yahwist and Priestly documents are important. The author of J is a
lucid, almost folksy story-teller whose writings include a natural intimate interaction with God and the freedom of human will. J believes
that there is a divine plan in how things unfold and is sympathetic for
victims of wrong. In contrast to J, P focuses largely on three main events
in the early chapters of Genesis: the flood, the blessing of Noah, and the
lineage of Abraham. P is interested in ritual sacrifice, festivals, the
sacred calendar, and the proper channel for appropriate interaction
with God via the priesthood ("the Lord said to Moses and Aaron ... ").
Priestly office is inherited in P, thus priests may marry and genealogies
are very important.

Once the students are introduced to the basics of the Documentary
Hypothesis, it is actually rewarding to review the initial chapters of Genesis with their new-found insight. I discuss the various themes and motifs
of Gen 1–2, and then ask the students to identify who might be the author
of Gen 3 and why. As the students move beyond the obstacle of multiple
hands in the process of biblical authorship, they usually begin to appreciate the distinctive literary characteristics of the authors of J, E, D, and P
and can more readily understand why they might have written their
respective stories.

William L. Lyons

83. THE DOCUMENTARY HYPOTHESIS AND SAMPLING

I have always found the task of introducing students to the "sources"
(i.e., the oral and literary traditions) of Israel's premonarchic history to be
a laborious task, especially in light of the lack of agreement among scholars regarding the separation of these sources. It is difficult to present the
topic in a way that is comprehensible and interesting to college students.
The objective of this exercise is to help students to understand the
premise of the Documentary Hypothesis by comparing it to the popular
music technique known as "sampling." Technically, sampling is defined
as the act of taking a portion of one sound recording and reusing it as an
element of a new recording (e.g., using the guitar riffs from Foreigner's

"Hot Blooded" in Tone-Loc's "Funky Cold Medina"). Other forms of sampling, however, include artists of a new song singing a few lyrics from another song in their new song or actually performing part of the music of another song in their song.

In preparation for class, students are divided into teams. Each team has to find a popular contemporary song that most of their classmates would know that contains pieces ("samples") of older songs within it. On the day of class each team plays its song for the class, and members of the class have to identify the pieces of the older songs that are in that song. Each team gets one point for every sample its song contains. The group also gets an additional point for each sample that students in the class are unable to identify (for the sake of time, each song should be no longer than five minutes). The team that receives the most points wins. In case the first team has difficulty leading the analysis of its song, I always come prepared with a song of my own for illustrative purposes. My favorite is The Sugarhill Gang's use of portions of Chic's "Good Times" as the basis for "Rapper's Delight." Since many of my students have never heard either of these 70s classics, I also bring a more contemporary example—most recently the 2004 release by DJ Danger Mouse of *The Grey Album*, which is a remix of the Beatles album *The Beatles*, commonly referred to as "The White Album," and rapper Jay-Z's *The Black Album*.

The strength of this exercise occurs in the analysis that happens afterwards. Members of the class that identified samples explain how it was they were able to recognize those samples. Each team has to be able to identify for the class the various samples that are within the selected song. Team members have to be able to discuss possible reasons why the artist may have used those particular samples. Included in that discussion are possible ways the samples function within the new song as well as what the samples contribute to the meaning of the new song. This of course leads to conversations regarding whether and how the meaning of the sampled pieces may have been changed within the context of the new song. The analyses of the songs help prepare the students to understand better the basic premises of the Documentary Hypothesis.

After the analyses, I then discuss how the "artists" of the Pentateuch have "sampled" older material within their new compositions and how that older material functions and contributes to the meaning of the new composition. I usually conclude by giving a brief introduction to J, E, D, and P and by presenting salient characteristics of J, E, and P. (I usually save comments about D for our examination of Deuteronomy and the introduction to Israel's tribal confederacy.) (For a similar exercise, see §160.)

Guy D. Nave Jr.

84. THE AUTHORSHIP OF THE PENTATEUCH

The purpose of this activity is to introduce students to the Documentary Hypothesis and to develop critical thinking skills. The activity takes one class period and requires that students read two short articles and write a short essay.

In preparation for the class, the professor assigns an article to be read that defends the Documentary Hypothesis and one that defends the Mosaic authorship of the Pentateuch. This assignment works best when the writers of the articles are committed to the view that they are presenting. For a defense of Mosaic authorship, see B. T. Arnold and B. E. Beyer, *Encountering the Old Testament: A Christian Survey* (Grand Rapids: Baker, 1999) or G. Archer, *New International Encyclopedia of Bible Difficulties* (Grand Rapids: Zondervan, 2001). For an explanation and defense of the Documentary Hypothesis and modifications, see S. L. Harris, *Understanding the Bible* (New York: McGraw Hill, 2002) or J. J. Collins, *Introduction to the Hebrew Bible* (Minneapolis: Augsburg/Fortress, 2004). The students write a short paper that evaluates the two articles and defends the view that the student concludes is most accurate. The students should also anticipate the strongest arguments for the position that they do not support in a paragraph in the paper. The paper should not simply restate the position but contain argumentation to support the student's conclusion.

In class, lead the students in a review of the articles. Afterwards, divide the class into small groups. The groups should be asked to give a defense of one of the two views as assigned by the professor. The students should be prepared to give the two strongest arguments to defend the assigned view. Roughly half the class will be assigned to defend the Documentary Hypothesis and the other half Mosaic authorship. Randomly assign a student in each group to keep a record of the group's discussion. Give the students five minutes to prepare their arguments. When the groups are finished, ask each group to evaluate their arguments by giving one objection to the argument from the opposing view. When they are finished, lead the groups in reporting and evaluating the arguments presented. You can conclude the class by discussing why the question of authorship is important and the implications it might have for understanding the nature of Scripture.

T. Perry Hildreth

Prophets

85. THE CONQUEST OF CANAAN

In this exercise students will be invited to think critically about the conquest narratives found in the books of Joshua and Judges. The objective of this exercise is to bring to light some of the editing processes involved in the writing of the Deuteronomistic History by demonstrating how discrete traditions have been brought together and shaped into a grand saga, not unlike the way that in Genesis two creation stories traditionally have been read as one.

Begin this exercise one class period in advance by dividing students into two groups. Assign one group the task of reading Josh 1–12 in advance of the next class period, urging them to return to class prepared to discuss the subject of the conquest of Canaan. Assign the second group the task of reading Judg 1–12 and ask them to come prepared to do likewise. The instructor may wish to have some fun with this assignment by pretending to involve the class in some detective work aimed at investigating the Bible's "take" on the origins of Israelite society in Canaan—without tipping the hand that multiple "takes" will emerge from the biblical text!

When the class meets again, allow the two groups about ten minutes to formulate a coherent statement about the conquest of Canaan on the basis of their respective reading assignments, something along the lines of journalism's traditional "Who, What, When, Where, and Why." (Note: Large classes should be further divided into sub-groups to allow for effective collaboration.)

The first group's statement might look something like this: Joshua, Moses' successor, leads a united Israel in a lightning-quick assault upon thirty-one Canaanite kings (city-states) in which (almost without exception) every possession is taken and every living thing killed, everything devoted to destruction. The Israelites, in effect, invade the country and almost entirely replace the Canaanite population.

The second group's statement might look something like this: After the death of Joshua, individual tribes team up one with another against various Canaanite cities. For the most part, the tribes are unsuccessful in vanquishing their foes and co-existence is worked out, usually with Canaanites serving forced labor.

Discuss the apparent contradictions. Lead-in questions might include: What cities said to have been vanquished in Joshua are mentioned in Judges as having remained undefeated? (Compare Judg 1 with Josh 12.) How does the tone of the writing compare for each version? What most reasonably seems to be the intent behind each of these (e.g., triumphant nationalism vs. theological observation, etc.)? Which of the two accounts seems to be more historically plausible? How have these differing versions been reconciled in the process of Deuteronomistic editing?

Attention should also be given to the leading scholarly models that have addressed the question of Israelite origins. (For a good summary of these perspectives, see L. Stager, "Forging an Identity," in the *Oxford History of the Biblical World* [ed. M. Coogan; Oxford: Oxford University Press, 1998], 90–131.) Discussing these perspectives, especially the reigning ruralization hypothesis, which sees Israelite society emerging as a rural phenomenon from within Canaanite culture, will help students appreciate the fact that the biblical writers are up to something else apart from writing a straightforward, factual account of Israelite origins.

Nicolae Roddy

86. THE BOOK OF JOSHUA AND ISSUES OF WAR AND PEACE

Our generation of students is bombarded, as it were, on a daily basis with images of the reality of warfare and its consequences. As described in the Hebrew Bible, the generation of Joshua lived the reality of warfare and daily faced its consequences. Is there an ethics of warfare or at least a set of moral rules by which, according to this biblical material, we should initiate, pursue, and conclude hostilities?

We begin with Josh 6. We first investigate how the traditional Hebrew or MT envisions the capture of Jericho and its immediate consequence; namely, the complete destruction of everyone and everything (with the exception of Rahab and her family). Students are asked how they feel about this and what possible justification there can be for such actions. We also look briefly at other ancient versions to determine if there are any major variations. We then turn to Deut 20 for a close reading and analysis of the material there. We note the integral connection between "religion" and "warfare"—a comparison with other ancient

Near Eastern peoples is relevant here—the criteria for exclusion from warfare (with some evaluation of them), and the procedures for waging war outside of the Promised Land and within the Promised Land, with an emphasis on the treatment of the defeated enemy in both cases.

At this point, the students are asked to explore their own feelings about what we have read, including how they feel about God's commanding these actions. We look in some detail at the categories of exemption, which may well strike a modern reader as very broad. Could a modern army function when exemptions from combat seem so easy to obtain? How would this have been possible in antiquity? Students observe that defeated nations outside of the Promised Land were dealt with harshly, but allowed to live so long as they agreed to admittedly severe terms of surrender. Within the land of Israel, annihilation or *herem* was to be the rule, not only among humans, but also animals. And there appears to be no provision for surrender. How do these commands coexist with our view of a loving God? Were the Canaanites inherently more guilty and less worthy of our sympathy than other humans?

We then return to the book of Joshua and follow the conquest, noting the degree to which the commands of Deuteronomy are, and are not, enforced—and how such actions or inactions are judged by the writer of Joshua. As the fighting proceeds from Jericho, it seems as if the provisions of Deuteronomy are less uniformly and strictly adhered to. Was Joshua acting on his own to keep his soldiers happy? Was he following a further, less stringent revelation from God?

In the process of considering these issues, we may discuss whether or not we think the book of Joshua contains "history" and whether or not, for our present purposes, it makes any difference. It is appropriate to conclude this lesson with a serious consideration of how this biblical view of warfare, and God's involvement in it, has been applied—or in some views misapplied—and should be applied in the modern world.

Among the anticipated outcomes of this lesson are (1) a fuller knowledge of how and why warfare was waged in ancient Israel; (2) a more complete understanding of the involvement of the divine in warfare and its outcome; (3) a consideration of the degree to which there is, or is not, a unified view of warfare in the material we are studying; and (4) personal and group reflection on the applicability—complete, partial, or non—of this material to today's world.

Leonard Greenspoon

87. THE BOOK OF JOSHUA AND POPULAR CULTURE

The Bible is not merely a document of the synagogue, church, seminary, and classroom. Rather, for better or worse, the Bible is part of our popular culture. The variety of such presentations and representations is wide indeed. In this lesson, we work with a few from the book of Joshua as illustrative of a far broader phenomenon.

I begin by asking students to consider whether they are at all aware of the book of Joshua or the figure of Joshua in popular culture. If, as is likely, there are few, if any positive responses, I rephrase the question to include the Hebrew Bible or the New Testament. After eliciting some examples from the Bible as a whole, we turn to Joshua. We listen to a rendition of the gospel hymn, "Joshua Fit the Battle of Jericho," and compare it to the biblical account. We also explore the relevance and power of the hymn for the communities in which it developed and among whom it was first sung and continues to be sung. We also listen to and analyze U2's *Joshua Tree.* I read from Frank Slaughter's 1956 pot-boiling novel, *The Scarlet Cord: A Novel of the Woman of Jericho,* about Rahab, and Joseph F. Girzone's more recent series. Students can explore the degree to which they appreciate "literary license" on the part of such modern writers and delve into the possible reasons for their modifications of and deviations from the biblical text.

We also spend considerable time on comic strips. In the case of the battle of Jericho, I have several examples (see especially the archives at Frankandernest.com under "Jericho"). We will discuss and analyze them to see how they relate to the biblical narrative and to the cartoonists' contemporary audience (see L. Greenspoon, "The Bible in the Funny Papers," *BRev* 7.5 [October 1991]: 30–33, 41). Students are then asked to create cartoons of their own. I assure them that they are not evaluated on their artistic abilities (or lack thereof) and even allow them to cut-and-paste from print and online sources, if so requested. Typically, I ask students to share their cartoons with the class; in so doing, they recount not only what they have done, but how and why. They come to see that their cartoons (and other expressions of popular culture) are not simply representations of the Bible, but new—and potentially valuable—creations. The results of an exercise such as this vary considerably, but that is also true for any written or oral assignment. At its best, this process is especially appealing to students who are comfortable with drawing (or art in general) as a means of expression.

On a more serious note, but still within the realm of popular culture, we examine the ways in which Joshua has been brought (dragged?) into the often heated and contentious debates about contemporary conflicts in the Middle East. The text has served the propagandistic purposes of groups on all sides, as we see.

Among the anticipated outcomes of this lesson are (1) an appreciation for the phenomenon of popular culture as it relates to religion, especially the Bible; (2) a sense of the value (or better, the values) of looking at the Bible in popular culture; (3) a recognition of the multiple ways in which the Bible can be presented, represented, or misrepresented for partisan or political purposes; and (4) the opportunity for students to create examples of popular culture on their own.

Leonard Greenspoon

88. THE BOOK OF JOSHUA AND BIBLE TRANSLATION

Very few, if any, of the undergraduate students I teach know the original languages of the Bible. They are dependent on translations, of which there are a considerable number in contemporary English. Using the book of Joshua as an example, I have devised a lesson to demonstrate to undergraduates how difficult and yet how vital translation is—and to what extent it involves interpretation, choice, and concerns for the intended audience.

Joshua 6:17 presents the first instance of the Hebrew root *herem* in this book. This root, repeatedly used as both a noun and a verb, then becomes an important element in the literary and theological development of chapter seven, which recounts the sin and punishment of Achan. We first look at a selection of translations—which range from "curse of destruction" (NJB) and "accursed" (KJV; see also "holy curse" [The Message]), to "devoted for destruction" (NRSV, ESV), to "proscribed" (JPS Tanakh) and "ban" (NAB; see also REB: "solemn ban"), to "consecrated property" (ArtScroll Tanach)—and try to discern what is common to these varying renderings. For this purpose, we also analyze a selection of the notes that accompany the translations of Josh 6–7 to see what additional information they provide.

We next turn to passages from the Torah, especially Deut 20, to look at the background of this expression and to see if, from Torah passages, we can understand better the concept that *herem* is intended to encompass—and then to evaluate the various translations offered and their accompanying notes. At this point students should be at least beginning to develop a sense of the challenges facing translators as they attempt to convey their understanding of the meaning of the ancient text to an audience contemporary with them.

I do not believe we can, or should, separate this linguistic emphasis from others. Thus, we look at the language of warfare elsewhere in the ancient Near East, and also its practice, to see if contemporary usage provides some guidance. We also examine, if only briefly, what other ancient translations have as a rendering for the Hebrew. Although it is not the main focus of this lesson, we should not exclude some discussion of the moral and ethical dimensions of declaring an entire land, including its people, *ḥerem*.

As a second part of this lesson, we look at Josh 6 as presented in the traditional Hebrew or MT and compare this with the oldest translation, the LXX. We note that this Greek text is ten percent shorter than the Hebrew. Many of the phrases that incorporate ritual or liturgical elements into the MT account are lacking in the LXX, and it is therefore tempting to picture the Greek text as developmentally and chronologically prior to the Hebrew. But even the Greek text is, in the opinion of many researchers, overloaded with features that defy easy placement in an overall picture of the capture of Jericho. So it is that we might posit an earlier "original" that was considerably simpler in its narrative than any extant narrative. On the basis of such analysis, students at least begin to see that translators often have a choice as to their starting point; that is, which ancient text (or combination of texts) they will render.

Among the anticipated outcomes of this lesson are (1) a broad understanding of what translation of the Bible entails and a respect for those who undertake this task responsibly; (2) a greater sense of how we, as responsible scholars, should evaluate contemporary versions of the Bible; (3) a knowledge of certain aspects of the nature of warfare as defined and described in the Hebrew Bible; and (4) a willingness to engage in a dialogue with the text over problematic issues and the applicability (or lack thereof) of such a text in the modern world.

Leonard Greenspoon

89. THE BOOK OF JOSHUA AND
JEWISH EXEGETICAL TRADITIONS

In my courses on the Bible, the text is the starting point. For that reason (also for economic concerns), I want my students to make use of what I term the most "stripped-down" format possible of their favorite English-language version; in my experience, more fully annotated study editions often overwhelm the biblical text itself for students and can serve to delimit and stifle their imaginative interaction with the Bible. Nonetheless, it is also the case that, outside of the classroom—in churches, synagogues, and assorted study groups—the Bible is read as part of a community with its own history (or better, histories) of interpretation.

Given the fact that I hold a chair in Jewish Civilization, I like to explore with students the exegetical traditions of Judaism. In order to do this, I begin with a quick reading of the first twelve chapters of the book of Joshua, to determine the course, direction, and strategies of the conquest they narrate. Then we look in more detail at Deut 20 and related passages that lay out the rules for engagement and for the treatment of conquered peoples. Our goal in this is to provide the necessary background for the Jewish exegetical developments that form the major emphasis of this lesson. Such a background becomes essential when this lesson is taught as part of a Jewish Studies course, where students may well have never read this material or read it several semesters earlier.

We then look at selected materials within Judaism from the Hellenistic and Roman periods (for example, 1–2 Maccabees and the histories of Josephus) to the Talmud through Elie Wiesel (for Joshua in Josephus, see L. Feldman, "Josephus's Portrait of Joshua," *HTR* 82:4 [1989]: 351–76; for Wiesel on Joshua, see E. Wiesel, *Five Biblical Portraits* [Notre Dame: University of Notre Dame Press, 1981], 1–31; for Joshua in these and other Jewish, as well as selected Christian, sources, see L. Greenspoon, "Joshua: A Man for All Seasons?" *ARCHAEVS: Études d'Histoires des Religions* 6 [2002]: 37–51).

In many of these sources, the students discover, Moses and Joshua are portrayed as distinctly more peaceable than God himself. Along these lines, Joshua is seen as offering peace even to the nations within the Promised Land, and this in spite of the clear prohibition in Deut 20. Thus, the annihilation called for in Deuteronomy (but only partially carried out by Joshua) is seen as a last step, rather than as a necessary consequence of the conquest of the Promised Land. We also look at the issue of fighting on the Sabbath, which became increasingly important as the enemies of the Jews learned more precisely the details of their traditions.

The Jewish tradition is not monolithic, but we limit ourselves to the main traditions. At the same time, we attempt to place these interpretations, and particularly these interpreters, within an historical and communal environment that would provide a reasonable context for rabbinic and later pronouncements, especially when they go against the plain reading of the biblical text itself. In so doing, we explore the range of interpretive tools available to later Jewish exegetes. As time permits, we compare developments within Jewish exegesis with selected examples from Christian interpretation. Students are encouraged to imagine themselves at the times of the interpreters and to develop interpretations of their own. Along these lines, I admit (or better, confess) to students that, with few exceptions we know little, if anything about the circumstances of the Jewish exegetes whose words and works we read and whose world(s) we try to reconstruct. I also inform students that such imaginative efforts on their, and my, part are not always accepted as "true scholarship" by all researchers.

Among the anticipated outcomes of this lesson are (1) an exposure to exegetical traditions that have guided the reading of the Bible within faith communities; (2) a particularly close acquaintance with Jewish exegetical traditions as they relate to war and peace; (3) an appreciation for the ways in which religious leaders read their Bible as a document of their present and future as well as their past; and (4) a sense of the difference between academic and confessional readings of the text, and the possibilities and limitations of their convergence.

Leonard Greenspoon

90. A SHORT STORY OF THE JUDGES

Students naturally find the various stories in the book of Judges quite fascinating, but because they are relatively independent of one another, it is sometimes difficult to present or discuss the book as a whole in introductory courses. True, there is a repeating plot shape (outlined in Judg 2) and broad themes that animate, and perhaps unify, the book in some sense. But how might one relate the individual stories to one another? To encourage students to think about the narratives collectively, and yet in detail—not merely in terms of general themes—I ask students to compose one story that creatively incorporates many of the characters from the episodes in Judges. This exercise is usually performed after we have considered the different stories in class—if only briefly. The instructions I distribute are as follows:

This is a creative writing assignment. Compose one story that incorporates at least seven of the following characters: Ehud, King Eglon, Deborah, Barak, Jael, Gideon, Abimelech, Jephthah, Jephthah's daughter, Samson, his Timnite bride, Delilah, the Levite, and his concubine. Provide a name for the anonymous characters. Look carefully at the portrayal of the character in the biblical text and do your best to retain the given character's traits in your short story. This, of course, will involve some interpretive decisions. Is Samson a hero or a buffoon? Is Gideon brave or timid? Is Delilah seductive? For your story, you should select a couple of main characters; they need not be the primary characters in the biblical narrative.

The general plot line can involve anything you wish, but be sure it includes some sort of conflict and resolution. The setting can be ancient or modern. Be creative and imaginative. Here are some starter questions to get you thinking: What would happen if Barak met Samson? What would the Levite's concubine have to say to Delilah? How would Jephthah have responded to the commands that God gave Gideon? Would Sisera's fate have been different if he wandered into the tent of Samson's Timnite wife, instead of Jael's?

This exercise works well as a take-home writing assignment where students have plenty of time to develop their thoughts. Students bring their stories to class and we conduct a contest to see who has written the best, most creative story. To do this, I put students in five or six different groups and give each group a set of papers to read; each group determines the best paper in its set and submits it to the final round. Thus students have an opportunity to read and evaluate the work of their peers. I then determine the overall winner and read that story to the whole class (in a subsequent session) or post it online. On other occasions I have employed this as an in-class activity, giving groups of three or four students about thirty minutes to create the story. This exercise stimulates creativity and offers an opportunity to work closely with the disparate stories in Judges.

Mark Roncace

91. EHUD AND EGLON: DRAMATIZATION

In this exercise, students are given the task of producing a dramatization of the unusual story in Judg 3:12-30. They are divided into groups and each group is given one supplemental reading to aid in the interpretation of the text. The supplemental readings are chosen from the following list: chapter two of Robert Alter, *The Art of Biblical Narrative* (New York: Basic Books, 1981), esp. 37–41; chapter three of Baruch Halpern, *The First Historians: The Hebrew Bible and History* (San Francisco: Harper & Row, 1988); idem, "The Assassination of Eglon: The First Locked-Room Murder Mystery" *BRev* 4 (December 1988): 33-41; Ferdinand Deist, "'Murder in the Toilet' (Judges 3:12-30): Translation and Transformation," *Scriptura* 58 (1996): 263-72; Lowell Handy, "Uneasy Laughter: Ehud and Eglon as Ethnic Humor," *SJOT* 6 (1992): 233-46; Marc Z. Brettler, "Never the Twain Shall Meet? The Ehud Story as History and Literature," *HUCA* 62 (1991): 285–304; Tom A. Jull, "MQRH in Judges 3: A Scatological Reading," *JSOT* 81 (1988): 63–75.

The members of each group are reminded that they need to clarify exactly what the biblical text describes as having happened, and to which audience the story is directed. They also should note which elements of the story are the focus of their supplementary article (e.g., literary features, historical and/or archaeological details, ethnic stereotyping, etc.). They, in turn, need to decide on the particular focus of their own dramatization.

After a suitable time for group discussion and preparation, the dramas are enacted in random order. (Usually, if the groups and readings are assigned in advance, one class period is required for the groups to plan their dramatizations; in the following class period the dramatizations are presented and discussed.) A plenary discussion follows, focusing on the similarities and differences between the various dramatizations. This discussion may focus on several different issues: (1) whether the biblical story is history, fictionalized history, historicized fiction, or fiction; (2) the theological difficulties in understanding the story from the perspective of contemporary notions of God and ethics; or (3) the uses and abuses of ethnic stereotyping and jokes about the other to construct one's own group identity. In any case, students come away from this exercise realizing that nailing down the details of what may seem straightforward "history" in the Bible is not as simple as it seems, that biblical stories are told from particular perspectives for particular purposes, and that the translation of a biblical story from its ancient context to the modern context is fraught with difficulties. And many enjoy dealing with a story that is a bit "off-color"! (For similar exercises, see §§72, 142, 199.)

F. V. Greifenhagen

92. THE UNITED MONARCHY (SAMUEL AND KINGS)

Teachers of American history advise us that one of the most effective ways to teach history to contemporary students is by approaching a topic or issue "backwards." For example, rather than beginning with the historical developments and manifestations of the civil rights movement in the 1960s, the teacher might begin with a discussion of the contemporary status of race-relations in the students' own community. After discussing something like current statistics on the students' life opportunities (life expectancy, likelihood of death by violence, probability of divorce, etc.) analyzed by race and social class, the teacher could lead the students to examine the historical developments and processes that contributed to the current situation (J. W. Loewen, *Lies My Teacher Told Me: Everything Your American History Textbook Got Wrong* [New York: Touchstone, 1995], 316).

To introduce the topic of the development of the monarchy within ancient Israel as reflected in the literature of the books of Samuel and Kings, I take the approach suggested by our history colleagues. Rather than beginning with the historical and social developments of ancient Israel in the tenth century B.C.E., I break the class into small groups and ask them to begin thinking about the topic at hand by reflecting on our contemporary global experiences. I ask the students to consider three specific questions: (1) What countries in our world have monarchies? (2) How did the kings or queens come to occupy that position? and (3) How do they imagine that a monarchy becomes established in the first place?

The small-group discussion naturally leads into a conversation with the whole class that allows the students to share their insights. The exercise immediately helps students identify more closely with a form of government that is less familiar and often hard to comprehend, particularly for students in the American context. Obviously for teaching Samuel and Kings, however, the last two questions are the most significant. By exploring the ways in which monarchies are maintained and initially come into existence, the teacher can move to the social, religious, and political aspects of the Bible's portrayal of the emergence of Israel's monarchy. Many of these aspects have parallels with contemporary experiences. Positively, for example, the development of a monarchy often involves a response to some immediate internal and external needs (in Israel's case, the social breakdown at the end of the book of Judges and the increasing Philistine threat in 1 Samuel). Negatively, however, the establishment and maintenance of monarchies both then and now often involves violence. Furthermore, the discussion of both positive and negative reactions to the idea of monarchy in contemporary society may provide a helpful transition into the next part of the biblical story that revolves around the different views of the monarchy (both positive and negative) from the perspectives of God, prophets, and people (see 1 Sam 9:1–10:16; 10:17–26).

Brad E. Kelle

93. WHO DECIDES WHAT'S IN THE BIBLE? THE CASE OF 1 SAMUEL 11

This exercise introduces students to the history of the biblical text and to questions of canon. Since few undergraduates have any concept of the MT or LXX and have only a passing knowledge of the Dead Sea Scrolls, learning that these versions of the Old Testament exist, that they vary as to which books they include, and that the content of the books themselves sometimes differs among the versions is surprising to most and quite shocking to some. First Samuel 11 provides an accessible example of how such issues affect modern translations of the Bible.

The first assignment is to read 1 Sam 11 in either the RSV or the JPS/Tanakh version and to answer the following questions: Does the story give any indication as to who Nahash was and why he would want to besiege Jabesh-Gilead? Does the story seem historically plausible? Why or why not? After considering these questions, the students then read the story in the NRSV, which includes an introduction to this story found in the Dead Sea Scrolls (4QSamᵃ) and apparently known by Josephus. Then, they answer the questions again.

At this point, the instructor has an opportunity to provide some basic information about the history of the Old Testament text and the relationship of Hebrew and Greek versions of the text to the Dead Sea Scrolls as well as to the texts of the Bible modern religious communities use. Armed with this introductory knowledge, the students can engage in thought-provoking discussion.

Students may notice that the passage in question has the benefit of providing more context for the story of Jabesh-Gilead and Saul's subsequent war against Ammon there, including the fact that Nahash was the Ammonite king. However, the prologue's assertion that "[n]o one was left of the Israelites across the Jordan whose right eye Nahash, king of the Ammonites, had not gouged out" (NRSV) may make the story appear more fantastical or less historical for some. The instructor can point out that the ancient historian Josephus modified the story and included an explanation to make the eye-gouging more plausible (*Ant.* 6.5.1). Also, students will often speculate that the Qumran/Josephus version of 1 Sam 11 is older and more original, and argue that therefore it ought to be included in modern translations. In response, the instructor could add to the discussion the example of Jeremiah and the presumption that the LXX and Qumran preserve an older version, one that is shorter and has a different arrangement from the version in most modern translations.

This discussion, of course, can lead to the question of whether or not modern translations, and by extension modern communities of faith, should include the prologue to 1 Sam 11 in the Bible. In order to distill students' thoughts on the subject, the instructor can ask them to imagine that they are on a committee given the task of advising their church or synagogue as to which Bible they should purchase for education and worship at their institution. What would they say in their memo to the rest of the congregation?

This exercise raises a number of questions for students and provides few answers, but in doing so it increases their knowledge of the Bible, opens their eyes to critical examination of the biblical text, and hopefully incites their interest in learning more about the complex processes that went into the Bible's formation. (For other exercises on text criticism, see §§19–22.)

Megan Bishop Moore

94. APOLOGY OF DAVID

I begin class by describing how 1 Sam 16—2 Sam 6 presents David in only a positive light. David does no wrong against Saul or his heir Ishbaal (Ishbosheth). The narrative presents David as a victim of Saul's jealousy; David seeks neither his own glory nor personal gain. The narrator uses other characters to speak on David's behalf: Jonathan confesses that David will become king (1 Sam 23:17); Abner acknowledges that God will make David king (2 Sam 3:18); Abigail extols David's virtues—claiming that he fights the Lord's battles and that the Lord has appointed him prince over Israel (1 Sam 25:26–31). When Saul calls up the ghost of Samuel from the dead, the ghost too proclaims that David will become king (1 Sam 28:17). Even Saul acknowledges his own guilt in relation to David and that David will become king (1 Sam 24:17–21; 26:21). One gets the impression that the narrative protests on behalf of David too much.

I then introduce the students to apologetic literature and suggest that the narrative in Samuel functioned as an apology for the Davidic dynasty—that is, defended the dynasty against the charges that David had usurped the throne from Saul. As an example of apologetic literature, I briefly discuss the "Apology of Hattusili III." Hattusili was a Hittite king who usurped the throne from his nephew, Urhi-Tesub. His "Apology" justifies the legitimacy of his reign by emphasizing six themes: (1) His ability to rule is demonstrated by his early military successes as a trusted commander of his brother, Muwatalli. (2) He enjoyed popularity and support among the people. (3) He used skill and restraint in waging the struggle which led to the succession of the throne. (4) The succession to the throne was not part of any grand scheme. (5) He was blameless in all his dealings with his predecessor, despite his jealousy toward him. (6) His rise to the throne was the result of Ishtar's special favor toward him.

As I discuss each of these themes from the Apology of Hattusili, I ask the students to identify similar themes in the story of David. Through class discussion, the students recognize the similarities between these two narratives and are willing to accept the Samuel narrative as a form of apologetic literature. But form is different from function. In the remainder of the class period, I lead the students to understand how 1 Sam 16 – 2 Sam 6 functioned as an apology.

Apologetic literature by its very nature assumes a defensive attitude toward its subject matter, addressing itself to issues exposed to actual or possible public censure. As an apology for the Davidic dynasty, we should expect this narrative to combat a number of charges that would have been leveled against the Davidic dynasty. Such charges are not cited directly in the narrative itself. They have to be reconstructed by "reading between the lines," noting the emphases of the story and imagining what possible accusations lie behind them. This would be a difficult task for the students themselves to accomplish. Instead, I divide the class into six groups and give each group one of the following hypothetical charges against the Davidic dynasty: (1) David tried to advance himself in royal service at Saul's expense. (2) David was a deliberate deserter from the court of Saul. (3) David was an outlaw leader. (4) David was a mercenary collaborator with the Philistines. (5) David established a rival kingdom to Saul in Hebron. (6) David was implicated in Saul's death, in the death of his general, Abner, and in the death of his heir, Ishbaal. (The last charge can be broken into three charges, if more than six groups are needed.)

I ask each group to address the following two questions and be ready to report to the whole class: (1) What evidence in the narrative suggests that the narrative is defending the Davidic dynasty against this charge? (2) How does the narrative defend the Davidic dynasty against this charge? After the groups have had sufficient time to answer the questions, I discuss each hypothetical charge with the whole class. Through this exercise, the students understand how 1 Sam 16—2 Sam 6 functions as an apology for the Davidic dynasty.

Ronald A. Simkins

95. DAVID'S RISE TO POWER

Students often think of the Bible solely as a theological document and so rarely expect stories of political maneuvering and intrigue between its covers. Overcoming readers' expectations often means assisting them in seeing the qualities the text and its characters share with more modern documents. The court history of Samuel—specifically David's rise to power—provides an excellent starting point.

I like to use what my students do know about political campaigns and the ways in which today's candidates seek office to illustrate the similarities between how the Bible generates a political image for David and how a campaign gives voters an idealized candidate in our own time. The almost constant cycle of elections in the United States familiarizes students with political conventions, campaign commercials, how politicians hit the trail, and the ways in which candidates rely on their experience, their connections, and good news coverage to win. This exercise relies on that knowledge by creating two campaign teams—both pro- and anti-David—and determining ways to "sell" his qualifications to be king to Israel as well as assessing where his opposition might produce effective challenges to his ambition.

After reading David's story from 1 Sam 15 to 2 Sam 5 (his anointing to his coronation as king of all Israel), the pro-David team or teams strive to find ways to show: (1) His experience for the position. I ask them to look for the positions that he has held, the kinds of leadership roles he has taken, and what qualifies him to become king. (2) David's associates are also in the spotlight. Who works for David and how does that recommend him? (3) Key endorsements: Who is on David's side and how can they speak to his qualifications? Finally, this group will also be prepared to answer any attacks leveled at their man.

The anti-David group seeks to find David's weaknesses. Where is his record questionable? Does he have a character problem? How can we see him as making claims that are not true? This team needs to locate where David's vulnerabilities as a candidate are and consider how they can be exploited.

Each group is charged with presenting campaign ads that lay out their information. Copy for thirty- and sixty-second spots is required. I also ask that both teams produce a list of "talking points" that stress the kinds of information they want others to make for or against David when speaking to the press. Ads that promote a candidate are allowed, as are attack ads; I have seen, for example, anti-David groups produce spots for Saul or for Ishbaal.

This exercise not only proves fun for most of the students, but also opens up a discussion of the ways in which the writers of the biblical text produce a David who comes across rather heroically. His deft handling of Joab's murder of Abner, for example, shows his ability to control his associates as well as potentially negative press. Similarly, his public mourning of Saul and Jonathan stands out as a carefully choreographed "photo op" where he shows respect for his rival while positioning himself to be his replacement. But students also note the manner in which David creates an alliance with Jonathan and uses Michal to gain access to Saul's family. Questions arise when they consider that the text mentions these siblings loving David, but never speaks of David loving them. Debate over whether David was sincere or conniving or some combination of both frequently ensues.

Of course, becoming a king and winning an election are two different processes. Nonetheless, I have found students appreciate the chance to see the ideological biases of the biblical writer here, and it certainly prompts them to look more carefully at texts typically read in only a cursory manner. (For similar exercises, see §§61, 65, 112.)

Sandie Gravett

96. DAVID AT THE MOVIES

Students live in a video world, and capitalizing on this can improve their interest in studying narratives in the Hebrew Bible. Most of my students who have heard anything about King David have a fairly romanticized view of him, so when I have them read 1–2 Samuel, they are shocked at David's brutality. They are also shocked by the different accounts of the young David that are stitched together in 1 Sam 16–17. But this reinforces the fact that the editor of the Samuel narrative drew from various sources when constructing his rendition of David. To help students experience more of the issues involved in such selection processes, I have them do a synopsis of a movie about David. I divide them into small groups and give the following directions:

I want you to pretend that you are screenwriters who have been given the task of writing a blockbuster movie script about King David. During the next few minutes you must decide what kind of movie you will write (drama, action, comedy, etc.), what material from 1–2 Samuel you will use, which contemporary actors you will have playing the major characters in the story of David, and what title you will give your movie.

They enjoy this task and always show a good deal of creativity in their work. The results are also revealing. Some of the groups are rather ruthless in what material they choose to omit. Like the Chronicler, they may choose to do a whitewashed version of David—if they include the incident with Bathsheba, she is portrayed as a temptress. Or some want to do a psychological drama that explores the tortured psyche of David, perhaps depicting him as dark and sinister. If the small group is primarily male in composition, I can generally expect them to propose an action movie that focuses on the battle scenes. One semester I even had a group propose a comedy using characters from *The Simpsons*.

Having each group explain its choice of movie title, main characters, and plot always reveals some of what they noticed when reading about David—which brings us back to the existing text in 1–2 Samuel. This exercise is both fun and educational for the students. They realize that one must be selective in the use of information when writing about people and events. For many of my students, realizing that biblical authors wrote with particular perspectives is a major hurdle. Using a movie approach to David puts the issues into a more familiar form and helps them to deal with the matter more objectively.

Michael R. Cosby

97. DAVID AND GOLIATH (1 SAMUEL 16–17): THE IDEOLOGY OF BIBLICAL POPULAR CULTURE

The dominant ideologies of the social, political, and economic context in which we do our teaching are strongest precisely when we do not reflect on them or, as so many do, dismiss them as trivial. It is therefore perfectly legitimate to examine it in the classroom. I recall the disdain with which my efforts were treated a few years ago in a seminary where the notion of "culture" was restricted by and large to "quality" literature. *That* was what you could relate to the Bible, not the popular trash I trot out.

So, how can one bring popular culture into play? Film is obvious, and now widely used, but I have always been struck by the way biblical narratives play themselves out in literature specifically targeted at different age groups. But with increasingly refined patterns of marketing, even the rough groups of children, teenagers, and adults break down into smaller ones of perhaps a couple of years at a time. And so when we get to the story of David and Goliath in my course on 1 Samuel, we spend a couple of weeks considering the interpretive moves made in (1) the "Little Golden Book" series, (2) the current form of daily Bible study notes produced by the Bible Society in Australia for different age groups from pre-teen to adult, (3) a teenage novel, (4) the Bible in comic strip form, (5) a children's Bible, and (6) a collection of finger puppets I once found at a local Christian bookshop. Of course, any other collection of texts could serve the same function.

We read through the Hebrew text first, in translation for those with no Hebrew, and then move immediately to the Little Golden Book and the children's Bible, along with any other of the numerous children's picture books available. This produces an immediate "estrangement effect" (I draw the strategy from Bertholt Brecht and the Russian formalists). The initial reaction by students is to note how the children's story plays loose with the Hebrew text, usually in a rather derogatory fashion. And yet, most agree that it is good for children to read stories like these, to become familiar with the biblical narratives—as most of those in theological colleges will have done as children. Even at this point I ask what ideological and political issues are at stake in the kinds of interpretations put forward in these children's versions of the story. Why do such stories insist on finishing with a moral? Why does David come off so well? Why is the market so large for these kinds of texts? Above all, why are children fascinated with the stone in Goliath's forehead?

From this point we wind our way forward through samples of daily Bible notes for age groups ranging from eight to fifteen years old. As the age increases, there is a greater emphasis on the active engagement of the reader with the text: questions, quizzes, invitations to camps, the insistence to read the Bible and pray daily. By now the class is attuned to the interpretive issues in question—the elisions, elaborations, gaps, and contradictions that may be generated by the biblical text itself or new ones that were not there before. But I ask them to focus on the framing elements (following Genette), the structure, layout, and the overt and covert context for this material. Above all, I am after the ideological effect of such literature. The estrangement effect of the children's material is still with them, and so they are still more critical of this material. Some with children (the seminary student being typically older) admit that they do not permit their children to read such texts, while others still think it worthwhile. Lastly we focus on the adult Bible Reading notes, whether provided by the Bible Society or perhaps the church to which most of the students belong. At this point we face a clash, for many use such notes, defending them as being more "liberal" or containing more spiritual depth. The major focus now is precisely on the function of these adult Bible notes in continuity with the earlier material. How is it that they are part of the ideological state apparatus (Althusser) called the church?

Finally, as a way of debriefing, I ask various members of the class to play the role of the characters in the story with the finger puppets. Surprisingly (to me at least), they seem quite willing to engage in the projection that this provides.

Roland Boer

98. DAVID AND BATHSHEBA: A CASE OF MIS-SENT POWER

Mentioning the name "Bathsheba" still readily conjures up negative stereotypes of adulteress and temptress in the popular imagination, as surely as Delilah and Potiphar's wife. Since this interpretive tradition has been bolstered by a spate of dramatic representations, I engage students by asking them to cast the Bathsheba role for a new film. I write their nominations on the board, and invariably it has been a predictable list of certain "types" of actresses with similar reputations at the time. For example, over a stretch of several years among hundreds of students in the 1990s, Madonna was the number one choice in almost every class (Sharon Stone and Pamela Anderson were also frequently mentioned). The popular image of Bathsheba was not hard to confirm.

But is this image supported by the biblical text? I promptly invite the students to look closely at the foundational story in 2 Sam 11:1–12:15, focusing on the sequence of "sendings" (and one critical non-"sending") that drives the plot. While on the surface, the notion of "sending" someone here or there seems rather prosaic, in the context of royal politics, it is a patent signifier of raw power (when the king "sends," things happen and people spring to action). I lead the class through a series of ten "sending" events illustrating King David's exercise of power, and soon the devastating effects of "mis-sent" power become evident. To encourage close reading, one might also assign the task of isolating ten episodes in which "sending" plays a pivotal role in the narrative.

1. "David *sent* Joab with his officers and all Israel" out to fight, while he "remained in Jerusalem" (11:1). What happened to the great champion of the people who led them into battle? Has he gotten too big for such dirty work?

2. In this leisured state, David gets up from a nap, strolls out on the palace roof, and spies Bathsheba taking a bath. He *"sent"* someone to inquire about her (11:3).

3. Learning that she was the wife of Uriah the Hittite should have put an end to David's "sendings." But he is just getting warmed up. From inquiring, he moves to acquiring: "David *sent* messengers to get her, and she came to him, and he lay with her" (11:4). Students are often surprised that this is all the narrative recounts about the famous adultery scene. They are even more surprised about the implications of the brief report. David is the initiator, the aggressor, throughout the story. To be sure Bathsheba "came to him," but what choice did she have? Is this really adultery or more like rape?

4. This is one of three key interruptions in David's sending spree, that is, where someone else gets in on the act or refuses to be sent and complicates David's scheme. Here is Bathsheba's only active contribution to the

story: "She *sent* and told David, 'I am pregnant'" (11:5). A bit of a nui-sance for David.

5. "So David *sent* word to Joab, '*Send* me Uriah the Hittite'" (11:6). Bathsheba's husband has been away fighting (for David!), and now David wants him home. We can be fairly sure David is not planning to tell Uriah what he has done to his wife.

6. David *sent* Uriah home to be with his wife, so her pregnancy will appear to be legitimate (11:8). A perfect cover-up, it seems.

7. Suddenly David seems thwarted, as Uriah *refuses to be sent* (this is the one non-sending). Instead, Uriah camps out one night on the king's porch and another on the king's couch. How dare he not follow orders! But Uriah has David over a barrel, because he refuses to sleep with his wife out of solidarity with David's men at the battlefront (11:9–13).

8. Now David is becoming desperate, but he still has his power to send. So he "wrote a letter to Joab and *sent* it by the hand of Uriah," instructing that Uriah be deployed at the fiercest zone of fighting (11:14–21). Uriah carries his own death warrant, and David soon adds the crime of murder to his increasingly blighted resume.

9. But at least this mess seems to be over. All that remains is for David to marry the widowed Bathsheba: "David *sent* and brought her to his house, and she became his wife, and bore him a son" (11:27). David can even appear magnanimous in the process—look how he has com-forted this poor widow.

10. However, for all his seeming control of the matter, David has failed to reckon on the surprise sending of one more sovereign than he: "But the thing that David had done displeased the Lord, and *the Lord sent* Nathan to David." And the Lord's prophet lowered the boom on David and finally brought him to repentance—and judgment as well. While for-givable, David's actions will have devastating consequences for generations to come (12:1–15).

This is all David's doing and David's fault. Bathsheba does nothing more than take an innocent bath in her own home; otherwise she is trapped in the vicious web of David's deceit and power, against which she is helpless. (For an important development in her character, how-ever, where Bathsheba finds her voice and flexes her muscle, see 1 Kgs 1–2.) Subsequent discussion may center on the possible reasons for the development of Bathsheba's bad reputation or on the place of this story in the larger Deuteronomistic History with its special interest in the Davidic monarchy.

F. Scott Spencer

99. A CONTROVERSIAL KING

This exercise is designed to assist undergraduate-level students acquire better understanding of the nature of the Deuteronomistic History (Joshua through Kings), navigating them from naïve acceptance of the biblical text as "history" (in the modern sense of the word) to a platform of engaged critical thinking about a very complex literary tradition. Objectives include equipping the student to (1) compare biblical and historical witnesses to a particular biblical king; (2) develop the ability to think critically about biblical texts; (3) become conversant in the subject of biblical historiography; and (4) develop greater appreciation for how it is that the Bible has endured as Scripture, gaining understanding of the nature of revelation as a testimony of ongoing human experience.

Begin by introducing students to the information scholars have gleaned from Assyrian imperial inscriptions concerning a certain, yet to be identified, ninth-century B.C.E. Israelite king, who joined a twelve-nation coalition of nations allied against the conquering advance of Shalmaneser III and his formidable Assyrian forces. (For more details, see E. F. Campbell, "A Land Divided," in the *Oxford History of the Biblical World* [ed. M. Coogan; Oxford: Oxford University Press, 1998], 206–41.) According to these records, endurably inscribed in cuneiform on baked clay, this Israelite king contributed 2,000 iron chariots—slightly more than half of the coalition's total number of chariots—and an army of 10,000 foot soldiers in the coalition's campaign against the Assyrian threat. The coalition, spearheaded by the Aramean (Syrian) king of Damascus, encountered the Assyrians at Qarqar, located in his country near the banks of the Orontes River, in 853 B.C.E. The battle ended in a kind of Pyrrhic victory for the coalition in that they successfully withstood the battle, but ultimately lost the war. Nevertheless, it was the mighty king of Israel who proved to be the decisive factor in Shalmaneser's inability to defeat the coalition and his subsequent temporary retreat from Aram.

After concluding the story of this Israelite king, divide students into small groups. Assign each group the task of compiling a brief but imaginative historical profile of this unnamed king from a ninth-century B.C.E. Israelite perspective, based on the Assyrian account. The profile should also include a hypothetical evaluation of what life under this king most likely would have offered its Israelite citizens in the way of such things as security, military or civil service, cultic options, and so on, and whether or not such a king would likely have enjoyed divine favor.

Once the portraits have been completed, inform the students that they are now to read the Bible's portrait of what is almost certainly this same Israelite king. Have them read 1 Kgs 16:29–22:40 and respond (either orally or in writing) to the following questions: (1) In which ways does the biblical portrait of Ahab differ from the portrait derived from the combination of Assyrian annals and student imaginations? (2) Where does the Deuteronomistic writer suggest one go for additional information about Ahab? (3) Under what historical circumstances was this additional document most likely lost to history? (4) What sort of information do you suppose this lost document may have contained? (5) Without resorting to inherently indemonstrable statements of faith, what factors might account for how it is the biblical portrait continued to survive informing living communities of faith, while the other, more historical documents did not?

Nicolae Roddy

100. PATRONAGE IN 1 KINGS 17 AND 2 KINGS 8

The social world of the ancient Israelites is embedded in the biblical texts. In order to understand the biblical texts in the social context of ancient Israel, it is necessary for students to understand how their social world differs from that of the Bible. A key institution in this respect is patronage, a system of social relations that are rooted in an unequal distribution of power and goods and expressed socially through a generalized exchange of different types of resources. Patronage in ancient Israel is the dominant structure of social relations among those of unequal status. Although patronage only rarely comes to the forefront of the biblical texts, its ubiquitous presence in the background emphasizes the importance of this institution for our students.

Many of our students are familiar with aspects of patronage from Mafia movies like *The Godfather*. Indeed, I begin class by showing the opening scene from *The Godfather*, where Don Corleone, the patron, is visited by three men on his daughter's wedding day. The first, Bonasera, asks Corleone to punish two men who had "ruined" his daughter, yet were released from jail on a suspended sentence. The second man, Nazorini, who is baking the cake for the wedding of Corleone's daughter, asks Corleone to arrange immigration for his daughter's boyfriend. Luca Brazi, the Don's assassin, finally meets with Corleone to thank him for inviting him to his daughter's wedding, to pledge his loyalty to Corleone, and to give Corleone a gift for his daughter's bridal-purse. All three men are clients of Don Corleone, and illustrate different aspects of patronage. I use the film clip to introduce a discussion of patronage in ancient Israel. I emphasize that patrons are those with resources and clients are those in need of resources. The patron-client relationship is based on the on-going exchange of tangible resources (access to markets, land for grazing, water rights, labor) and intangibles (loyalty, protection, and honor). This exchange builds friendship and entails obligations for both parties; it is a means for maintaining one's status in the inequitable world of limited goods. The patron-client relation is also an expression of honor and shame. The patron displays his honor by providing for the client. The client's dependence upon the patron is an expression of his shame (that is, concern for his reputation; the alternative is that he would lose status and be dishonored), and he publicly upholds the honor of his patron. The client's honor is embedded in the honor of his patron. (Cf. S. N. Eisenstadt and L. Roniger, *Patrons, Clients and Friends: Interpersonal Relations and the Structure of Trust in Society* [Cambridge: Cambridge University Press, 1984].)

Two biblical stories in which patronage is at the forefront are the similar stories of Elijah and the widow of Zarephath (1 Kgs 17) and Elisha and the Shunammite woman (2 Kgs 8). Students often interpret the first story in the context of hospitality. After all, Elijah lives as a "guest" in the home of the widow, whom God had commanded to feed him. Yet, many of the details of Elijah and the widow's relationship do not fit the students' understanding of hospitality: Elijah makes demands on the widow, and the widow does not have the resources to provide for Elijah. Thus, when I divide the class into groups, I first ask them to assess whether hospitality or patronage is the appropriate model by which to interpret this story. To aid their assessment, I ask them to consider the following questions: (1) If God commanded a widow to feed Elijah, why is she unaware of the command and unable to feed him? (2) Why does Elijah make demands on the widow? (3) Why does the widow yield to Elijah's demands? (4) When the son of the widow dies, why does she blame Elijah? (5) Why does Elijah blame God? After the groups have had time to discuss these questions, I ask each group to report its assessment. Most groups recognize that patronage is the appropriate model for interpreting this story, and as I question them about their assessment, interpretive issues in the story are uncovered and discussed by the class.

The story of Elisha and the Shunammite woman is more complicated than the previous story, in spite of the similar plot in each. Rather than asking whether hospitality or patronage is the appropriate model for interpreting the story, I focus instead on the different social expectations between Elisha and the woman. The Shunammite woman, who is a "great woman," offers Elisha hospitality and expects the relationship to remain at this level. Elisha, in contrast, prefers a relationship of patronage and imposes this relationship upon the woman. When the woman's son dies, however, Elisha is unaware of the tragedy. The woman demands that Elisha live up to his obligations as her patron. To explore these complexities, I ask the students in their groups to address the following questions to form an interpretation of the story: (1) Why does the woman offer Elisha hospitality? What are her expectations for the relationship? (2) Why does Elisha offer to do something for the woman? (3) What does the woman mean by the statement: "I live among my own people"? (4) Why does he speak to the woman through Gehazi rather than directly? (5) When Elisha promises the woman a child, why does she think Elisha might be deceiving her? (6) What are Elisha's expectations for the relationship? (7) After her son dies and the woman goes to Elisha, why does she ignore Gehazi and proceed directly to Elisha? (8) Why does she cling to Elisha and demand that he return with her? Because of the complexity of this story, many more issues will be raised in the class discussion than for the first story. After the groups have formed an interpretation of the story, I ask that each group report its interpretation to the class. As the groups report, I take note of the significant interpretive issues raised by the students' interpretations so that I can return to these issues once all groups have reported, as time allows.

Ronald A. Simkins

101. THE SIEGE OF JERUSALEM: BOTH SIDES OF THE STORY

Historians get excited whenever they acquire access to more than a single witness to any important historical event, for competing perspectives allow the historian to weigh the event in favor of what actually happened. The Assyrian siege of Jerusalem (701 B.C.E.) offers such an occasion (cf. M. Cogan, "Sennacherib's Siege of Jerusalem," *BAR* 27 [2001]: 40–45, 69). The goal of this exercise is to help undergraduate-level students acquire a better understanding of the nature of the Deuteronomistic History (Joshua through Kings), moving them from naïve acceptance of the biblical text as "history" (in the modern sense of the word) to engaged critical thinking about a very complex literary tradition. Objectives include equipping the student to (1) compare biblical and historical witnesses to a particular biblical event, (2) develop the ability to think critically about biblical texts, (3) become conversant in the subject of biblical historiography, and (4) develop greater appreciation for how it is that the Bible has endured as Scripture, gaining understanding of the nature of revelation as a testimony of ongoing human experience.

First, assign the reading of Sennacherib's account of the Siege of Jerusalem. A translation of Sennacherib's Prism is available in M. Cogan and H. Tadmor, *II Kings* (AB 11; New York: Doubleday, 1988), 337–39. Upon completion of the reading, invite the students to discuss the event from the Assyrian leader's perspective, asking them especially to identify which aspects of the account seem plausibly to be historical and which appear to be overly inflated. Next, have the students read the biblical account of the event (2 Kgs 18:13–19:37) and encourage them to discuss the pericope in like fashion. After this discussion, have them compare the more plausible historical data from each account and have them reconstruct what most likely actually happened. Finally, have students compare (orally or in writing) the seemingly non-historical elements of each in order to determine the primary concerns of each writer.

An additional point of discussion, especially suited for an academic theological setting might include the following question: Without resorting to inherently indemonstrable statements of faith, what factors might explain how it is that biblical writings continued to survive and come together to inform living communities of faith, while other, more historical-type documents did not? Aimed at fostering greater appreciation for the Bible among students, the key to unlocking this discussion is found in developing increased textual and contextual sensitivity to certain biblical themes that modern Western readers often downplay, undervalue, or simply take for granted. Surveying the intricate and colorful fabric of the Bible, students may choose to trace such threads as (1) development of the idea of ethical, transcendent monotheism arising from human experience; (2) elevation in status of the human person (e.g., image of God, model of Abraham as Everyman, etc.); (3) promotion of the twin principles of justice and righteousness (*mishpat vezedekah*) as obligatory for everyone; (4) exercise of the moral critique of human institutions (kingship, Israel's defenses, the city, etc.); and (5) affirmation of the deity's steadfast lovingkindness (*hesed*) even in the wake of near extinction. At the very least, any discussion should be based upon sustained and careful reading of the biblical texts, with an expectation that such reading will lead to informed analysis of the nature of the so-called historical books, through which students will be able to determine for themselves that history, at least in their usual sense of the word, is not what the Bible is about.

Nicolae Roddy

102. WHAT IS A PROPHET?

A basic misconception that many students unknowingly carry with them has to do with the definition of prophecy. The culture tends to think of a prophet as a predictor. Another common definition has it that the prophet is an ethical progressive. Neither of these unhelpful labels does justice to the public practices or the proclamations of the biblical prophets. I have used two interactive exercises to help students live into a more full understanding of what a prophet was.

The first activity I call "Meet the Prophets." I use this activity at the start of a course or unit on the prophets. I divide the class into small groups and assign each group texts representative of different prophets. Each group is directed to investigate their passages with several questions in mind: Can you answer who the prophet was or what his self-understanding was? What was the content of the prophet's preaching? What was the prophet's attitude toward the nation? What was the prophet's attitude toward the priesthood and other prophets? How and where did the prophet see God at work? What future did the prophet see? How did the prophets communicate their messages?

Some of the texts that I have used are: Amos 7:1–6, 10–17 (Amos intercedes on behalf of the people and announces that judgment is averted; he describes his call and announces judgment); Hos 1:1–8; 4:1–3; 11:1–9 (Hosea uses his marriage and children as messages of judgment; condemns both people and religious leaders for ethical and faith violations; he announces a future with hope); Isa 6:1–13; 11:1–9 (Isaiah reports his call and the message of judgment; he announces a future reign of peace brought about by the ideal Davidic king); Jer 1:4–10; 5:13-15; 20:7–12; 31:31–34 (Jeremiah reports his call, condemns false prophets, laments the prophetic calling, and announces a future with hope); Isa 40:1–5; 44:9–20; 45:1–8 (Second Isaiah reports his call and the message of hope he was to deliver; he condemns idols and speaks of Cyrus as God's servant); Joel 1:13–20; 2:18–27 (Joel calls for repentance and announces a future deliverance); Hab 1:1–2:5 (Habakkuk pleads with God to avert judgment and announces that even though judgment will come, God is nevertheless present).

I then ask for a volunteer from each group to come forward. Each volunteer is given a sign with their respective prophet's name and is told to play the part of the prophet for an impromptu "Jerry Springer Show" performance. I play the show's host and interview the different "prophets." It works best if the volunteers are students who can play (literally) and will get into the exercise, so I often single out students ahead of time and ask them to volunteer. Afterwards, the class discusses the exercise.

A second exercise that has effectively helped students explore the idea of what a prophet was draws on an article by Gene Tucker ("The Role of the Prophets and the Role of the Church," in *Prophecy in Israel* [ed. D. L. Petersen; Philadelphia: Fortress, 1987]). Part of what Tucker does is to explore six common ways in which people have tried to understand prophetic identity, showing how each includes both a grain of truth and some inadequacies. The six ways he presents are: mystics/visionaries, literary giants/poets, great theologians/religious philosophers, social reformers/ethical radicals, seers/predictors, preachers of repentance. To his list of six, I add the rubric of prophet as messenger. The class is divided into seven groups and each group is assigned to perform for the class the following week a presentation exploring the rubric they were given for how a prophet is to be understood. Again, the class processes the exercise as a large group.

I have found that these exercises help the students to understand the prophetic literature much more deeply and thus to obtain a better sense of how to interpret this literature and how to begin to apply it to the church today. Students begin to understand that prophetic identity was too diverse for a single label; that prophecy was a complex phenomenon and that prophets had different self-understandings and different ways of relating to Israel's institutions; that each prophetic book needs to be interpreted on its own merits and not dissolved into a generic prophetic stew; and that different prophets experienced God in different ways and delivered their messages differently.

Rolf Jacobson

103. THE PROPHETS AND TWO GOOD DOCTORS

The prophets are a strange genre for beginning students for many reasons, not the least of which are (1) that they are largely poetic in form and (2) that students often operate with a default understanding of prophets as fortune-tellers or futuristic visionary figures like Nostradamus. The first problem is best dealt with over an extended period of time by helping students develop poetic sensibilities and sensitivities. The latter problem, however, can be dealt with more economically and should be addressed at the outset. I have found that discussing "two good doctors" with whom students are familiar often proves helpful in disabusing them of popular conceptions and shifting them toward biblical examples of the genre.

The first doctor is Dr. Martin Luther King Jr. and his work in the civil rights movement. Virtually any incident in King's career will do the job, but I focus on the Montgomery bus boycott and how his preaching in this context was quite different from earlier black preaching, which tended to be more accommodating toward social oppression, favoring eschatological or apocalyptic rather than prophetic stances (see G. S. Selby, "Framing Social Protest: The Exodus Narrative in Martin Luther King's Montgomery Bus Boycott Rhetoric," *Journal of Communication and Religion* 24 [2001]: 68–93). King's preaching and practice obviously changed all that.

The second, more humorous, doctor is Dr. Seuss (Theodor Seuss Geisel), the famous children's writer, who was also involved in political issues at various points in his life, especially by means of political cartooning in *PM* magazine during World War Two. I read to my students Seuss' short and ecologically-conscious book, *The Lorax* (1971). Besides bearing a striking resemblance to the prophet Amos of Tekoa (!), the Lorax speaks on behalf of the powerless entities (the Truffula Trees, the Swomee-Swans, the Brown Bar-ba-loots) that are being destroyed by an overly-eager entrepreneur named the Once-ler, who will stop at nothing, including total ecological disaster, for his economic gain. The book hinges on a message of responsibility and activity: "Unless someone like you cares a whole awful lot, nothing is going to get better. It's not."

The publication date of *The Lorax* in the 1970s and the rise of ecological concerns is notable, but in many ways the prophetic theme here is already figured in Seuss' much earlier work, *Horton Hears a Who!* (1954). In that volume, the elephant Horton hears a small voice—a Who!—that no one else can hear coming from a speck of dust. His attention to that voice, which turns out to be an entire community of *Whos* in *Whoville*, is what saves them from certain destruction. As Horton says: "A person's a person, no matter how small." Finally, by means of intertextual linkage, one might tie these themes to what is probably Seuss' most famous book, *How the Grinch Stole Christmas!* (1957). The protagonists in this story are also called Whos, also live in a town called Whoville, and prove to be, in the end, prophetically (at least in contemporary American culture) non-consumerist in their understanding that Christmas is not about products but about their fellow townspeople.

Both doctors work well and using them in tandem has some advantages. King's work, not to mention his assassination, and the ongoing legacy of the civil rights movement highlight the real risks and gravity involved in the prophetic task. This example also finds its place within a religious community, specifically King's status as a Baptist minister, even though the civil rights movement extended beyond that denomination to other groups (e.g., Nation of Islam). The Seuss materials seem to work well because his writings are humorous and are often more immediate to the students' experience and memory. But *The Lorax,* in particular, also illustrates in brief and concise fashion the speech of the prophets on behalf of the powerless. Both good doctors, therefore, have proven helpful in redefining the prophet and the prophetic task away from Nostradamus and toward more biblical exemplars. Indeed, it is quite easy to move from King and Seuss to Walter Brueggemann's work on the prophets, which stresses the origins of the prophetic in grief and suffering and in the capacity to criticize and energize so as to create a vision alternative to that of the dominant culture (see *The Prophetic Imagination* [2nd ed.; Minneapolis: Fortress, 2001]).

Brent A. Strawn

104. ON BECOMING PROPHETS

In lieu of a research paper on prophecy, students in an upper-level course on Hebrew prophecy are asked to choose a contemporary issue and to apply the elements of prophecy about which they are learning to that issue in a contemporary setting. The venue for this project typically is a 20–45 minute class presentation that is to be as powerful as possible. Topics are left to the students to choose, and the issues their "prophets" confront have varied from a shoe factory in Indonesia, the confrontation between contemporary and traditional Christian music, homosexuality (several sides of the debate), the pervasiveness of complaining on campus, the contrast between enthusiasm for sport and enthusiasm for Christ, and the lack of diversity on campus (several years ago), to the L'Arche community for people with disabilities. Topics range as widely as students' interests.

For this project, students must carefully incorporate the elements of prophecy that we have studied throughout the course:

The assiduous study of scripture (e.g., Amos's use of Torah in Amos 1–2; Hosea's condemnation of kingship [9:15], which is based upon the story of Saul in 1 Sam 11:14–15 and 13:8–15; Jeremiah's dependence upon Hosea in Jer 1–7). This element is absolutely essential for students who may labor under the popular assumption that prophets received everything by direct revelation. In my introductory class, I illustrate this misconception by wearing a baseball cap with a funnel taped to the top of it. I drop a ping pong ball into the funnel and spit across the classroom another ping pong ball, which I have inserted into my mouth, as if the same ball traveled through my head and out of my mouth. Though this is hardly sanitary, it does help students to conceptualize that the prophets were not "funnel-heads," or they grasp that I, at least, do not think prophets were funnel-heads.

The turning of traditions on their heads (e.g., Amos's transformation of the priestly call to worship [4:4–5]; Jeremiah's condemnation of the conviction that Judah was protected because of the temple in Jerusalem [Jer 7]; Ezekiel's vivid and sexually explicit revision of Israel's history in Ezek 17, 20, and 23).

Vivid metaphors and similes (e.g., "Let justice roll down like waters" in Amos 5:21).

A personal experience or a lack of personal experience (e.g., some sort of call or non-call; cf. Amos 7–9; Hos 1, 3; Isa 6; Jer 1; Ezek 1–3).

In developing creative prophecies that are well-researched, reflective of the traditions and values of the recipients, personally significant, and vividly portrayed, students have created stunning prophecies, including, for example: a vivid indictment of health-care by a nursing student who exposed the tendency to take emergency patients to Cook County hospital even when other emergency rooms were much closer; the use of a fan to disseminate the putrid stench of injustice; a mock student directory that, well, mocked the lack of racial diversity on our campus; a model airplane crashed into a four-foot model of the Empire State Building which it took the student weeks to build (as an analogy to the high level of detail in Ezek 40–48); an urgent plea for the church to be more enthusiastic, in the format of a Seattle Mariners program, replete with advertisements; a PowerPoint presentation on a sweatshop sneaker factory in which the Nike logo "Just Do It!" is morphed, through successive images, into the counter-logo "Just Don't Think!" about the deplorable conditions of the factory; an invitation to people with disabilities in which a student reads from her own experiences of excluding others while she meticulously sets a lovely table to invite the disabled, such as those in the L'Arche community, to a feast; and an original CD rich with music intended to demonstrate the sad foolishness of the impasse that exists between proponents of classical and contemporary Christian music—the CD ends in the valley between the warring cliffs with a moving and rhythmic South African street song.

The degree to which the rest of the class participates depends on the project. The interaction between the "prophet" and the "people" opens up additional avenues for reflection on the similarities and differences between ancient and contemporary prophetic critique. (For a similar exercise, see §227.)

John R. Levison

105. PROPHETIC CALL NARRATIVES

When I present the prophetic call narratives and the experience of the prophetic call as reflected in the text, I draw upon a long-running staple of popular culture: *Monty Python and the Holy Grail*.

To begin the discussion about the phenomenon of the call, I play the scene in which Arthur and his knights have their initial direct encounter with God and receive their "sacred quest" for the holy grail. Along with obviously comedic (and somewhat sacrilegious!) aspects, this scene presents several key elements of the prophetic call narratives. When God first confronts the group, their initial reaction is to grovel, "avert their eyes," and proclaim their unworthiness to be in God's presence, an action to which God responds with no small amount of displeasure. After reassuring them of their standing before him (God is portrayed as an elderly male), God gives them the direct task of searching for and finding the holy grail. By the end of the encounter, Arthur and friends are seemingly convinced of both the legitimacy of the quest and their ability to complete it successfully with God's help.

My primary reason for using this clip is to provide a link between popular culture and the biblical text in a light-hearted way. The clip also provides, however, an illustration of the typical elements found in the call narratives in the Old Testament. To present these elements, I ask the students to divide into groups and compare what they have just viewed with one of the call narratives from the Bible (e.g., Exod 3:1–22; Judg 6:11–24; Jer 1:4–10). This discussion generally leads the students to identify the four typical elements involved in the call experience: (1) encounter with God, (2) call, (3) objection, and (4) reassurance or sign. Furthermore, the comparison allows the teacher to broaden the discussion and highlight the way the call experience functions in both the movie and texts. In both cases, the call serves to authenticate the recipient to himself and to others and to equip the prophet with a specific task or message that then dictates subsequent actions. An additional by-product of this comparison, however, includes the ability to discuss the ways in which biblical imagery can be adapted and represented within the different venues of contemporary culture. This discussion may be especially fruitful given the continuing fascination with prophets and prophecy, particularly within evangelical Christianity and its television programming.

Brad E. Kelle

HEBREW BIBLE

106. M&MS, PLAY-DOH, PLUMB BOBS,
HOW YOU GOT YOUR NAME–AND PROPHETS

A teacher once admonished me, "The room starts to teach before you open your mouth!" Based on that wisdom, I strive to arrive to class early and set up an implicit learning environment that will greet students as they arrive. A friend who is more deeply trained in pedagogical terminology than I explained to me that what I am doing is constructing "anticipatory sets." That may be so, but what I really am doing is tricking the students into learning. I have found this strategy particularly effective as a means of opening up various of the minor prophets. Here are some examples:

Hosea. As students arrive, I ask them how they got their names and what their names mean. (A surprising amount of students report that their name means "I don't have any idea." A colleague of mine who uses this exercise reported that an African student described how he had many names, but one of his names was "Don't Touch That." His father had been a tribal chief and received many visitors. In his culture, it is considered rude to tell guests not to handle one's property. So when visitors started to pick up various items in the home, his father would call him and guests would get the idea.) The point of the exercise is that it gets students thinking about names, which leads naturally into Hosea and the colorful way that the prophet used his children to deliver his prophetic messages—"He sows," "Not My People," and "Not Pitied." (This exercise would also work with Isa 1–39 or the beginning of the Gospel of Matthew.)

Amos. Prior to the arrival of students, I set up two brick towers—one as straight as I can make it and one as crooked as I can manage. Between the two towers, I hang a plumb bob. As the students arrive, I give them a handful of M&Ms and direct them to make a line with their M&Ms on the desk in front of them. The use of the towers and plumb bob is obvious— it leads to a discussion of Amos's oracle in 7:7–9 (and it is easier than bringing in a swarm of locust [7:1–3]!). But I have found that many students will read these oracles and not reflect on their meaning—it is almost as if reading means moving your eyes over words rather than understanding them. But the M&Ms! Inevitably, some of the students use the different colored M&Ms to make designs—often elaborate chiastic arrangements, ROYGBIV rainbows, and so on. I ask the students to notice the inevitable urge of some people to create some order out of a series. I also note how other people never have this urge—toward this end I pretend to notice an intentional arrangement in a case where a student clearly just lined up the M&Ms randomly. I use this teaching point to talk about prophetic books as collections of oracles that the prophets spoke but that other people arranged into (what we call) books. In the case of Amos, this leads to talking about the arrangement strategy of first condemning all of Israel's neighbors and then lastly lambasting both Judah and Israel. This arrangement is clearly intentional; the question is why and what does it mean? This also leads to a discussion of the three praise fragments that some scholars have perceived as located strategically throughout the book (4:13; 5:8–9; 9:5–6)—but I ask whether this arrangement is intentional (and thus evokes meaning) or accidental (and thus any meaning assigned is imposed by modern scholars). I remind the students here of the arrangement that I had "perceived" in the M&Ms of the student who arranged her line randomly. I also note how books such as Amos and Hosea are filled with judgment texts but end with messages of hope. Why? I have also found that students like the M&Ms.

Jeremiah. As students arrive, I give each one a jar of play-doh and instruct them to mold it into a symbolic message of what God has to say to the world, church, or school today. On my table at the front of the classroom, I have a pottery vase that a former student made for me. On it are inscribed some Hebrew words. This exercise then leads into a discussion first of Jer 18 in which Jeremiah likened God's work to a potter forming and reforming clay. Then I describe how the pottery vase is a symbol of how God views the seminary where I teach—and I smash it (the former student made many of these for me). This leads to a discussion of Jer 19 in which God directs Jeremiah to buy and then smash a pottery vessel as a message of what God was going to do to the city. These two exercises are fun (as is bringing in a soiled diaper from one of my children to illustrate Jer 13!), but the real pedagogical point is to open for discussion the prophetic practice of performing symbolic actions as a means of conveying prophetic messages. I drive the class to grasp how the prophets were paradoxically limited in what they could say but also free in how they said it. This leads to a discussion of what we are called to say and how we are free to say it.

Rolf Jacobson

107. MODERN POETRY AND PROPHETIC FORM CRITICISM

While few, if any, students come into an Old Testament survey class having the ability to read the text in the original language and challenge a particular English translation, they seem to be unwilling to challenge even the formatting or paragraphing of a text in, for example, *The Harper-Collins Study Bible* or *The Oxford Annotated Study Bible*. This exercise attempts to help the students see that formatting and paragraphing are interpretive acts in themselves, particularly in the texts of the poetry of the prophets. Once the students recognize this, hopefully, they will be more willing to question and consider how an interpretation of a passage changes depending on how it is segmented.

I note that, although most modern English translations of the Prophets divide up the various oracles and clearly format them on the page with space or, very often, titles to the different oracles, the Hebrew text does not divide them up so clearly. When one interprets the Prophets, therefore, it is important to be aware where one oracle might end and another begins. If one starts "lumping and dumping" the various oracles together and tries to interpret long sections of prophetic material, the meaning of the passage will usually be confusing or nonsensical. And even if one can make sense out of a long oracle, where one chooses to begin and end it will necessarily affect the interpretation.

To illustrate, I pass out a section of poetry, in which I have chosen four relatively short poems by Jane Mayhall. (I use Mayhall because most students do not seem to be very familiar with her work, her poetry is non-rhyming, and the line length of the four poems is generally equal. Any combination of poems by any author having a similar, non-rhyming meter and "feel" would work.) To form the section of poetry, I have taken the titles off the poems and have connected them together into one long poem. I do not tell the students how many separate poems are in the section; I simply say there are a few. I then ask the students to read through the long poetic section and try to discern where each of the poems ends and another begins. After a few minutes, I ask them to confer with two or three other people to see if they agree.

We then go through the poetic section and I ask where the first poem ends. Inevitably, there are at least two different opinions presented. Similar results occur with the other three poems. I ask the students to defend their decisions. Why were certain choices about the ending of the first poem made? What are the conventions of poetry that they are using? What provides the coherence for the poem with each of the options?

Then, when the various options and their rationales are clear, we go back through the section and I ask about what the first poem is "about," what it "means." Depending upon what the final line of the poem is, the meaning of the poem slightly changes. We continue this type of analysis throughout the section. In this way, students are better able to evaluate the formatted poetic text in their Bibles and can better appreciate both the poetic nature of prophetic oracles as well as their possible meanings, both historically and theologically.

Roy L. Heller

108. VICTIMS' TESTIMONIES AND PROPHETIC LITERATURE

The study of the prophets at many Christian colleges is limited to those passages that, according to the New Testament writers, predict the coming of Jesus. This method of study misses much that is important about the prophets and about the God for whom they spoke. The prophetic books show God's love, mercy, and desire for justice in a world where the powerful oppress the weak. A major emphasis of prophetic literature is the call to social justice. The prophets confronted the upper classes of Israel, and other nations, in the name of Yahweh who defends the powerless, such as the poor, widows, and orphans (Ezek 34; Isa 1:11–17; Amos 5:7–15; Mic 6:6–8). The prophets were able to challenge the people and leaders because they, like Yahweh, empathized with the outcasts of society. As Carol Dempsey states, the message of the prophets "cuts to the chase to sting people with its moral consciousness and to call them to responsibility" (*Hope Amid the Ruins: The Ethics of Israel's Prophets* [St. Louis: Chalice, 2000], 47). How can college students come to see their role as something like that of modern prophets? Rather than focusing solely on the history and exposition of the texts, students need to be moved to anger, compassion, and righteousness.

In pursuit of this objective, I have the students read two or three written testimonies by abuse victims followed by a class period where we hear a personal testimony of an abuse victim or watch one of the videotapes produced by the Faith Trust Institute in Seattle (www.faithtrustinstitute.org). This domestic violence prevention center has produced videos concerning sexual abuse, physical abuse, and abuse by clergy. The video *Not In My Church* is the story of an adulterous pastor and the reaction of the congregation and victims to his crimes. This is an excellent movie which challenges the students to consider what it means to be prophetic and to confront abusive personalities. Another video, *Hear Their Cries,* deals with child abuse and the faith community. (Whatever their shortcomings, many television talk shows also feature similar stories quite frequently.) In the next class period we discuss how the prophets would have addressed these situations. Not only are students provoked to consider the role of the community of faith in the pursuit of justice, but they are also exposed to the emotions faced by victims and the horrors of human-induced trauma.

Throughout my course on the prophets we refer frequently to these stories, and the students are driven into the prophetic texts to find hope, comfort, and justice for the afflicted and oppressed. All assignments have some component concerning justice and the oppressed. As they are now acquainted with stories of abuse (and I find that many eventually share their own stories as victims), students are expected to discuss their roles, and the roles of the faith community, in providing justice for the oppressed. I refer to them as "little prophets" and remind them that prophets are not without emotion. Victims' testimonies encourage the student to understand and to feel the passion of the prophets and of Yahweh for the humiliated of society. The students see their role as modern prophets, calling their communities to work for social justice and freedom for all people.

Ron Clark

109. INTRODUCING THE BOOK OF ISAIAH

The task of introducing the book of Isaiah is an arduous one. The best of recent scholarship demands that we find some way to integrate both the classic scholarly approaches to the book that have identified "First," "Second," and "Third" Isaiah with newer approaches that stress the possibilities and benefits of reading the book as a whole. In order to move in this direction, I begin the class session on Isaiah by showing a clip from the original *Star Wars* trilogy (any clip that will get the discussion focused on *Star Wars* will do). From this clip, I ask the class to think about the nature and making of the series of original *Star Wars* movies. In the discussion, I highlight several significant facts for the intersection with Isaiah. The *Star Wars* movies consist of three different episodes that were made by different teams of people in 1977, 1980, and 1983 respectively. As a result, each of the three original movies can be viewed independently as a complete film in its own right. The three movies can also be viewed together, however, as part of the larger story of the *Star Wars* saga (the rebellion versus the empire, the redemption of Anakin Skywalker, etc.).

From this starting point, I turn to the composition of Isaiah. My basic point is to emphasize that this type of "Star Wars composition" has long been acknowledged to be at work in the book and to give the students some kind of contemporary analogy (loose though it may be) to the nature of the biblical text. Thus, I point out that nineteenth-century biblical scholarship identified three separate works from different authors and settings that now make up the biblical book, and the book as a whole includes expansions and additions that move beyond the "original" (not unlike new episodes of the *Star Wars* trilogy). At the same time, I bring out that, much like the *Star Wars* saga, more recent scholarship has emphasized the ways in which the whole book hangs and functions together as a whole.

From here, the teacher can move into a more detailed presentation of the traditional multi-authorship approach, the more recent studies of the book's literary and theological unity, or illustrative discussions around representative texts. One may continue to refer back to the similarities and dissimilarities between the composition processes of *Star Wars* and Isaiah to enhance a variety of points that come up in the discussion.

Brad E. Kelle

110. ISAIAH AND BOB DYLAN ON THE WATCHTOWER

One of the goals in my biblical studies classes is for students to become aware of the ways that the Bible interacts with popular culture. I often assign an essay in which they are required to identify a popular song which makes reference to a specific biblical passage. By the time this assignment comes along in the semester, I have played a number of songs that are clear examples of this phenomenon, such as Natalie Merchant's "Our Time in Eden," Nick Cave's "The Mercy Seat," Leonard Cohen's "Hallelujah," and Joan Baez's "Isaac and Abraham." As an example of a song that makes a more veiled reference to the Bible, I use Bob Dylan's classic song "All Along the Watchtower." The beauty of this selection is that the related biblical text is from Isa 21:1–12, and both the song and the prophetic oracle reveal the ambiguity of such poems and their dependence upon a social or literary context.

Before turning attention to the song, I display the KJV of Isa 21:1–12, one of the "Oracles Against the Nations" in Isa 13-23. It is essential to use the KJV to illustrate the numerous verbal connections in the song. After reading the text I talk about the oracles and their place in Isaiah. Then we review the relationship between Israel and Babylon, which has already been encountered in our reading of 1–2 Kings.

The version of the song I play is usually a live Bob Dylan version. I find that my current students are familiar with either the Jimi Hendrix version or the live U2 version, though the lyrics are slightly altered on the latter. While playing the song, I display the lyrics (see http://bobdylan.com/songs/watchtower.html). After the students hear the song and laugh at Dylan's voice, I ask them to list the verbal connections they observe between the song and the Isaiah text. This works best if the song lyrics and the King James text can be displayed simultaneously. They should come up with a list that includes some of the following: (1) "whirlwinds" in the Isaiah text and "wind" in the song; (2) "watchtower" in both; (3) "princes" in both; (4) "drink" in the Isaiah text and "drink my wine" in the song; (5) "couple of horsemen" in the Isaiah text and "two riders" in the song; (6) "lion" in the Isaiah text and "wildcat" in the song; (7) "whole nights" in the Isaiah text and "hour is getting late" in the song; (8) "watch" in the Isaiah text and "kept the view" in the song; (9) "pain," "bowed down," and "dismayed" in the Isaiah text and "confusion" and "no relief" in the song.

Looking for these verbal connections will force them to pay careful attention to both the biblical text and the song. At this point some more complex questions can be asked:

How would you describe the general mood of the Isaiah text and the song? How do they compare? What themes are present in the text and the song that might not be reflected by actual verbal connections? (Both Bob Dylan's song and the oracle in Isa 21 see and hear something fearful approaching. The awareness of coming upheaval is painful and difficult for the prophet and the singer.)

Bob Dylan wrote "All Along the Watchtower" in the mid 1960s. What was going on in America at this time? How might his social situation have been similar to or different from Israel's in the Babylonian period? (The social fabric of America in the 1960s was torn by the civil rights movement and the controversy over the Vietnam War. Even for those who desired change, the turmoil that came with it was difficult. Israel was first destroyed by the Babylonian Empire. Isaiah 21 speaks of the overthrow of this empire. Though this turn of events would be satisfying to Israel in terms of revenge and potential liberation, it also brought with it another wave of social upheaval.)

In what ways is Dylan similar to or different from the prophets of ancient Israel? (For the most part, the lives of the Israelite prophets are obscured behind their words. Their words take on much greater importance than their personal lives. The prophets were also performers. The texts of their prophetic speeches are only partial remains of prophetic events. Like the bare words of a song, these texts lack the settings, sounds, body language, and facial expressions of the actual performance. In a recent interview, Dylan displayed an aversion to being labeled a prophet. Some of the biblical prophets demonstrated a similar reluctance.)

Why might musical artists use biblical images, phrases, or characters in their songwriting? (A literary work with the cultural weight of the Bible offers a tremendous reservoir of images and ideas. In some cases, the mere mention of a name or place, like Eve or Jerusalem, pulls an enormous amount of information or emotion into a song with a single word. This case is a little different because the text is not a familiar one. The effect may have done more for the writer than the casual listener. The connection of these two distant moments of crisis may shed light on both of them.)

Mark McEntire

111. SECOND ISAIAH AND THE EXILIC IMAGINATION

If prevailing scholarly opinion is to be believed, the exile is an event of singular importance in biblical history and for the composition of the many biblical books or traditions that can trace their origins or motivations to this experience. Most students in North America have not, however, experienced anything like the exile and can barely imagine such an event let alone begin to sympathize with its impact on virtually every level of Israel's life, culture, and psyche. That being said, the events of September 11, 2001, may provide a window into the trauma of exilic experience that is quite near and immediate. More removed in actual experience, but not in cultural memory and societal aftermath, is the horrible history of slavery in America.

Despite both of the latter items, which can provide powerful entrées into Israel's exilic experience, I have found it helpful to draw on the motion picture *The Shawshank Redemption* (1994; based on a short story by Stephen King) to introduce students to the "exilic imagination." The clips I use have been carefully and specially edited for just this task so as to flow seamlessly in a short film of approximately eighteen minutes, but jumping around the film by means of the chapters on a DVD (or a counter on a VHS) could do the job just as well. In the absence of technology for video or DVD playback, a simple description of the story, if well done, can be just as effective. In any event, the clips I show focus on the character of Red (Morgan Freeman) and his transformation from "an institutional man"—one completely accustomed to, even dependent upon, prison and prison life for his existence—to someone who has hope, not just for a life outside of prison but for life in general, even in prison. Red's are the last words of the movie and the last of his words are simply "I hope"—tellingly and importantly without any indication of a direct object.

The change in Red's character, from institutionalized prisoner to one who hopes, is sparked by Andy Dufresne (Tim Robbins), a man who has been falsely imprisoned and who finally escapes. But before doing so, Andy enables an escape of sorts among his fellow inmates—an escape and transformation of their imaginations. Andy affects the lives of Red and several others in significant ways. One of the most notable moments is the scene where Dufresne uses the prison public address system to broadcast an Italian aria throughout the whole prison—an event that brings the entire complex to a standstill. In Red's word, in that experience, "for the briefest of moments, every last man in Shawshank felt free." Dufresne's seminal wisdom in the film for Red and the others is found in his line: "Hope is a good thing, maybe the best of things, and no good thing ever dies."

The story is extremely helpful in giving a sense of the exilic imagination. If D. N. Freedman is correct, Deuteronomistic retribution theology was the ideological status quo of exile ("'Son of Man, Can These Bones Live?' The Exile," in idem, *Divine Commitment and Human Obligation: Selected Writings of David Noel Freedman* [2 vols.; ed. J. R. Huddlestun; Grand Rapids: Eerdmans, 1997], 1:171–86). This theology—simplistically summarized—casts the history of Israel as a history of failure and apostasy leading to inevitable judgment, doom, and destruction. The *apologia* of the Deuteronomistic History, in this perspective, is a national confession of sin that broadly construes the destructions of Israel and Judah as deserved punishments. Surely this is a powerful prison of the imagination! But even if this theory (largely Martin Noth's) is in need of nuance and revision, the exile itself was massive in terms of cultural, societal, and psychological impact. Simply put, the Babylonian exile was a prison from which most, if not all, Judeans would never return. There can be little doubt that many became, in Red's words, "institutionalized."

In this context, Dufresne's "ministry" and his ethic of hope find a powerful parallel in the preaching of Second Isaiah, the prophet of hope to exiles who seem well on the way to institutionalization. (Consider, e.g., the prophet's citation of the exiles' speech in Isa 40:27.) But it is into this context, this prison that is both bodily and imaginational, that the aria of the anonymous prophet sings. And for a moment, or at least for a few chapters, every exile in Babylon felt free. And small wonder. It is, after all, the Shawshank *redemption*. It is, after all, the good news of comfort that the prophet announces (Isa 40:1; cf. 40:9).

I have found that the movie clips work equally well as a conclusion to a lecture on various perspectives on exile (culminating in Second Isaiah), or as the beginning of a lecture, in which case the movie functions as an engaging, multi-media introduction that is a wonderful discussion starter for the topic of the day.

Brent A. Strawn

112. THE DEPICTION OF JEREMIAH

The book of Jeremiah paints a complex image of the prophet. In order to help students appreciate the depth and sophistication of his portrayal, I ask one half of the class to argue that the text invites a sympathetic reading of Jeremiah (i.e., play the role of his defense lawyer) and the other half to argue that Jeremiah's role as a prophet is undermined and challenged (i.e., the prosecuting attorney). I ask them to deal with the following texts. Here I include some brief comment on the issues that students might address. Depending on the level of the class and time devoted to the exercise, I may include some of these prompts along with the references; other times I simply list the texts.

The Laments/Confessions: 11:18–20 (and God's response in 11:21–23); 12:1–4 (and God's response in 12:5–6); 15:10–18 (and God's response in 15:19–21); 17:14–18; 18:18–23; 20:7–13; 20:14–18. What is Jeremiah "lamenting"? Or is he "confessing"? What sorts of things does he say to and about God? What is the overall image of Jeremiah in these passages? What is the nature of God's response to the prophet—consoling and reassuring or harsh and defensive? How would you describe the relationship between God and Jeremiah? Is there any significance to God's silence in response to the last four laments/confessions? What do you think of Jeremiah's final lament in 20:14–18? How might this connect to Jeremiah's call to be a prophet in chapter 1? Do your sympathies lie with God or Jeremiah or neither or both?

Jeremiah 27–29: How could Jeremiah's message of submission be understood as treason (cf. Isa 36–39)? How could the people listening to Jeremiah and Hananiah know who was correct? How does Hananiah's fate (death) and the curse against Shemaiah (29:29–32) reflect on Jeremiah? Are Jeremiah's predictions always right (29:10)? What are the implications of this?

Jeremiah 37–40: Is Jeremiah more concerned about his own safety and well-being than he is about delivering the message of God? How is one to interpret the prophet's physical sufferings in light of God's message to Jeremiah in 1:17–20? Is Jeremiah a liar (38:14–28, esp. vv. 24–28)? Does his message turn out to be at least somewhat inaccurate (cf. 38:2 and 39:9)? Why are the Babylonians so kind to Jeremiah (39:11–15; 40:1–6)—does this imply he was a collaborator?

I have used the exercise as a homework writing assignment or as an in-class project; in the case of the latter the discussion can be set up as a debate, with the instructor serving as the judge. Some possible concluding questions include: What other prophets are portrayed ambiguously? What social, ideological, or religious perspective would lead to this kind of depiction of Jeremiah? What are the implications of a "prophet of God" being portrayed in this fashion? (For similar exercises, see §§61, 65, 95.)

Mark Roncace

113. DIAGNOSING EZEKIEL

The dual objective of this exercise is (1) to gain an appreciation for the bizarre and sometimes disturbing images of the book of Ezekiel and (2) to discuss whether madness and divine inspiration are distinguishable states or, rather, are points on a single continuum and thus "in the eye of the beholder."

We begin by discussing mental medical conditions and their characteristics, with a focus on defining and describing such conditions as paranoia, schizophrenia, delusions of grandeur, and hallucination. Sometimes I prepare clipboards with ready-made "diagnoses" made by an imagined predecessor attached to them, which list characteristics of mental illness and instructions such as, "the patient Ezekiel demonstrates signs of sexual perversion, self-destructiveness, self-mutilation, antisocial conduct, excessive revulsion for women, violent tendencies, catatonia, periods of prolonged silence, delusions, and self-aggrandizement—please assess," or, "the patient Ezekiel complains of odd physical symptoms and of receiving divine messages—please assess."

After going over any words or conditions that are unfamiliar, I ask students in small groups to read excerpts from the text of Ezekiel, imagining that these excerpts are the reports of an individual whose mental state is being assessed. Their task is to collect symptoms of and evidence for a diagnosis of mental illness. Excerpts that lend themselves particularly well to this exercise are Ezek 2:9–3:15; 3:24–4:15; 5:1–11; 8:1–14; and 12:1–7. Chapters 16 and 23 can also be used effectively if they are treated as outbursts by Ezekiel. (It is a good idea to prepare students for the obscenity of these chapters.)

After this, the groups each report back to the class and "case notes" are compared. The exercise stimulates careful reading of the texts and, in my experience, drives home the point of how odd and also how disjointed the early chapters of Ezekiel really are.

From here there can flourish an interesting discussion on the similarities and distinctions between mental illness and madness on the one hand and divine inspiration and prophecy on the other. I find this exercise to be an excellent introduction both to psychoanalytical criticism of biblical texts and to discussing such phenomena as claimants of messiah status, such as Shabbetai Zewi in the seventeenth century or, in contemporary times, Vissarion Christ, who considers himself the incarnation of Jesus (see www.vissarion.org and www.wie.org/j23/vissarion.asp). Do we dismiss these people as madmen? If yes, what makes *them* mad but Ezekiel (or Jesus) not mad? *Is* Ezekiel mad? Is the difference purely subjective? Is the deciding criterion whether a person is in fact divinely chosen or sanctioned? Is it simply a matter of what one believes about the legitimacy of the phenomenon of prophecy? Such discussions frequently venture into interesting territory.

Johanna Stiebert

114. EZEKIEL'S INAUGURAL VISION

Much prophetic writing is characterized by bizarre imagery. This is especially true of parts of Ezekiel and of apocalyptic prophecy. I use the following exercise in order to draw students' attention to the magnificence, peculiarity, mystery, and sheer precision and detail of Ezekiel's inaugural vision. The exercise works best with beginner-level groups, can be conducted with small as well as large groups, and serves as an excellent "icebreaker."

After introductory comments about the prophet Ezekiel, his situation of exile in Babylon, and his receiving a vision of God (theophany) in a foreign land, I distribute sheets of blank paper and announce that I am about to ask them to try to draw what Ezekiel purports to have seen in chapter one of the eponymous book. I warn them that the vision is very strange and detailed and that it involves four creatures, four wheels, and above this, God enthroned.

I read Ezek 1:4–28 very slowly. The exercise works even better with some background music—particularly something instrumental and suitably dramatic, such as the readily available soundtrack for *2001: A Space Odyssey*. Meanwhile, the students try to draw what Ezekiel describes. The exercise highlights the incongruous and superbly vivid elements of the vision. It also encourages listening, visualization, and creativity. Students tend to enjoy getting actively involved and delight in swapping and comparing drawings.

Following on this we discuss the sensory features of the vision. How does Ezekiel stimulate the visual and auditory senses? How does movement enliven the vision? What is the effect of the vision on the prophet? Is there evidence of his struggling to accommodate in words what he sees?

Sometimes I show the class artistic renderings of Ezekiel's vision, such as the one from the sixteenth-century *Biblia sacra* and the seventeenth-century Kitto Bible. Both are reproduced in Michael Lieb's *Children of Ezekiel* (Durham: Duke University Press, 1998), 9–10. Finally, I explain that a major focus in Jewish mysticism is experiencing God, or achieving union with God. I point out that Ezekiel's inaugural vision is featured prominently in Jewish mysticism and then invite comments on why this might be. In this way, the inaugural vision can become a useful and concrete starting point for introducing the particularly difficult topic of mysticism.

Johanna Stiebert

115. THE ABUSIVE GOD

The objective of this class is to help students cultivate strategies that deal with the troubling biblical depiction of God as abusive spouse found in Ezek 16 and 23. I have found that this topic is an excellent means to help students understand that all language for God is contextual, growing out of the particular socio-cultural circumstances of its writers. Moreover, this topic may help nurture a healthy hermeneutics of suspicion. Finally, this class provides a good opportunity to convey something of feminist theology's concern for the full humanity of females.

As a first step, students are introduced to the way the biblical text portrays God as an abusive spouse. Students are asked to read the text together in small groups and identify how the metaphor is worked out in the biblical text. Students are then asked to consider how these troubling images would be heard by somebody who is or has been the victim of abuse. In an effort to identify the difficulties involved in using these images, I have fruitfully used an excerpt from the book by David Blumenthal, *Facing the Abusive God* (Louisville: Westminster-John Knox, 1993), which includes correspondence between an anonymous abuse victim, himself, and the theologian Wendy Farley.

At this point, most students realize that the image of God as an abusive spouse is problematic. Many of the students do not even know that this image for God is in the Bible. I ask students what this troubling image for God does to their own image of God. I have found students to be quite upset by this image—particularly as they tend to have a more loving image of God in mind. Students are thus challenged to reconcile these images with the biblical text as God's word.

We then proceed as a class to come up with different strategies for dealing with this problematic image. I ask students to think about the advice they would give to a friend who stumbles across these pages. Some students may want to explain the problem away, saying that this image is just a metaphor, or that the punishment is justified on account of the woman's adulterous behavior. It would be important to identify the difficulty with both of these justifications. Feminist theologians like Elisabeth Johnson argue that images for God are not peripheral or innocent, but function in "social and personal life to sustain or critique certain structures, values, and ways of acting" (*She Who Is: The Mystery of God in Feminist Theological Discourse* [New York: Crossroad, 1992], 36). Thus the images we use for God are exceedingly important as they may affect the way we think and act—in this instance creating an environment in which violence against women is acceptable. Moreover, to justify the abuse due to the behavior of the women could be considered a case of "blaming the victim."

Students are encouraged to understand something of the socio-historical and literary context in which this image occurs (cf. the secondary reading in the essays on Hosea and Ezekiel in the *Women's Bible Commentary* [ed. C. Newsom and S. Ringe: Louisville: Westminster-John Knox, 1992] and, more generally, Renita Weems, *Battered Love: Marriage, Sex, and Violence in the Hebrew Prophets* [Minneapolis: Fortress, 1995]). It is important for students to understand that the image of God as abusive spouse arose out of a patriarchal context governed by a different set of values concerning women.

Students are further encouraged to think about whether this troubling image should be used today. This is a good opportunity to introduce the notion of a hermeneutics of suspicion. It may well be that some troubling images like the one of God as abusive spouse are irredeemable, and that we may want to look for alternative metaphors that better express the theological message of Ezekiel.

Toward the end of the class, it may be worthwhile to inform students about the reality of domestic violence. It is particularly important for college-age students who are entering into new relationships to be aware of the persisting reality of domestic violence. Raising awareness is even more important in a seminary setting, in light of the fact that pastors often have to recognize victims of domestic violence. Helpful statistics are to be found on the Rape, Abuse and Incest Network website (www.rainn.org).

L. Juliana M. Claassens

116. HOSEA MEETS HANK WILLIAMS

For a class session on the "marriage metaphor" in an upper-level course on Israelite prophecy, I have students read biblical passages that present the metaphor, especially Hos 1–3. I also have them read Renita Weems' "Gomer: Victim of Violence or Victim of Metaphor?" (*Semeia* 47 [1989]: 87–104). This article prepares them to think about the ways metaphors work. In class discussion, I try to develop all the various ramifications of using marriage as a comparison—what can marriage "mean"? And, in light of the answers to that question, how does the marriage metaphor characterize God/Hosea and Israel/Gomer?

I then provide a second treatment of an unfaithful female and forgiving male: Hank Williams' "You Win Again." The lyrics to this song are available online (www.asklyrics.com). Williams' rendition of the song, in that voice crackling with intensely emotional self-pity, is available on a number of CDs and over the Internet in MP3 form. The song relates the narrator's musings to himself regarding his significant other who has been "a runnin' 'round," including protestations of pity for the man she is currently with, who will soon experience her deceit. Despite this mistreatment, the narrator admits that he cannot do anything but love her: "I just can't go, you win again."

This song presents an alternative view of a man fully committed to a relationship with a wayward woman, but in this case the power equation is completely different. The woman controls the man's emotions so completely that the man cannot take action. Discussing this song leads students to see the correspondences with the story of Hosea/God and provides, in a sense, an alternate explanation for their "mercy" regarding Gomer/Israel. I use Isa 54:7–8 as an especially apt parallel to Williams' lyric: "For a brief moment I abandoned you, but with great compassion I will gather you. In overflowing wrath for a moment I hid my face from you, but with everlasting love I will have compassion on you, says the Lord, your Redeemer." Hearing Deutero-Isaiah after Williams' song changes students' readings of the metaphor. In short, Hank Williams raises the question of power in the text. I believe this then provides insight into how Hosea (and the other prophets) may be at some pains to prevent their metaphor from being read as if it were this song. This may explain, at least in part, the violence of the metaphor: the violence tips the balance of power back toward the (captured?) male.

Donald C. Polaski

117. AMOS AND "ECONOMIC JUSTICE FOR ALL"

I have students read excerpts from the U. S. Catholic Bishops' 1986 Pastoral Letter, "Economic Justice for All," in concert with the book of Amos, an idea suggested to me by my colleague Carleen Mandolfo. I find that having students read at least parts of both documents helps them to reflect on the context, style, and implications of Amos's critique of eighth-century Israelite society. Students should read, at a minimum, Amos

1:1–2; 2:6–8; 3:1–2, 13-15; 4:1–6:7; 6:14; and 8:4–12. In class, we discuss the imagery and references in the text (e.g., economic injustice, debt slavery, bribery) and attempt to reckon with Amos's argument that piety divorced from justice is worthless.

Once students have encountered Amos's approach and the historical-political context out of which his message arose, we talk about the 1986 Bishops' Letter, a major publication in its own right. The bishops call for a "new American experiment" in which the economy would be viewed as a moral issue. They bring attention to the widening gap between rich and poor both in the United States and around the world, and they urge American Catholics to reflect on the biblical and theological resources of Catholic Social Teaching as they seek to live as faithful people in the context of modern economic realities. The invitation to dialogue and partnership is extended to non-Catholics as well; everyone is encouraged to work together to seek justice in the marketplace. Although the document and the statistics are dated, I still find that the text is useful, inasmuch as students can analyze how the bishops thought through a particular problem and how they sought to speak to a diverse group of potential readers. Copies of "Economic Justice for All" are easily located on the web (http://www.osjspm.org/cst/eja.htm). The entire document is huge; I cut and paste together my own eleven-page handout of excerpts that seems to work fairly well (including the introduction, theological rationale, and some of the policy recommendations).

I ask students to reflect, before they come to class (and often on our course's online discussion board), what they find to be the most significant themes or concepts in the document. Moreover, I ask them to compare the Bishops' Letter with Amos. In what ways are the documents similar? How are they different? I have students consider style and tone, major themes, images of God and God's people, and the historical context out of which the texts seem to arise. Finally, I ask students to be prepared to share their own reactions to and assessment of the Bishops' Letter, with their reasoning.

During class, I may divide students into small groups and ask them to share their reflections prior to a large group discussion. Students often have widely different responses to the material. Many prefer the gentler tone of "Economic Justice for All" to the acerbic Amos. Some find the Bishops' Letter highly persuasive and appealing; others find the bishops' case to be hopelessly idealistic and unrealistic. Wonderful discussions can grow out of this variety. We can wrestle with questions of social location, hermeneutics, economics, and politics. We can consider ways in which religious faith and the public sphere intersect. Perhaps most importantly with regard to Amos, we can ponder the challenge that economics is to be understood as a moral issue. We discuss the way in which the bishops seem to place a higher premium on what they see as God's value system than they do on the feasibility of implementing a particular policy. In the end, they suggest that doing what is right is more important than doing what is possible. Whether or not one agrees with the bishops, it is worthwhile to make sure students see that practicality is not their primary concern.

As a non-Catholic professor teaching at a Catholic institution, incorporating the Bishops' Letter assists me in linking biblical content and themes with a larger confessional tradition. Ultimately, using Amos and "Economic Justice for All" allows the class to consider not only moral questions regarding the economy, the common good, and so forth, but doing so allows students to consider how they "hear" such texts. Many find "Economic Justice for All" to be offensive. This exercise helps them imagine how ancient Israelites might have "heard" Amos as well.

Michael Barram

118. PREACHING AMOS: THE RHETORIC OF AMOS 1:3–2:16

The rhetorical form and performance of a text shapes its meaning. By performing a text, a teacher can bring to life textual dynamics and effects that otherwise might be missed in the secondary literature. The idea of this exercise is to get students to understand how rhetoric affects the meaning of the biblical text in general and one of Amos's judgment oracles (Amos 1:3–2:16) in particular.

At the beginning of class, I provide a map that has the geographical locations mentioned within the oracle. As we look at the text of Amos 1:3–2:16, I encourage the students to follow along with the map so that they can trace the circuitous movement of the prophet's geographical references. I read the text as a revivalist preacher, and I ask the students to be an interactive congregation of Israel, encouraging them to boo and hiss when other nations are mentioned and to give a hearty "Amen!" or "Preach it!" when judgment is proclaimed on their enemies. When reading the text, one must allow for dramatic pauses so that the students can chime in with their responses. Below is a sample interaction using Amos 1:3–5 (NRSV):

Teacher:	"Thus says the LORD: For three transgressions of Damascus ... (pause)
Students:	(Chorus of booing and hissing)

Teacher:	"… and for four, I WILL NOT REVOKE THE PUNISH-MENT!" (pause)
Students:	(Responses of "Amen," "Preach it," "Speak," etc.)
Teacher:	"Because they have threshed Gilead with threshing sledges of iron." (pause)
Students:	(Boos and hissing)
Teacher:	"SO I will send a fire on the house of Hazael, and it shall devour the strongholds of Ben-hadad (building cadence). I will break the gate bars of Damascus, and cut off the inhabitants from the Valley of Aven, and the one who holds the scepter from Beth-Eden (cadence and volume reach crescendo); AND THE PEOPLE OF ARAM SHALL GO INTO EXILE TO KIR, SAYS THE LORD!"
Students:	(By this time, the students are responding loudly and affirmatively.)
Teacher:	And all God's people said …
All:	"AMEN!"

It is not necessary to write out a script for the reading and response. The students will catch on quickly. Usually the key to an effective performance is tied to the teacher's willingness to preach with conviction and good cadence, allowing well-timed pauses for the congregation of students to respond.

When Amos finally makes his way to Judah and Israel in the last two movements of the text, the point of the prophet's rhetoric becomes clear. Usually the students' reaction to Amos's judgment on Judah is mixed. Some of the students find themselves booing and hissing louder and more vigorously, and some of them are responding half-heartedly. At this point, I pause to explain that a mixed response is appropriate since Judah's proximity to Israel makes the hatred for this enemy more intense and conflicted. The closeness of Judah also suggests that Amos's words are hitting near to home, literally. By the time that v. 6 is read, describing Yahweh's judgment on Israel, the audience has fallen silent, and Amos's rhetorical point is heard loudly and clearly. I follow up the sermon with a brief discussion of how Amos's rhetorical gesture affects the meaning of his message. I also discuss how the performance of a text—whether it be sung, preached, read dramatically, or prayed through—can greatly affect the text's meaning.

Frank M. Yamada

119. JONAH AND A NEW PAIR OF GLASSES: AN INTRODUCTION TO HERMENEUTICS AND HUMILITY

To establish an atmosphere of curiosity, I eschew the usual pedagogical comfort food of first-day-of-term protocol, such as the distribution of syllabi and the reading of the professorial riot act about daily preparation, and turn immediately to the matter of hermeneutics. Not hermeneutics per se, of course, but the matter of critical self-awareness about the assumptions and expectations we bring to the text. From the start, I attempt to present in a dramatic way one of the clear purposes of the course: to let students know that they will need to give up many of the childhood ways of reading the Bible they may have inherited and begin in earnest to read it as university-educated adults.

To this end, class begins with a simple oral association quiz: Adam and ____; Sarah and ____; Mary and ____; etc. The quiz concludes with "Jonah and the ____." This leads to the question, "Why is the fish so important?"

While administering this quiz—and throughout the class period—I employ a gimmick, pure and simple. I begin, without explanation, to switch glasses every few minutes—from cool sunglasses to nerdy glasses with black tape to kids' rose-colored glasses to safety glasses (the big, clunky ones that carpenters wear) to real reading glasses. This activity continues throughout the remaining portion of the class period.

The students are then given the task of studying Jonah—printed on a single page—in small groups. They are asked to look for key themes, prominent figures, major character contrasts, as if they were reading the book for the first time (which, of course, many will be). When the students return to the large group, I—all the while exchanging glasses without explanation—briefly elicit several observations from the students, such as: how little the fish features in the story in comparison with sailors and the other animals; how rote Jonah's prayer is in its quotation of the psalms but how impoverished it is; how Jonah is self-absorbed, unwilling to face his mistake, and unable to take responsibility; how little Jonah himself repents, how petulant he remains after his experience in the fish, and how laconic his speech is ("yet forty days, Nineveh destroyed"); how overwhelming the response of his enemies, the Ninevites, is by comparison; even how responsive the animals (the fish, the worm, the animals) and plant life (the vine) are in comparison with Jonah.

All of these observations are preparatory to the most significant observation of all: the climax of the story occurs in chapter 4. This raises the pivotal question of the entire class period: Why have we heard so much about the fish and so little about chapter 4?

The answer to this question, which occupies us throughout the term, lies in two realizations which I hope the students will grasp. First, students must realize that the disproportionate attention paid to the association of "Jonah and the fish" has its roots as far back as their proverbial mothers' knees in the children's Bibles that may have been read to them—children's Bibles that reflect popular but errant construals of Jonah. To make this point cogently, it is extremely useful to sit on a chair in the middle of the room and read from three or four children's Bibles, all of which, of course, focus upon the fish story. This can be followed by the highly imaginative scene of Jonah's alleged conversion in the belly of the fish in the Veggie Tale film, *Jonah and the Big Fish.* The second realization to which students ought to come is that the unwitting and inappropriate focus upon the fish may be due to its benign nature as a delightful miracle of happy rescue; the fish story hardly evokes the personal discomfort that the final chapter does, in which Jonah's selfishness, petulance, and ethnocentricity (4:2–3) may well mirror a reader's own.

It is at this point that I finally explain the glasses. Glasses, of course, represent the hermeneutical lenses that readers have inherited and adopted. The various glasses illustrate various lenses. Sunglasses, for example, can be made to represent the tendency to shield the reader from the harsh self-revelations that may transpire in the reading of Jonah's true character. Safety goggles reflect the tendency of the reader to protect him or herself from the global sweep of Jonah—with its clear appreciation for the pagan sailors, for Ninevah, for the vine, even for the compliant worm and, in the tale's last line, the animals for which God cares. The lessons of the glasses, of course, can be extended to accommodate as many pairs as the instructor can collect. The theme of putting off inherited childhood perspectives can be brought up daily during the successive weeks of the course. During those moments at which students become uncomfortable with my interpretations, I explain that this may be a difference in lenses rather than my effort to launch an overt challenge to the Bible. And as the case of Jonah shows, the lenses of biblical scholars are not infrequently more biblical than those of their students.

John R. Levison

120. JONAH: HOW THE BIBLE TELLS A GREAT STORY

This exercise uses the book of Jonah to sharpen students' awareness of the literary features of biblical stories. The story of Jonah is familiar to many students, making this an exercise that can pique students' interest, because as they perform it they learn new details and recognize new angles in a story they thought they knew.

I begin by discussing characterization, setting, and plot as features of narrative. Characterization, I say, can be found by looking at the way a character is described, his or her actions, and the contrasts between characters. Setting has to do with geography and time as well as mood—if put in terms of a play, it would encompass the costumes, the set, and the lighting. Plot is, of course, the "action." Then, I have students read Jonah as homework and ask them to make a page of notes on how characterization, setting, and plot work in the book.

At the beginning of the next class, I collect on the board students' general impressions about each category. Common reactions to the book include the idea that Jonah is characterized as stubborn, afraid, and bitter, and that the sailors and the people of Nineveh are surprisingly good and faithful to God. Readers usually recognize that the setting is dramatic— the big storm and the large city of Nineveh stand out—and that the plot moves rather quickly. I then attempt to organize and re-cap the discussion by offering some keywords that, not coincidentally, all begin with the letter "H." Sometimes I give them the "H" words and ask them to comment on how they relate to Jonah. On rare occasions, if I think the group is up to it, I simply announce that I have five "H" words that can sum up the discussion of Jonah and let students see if they can figure out what the words are. Of course, they usually come up with many "H" words that are not on my list, which often leads to interesting discussions I had not anticipated.

Drawing on the students' own observations, I argue that *heathens* are key to characterization in Jonah. Of course, I use this term with tongue firmly in cheek, but its point is that in Jonah, the contrast between non-Yahweh worshippers and Jonah, Yahweh's prophet, is shown in strong relief. Jonah tries to run away and to get himself killed in order to avoid doing what God wants, while the heathens recognize God's sovereignty and power by praying to this foreign god and willingly undertaking repentance for their sins. This point can also be an entrée into the *history* of the book, that is, its likely emergence at a time when ancient Israel and Judah were faced with domination by foreigners who worshipped other, and seemingly more powerful, gods.

The setting and mood, as most classes note, is overdrawn, or *huge*. To quote the NRSV, the wind in the story is "great," the storm is "mighty," the fish is "large," Nineveh was "an exceedingly large city," the king of Nineveh decrees that the people "shall cry mightily to God," and, at the end, Jonah is "angry enough to die." I note here that language and word choice help create this setting, and I add a few specific examples from the *Hebrew*. The potential double-entendre of Nineveh's description as '*iyr gedôlah le'lohiym* (3:3) is lost in translation, and I encourage the class to come up with another description. Also, the Hebrew word *hašab*, used when the boat "thinks" it will break up, makes the boat itself a character and contributes to what one might call the fantastical setting of the action.

Finally, I contend that the characterization, the overdrawn setting, and the fast pace of the story combine to offer a story that is full of *humor* but uses this humor to point readers to *hard questions*. It is difficult not to smile when the first verse of chapter three dryly repeats the beginning of 1:1, only after Jonah has been through much calamity and has been vomited up by a fish. Students also pick up on the absurdity of Nineveh's animals repenting in sackcloth, Jonah's waiting for the city's destruction and pouting about the city's redemption, and God's toying with Jonah through the bush and the worm. Nevertheless, both the last verse of the book and the entire story ask readers to consider God's relationship and response to people not of their own religion, as well as their own personal responses to God, and these questions can engender thought-provoking discussion.

Megan Bishop Moore

121. "GO STRAIGHT TO SHEOL!": A DISCOVERY EXERCISE ON SHEOL USING JONAH 2

Most of my beginning-level students enter class biblically illiterate, yet confident that they know what is and is not true about the Bible. I teach in a Christian liberal arts college where the majority of students are "churched," which means that most have to unlearn a lot before they begin to read the Bible to see what it actually says—not what they want it to say. Nearly all have some sort of belief that everything in the Bible is consistent with everything else in the Bible. They have no concept of intra-canonical dialogue, and this hampers their ability to take each book's content seriously. Getting them past this mindset requires finesse. If, for example, early on in the semester, I lecture about how beliefs concerning afterlife develop and change as one progresses through Scripture, many students will write me off as "another one of those liberal professors." However, if they see these same things for themselves, they view it as a challenge and are stimulated by it.

Jonah is the first story that I have students read in my "Introduction to Biblical Studies" course. I choose this brief narrative because it works very well in getting them to look for plot and character traits instead of trying to interpret verses in isolation from context. As we discuss the story of this stubborn, bigoted prophet, I lightheartedly ask, "If you were thrown into a raging sea and were swallowed by a huge fish, when would you start to pray?" Of course, they throw out comments like "Immediately, if not sooner" or "I would have been praying long before I got pitched overboard." Then I ask, "How long was it before Jonah began to pray?" They look at the text, laugh at what they see, and then we analyze the prayer in Jonah 2: "Then Jonah prayed to the Lord his God from the belly of the fish, saying, 'I called to the Lord out of my distress, and he answered me; out of the belly of Sheol I cried, and you heard my voice. . . . I went down to the land whose bars closed upon me forever; yet you brought up my life from the Pit, O Lord my God'" (NRSV).

At this point, I begin a discussion of Sheol. Usually no one in class has a clue about Sheol, so this gives me a chance to help them do a bit of detective work. I put them into small groups and give the following directions: "I want you to look up these passages in your Bibles and answer the following questions: (1) What is Sheol? (In other words, what characteristics does it have?) (2) Where is Sheol located? and (3) Who goes to Sheol? Consult Num 16:30; Ps 6:4–5; 30:9; 88:3-6, 10–12; 89:48; 94:17; 115:17; Job 3:13, 17–19; 7:9–10; 10:20–21; 16:22; Eccl 9:2-6, 10; Isa 5:14; 14:9; 26:14; Jonah 2:2, 6."

As the students read these passages, they almost always begin by trying to interpret Sheol in light of their own understandings of heaven and hell. Of course, this does not work, and they get agitated. I let them struggle along in their groups and voice their objections to each other's ideas. Then we discuss their findings as a whole group. By letting students explore on their own this strange new thought world that includes Sheol, I help them begin to see that they need to take biblical scholarship seriously. They typically leave class full of questions, and conversations about Sheol and heaven and hell continue beyond the classroom.

Michael R. Cosby

122. THE MANY VOICES OF PROPHECY (MICAH 6)

This exercise seeks to enhance students' appreciation for prophetic literature by illustrating the interplay of the divine voice, the prophet's voice, and the voices of the people in typical preexilic oracles. A choral reading of Mic 6 by the class is the primary vehicle for exploring this interplay. This approach to prophetic literature helps to advance students' understanding of prophecy beyond the ideas of simply predicting the future or condemning sin, and opens up the possibility of discussing the liturgical, social, and literary aspects of the prophetic phenomenon. This session works best if students are familiar with the idea that the prophets were God's representatives to the king and people of Israel and Judah.

First, have a student volunteer read Mic 6 aloud, straight through. Ask the class whose voice they heard in the text. Several answers (Yahweh, Micah, perhaps the people) are possible. Suggest, if necessary, that there are several voices present in the oracle as preserved.

Next, distribute a "script" version of the chapter to each student. Each script should be marked "Micah," "Yahweh," or "People." Distribute these voices as you see fit, typically one "Micah," one "Yahweh," and the rest "People" (though there are interesting discussion possibilities inherent in the assignment of multiple voices for Yahweh). Each script should have the lines spoken by that "character" in bold or highlighted. Micah speaks vv. 1a, 2, and 8; Yahweh speaks vv. 1b and 3–5; and the people speak vv. 6 and 7. Have the class read through the script, each reading aloud their assigned parts. Encourage as much expression in the reading as possible. This can be facilitated by minimal staging of the "performance," with the "People" grouped together, "Yahweh" seated on high (perhaps atop a desk or table) and "Micah" standing between them.

Discussion may begin by asking students to articulate the differences between their reactions to the first, solo reading of the chapter and the choral reading. Often, student responses here will be enough to drive the rest of the discussion. If needed, possible discussion topics include: insights gained into the character of prophecy as performance or "street theater"; the relationship between the prophetic books and the actual proclamation of the prophets; the liturgical elements of the oracle, with connections to the use of prophetic texts in general, and Mic 6 in particular, in various worship traditions; the dynamic between the words spoken by God in the text and the character of the whole text as "the Word of God"; and the implications of various options for "casting" the voice of Yahweh (male or female, solo or multiple, etc.).

D. Matthew Stith

123. TITHING IN MALACHI 3

Whether it is politics, history, or religion, readers are often not inclined to ask about the social location of the writer and the possible interests served by the writer's words. While all texts should not and cannot be reduced to socio-economic concerns, those concerns are often present in one way or another. Learning to interpret biblical texts critically involves

asking key questions about such concerns. Can the writer's social location be discerned from the text, and does the text serve the
socio-economic interests of the writer? When these interests are
addressed, how do they affect the situation of the writer and the writer's
audience? A look at tithing in Mal 3 affords an opportunity to consider
some of these questions.

In a class on Malachi, after discussing the prophet's setting in the
Second Temple period, I note how almost every section of the book
touches on temple worship in some way. There are many references to
"priests," "the altar," "offering," "sacrifice," and "revere/reverence."
Malachi is very concerned with covenant faithfulness, especially as it is
expressed in temple worship. Malachi chastises the priests for unfaithful temple service and the people for a lack of devotion to the temple.
Although Malachi criticizes the priests (1:6–2:9; 3:3), the writer is sympathetic with the position of the priests and advocates obedience to the
covenant of Levi (2:4, 8). Toward the end of the book's disputations,
Malachi uses the rhetorically effective claim that the people are "robbing" God. And how are they robbing God? They are robbing God by
not giving tithes and offerings to the temple (3:8–12). The writer is calling for the people to be faithful to the law that required giving a tenth of
all produce as a temple tax, which supports the priesthood and may
also support charity for the poor (cf. Lev 27:30–33; Num 18:21–24; Deut
14:22–29).

With these textual observations in mind, ask students to consider the
following questions: What is the probable social location of this writer?
How does the writer know about priestly misbehavior? How does he
know that some are oppressing the poor? How does he know sufficient
tithes are not coming in to support the temple? Whose interests are
served by the tithe requirement? Why do you think the law required a
tenth? Why not more or less? If people are not consistently giving a tenth
to the temple, why do you think that was the case? Is it possible that the
average family leader in Judah at this time cannot afford to give a tenth of
his produce? Is the requirement of a tenth reasonable for everyone? Do
some have a greater ability to pay than others in Judah? Is the tenth a
"flat tax" that overburdens some in Judah? Would it be fairer to allow the
poor to give less than a tenth? What are the tensions between equity and
efficiency when a tenth is required for everyone? Is it reasonable to ask
these questions of this ancient text?

If one is teaching students preparing for service in particular religious communities, one can ask further questions: How is Mal 3 used in
contemporary religious communities? Considering the modern economic context, how should Mal 3 and similar passages be used? In our
modern income-based society versus an ancient agricultural society, is

the requirement of a tenth for everyone equitable? What do you know about modern debates regarding proportional taxes, progressive taxes, and regressive taxes? How should these debates inform our thinking on these questions?

These kinds of questions should create a great deal of discussion and debate, and it should help students think about the real life situations of both writer and audience in the original ancient context as well as issues of appropriation in modern contexts. (For another exercise on tithing, see §76.)

Joseph F. Scrivner

H
E
B
R
E
W

B
I
B
L
E

Writings

124. CREATIVE WRITING AND INTERPRETING BIBLICAL POETRY

Almost all beginning students of the Bible—and many advanced students—struggle with understanding Hebrew poetry. When I taught an undergraduate Bible survey class, I noticed that semester after semester, student comprehension dropped off once the curriculum moved from the narrative to the poetic material of the Old Testament. The first part of this lesson uses creative writing to introduce basic features of biblical poetry.

This lesson assumes that the students understand the basic nature of Hebrew parallelism. To afford students this basic knowledge, I begin class with a mini-lecture on basic features and theories of parallelism (cf. Adele Berlin, "Introduction to Hebrew Poetry," *NIB* 4:301–15). Following this presentation, I ask the students to try their hand at writing some poetic phrases. Using a data projector or a blackboard, I supply the first phrase (or "A phrase") from a number of different psalm verses and I direct the students to write the second phrase (or "B phrase"). Here are some examples of verse a teacher might use for this exercise: "I will sing of loyalty and of justice" (101:1a); "Moses and Aaron were among his priests" (99:6a); "My heart is steadfast, O God, my heart is steadfast" (108:1a).

After letting the students try their hands a few times at writing just the "B phrase" of a verse, I then give them a few opportunities to see an entire verse and ask them to compose a verse that might follow. Again, here are some examples:

"Gilead is mine; Manasseh is mine;
    Ephraim is my helmet; Judah is my scepter" (108:8).

"Those who trust in the Lord are like Mount Zion,
    which cannot be moved, but abides forever" (125:1).

As I do this exercise, I give a few students a chance to read their work out loud. Some students are eager to do so, while others are horrified at the thought. I have to remind the students continually that the idea is not to get the right answer but to understand the nature of Hebrew poetry. After a few students have tried each example, I then show them the actual verse as it exists in the Bible, and—this is critical!—we then discuss how the poetry of the actual verse functions. Through this exercise, I have found that students gain a much clearer conception of the literature that they are reading, and thus they are better equipped to interpret it.

Toward the end of a term, I use a similar exercise and direct students to write their own psalm. I give them two lists: one consists of poetic devices commonly found in the psalms (such as chiasm, repetition, refrains, abstract for concrete, metaphors and similes, inclusio, poetic reversals, etc.) and the other consists of the common psalm genres (lament, praise, etc.). I direct students to write a psalm—they must pick one of the genres and must include at least five different poetic devices. Volunteers then read their psalms and the class is asked to identify the genre, describe the poetry of the psalm, and discuss its meaning. Neither of these exercises is graded, but each exercise affords students the opportunity to inhabit basic concepts that are crucial to interpreting the psalms.

Rolf Jacobson

125. SEARCHING THROUGH THE PSALMS

A great deal of work has been done in recent decades concerning the organization and development of Psalms as a book. This activity leads a classroom of undergraduate students on a process of discovery that will allow them to make significant observations about the structure of the book of Psalms.

I begin the lesson with a brief explanation of the titles at the beginning of most of the psalms. Using the first four or five psalms as examples, I illustrate to the class that some psalms, like 1 and 2, do not have titles, but most of the psalms, like 3 and 4, do. Some English editions of the Bible have added captions at the beginning of each psalm, so these must be carefully distinguished from the titles that are actually part of the psalm text, usually presented in small print just below the psalm number. Some psalm titles are longer than others, but most contain a phrase like "A Song (or Psalm or *Maskil*) of _____." This is the feature upon which I want students to focus. In the case of Ps 3, "David" is the name that fills the blank. Often, but not always, the blank is filled by a name. We do not know who produced and placed the titles, or when they did it, but these titles have become part of the vast majority of the biblical psalms. In the

Hebrew text, the title is usually numbered as the first verse. Our English verse one is then verse two in the Hebrew text.

Next, I ask each student to select randomly a number between 1 and 50, a second number between 51 and 100, and a third number between 101 and 150 and to write these numbers down. I then divide the chalkboard into three columns with those numerical headings. I ask each student to look up the psalms corresponding to the three numbers they have randomly chosen and find the name or word that fills in the phrase "A Song of _____" in the title. They are then to go to the board and write in the appropriate column the number of the psalm followed by the name or word. With my class of about twenty-five students, that will mean that about seventy-five psalms, half the Psalter, will be represented in the sample on the board

The next step requires dividing the class into groups of five students each. Ask the class if they notice any patterns in the lists of names and words that appear on the board. They should notice that certain groups or sequences of psalms contain the same title. Assign each group one or two of the names that appear on the lists and ask them to look carefully through the whole book to find the precise boundaries of each of these sequences. Once each group has finished its work, they should send a representative to the board to write down the sequences they have found. The resulting list should include the following: 3–41 (except for 10 and 33)—David; 42–49 (except 43)—Korahites (or the sons of Korah); 51–71 (with a couple of exceptions)—David; 73–83—Asaph; 120–134—Ascents.

When this list is finished, ask the groups to look at the psalms that are not included in any of these sequences to see what their titles say. Record their observations on the board. Ask the groups to discuss among themselves what these patterns might indicate. While they are in discussion, record the five book division of the book of Psalms on the board. After a few minutes, ask the groups for their conclusions and record them on the board.

Using all of the data that has now been collected, the class can now address some of the following questions. What might the process of the formation of the book of Psalms have been like? How does the five book division of Psalms compare to the title sequences that have been observed? Where do the unusual psalm titles, such as those containing Moses and Solomon, appear? What does it mean that there are multiple David sequences, especially in light of the final statement in Ps 72?

Mark McEntire

126. IMAGERY AND THE PSALMS

The psalms do not simply speak their meaning, they paint it. In order to interpret the psalms, the interpreter must be equipped with the capacity to unfold the possibilities of the images, metaphors, and similes of the Psalter: The righteous are likes trees planted by water (Ps 1); the Lord is a shepherd (Ps 23); the praying believer is like a weaned child with her mother (Ps 131). But modern and postmodern readers are not used to exercising their imaginations on images. Most of the images that we encounter are already digested for us by some visual media. So interpreters must be taught to knead the textual dough with their imaginations so that the images rise and give life. This lesson outlines a two-part exercise in how to work with a psalm's imagery.

The first part of the exercise is to assign students the task of drawing or painting a psalm. The instructions that I give are intentionally cursory: "Draw a picture of Ps 8, in as much detail as possible." I use Ps 8 because it is brief yet overflows with imagery. The reason I give only curt directions is that I want to refrain from shaping the students' drawings as much as possible. Some students always ask for more direction, which they are immediately denied. The only exception to this rule has been when I worked with undergraduate students and required them to include at least five elements from the psalm in their drawings. I have asked students to do this work in class, but results have been much more spectacular when students get to work on this at home. (One regular outcome of this exercise is that a student reports that they worked on the project with a child, whose interpretation differed from that of the parent, which then led to great discussion.)

In class, I divide the students up into groups and direct them to describe one at a time how the drawings are visual interpretations of the psalm in question. I have to reinforce constantly with the students that the point is not to create a quality drawing, but to begin to think about the drawings as visual interpretations of the psalms. I ask them to think about which elements of the psalm were foregrounded and which left out? Were there concepts or symbols that the artists introduced that were anachronistic or foreign to the world of the authors? Did the picture present the psalm using linear thought or more random thought? Back in the large group, a few students are given the opportunity to show the work of one of the other group members and describe what the picture taught them about the psalm. This exercise can be augmented by the professor showing paintings, stained-glass windows, and other visual images of different psalms. Similarly, I often stop when a particular psalm evokes an image and ask students to close their eyes and picture the tree of Ps 1, the child of Ps 131, and so on.

A second exercise that I have used to help students learn to interact with the visual images of the psalms involves movies. Psalm 23 is heard in many movies. I often use scenes from two Westerns—*Rooster Cogburn* and *Pale Rider*. In *Rooster Cogburn*, Katherine Hepburn's character stands before the movie's antagonist. As he threatens her, she confidently recites Ps 23 as if the words themselves could turn away bullets. In *Pale Rider*, an adolescent girl named Meghan carries the corpse of her dog, which has been killed by the movie's antagonists. Kneeling over the grave, she mournfully prays parts of Ps 23—between each petition, she speaks a word of prayer. I then lead a discussion in which students are asked to comment on the psalm's use in these scenes.

These two exercises allow students the chance both to exercise their own imaginations and criticize the imaginations of other interpreters. One benefit of this exercise is that it appeals to students who are visual learners rather than verbal learners. When I employ such exercises, it almost never fails that students who have been quiet in class up to that point in the semester are turned on and continue to participate for the remainder of the term.

Rolf Jacobson

127. PSALM 13 AND PSALMS OF LAMENT

A one-semester introduction to the Bible leaves little time to study the Writings in general much less the book of Psalms in particular, a constraint that usually contrasts with students' level of interest in and knowledge of the psalms, at least relative to other portions of the canon. If more than one day is not available for the book of Psalms, the professor can provide a hand-out that offers a general overview of the historical, canonical, religious, and form-critical questions of psalm study. The majority of the class session may then be given to interpreting an individual psalm. In light of their prevalence, I focus on lament psalms as a way of putting students in touch with the biblical text.

I use Ps 13 as the paradigmatic example of a psalm of lament. Scholars have identified the basic elements of the biblical lament form in different ways; your course's introductory text book will probably mention some of these elements: address to God; complaint about circumstances; petition (usually stated in imperative form); some justifying clause to motivate God; an expression of trust; a word or vow of praise. Students first work individually, identifying these elements in Ps 13 and comparing them to a few short individual laments (e.g. Pss 3; 4; 6) on handouts I provide, from texts like the NIV or NRSV. Students then look for key repetitions, literary structure, expressions of emotion, and so on. By placing the text on an overhead transparency, I am able to highlight these features as the whole class identifies and discusses them.

We also explore the ways in which contemporary cultures continue to have forms of lament prayer and to what extent this is true in Western culture. I play the song "Bring Him Home" from the Broadway production of *Les Miserables* and ask the students to draw comparisons and contrasts to the biblical lament form. It may in fact be helpful to place the lyrics on an overhead projector. Some elements will be easily identifiable from the opening line: "God on high" (address); "hear my prayer" (petition); "in my need, you have always been there" (trust or motivation). Students usually call attention to musical features like tempo that add to the pathos. They may also notice the absence of the traditional vow of praise, a factor that points to the special character of Hebrew lament and Claus Westermann's observation about the Psalter in general moving from lament to praise.

Such similarities and differences with our own forms of personal prayer generally raise questions of theological interpretation. I ask students to work in groups on two questions: (1) What theological insights into Hebrew faith are gained from the fact that the largest group of psalms are in the lament genre? (2) Does our culture have opportunity for and examples of community lament? Depending on the institutional context, it may be possible to explore more specific religious practices, such as the liturgical use of the Psalter. Then, too, students may wish to discuss expressions of lament in the New Testament, such as Jesus' words from the cross or prayers of the early church in the book of Acts.

James K. Mead

128. LAMENT PSALMS

In *Spirituality of the Psalms* (Minneapolis: Fortress, 2002), Walter Brueggemann discusses the Psalms in three categories: "orientation" (full of confidence in the reliability of God's good creation and God's just rule), "disorientation" (expressing the hurt, anger, feelings of betrayal, and questions that surface when the orderliness and goodness of the world are not being experienced), and "new orientation" (when disorientation yields to healing, a fuller understanding, and a renewal of relationship). Brueggemann points to the lament psalms as expressing "disorientation" and discusses their spiritual direction and structural components.

In this exercise, students, working in groups, are assigned to identify a contemporary "psalm" of disorientation to present to the rest of the class. Their presentation is to demonstrate the disorientation and to identify the audience and the purpose of the lament. Each member of the group is also to turn in a written analysis of their "psalm." The write-up gives each student equal opportunity to present an analysis of their "psalm" since they will divide up the tasks in making the presentation.

Students enjoy this assignment because they can draw from their own culture and can count on many of the other students in the class being familiar with the material they will present. For the instructor it offers a crash course in pop culture. Requiring students to inform the instructor of their topics in advance prevents duplication and allows the instructor to be prepared. The uncensored language in some contemporary expressions of disorientation provides an occasion for discussing the frankness of language in the biblical laments and room for such frankness in contemporary worship and religious life.

The examples students choose vary widely. In the mix, typically, are songs appealing to lovers who have walked out on a partner and rap songs raging against individuals, institutions, and social or economic systems. Some groups present websites that are collective expressions of grieving, others present art that visualizes suffering (e.g., the works of Frida Kahlo), and others scenes from films that capture the anguish heard in the laments. One student shared a poem she had written at the trial of the man who had murdered one of her relatives. Students have examined web-blogs as a new media for expressing disorientation. Sometimes the laments are less familiar to the class as a whole—such as those appealing for relief from oppression in South Africa or other parts of the world— providing an opportunity for students to see the power of lament to sustain hope in seemingly hopeless times.

Because the assignment is to bring in a contemporary "psalm" of disorientation, not every example fits the definition of a lament. In their presentations students will generally identify the elements of a lament psalm (e.g., address, complaint, plea, motivation, imprecations, praise) that they see represented in their example. That turns out to be very useful in helping students become familiar with the parts of a lament psalm and understand those components. If a group has mislabeled a part of their "psalm," other members of the class will question it. The discussion that results can provide the instructor insight into how the students are understanding what they have read about laments as well as opportunity to provide any needed clarification.

Most of the examples presented are, in fact, not laments. They are expressions of disorientation and, frequently, extended complaints. That distinction—which frequently only becomes apparent in the class discussion after all the presentations have been made—is important for helping students understand the theology and the function of the biblical lament psalms, which not only appeal to the offender (God) but call for a response, and sometimes even end in blessing. In many of the contemporary "psalms" no one is being addressed and no change is called for.

Students are often struck by the pervasiveness of complaint and the lack of lament in their own culture. This generally prompts discussion of the audience and purpose of these contemporary "psalms" of disorientation. Students have frequently been able to distinguish between the commercialization of complaint and "psalms" of disorientation that have helped the society as a whole hear the cries of those in need, such as those persons suffering from depression and mental illness. One group of students argued that the movie *John Q* (2002)—which depicts the frustration and rage of a father whose son is not going to be placed on the list to receive a heart transplant because the father lacks sufficient insurance coverage—not only contains the father's lament but is itself a lament appealing to the general public to do something about health care in the United States.

The discussion of contemporary "psalms" of disorientation enables students to reach a deeper understanding of the forms of expression of these emotions in both ancient and contemporary contexts. It also brings to the reading of the ancient psalms the needs and hopes of the contemporary readers.

Elna K. Solvang

129. LAMENT AND PRAISE, TOP FORTY AND PSYCHOLOGY

In discussing the lament psalms and particularly their famous shift from lament and petition to confidence and praise, I frequently play a track from Alanis Morissette's award-winning album, *Jagged Little Pill* (1995; virtually any track will do, but "You Oughta Know" and "Perfect" are favorites). This album won "album of the decade" honors from MTV. The album reveals the singer on the warpath with song after song of truly inspired rage. Her follow-up album, *Supposed Former Infatuation Junkie* (1998), was somewhat less commercially successful and its big hit, "Thank U," quite different from the first outing. "Thank U" is true to its title: in it, Morissette moves from blaming the anonymous "you" for everything and tries to move toward more healthy attitudes and responses, punctuated by the chorus where she thanks a litany of items that have facilitated this move (including terror, disillusionment, frailty, clarity, and silence). In the former album the oppressive "you" was the source of virtually every problem and pain Morissette recounted.

I play "Thank U" after the first track and then ask the students to think about what might have caused Morissette to go from the first song's perspective to the second. The exercise is somewhat speculative, but also draws on critical-thinking skills. The point is to generate possible reasons for the switch to a thankful, more grateful, even happy attitude from a previously angry, even lament-full attitude. Various ideas will be offered, including—for those who know something of the singer's biography—a spiritual awakening during a trip to India. Other ideas usually include Morissette's mellowing due to the passage of time or, perhaps, that the songs are from different songwriters (not the case here: all lyrics on both albums are Morissette's). Another idea that is often presented is that of catharsis: maybe she simply felt better after the vocalization of the first album.

Interestingly, all of these student-generated answers have also been offered as explanations of the shift from lament to praise in the lament psalms. (The still-regnant explanation, however, is that a priest or cultic functionary delivered an oracle of salvation to the psalmist between the petition and praise sections of the psalm [see, esp., the work of Sigmund Mowinckel and Joachim Begrich]. For obvious reasons, this option, or an analogous one, is typically not mentioned by students in the music exercise. Even so, the less-than-obvious nature of the oracle explanation—at least in the case of the music example—might be information that can be used to assess the oracle theory.) Each of these student-generated answers can thus be incorporated into the subsequent lecture and discussion on the lament psalms since the musical example provides a contemporary illustration of the shift from lament to praise. A key difference, of course, is that the lament psalms tend to make this shift within one (musical/poetic) composition, whereas the example provided above utilizes two discrete songs (but compare, perhaps, Pss 9–10, 42–43, 88–89).

I usually hold the catharsis idea for last because, while it is not an exhaustive explanation, it is interesting insofar as the vocalization of anger, disappointment, and rage that characterizes *Jagged Little Pill* also characterizes many of the lament psalms at their rawest. As many psychoanalytic therapists (especially those working in object-relations) would remind us, giving voice to grief is often what permits a move to new hope. In this regard, it is interesting to note that the art on the CD to *Supposed Former Infatuation Junkie* depicts Morissette in a dark area, naked, in the fetal position. It is as if she has been reborn in the new album through her grief in the first. Perhaps the same might be said for many of the psalmists who wrote and prayed the laments. Perhaps they too would look back and say "thank you" to the terror, disillusionment, and solitude that they experienced in the dark night of their souls, even as they give ultimate credit and praise to the One who brought those souls up from Sheol and restored those lives from among those gone down to the Pit (Ps 30:3).

Brent A. Strawn

130. IMPRECATORY PSALMS: ANCIENT AND MODERN

The imprecatory psalms (cf. Pss 58, 83, 94, 109, 137, 139) are often difficult for moderns, especially in so-called "first world" countries, to understand. Many readers in these (comparatively speaking) highly affluent contexts simply cannot appreciate the cry for vengeance and justice that is these psalms' major staple—mostly because they have never been on the opposite end of oppression like so many of their "third world" or "two-thirds world" neighbors.

To explain the imprecatory psalms and the powerful emotions contained therein, I have taken a clue from the work of Carol Antablin Miles ("'Singing the Songs of Zion' and Other Sermons from the Margins of the Canon," *Koinonia* 6.2 [Fall 1994]: 151–73). Miles has suggestively compared the dynamics of Ps 137 with protest music of various types, including Bruce Cockburn's "If I Had a Rocket Launcher" (*Stealing Fire*, 1984; written after a tour of Central America) and Ice-T's "Cop Killer" (*Body Count*, 1992; note the proximity to the Los Angeles riots and the Rodney King verdict). These songs could be seen as contemporary *midrashim* on the imprecatory psalms. Cockburn's song is particularly striking when set next to Ps 137; Ice-T's song is equally fascinating given the existence of a good deal of secondary discussion on it following the controversies surrounding its release. To these two songs of Miles's, I often add Public Enemy's "Burn Hollywood Burn" (*Fear of a Black Planet*, 1990), which rages against the mistreatment of African Americans in the entertainment industry. The song wishes destruction on Hollywood. The background music is frenetic with sirens blaring behind the chorus "Burn, Hollywood, burn! / Burn, Hollywood, burn!"

Setting these songs alongside imprecatory psalms does a number of things: it demonstrates (1) that many people, not just ancient exiled Israelites, experience emotions and rage like those encapsulated in these texts; (2) that such emotions are felt even today—probably everyday by someone somewhere around the world; and (3) that such

H
E
B
R
E
W

B
I
B
L
E

feelings often arise out of experiences of extreme grief and injustice, not just from violence for violence's sake. Moreover, (4) the exercise opens a window onto such experiences and emotions for those who have not, for whatever reason, (yet) experienced those for themselves; and (5) it raises the issue of genre (song, poetry, prayer) and how best to read or hear or act on such lyrics. At this point Miles's discussion of an interview with Ice-T about "Cop Killer" is quite revealing. Miles uses the rapper's own assessment of the song there (namely, that he wrote a song of anger and hate, not one that actually advocated specific acts of violence against the police) to argue for the importance of "instructions for reading or hearing." That is, some material—biblical, poetic, or otherwise—is highly volatile and should come with an instruction manual of sorts or warning label. In this case, contrary to the contemporary practice of the record industry, the label is not simply warning a consumer (or consumer's parent) *that* there is violent material on the record, but instead goes further: there is such content here and it ought to be read or heard *in this specific way.* In the case of the imprecatory psalms, that way is the way of prayer where the cry of rage is lifted, not in an angry fist against a human enemy, but in prayer to the God who claims sole proprietary rights to vengeance and payback (Deut 32:35; cf. Rom 12:19; Heb 10:30).

Appreciating the volatile nature of the very real and very raw human emotions captured in the imprecatory psalms (and their contemporary parallels) and having suitable instructions for reading and listening also helps one understand why such compositions often permit their violence to leak out in inappropriate ways. The emotions are too hot to be controlled easily. Once they are voiced, they have a way of taking over and going to places and targets previously unimagined or unimplicated. So it is that the Public Enemy song moves from rage against Hollywood to violence against the police to derogatory terms about women, and Ps 137 moves from grief over Jerusalem's devastation (vv. 1–6) to rage against Edom's role in the destruction (v. 7) to Babylon (v. 8) and then, suddenly, to Babylon's babies (v. 9). The contemporary imprecations show us that the genre is alive and well, controversial and powerful, and in urgent need of attention and (re)interpretation whenever it is encountered: in the pages of Holy Scripture or on the radio.

Brent A. Strawn

131. PSALM 23 AND MODERN WORLDVIEWS

When discussing Ps 23, I play "Gangsta's Paradise," a 1995 rap song by Coolio which begins with the words, "As I walk through the valley of the shadow of death, I take a look at my life and realize there's nuthin' left." I print out the lyrics and give them to students to follow along (the lyrics are available online: www.getlyrics.com). Most students are familiar with the song, which was also the soundtrack for the movie *Dangerous Minds.*

After playing the song, I ask students to identify the "Gangsta's Paradise" that Coolio is describing. Answer: life in the ghetto or inner city. Coolio's "valley of the shadow of death" is life on the streets. I then ask on whom Coolio relies on as he walks through his valley. Answer: himself. As several lines in the song clearly demonstrate, he feels that he must depend on and defend himself. Coolio relies on the "tin" in his hand—his gun—for protection while the psalmist trusts in the Lord's "rod and staff." Whereas Coolio threatens to kill his enemies ("you might be lined in chalk"), the psalmist relies on God ("you prepare a table before me in the presence of my enemies"). Coolio, then, as a representative of a "modern" worldview, relies on himself and sees things happening according to fate or chance ("I know my life is out of luck"). By contrast, the psalmist, as representative of a biblical worldview, depends on God to take care of him and believes in the sovereignty and providence of the deity.

Furthermore, I contrast Coolio's reaction to his "valley" ("I take a look at my life and realize there's nuthin' left") to that of the psalmist ("I will fear no evil, for you are with me"). The mood or tone of the song is one of despair and hopelessness ("Death ain't nuthin' but a heartbeat away"), whereas the psalm is marked by confidence and trust in God. Thus, Coolio rewrites a psalm of trust into a lament Psalm. His worldview is reminiscent of another popular take-off of Ps 23: "As I walk through the valley of the shadow of death, I will fear no evil, 'cause I am the baddest SOB in the valley." The speaker demonstrates a high degree of self-reliance and is much more confident than Coolio that he can take care of himself. Here I bring in Walt Whitman's "Song of Myself" as another representative of a modern, self-reliant, confident worldview. I quote Whitman: "I celebrate myself, and sing myself... Walt Whitman, a kosmos... Divine am I inside and out, and I make holy whatever I touch... The scent of these arm-pits aroma finer than prayer, This head more than churches, bibles, and all creeds." (This comparison is drawn from R. Walsh, *Reading the Bible: An Introduction* [Notre Dame: Cross Cultural Publications, 1997], 306. Walsh's book makes a number of insightful comparisons between the Bible and modern texts.)

The last part of the discussion underscores the fact that as modern Westerners we are taught to rely on ourselves. We are supposed to trust and believe in ourselves. But the psalmist illustrates a different world-view: utter dependence on God. I mention that Jesus in the Sermon on the Mount also advocated the same radical, complete dependence on God to meet one's needs. I then conclude by asking if class members identify more with Coolio or the psalmist? And which worldview is more robust, noble? Is Coolio a hero or a fool? Is the psalmist a great person of faith or terribly naïve? Students often advocate some mediating position ("God helps those who help themselves"), which can lead to a discussion of the subtleties among differing worldviews.

Mark Roncace

132. CANONICITY, MUSICAL POLYPHONY, AND THE BOOK OF PSALMS

One of the salient contributions to biblical studies made by Russian literary theorist Mikhail Bakhtin is the idea that truth is dialogic. His descriptions of polyphony in a text provide an insightful way of discussing what biblical scholars have long recognized in the canon: that different voices and theologies are bound together in one book, and truth is more fully represented in the dialogue of these voices as they are heard together than in a monologue. Walter Brueggemann expresses this understanding in his *Theology of the Old Testament* (Minneapolis: Fortress, 1997) through his central metaphor of the text as Israel's testimony to, for, and against God. There is a core testimony that affirms God's faithfulness, constancy, and care for God's people, but there is also a countertestimony expressed in texts that speak of God as hidden and unpredictable. The core testimony dominates, but the countertestimony cannot be ignored. Together, both testimonies better approximate the truth about God than either would by itself. This exercise uses an example of musical polyphony to help students understand the literary-theological polyphony heard in the Bible.

Music has always had an easier time with polyphony than texts. Two voices reading words out loud are polyphonic, but also cacophonic. Multiple voices expressed musically, however, are richer and fuller than a single voice by itself. A chord is richer than a single note. Moreover, musical notes do not have to be expressed in harmony; dissonance can be musically profound and sometimes more interesting than simple harmonies.

A wonderful example of musical polyphony illustrating textual polyphony is Leonard Bernstein's *The Chichester Psalms*. Bernstein weaves together all or part of six psalms in three different movements. I use the movement where he juxtaposes Ps 2:1–4 and Ps 23. Students first read through each of those texts to familiarize themselves with the content and are asked to summarize the main theological claims made by each text. Then, they are asked to listen to the music and identify when and where Bernstein switches from one psalm to another. Because the lyrics are in Hebrew, most cannot hear where the switch is made by listening to the words. Even those who know Hebrew have a difficult time following the words, because the musical setting and rhythm of the words is so complex. This requires the students to listen carefully for changes in the music, which are obvious enough that they have no difficulty noting the change in melodies from one psalm to another.

Bernstein begins with Ps 23, sung liltingly by a boy soprano and accompanied by a harp. This melody is then echoed by a chorus of women who repeat and build on the tune. The words of the peaceful, pastoral theology ("the Lord is my shepherd, I shall not want") are expressed in music that matches that peace in tone and tune. After the women have sung for several measures, Ps 2 begins with a crash of percussion, interrupting the peace. It is sung by male voices in dark, dissonant and sinister tones ("Why do the nations rage, and the peoples plot in vain?"). Both melodies continue in an uneasy counterpoint for several measures, until finally the male voices disappear, and Ps 23 is once again sung by itself. But even though Ps 2 is overcome by the music of Ps 23, the grumbling percussion of Ps 2 returns at the very end of the piece. Therefore, although the concerns of Ps 2:1–4 are answered and resolved by the affirmation of Ps 23, they are not ultimately silenced. Bernstein's composition gives a musical illustration of how, although a dominant voice prevails, the countervoice never ultimately goes away.

It may be easier for students to understand ideas of biblical polyphony by using music than by simply talking about texts. In Bernstein's piece, they hear the juxtaposition audibly. The exercise can also illustrate Brueggemann's ideas about testimony and countertestimony, and thereby lead into a greater discussion of multiple voices in the biblical canon. The core theological testimony, like the dominant melody in the music, is challenged and enriched by a countertestimony.

Sara Koenig

133. INTRODUCTION TO WISDOM LITERATURE

The objective of this exercise is to introduce students to biblical wisdom traditions by helping them develop an understanding of the basic purpose and typology of wisdom in the Bible. Wisdom is often arcane and unfamiliar to students and can be very intimidating as a result. The activity that begins this session aims to break through this unfamiliarity by "personalizing" the idea of a wisdom tradition. Once the students have discovered that wisdom is something that is already a familiar feature of their own context, they have a point of contact with the biblical exemplars of Wisdom literature that will allow them to engage the material with at worst an open mind, at best enthusiasm.

Begin the discussion by posing the general question, "Who here has a wisdom tradition?" Most likely, no affirmative answers will result. In any case, propose that each of them does, in fact, have such a tradition. Prove it by going around the room, asking each of them to recite, and, if so inclined, briefly interpret one of those old sayings or instructions that someone in their family is always using, or that they learned from a grandparent, or that they heard in a movie and really liked. I usually kick things off by citing a couple of my own examples, usually one from my grandfather and one from Yoda in *The Empire Strikes Back:* "Do, or do not. There is no 'try.'" Once the proverbs and sayings start flowing, if adequate board space is available, record each student's contribution for later use.

Next, students hash out, based on the examples given, some basic descriptions of wisdom. Ideally, they will provide a transition into the more systematic discussion below, but in any event, try to draw connections with the students' wisdom examples and descriptions throughout what follows.

To help students synthesize the discussion, offer the following descriptions as different ways of thinking about the phenomenon of wisdom, each of which contributes to the production and understanding of wisdom literature:

a. Wisdom as the intellectual/scientific tradition of the biblical world (observation and experience-based, somewhat systematic in approach, very mundane in view and application)
b. Wisdom as instructional/pedagogical literature
c. Wisdom as a theological/cosmological perspective (a distinctive way of looking at God's way with the cosmos)
d. All in all, wisdom offers strategies for survival—how best to live life in the world with which human beings are presented. From these brief descriptions one may derive a simple typology for clas-

sifying particular wisdom books, emphasizing that the categories are not ironclad and each book is likely to have features of both types, while primarily falling into one or the other:

a. Practical Wisdom—Material that focuses on how best to live life, day-to-day. Typically conservative in outlook, pedagogical in form. The prime biblical example is Proverbs.
b. Speculative Wisdom—Material that focuses on how the world works, with particular interest in issues of life and death, justice, and the like. Typically more radical and questioning in outlook, dialogic or even abstract in form. The best biblical example is Ecclesiastes. Job, the third wisdom book in the canon, incorporates lengthy blocks of material drawn from the practical strain within an overall structure that is profoundly speculative.

Subsequent discussion may focus on additional issues, such as the "international" or universal character of this ancient Israelite literature or on the degree to which wisdom is or is not relative to culture.

D. Matthew Stith

134. THE SOCIAL SETTINGS OF ANCIENT AND MODERN WISDOM

I thought of this assignment when, some years ago in a bookstore checkout line, I picked up a calendar ("Life's Little Instruction Calendar, Volume IV," by H. Jackson Brown [Andrews & McMeel]). I was struck with how its way of speaking was quite reminiscent of the book of Proverbs (a fact also not lost on another press, which published snippets from Proverbs in "God's Little Instruction Book.") I also noticed that the calendar's intended audience could easily be derived from its bits of advice. This audience is, among other attributes, wealthy enough to have considerable possessions ("Use your best manners and best silver and china for your family—the ones you love") and access to frequent travel ("Attend a baseball game at Skydome in Toronto"), American ("Once in your life see a U.S. shuttle launch; it will renew your faith in America") and married straight male ("Kiss your wife at midnight on New Year's Eve, even if you have to wake her up").

I assign students to read selections from Proverbs and the last three months of "Life's Little Instruction Calendar, Volume IV," which I have transcribed. For fun, and to make the calendar a better parallel, I represent the month as a chapter number and the days as verse numbers, printing it in "biblical" format. I assume any section of a book or calendar of this genre would work equally well. They then write a brief essay determining what can be known about the audience and the author: What author and audience does each selection imply? How do the respective audiences compare? This sets up a discussion at the beginning of the treatment of wisdom in class. In general, it is relatively easy for students to figure out the assumptions which animate the Instruction Calendar. They then bring that knowledge to bear on Proverbs, noting, for example, its male focus and its possible settings in the family or at court.

It would also be possible to do this assignment by doing the reading in advance without requiring writing, though writing aids the reflection process. The material could even be done "on the fly" by passing out a smaller selection of the calendar, discussing it, and then using some of the conclusions to shape a lecture on Proverbs.

Donald C. Polaski

135. SAYINGS OF THE WISE (GUYS): AN APPROACH TO THE BOOK OF PROVERBS

Among the challenges in an introductory Bible course is to make rather complex scholarly arguments accessible to students who are familiar with the text in a devotional way that often makes them less amenable to the academic study of the Bible. One text that I have found particularly good in overcoming the barrier between the scholarly and the immediate is the book of Proverbs. Proverbs raises questions of authorship (an anthology), provenance (scribal traditions in the ancient Near East) and genre (wisdom literature), but it also raises the larger questions of how young people learn and from whom they learn, including both parents and teachers. Most of the instruction in Proverbs is intended for young men presumably about the age of many traditional students. The inclusive language of the NRSV often mutes the gender of the recipient—happily in a class that is of mixed gender, unhappily when gendered issues like advice about the Strange Woman and the feminine gender of Wisdom get obscured. In an introductory course, however, where one might have an hour or less to discuss Proverbs, attention to these and other ideas may have to be perfunctory at best. I focus on the "sayings of the wise" (Prov 22:17–23:11) to help students appreciate how they are generated and what role they play in giving advice for a "good life."

I usually assign three sections of the book (Prov 1–9; 22:17–23:11; 31), but even when they use a study Bible with good footnotes, I have found that students rarely read them. Consequently, they read with very little commentary at all, a method that is not necessarily a bad thing, as they also read without the bias of the footnotes. My task is nonetheless to prevent a perfunctory reading, introducing students to scholarly ways of seeing a text while at the same time engaging them in it. But those students who balk at technical terms like *mashal* will not readily appreciate the influence of Amen-em-ope on Prov 22:17–23:11. As one student told me, she did not see why she needed to learn words like *mashal* because she would never again use them in her life. After I recovered from my consternation, I realized that she was probably right.

Hence I devised a method of involving students, if only momentarily, in a type of "scribal wisdom tradition" in which they act as scribes (literate people who write things down), remembering and passing on wise sayings (or at any rate, bits of advice). I pass out three-by-five note cards to the students in the class and tell them that they are going to be acting the part of scribes. On the front of the card, they are to write a piece of advice that an elder (parent, grandparent, older sibling, friend, or neighbor) gave them before they came to college. Then, on the back of the card, they are to write a piece of advice that (in their vast wisdom after the first semester in college) they would pass on to a younger sibling or friend still in high school. The writing part of the exercise takes about ten minutes, and the size of the card prevents the "sayings" from being too lengthy. When all are done inscribing their "wisdom," each student in turn reads aloud from the advice of the elders, and I try to group these sayings in categories on the board. Not surprisingly, there are some favorite categories, not unlike those in Proverbs, albeit modernized: study, dating (and marriage; one man's uncle told him, "Don't marry the first woman you fall in love with"), prudent behavior regarding alcohol, and socializing. When the "sayings of the elders" are finished, the student-scribes then read their own advice to their juniors. Again, there are some familiar categories, the wisdom of the elders updated.

What this exercise achieves is to involve the students, albeit in a tenuous way, in the process of scribal collection and reproduction. It gives them an appreciation, moreover, of the kind of moral and social education that goes on informally in their own lives and perhaps some recognition that they are themselves custodians of tradition and preservers of common sense. "Gnomic wisdom" means a lot more to them after the exercise.

Gail P. C. Streete

136. PROVERBS AND PROVERBS OF THE WORLD

The reaction of most students to the collection of sentence sayings that comprise Prov 10–29 is usually a strange mixture of confusion, boredom, and aversion. These chapters present any teacher of the Hebrew Scriptures with a pedagogical challenge. One way to address this challenge is to bring the biblical text into dialogue with aphoristic material from different cultures and different eras and in different mediums and forms.

To pique students' interest in the study of the sentence sayings of Prov 10–29, I begin a class session on the aphorisms of the book of Proverbs by having the students consider a painting by Pieter Brueghel (1525–69) entitled *Dutch Proverbs*. Keys to the proverbs Brueghel illustrates in the painting are widely available (cf. the Taschen edition of *Bruegel* [Köln: Benedikt Taschen Verlag, 1994], esp. 30, 35–37). Generally I project an image of Brueghel's painting onto a large screen for the entire class to view and ask the students to identify a handful of the over one hundred Dutch proverbs that Brueghel illustrates, many of which are just as "colorful" as Brueghel's palette.

Students are generally able to recognize in the painting several proverbs with which they are familiar. Subsequently I indicate to the class that the use of proverbs is, in fact, a broadly attested phenomenon cross-culturally, and I hand out examples of proverbs from a variety of cultures, for instance, Mexico, Korea, Ireland, and a variety of African societies. (Collections of proverbs from these and a multitude of other cultures are all widely available on the Internet.) I also include in my handout a brief excerpt from the *Panchatantra,* an Indian Sanskrit collection of stories and animal fables likely compiled before the fifth century C.E. and attributed to Vishnusharman. The text, which was probably intended to instruct princes in choosing friends and ministers and in managing daily life, makes broad use of aphorisms to drive home its teaching.

After the class reads together some of these proverbs, I ask students to share any proverbs from their own cultures with which they might be familiar. Next I ask them to reflect on all the types of proverbs we have been discussing—from the Dutch proverbs illustrated by Brueghel, to the Mexican or Irish or Yoruba proverbs we read together—and to relate them to the sayings they shared from their own cultures. Specifically, I ask them to consider when and where these sorts of proverbs are deployed and by whom, as well as who might be considered the author of such sayings. This conversation permits the students to realize that proverbs are primarily an oral speech genre which, though capable of being employed in a variety of settings, nonetheless often have a didactic intent and transmit the unique values and virtues of a particular culture or subculture. Often at this point the class is able to translate insights from the discussion into a working definition that incorporates the literary observation that a proverb is a short, pithy saying whose "author" is a "community" rather than an individual. This exercise also permits the class to begin considering questions of the social setting and function of proverbial speech.

At this point I ask the students to compare and contrast the sayings of Proverbs with the proverbs we have been considering. Points of similarity in terms of literary structure, subject matter, and the like are regularly forthcoming. Points of contrast, however, generally require more prodding. In order to get at these differences I ask the students to consider, for example, the fact that Proverbs appears to make more persistent use of highly charged moral and intellectual categories—such as "righteousness" and "wickedness" or "wisdom" and "folly"—than the other proverbs we have considered. Most effective, however, is to ask the students to consider who it is that put together most of the collections from which we read and who it is that might have put together the sayings of the book of Proverbs. This line of inquiry helps the students realize a significant distinction: namely, that the collections of sayings from the different cultures of the world that we read have largely been compiled and categorized by modern anthropologists and folklorists, while the sayings of the book of Proverbs were compiled into a book by ancient scribes whose anthological strategies are not immediately clear to us in the twenty-first century.

It thus becomes clear to the students that Proverbs is, in some sense, much more akin to the *Panchatantra*—an instructional text that provides a clear literary context of interpretation for the aphorisms it deploys—than any compilation of proverbs put together by folklorists. With these insights that the class has collectively discerned, it is then possible to offer suggestions about a range of issues related to the study of Proverbs, including the anthology's literary and instructional integrity as well as the possible social settings out of which the various collections in the book may have emerged (e.g., the world of the family and the clan, the world of elite scribes, and so forth).

Timothy J. Sandoval

137. FEELING THE HEAT IN JOB BY REWRITING THE SPEECHES WITH MODERN EXPRESSIONS

My students are so programmed to look for theology that they often do not see important human dimensions in biblical stories. The poetic dialogues in

Job provide an excellent opportunity to let them experience a fiery debate that is filled with name calling and insults. They love it.

In my introductory course, I devote two class periods to Job. In preparation for the first session, I have students read Job 1–21 and write brief answers to the following questions: (a) How is Job portrayed in Job 1–2? (b) How is he portrayed in chapters 3–21? (c) What perspective on the theology of retribution does each of Job's opponents present? (d) How does Job's understanding of divine justice and intervention in the world differ from theirs? (e) How do Job's beliefs on rewards for wise and righteous living compare with the viewpoint presented in Proverbs?

I spend a few minutes during the first part of the class session listening to what they say about the way chapters 1–2 depict Job and how chapters 3–21 depict him. Then we move to an exercise that captures their imagination because it allows them to feel the heat rising off the pages of Job. I divide the class members into small groups and assign each group a single discourse from Job. I tell them to condense their assigned speech and to word the argument with modern colloquial expressions. They really enjoy this task. When they are finished composing, I go around the room and have one person from each group do a dramatic presentation of the speech they have composed. I begin by letting the first "Job" moan about ever being born (Job 3); then I let the first "Eliphaz" answer (Job 4–5); then I say, "How does that make you feel, Job?" and let the next group answer from Job 6–7. We continue this process until we get through chapter 21.

Students gain an immensely different feel for the text by participating in this exercise. They feel the emotions and they begin to see the major theological issue that Job raises. They can be pretty creative with their speeches, which leads to a lot of laughter. But this exercise seriously improves their ability to read Job as literature. Because I have them read Job after we have dealt with Proverbs, they also get a better feel for intra-canonical dialogue when they see Job challenging the dominant theology of retribution.

During the second class on Job, we finish the debates in the poetic section and also analyze the way the speeches of Eliphaz, Bildad, and Zophar escalate their rhetoric. Students come ready to do the remaining speeches in modern vernacular. Then we explore the seriously challenging question that emerges from the text: God is powerful, but is God good? Thus we go from a fun time of writing and delivering insult-filled speeches to asking big questions about God and life.

Michael R. Cosby

138. JOB: PUTTING GOD ON TRIAL

This exercise will work if the biblical book of Job is extensively studied in the particular course in which it is attempted. I use it successfully in a course in which Job is the subject of about four weeks of study and which makes use of Robert Sutherland's *Putting God on Trial: The Biblical Book of Job* (Victoria: Trafford, 2004). Sutherland, a lawyer by training, approaches the book as a legal drama: God puts Job on trial, the Satan puts God on trial, Job's friends put Job on trial, Job puts his friends on trial, and everything culminates with Job's attempt to put God on trial. Job submits an oath of innocence (a legal procedure for which Sutherland finds ancient Near Eastern parallels) and refuses to acquit God of blame.

As a culmination to this study, students are divided into four groups: (1) The first group represents the prosecution and prepares arguments for Job's innocence and God's culpability in Job's suffering. (2) The second group represents the defense and prepares arguments to justify God's actions and Job's experience of suffering. (3) The third group represents the interveners in the case, that is, Job's friends, and prepares arguments from their perspective. (4) The fourth group represents the judges who will hear and decide the case, and prepares a set of criteria by which they will evaluate the various arguments and come to a decision. It also decides on the agenda and procedure of the trial. For ideas, students draw on the biblical text as well as Sutherland's book and various commentaries on Job. The students then enact the trial: the prosecution, defense, and interveners present their arguments, there is opportunity for rebuttals and cross-examination, and closing statements are given. Finally, the judges privately convene, come to a decision, and announce and explain their verdict to the entire class. A general discussion follows.

Obviously, this is an extensive exercise but it works extremely well in giving students the opportunity to really sink their teeth into the various arguments presented in Job, and it inevitably leads to a discussion of the contemporary ramifications of the enduring issues that Job raises: the cause and meaning of innocent suffering, the justice and mercy of God, and the relationship between the transcendent and the human.

F. V. Greifenhagen

139. EDITING THE END OF JOB

One fairly simple way to develop creative thinking abilities is to have students rewrite biblical stories. This could be done with just about any text—Judg 19–21, the books of Jonah and Esther, or the parable of the Prodigal Son, for example—but one that serves the purpose particularly effectively is the book of Job.

After discussing Job 38–42—the divine speeches from the whirlwind, Job's response to God, and the conclusion to the book in which God restores Job—I announce that I am directing a screenplay based on Job and I find the canonical version confusing (what exactly is God trying to say to Job?) and not very compelling (how can God simply return everything to Job and think that will make amends?). So I ask students to rewrite this part of the book. They are to write an alternate ending—for the DVD version—and tell me, the director, why their version is to be preferred over the canonical one. I usually let students think on their own for a few minutes to sketch some ideas, and then they form small groups to pool their thoughts. Each group then decides on one alternate ending. In addition to stimulating creativity, this format gives students the opportunity to hear ideas from their peers and then to work together to formulate the best ending.

Students have come up with a variety of scenarios, such as: (1) God tells Job about the bet, Job curses God, so God loses the bet with the Satan, but the Satan then decides to restore everything to Job. (2) God does not restore Job because the Satan objects, so Job commits suicide, and God repents. (3) Job wakes up at the end and realizes the whole ordeal has been a dream. (4) Job is not satisfied with God's restoration because he has still suffered the loss of his original children (which his wife points out), so in an act of defiance he gives away all of his possessions to ensure that the same thing will not happen in the future.

It is crucial for groups to argue the merits of their rewritten version, as this typically leads to fruitful discussions about the biblical text. As can be seen, each of the alternate endings mentioned above is wrestling with certain "problems" in the canonical version. One other note: If students object to "rewriting the Bible," I point out that the Bible itself is already in the process of revising (as in the various law codes in the Pentateuch, the Chronicler's History, or the editing of Mark one sees in Matthew and Luke). That is, the class, faithful to the biblical model, is redacting the story.

Mark Roncace

140. ON COVERING (THE SONG OF) SONGS AND THE IMPORTANCE OF (CANONICAL) CONTEXT

A familiar phenomenon in music is called "covering"; it is when one band sings a song that is not its own but that was made famous by another artist and does so with little or no alteration to the tune or lyric. Although the practice is widely known and employed, it may at first be surprising to discover that contemporary Christian music has recently covered a number of songs that have been immensely popular in "Top 40" radio. Recent artists who have covered famous songs include Delirious? ("Pride [In the Name of Love]," originally by U2), Kristy Starling ("I Need You," by LeAnn Rimes); Nichole Nordeman ("Time After Time," by Cyndi Lauper, and "In Your Eyes," by Peter Gabriel); Mark Schultz ("Kyrie Eleison," by Mr. Mister); Jim Witter ("Turn, Turn, Turn," by The Byrds). An entire CD entitled *In the Name of Love,* by Artists United for Africa, is a collection of U2 songs covered by contemporary Christian artists.

After selecting one of these songs and playing both the original and the Christian "covered" version, I ask my students to talk about what is different in the songs. At the start, the answers tend to be "nothing" or "very little" and might focus on fine points of phrasing, production, or nuancing of lyrics or tune. If the discussion goes no further, I prompt by asking why they think a Christian has remade a "secular" song and if there is any significance to that. At this point, the quasi-"religious" nature of the original composition is usually mentioned. My ultimate teaching goal with the exercise, however, is to guide the discussion so as to get at three central issues: (1) point of *origin* (who is singing?); (2) point of *delivery* (who is being sung to?); and (3) *context* (what else is on this album? are there other songs that clarify the lyrics of this particular song or the points of origin and delivery?). The last point, which may well be the most important, can be helpfully illustrated by having a copy of the liner notes for each album and a sense of the content of each.

This last point, in turn, can be a wonderful entrée for students to think about the importance of context for canon and canon formation. To give but one example: According to many scholars, the Song of Songs is originally a collection of "secular," erotic love poetry. Even if this is correct, such a collection "reads" differently when it is covered in an "album" (Scripture as a whole, or even just the Writings/*Kethubim*) that has a lot of other tunes and lyrics that have much to do with God. In this light, it is easily seen that the other "tracks on the (biblical) CD" lead one to read the Song of Songs in ways quite different from the way one would in a local bookstore in the human sexuality section (witness the extensive allegorical interpretation of the Song in both Jewish and Christian circles). A similar judgment may also hold true for Esther, which never mentions the name of God in the Hebrew version of the book, but, in the sweep of the canon, finds its fitting place as a testimony to clever and faithful members of the Lord's people. The "tracks" elsewhere on the "album" fix God on the brain—so much so that readers are tempted to find God even in Hebrew Esther, perhaps in the famous but oblique reference to help arising for the Jews from "another place" (4:14).

In brief, the phenomenon of covered songs demonstrates that all kinds of different material—even the "secular"—can be canonized. But once this occurs, the canon exercises a degree of reciprocal influence that molds and shapes subsequent perception and interpretation of what is now canonical. At this point the work of scholars like B. S. Childs and J. A. Sanders can be compared and provide material for further reflection. (For a similar exercise, see §176.)

Brent A. Strawn

141. READING THE SONG OF SONGS

When students read through the Song of Songs silently, it is sometimes difficult to "hear" the different voices in the text. To overcome this problem, I have photocopied the entire text and have highlighted in one color the verses spoken by the male and in another color the verses spoken by the female. I then ask for one male and one female student to volunteer to read the poetry to each other. I usually have the two students sit facing each other in the front of the class, each with a copy of the highlighted text. In addition to a male and female voice, a narrator reads 1:1; 3:6–11; and 5:1b. The "daughters of Jerusalem" are played by the women of the class who read in unison 1:8; 5:9; 6:1, 10. The maiden's brothers are read by the men of the class; they speak in 8:8–9. (Of course, it is not always perfectly clear from the text who is speaking, so some editorial decisions must be made.) Thus, the whole class is involved in the reading. It takes about twenty minutes to read the entire book aloud.

In the subsequent discussion I usually address several topics. First, we compare the conversational nature of the Song of Songs to the conversational nature of the book of Job (Job and God; Job and his three friends) and the book of Proverbs (the father/teacher and the silent son, thus no "authentic dialogue") since we have just studied those two books. Second, we compare the role and portrayal of the woman in the Song of Songs to the portrayal of the Strange Woman in Proverbs, noting who speaks, what is said about them, and so forth. Third, I point out that the male and female in the Song draw from the worlds of flora and fauna to describe each other and the passions of erotic love. While the specific ways in which they do this ("your hair is like a flock of goats") is quite strange to students, I suggest that it is not all that different from the way in which people talk today. I ask for modern examples of terms of endearment from the world of flora, pointing out that in the Song the references to flora appeal to the sense of taste. Terms like "honey," "sugar," "sweetie," "cupcake," and "pumpkin" are often mentioned. For animals (fauna), modern examples include "chick," "fox," and "stud." (Students usually mention some of the less-than-flattering terms that fall into this category.) This third topic can lead to a broader comparison of the Song with modern love language, often found in songs.

Mark Roncace

142. PERFORMING THE BOOK OF RUTH

On one level, the book of Ruth is a simple story of two widows who find happiness and a future through marriage to a wealthy man and the birth of a son. It is also a complex story in which each action of each character causes the reader to question: Why does Ruth insist on returning with Naomi? What would Naomi have done if Ruth had not returned with her? Why does Boaz not tell Naomi about the land? What does Naomi intend when she sends Ruth to the threshing floor? Is Boaz the redeemer in the story or is Ruth? Through a system of gaps and clues the writer has constructed a story that forces reflection not only on individual actions but on the process through which a community learns loyalty from a poor, widowed foreigner and finally extends redemption to her. The challenge in teaching this book is to preserve the simplicity of the storytelling without eliminating its mystery or glossing over the complex questions the story raises.

I have found it helpful to have four groups of students act out the story in four scenes corresponding to the four chapters. The script is the text of Ruth, which I print out with the various character roles labeled (Ruth, Orpah, narrator, Boaz, women of Bethlehem, etc.). Before they meet in their groups I lead the students through the biblical passages that describe the relationship between the Israelites and the Moabites in order to help them recognize the twists and surprises that run from the beginning to the end of the story. I also introduce students to the laws about gleaning, redemption of land, and levirate marriage. Then I give them time to discuss, plan, and practice their scenes. I make available a few props that they can use if they want (e.g., a basket, apron, shawl, bag, and blanket).

Having to act out the scene forces students to examine the clues in the text and to make choices about how to interpret the actions and reflect the motives of the characters. Since there are four different groups

H
E
B
R
E
W

B
I
B
L
E

there are varying interpretations, prompting discussion between the groups about interpretive choices and alternative possibilities. The acting draws attention to Ruth's role in initiating actions that require others to respond. The transformation from emptiness to fullness that is crucial to the structure of the story also becomes visible. Although each scene is presented by a different group, the text itself provides for continuity since the end of each chapter provides a piece of information that anticipates the next one.

When students act out the book they are less focused on the morality of Ruth's visit to the threshing floor and more on the change in the community around her and how Ruth inspires them to initiate acts of "redemption" that go beyond what is required by the law. (For similar exercises, see §§72, 90, 199.)

Elna K. Solvang

143. QUESTIONING RUTH

This is a discussion-based exercise for small groups that provides an overview of the concerns of the book of Ruth in a single class session. One student reads the following script in this present form. It is important that the reader stop at each question mark to allow the other members to respond because the script is designed to have a narrative flow:

Chapter 1. Verses 1–5 frame the story of Ruth. In this book names have symbolic value (Elimelech="my god is king"; Mahlon and Chilion="sickness" and "consumption"; Naomi="pleasant"; Orpah="back of the neck"; Ruth="companion" [probably]). Along with these names, what type of nouns appear in these verses? What does this say about the concerns of the author? At this point, what do you know about the various characters?

In the rest of chapter 1, the women take center stage and start to gain individuality. Up until Orpah's departure, Ruth and she are as indistinguishable as their dead husbands. Much of this chapter is taken up with dialogue—Naomi's two speeches surrounding Ruth's. Take a look at the language of Naomi in vv. 8–13. What are the motifs that appear in her charge to Ruth and Orpah? What are the verbs that dominate vv. 6–22? How do these verbs impinge upon the overall concerns of the narrative?

At the end of chapter one, how would you describe Naomi's situation, and what is the significance of v. 22?

Chapter 2. This chapter introduces Boaz, whose name possibly means "in him is strength." Look at the way in which Ruth is described in this chapter, both by the narrator and by Boaz. What are the most important characteristics of Ruth for the narrator and for Boaz? This chapter also raises issues about man/woman relationships. Compare vv. 8, 9, 21 (in which "servants" is masculine), and 22. Verses 8, 9, and 22 all are about Ruth's activity in the fields and with whom she should interact. Why the difference in v. 21? Is this significant?

Another issue raised in chapter 2 is the role of God in the unfolding action. Is God involved in the fates of these people? What is the textual evidence for saying God's providence is present or absent?

Chapter 3. This chapter is in many ways the climax of the book. First of all, Naomi governs the actions to follow. What are her reasons for exhorting Ruth to take the actions of vv. 1–4? How do you know Naomi's motivations? To this point, what else seems mysterious about the actions and speech of Boaz, Ruth, or Naomi?

The encounter with Ruth and Boaz presents difficulties in terms of knowing exactly what transpires between them. Some helps—"threshing floor," at least in Hosea, is a place associated with illicit sexual activity; "feet" is often a euphemism for genitalia; "lie down" has the connotations of sexual intercourse, as does "know." Based on the text in front of you, try to map out what occurs in vv. 6–13—step by step. Especially interesting is Boaz's reaction—what exactly is he doing when he puts his cloak over her, and how does his statement in v. 13 affect the way in which the reader judges his actions?

Chapter 4. In chapter 4, all the events of the past night come to light, and, if we read it with somewhat prurient eyes, we have the potential for a one-night stand or for Boaz doing the right thing. The chapter starts smoothly with vv. 1–2 and then continues jarringly with vv. 3–4. What is the narrative effect of these verses? Is Boaz telling the truth? Of course, Boaz throws a wrench into the contract in v. 5. One can read this either as playing loose with Ruth's affections or a stipulation that the other kinsman simply would be unable to follow. What do you think?

When Boaz announces publicly his gains in the bargain, what does he emphasize? How is this different from what he had said to Ruth the night before? Furthermore, what is Boaz's relationship to Naomi, and how does she play into this agreement? What happens to the gender roles as the narrative moves to its end?

Synthesis. In a summary of her exegesis of Ruth from *God and the Rhetoric of Sexuality* (Philadelphia: Fortress, 1978), Phyllis Trible writes,

> As a whole, this human comedy suggests a theological interpretation of feminism: women working out their own salvation with fear and trembling, for it is God who works in them. Naomi works as a bridge between tradition and innovation. Ruth and the females of Bethlehem work as paradigms for

radicality. All together they are women in culture, women against culture, and women transforming culture (196).

Based on your reading, does Trible's interpretation seem justified?

Kyle Keefer

144. WHAT IS THE ANGLE?

Beginning students generally have a limited view of the range of interpretive issues raised by different texts. They tend to assume that the primary concern of the book of Ruth, for example, has to do with family and faithfulness, especially due to its use in Christian wedding ceremonies and in genealogies of Jesus (Matt 1:6, Luke 3:32). This exercise uses Ruth to alert students to the ways in which a variety of interpretive issues engaged in biblical texts derives from the perspectives and interests of the interpreter.

In a plenary session, place a variety of popular newspapers and periodicals on a table (e.g., *National Enquirer*, *Ladies' Home Journal*, *Wall Street Journal*, etc.). Ask students to describe the material that they expect to find in each publication and the general perspective of the publication based on the name, subtitles, cover photo, or previous knowledge of the publication. For example, students may describe the *National Enquirer* as a tabloid magazine that focuses on sensational stories of unlikely events. Even students who are not familiar with the publication will be able to contribute based on the features mentioned above.

Divide students into small groups. Each group is to select one of the publications discussed in plenary. Assign each group to assume the role of reporters for a fictional publication modeled after the publication selected and its perspective. Using the text of Ruth as material for their story, students will determine the angle of the article, as well as the particular features of the text on which their article would focus. Students will not write an article but sketch an idea for an article, which they will "pitch" to the plenary group. For example, with some suggestions from the instructor, the group that selects the *Wall Street Journal* may develop the following pitch: "We are reporters for the *Grain Path Journal*, which highlights financial news in the ancient Near East. The angle for our story will involve the socio-economic elements of the text. Based on the available material, we will focus on marriage and property negotiations, as well as the impact of the famine on women." After allowing students time to work together, have the groups return to plenary and pitch their ideas.

In the follow-up discussion, invite students to share their responses. Point out that students may see a variety of publications together at a newspaper stand. Yet, they would have differing expectations for the perspective taken by those publications even if they covered the same events, such as the Grammys or a national election. Highlight the number of different approaches that each group used with the book of Ruth and stress that the text is not "about" one single thing.

As an additional component of this exercise or as a follow-up homework assignment, have students read brief selections from overview material in commentaries on Ruth written from varying ideological and faith perspectives. Ask students to compare and contrast the angle of the author, how explicit the author makes that angle, and which elements of the text the author highlights. Impress upon the students that just as they utilize their interpretive skills when reading popular publications, they can use those skills when reading biblical scholarship.

Nyasha Junior

145. "WHY WOULD I WANT TO MARRY MY SISTER-IN-LAW?": CULTURAL DIVERSITY AND LEVIRATE MARRIAGE

In my "Introduction to Biblical Studies" course, I begin by having students read the short stories of Jonah and Ruth. I have them contrast the portrait of Ruth, the virtuous foreigner, with the depiction of Jonah, the bigoted prophet. They enjoy seeing the striking contrasts, but they are somewhat troubled by the characteristics that make Ruth such an endearing character for ancient Israelites. In the story about this hard working, loyal Moabite, students encounter what—from their own cultural perspectives—seem like completely bizarre beliefs and customs. This shocks them into the realization that they simply cannot assume that biblical characters basically thought the way modern Western Europeans do.

I discuss the story of Jonah with my students before we turn to Ruth, because Jon 2 gets us into Israelite beliefs about Sheol—which is important background for understanding why Ruth needed to marry someone near of kin to her dead husband. As we discuss the major plot characteristics of the story of Ruth and explore how the characters of Ruth, Naomi, and Boaz are presented, some of the dimensions of the narrative simply do not make sense to students. They are intrigued by remarks like that of Naomi to her daughters-in-law:

> Turn back, my daughters, why will you go with me? Do I still have sons in my womb that they may become your husbands? Turn back, my daughters,

H
E
B
R
E
W

B
I
B
L
E

go your way, for I am too old to have a husband. Even if I thought there was hope for me, even if I should have a husband tonight and bear sons, would you then wait until they were grown? Would you then refrain from marrying? (Ruth 1:11–13)

When it dawns on them that Naomi was not merely joking when she said this to Ruth and Orpah, the students respond that this is "just too weird."

I have them turn to Deut 25:5–10 and ask how this law of Levirate marriage helps them to understand the story of Ruth. We get some good laughs by discussing the implications of this law that seeks to dissuade a man from refusing to get his dead brother's widow pregnant. Students particularly laugh when I dramatically read the shame-based conclusion: "Throughout Israel his family shall be known as 'the house of him whose sandal was pulled off.'" We talk about the ancient Israelites' belief that it was best to keep a widow as part of her dead husband's family by giving her to a surviving brother. I point out that the reason for the law is stated in Deut 25:6: "so that his name may not be blotted out of Israel." Once they understand that ancient Israelites had no developed belief in afterlife but thought that a man lived on through his sons, they begin to see the rationale for the custom of a sonless widow being impregnated by her brother-in-law—or in Ruth's case by Boaz, her husband's near of kin. At this point they see the connection between Sheol and levirate marriage.

This exercise proves to be significant in helping students make the transition between reading ancient texts in light of their own cultural presuppositions and seeking to discover how biblical cultures functioned. It enriches their reading by opening a window to the ancient Near East. It also opens up valuable conversations about cultures today in which parents arrange marriages for their children. Often this becomes a good avenue to discuss cultural diversity and sensitivity to the ways that other people do things—customs that seem strange because of personal experiences in our own society.

Michael R. Cosby

146. LAMENTATIONS THROUGH MUSICAL INTERPRETATION

The book of Lamentations has inspired numerous musical pieces, evidence of its profound theological and emotional importance in many artistic imaginations. I have used Leonard Bernstein's Symphony No. 1, "Jeremiah" (1942), to introduce Lamentations and have found the symphony pedagogically useful in several ways. First, the music helps students who are better at hearing texts to approach the written text from another angle. Second, even students who are adept at reading and interpreting written texts often discover something new in the text when they approach it with other senses. Third, I have found that the form and content of the book become anchored in students' minds when they encounter the text in another medium.

The symphony has three movements. The first two movements are instrumental, entitled "Prophecy" and "Profanation," and are based on Jeremiah's prophecy about the fall of Jerusalem. The third movement, "Lamentation," includes vocalization of the Hebrew text of Lamentations, focusing on the aftermath of the fall of the city. I use the most relevant final movement at the beginning and end of the class to bracket discussion or, in some cases, a more detailed lecture about the book. The first experience of the music sets up discussion of Lamentations and the second hearing gives students an opportunity to integrate other students' observations about the text and the music with their own interpretations of both. Though the movement lasts a little over ten minutes, in my experience it is worth playing fully at least once. Using a portion of the piece, however, may also be effective.

I set up the first "hearing" of the music with a brief introduction to Lamentations to orient students to the historical context of the book, its connection with the Ninth of Ab, its acrostic structure, the presence of three different voices (the first person "I", personified Zion, and the communal "We") and its inclusion of elements of the lament and the dirge. The title of Bernstein's piece implies that the prophet Jeremiah wrote Lamentations and therefore provides an opportunity to talk about the LXX tradition of authorship, the fact that the Hebrew Bible does not attribute Lamentations to Jeremiah, as well as similarities and differences between the books of Jeremiah and Lamentations. Finally, because many students are unaccustomed to listening to this kind of music, I offer guidance about what I would like them to notice. Most importantly, I ask them to be sure to notice how the music makes them feel, and ask them to make notes about their thoughts while they are listening. What is the tone of the music? Is it angry, comforting, despairing, or hopeful? I also ask students to listen for the repeated orchestral motif and the quality of the conclusion of the symphony as a whole. My intent is to lay the groundwork for later discussion of the range of emotions expressed in the book itself, as well as the means by which both the music and the written text organize that expression of emotion.

I then ask students to reflect on the music. During the ensuing conversation, my goal is to connect the students' experience of the music to elements in the book. For instance, the repeated motif in the music functions much the same way as the acrostic form of the poetry; both operate as a grounding structure that offers boundaries for the vocal expression of overwhelming pathos and the words in Lamentations of desperation, violence, and despair. The expression of emotion in the text, as in the music, happens within a structure that provides a way of containing, expressing, and finding relief for suffering. The emotional quality to the music helps students understand on an experiential level the emotional and theological work of the text as it organizes grief and communicates it in a recognized cultural form. In addition, students inevitably hear different emotions in the music, which provides a way of recognizing the variety of emotions expressed in Lamentations, including the hopeful words in 3:21–39. The ending of Bernstein's composition is especially significant, I think, because rather than a decisive and pointed resolution, the music fades and diminishes, expressing ongoing despair as opposed to promise. Likewise, the ending of Lamentations is decidedly not hopeful. Students should recognize this ending of the text as a significant manipulation of the standard lament form that often concludes by pointing the reader in the direction of hope.

My hope is that students will leave the class with a better understanding of the theological and historical significance of Lamentations, as well as the importance of the book in a longer tradition of interpretation that extends, in the case of Bernstein's symphony, into the twentieth century.

Amy C. Cottrill

147. ENTERING INTO LAMENTATIONS

The book of Lamentations poses distinct challenges in introductory courses on the Old Testament. In seeking to avoid the uncomfortable questions and horrific images Lamentations evokes, students may fail to hear and appreciate its rich testimony of pain and hope. In my course for divinity students I spend two sessions on the book of Lamentations. In these sessions I have four main goals: (1) to convey an appreciation for the events, experiences, and questions to which the book gives witness; (2) to introduce the genre of lament; (3) to explore the significance and function of the acrostic, or alphabetic, structuring devices used in the poems; and (4) to invite students to enter into the laments, hear their testimony, and address questions of actualization.

To achieve the first goal, I read aloud Nathan's oracle to David in 2 Sam 7:12–16, and Isa 4:12. We discuss the centrality of the Zion traditions, their relation to the David traditions, and the significance of the belief that Jerusalem was inviolable. We then discuss the fall of Jerusalem and the theological problems raised by this event. I compare the fall of Jerusalem to the more familiar war-time devastation of modern cities such as Baghdad or Hiroshima, to help the students gain a more visceral appreciation for the horrors described in the text.

To introduce the lament genre, I discuss the Sumerian laments over ruined cities and temples (1950–1700 B.C.E.) and their literary and liturgical legacy in the ancient Near East (translation of the lament over Ur available online: http://etcsl.orinst.ox.ac.uk/cgi-bin/etcslmac.cgi? text= t.2.2.2#). After identifying key similarities between these laments and the book of Lamentations, I read aloud excerpts from the lament over Ur. I ask students to listen for similarities as well as differences, which we then discuss. When students note the shift from polytheism to monotheism, they see some of the unique theological problems posed in Lamentations. For example, they note that in the lament over Ur, patron deities intercede with the destroying god, while in Lamentations, the "patron" God *is* the destroying God, with whom Mother Jerusalem/ Daughter Zion pleads.

As we turn to the text of Lamentations, I describe for the students the acrostic structuring devices used in the poems. I suggest to the students a variety of ways the acrostics might function, including as a memory aid, a compositional aid, a compositional constraint, an aid to catharsis, and a way of limiting horror, grief, or anger. I ask students to consider why the poet abandons the alphabet in the final chapter. Then as an extra credit assignment I offer my students the opportunity to compose their own acrostic lament or complaint. The goal of the assignment is for students to experience and explore how this use of the alphabet functions in the composition process. I allot time on a later date for in class discussion of the students' observations and a few dramatic readings.

The acrostic structuring of the poems introduces the idea of movement within the laments (e.g., from question to complaint, complaint to hope, curse to blessing, and so on). I sketch the contents and structure of the book, tracing the movement within and between each of the five chapters. I then invite students to break into small groups and assign one chapter to each group. Each group is to read their assigned lament together out loud, then address the following questions (note that questions 8–10 are tailored for divinity students):

(1) Who is speaking, and at what points in the poem? (2) What is the effect? For example, are there multiple viewpoints? Do voices change within the poem? If so, do they interweave, interrupt, ignore, contradict, answer one another? Are there missing voices, and if so, what is the effect? Would a canonical or liturgical context supply voices that are

missing? (3) What are the dominant emotions? (4) What is the tone? (5) Is there movement in the poem? (6) What are the themes? (7) What imagery is used to convey them? (8) How might a community of faith benefit from praying or reciting this text? (9) What pastoral resources might one find in it? What is the value of recreating suffering? Confronting the reality of death? When is it too much? What is the relationship between personal grief and communal grief? How do conventional modes of expression or shared language make it easier to deal with grief? (10) Would you preach this text, and if so, how?

After allowing sufficient time for small-group discussion, we return to the larger group format and I invite the students to discuss each chapter in turn, sharing insights from their small-group discussions.

Anathea Portier-Young

148. LAMENTATIONS: READING POETRY OF DISTRESS IN DISTRESSING TIMES

The aim of this exercise is to convey a sense of the horror and distress attending the destruction of Jerusalem in 586 B.C.E. and the subsequent experience of exile. Without an appreciation of the magnitude of this seminal event, much of the literature of the Old Testament, including most of the prophetic writings, fails to resonate or even make sense.

The book of Lamentations is redolent with visceral images of terror, loss, and suffering, but in order for students to register their full impact, these images need to be moved from the page and related to situations that are more immediate and observable. Ideally, the compassion for contemporary victims of war and displacement can then be re-directed also at the suffering speakers in Lamentations.

One very effective strategy is to frame the topic within a unit about South Africa and, more particularly, its very public process of healing exemplified by the Truth and Reconciliation Commission. The reports brought before the Commission's Human Rights Violations Committee often have an eerie resonance with passages in Lamentations. If I am unable to get a speaker I use excerpts from Antjie Krog's *Country of My Skull* (Johannesburg: Random House, 1998), a book which recounts a journalist's experiences of the Truth and Reconciliation hearings. An excellent film resource, meanwhile, is the very moving documentary profiling four amnesty cases brought before the Commission, *A Long Night's Journey Into Day*, directed by Frances Reid and Deborah Hoffmann.

The advantage with this focus topic is that students usually have some prior knowledge about the apartheid era, as well as sympathy for the oppression suffered under a policy of institutionalized racism. Also, there is a veritable flood of recent biblical interpretations from a southern African context, most notably those contained in the recently published volume, *The Bible in Africa* (ed. G. O. West and M. W. Dube; Leiden: Brill, 2000). These provide plenty of scope for subsequent analysis of reading from different perspectives and contexts.

Once, for a change, I used the example of the Dalai Lama and his moving accounts of life in occupied Tibet and then in exile. These are available both on his official website (www.tibet.com) and in his autobiography, *My Land and My People* (New York: Warner Books, 1997). While this focus also worked well, students were less familiar with the tragedies of the history of Tibet.

Most effective of all by far has been having a guest speaker from a country where there have been recent wars and human rights atrocities. Most large universities are sufficiently international to have on campus students or professors from such countries as Uganda, Ethiopia, South Africa, or Zimbabwe, and often they are only too happy to share their personal experiences. I have also located speakers through local Amnesty International groups. Students respond very well to hearing autobiographical accounts of experiences most often radically different from their own. Again and again it is the exchange with visiting speakers that is singled out by students as their favorite part of the course.

After this I divide the class into small groups. Each group discusses a separate chapter of Lamentations and identifies images of suffering and verbs denoting violence (there are plenty and they are gruesome). This activity encourages close examination of discrete texts. Afterwards, each group reports back to the rest of the class, cataloging their findings. Next, we make links with what we have learned about suffering in South Africa and decide how realistic the depiction in Lamentations is. We also try to imagine what the occupation of Jerusalem may have been like and how a reader from a background like that of our speaker, who may have experienced similarly terrible circumstances, might respond to these images. Do these images acknowledge or affirm his or her experiences, or do they unnecessarily open old wounds? By the end of this discussion the brutality and enormity of the destruction of Jerusalem as depicted in Lamentations is much more tangible and lifelike.

Johanna Stiebert

149. THE CHARACTERIZATION OF
QOHELETH IN ECCLESIASTES

The notion of characterization, popular within literary and narrative criticism, provides a useful lens through which one can explore the shape and meaning of Qoheleth's message in the book of Ecclesiastes. The opening verse of the book provides the reader with a particular understanding of Qoheleth, namely, he is a "son of David, king in Jerusalem." The reader uses this information to construct an image of a sage who has acquired wisdom and knowledge through experience. The discourse that follows (1:12–17) also helps to round out this characterization. Since human experience has a pronounced role in Qoheleth's reflections and in wisdom literature more generally, I lead my class through an exercise that seeks to accomplish two tasks: (1) to explore the importance of experience in establishing wisdom; and (2) to show how a person's characteristics—age, experience, social location, gender—shape the way that we hear that person's message.

After briefly providing some introductory material on Ecclesiastes, I begin the exercise by asking the students to share how their own experiences or the experience of others have made them "wiser." This can include asking them to recite pithy proverbs that represent such wisdom (e.g., "The early bird gets the worm"). I also ask them to what extent factors such as race, age, and gender affect the shape of such knowledge. This last step helps to bring out aspects of experience that are particular to different social locations. The class easily comes to the conclusion that human experience makes a huge difference in our contemporary understandings of wisdom.

In the second part of the exercise, I play two renditions of the song, "Hurt," written and performed by Nine Inch Nails and covered by Johnny Cash. The videos actually work best. As introduction, I provide background information about the Nine Inch Nails (NIN) song. Trent Reznor wrote this song, which vividly describes the pain and despair of heroin addiction from the perspective of an addict. The video is a live NIN performance with a barrage of images depicting death and decay in the background. Cash's cover of the song takes on a much different tone even though he does not change the words. The message seems to be one of an old cynic who is wrestling with the meaninglessness of life. His aged voice and face provide a clear characterization of this musical icon's wrestlings at the end of his life. I then ask the class to discuss their reactions to the two versions of the song, focusing on the ways in which the different characterizations of the performers determine the meaning of the song. It is fine if students make value judgments on the different renditions, though I prefer to push the students to see the particularities and contextual nature of the two performances.

The themes in the song—hope, despair, meaningfulness, meaning-lessness, emptiness, and soulful reflection—and the relation of these themes to lived human experience lead very naturally into a discussion of Eccl 1–2. I end the class session with a close reading of the text, empha-sizing the importance of the characterization of Qoheleth as an old king and wise sage for understanding the shape of this wisdom text. To drive home the point made by the two versions of the music video, it may be fruitful to consider whether or how particular passages from Ecclesiastes would communicate a different message if the author were to assume a different persona.

Frank M. Yamada

150. QOHELETH SINGS STAMPS-BAXTER

I begin discussing Qoheleth with a discussion of theodicy (a bridge to the lecture on Job which has preceded it). I point to the way the tensions are resolved in some theodicies by an appeal to knowledge. I end this section with the hymn "Farther Along" as an example. This song, first published by those patrons of Gospel music, the Stamps-Baxter Publishing Com-pany, in 1937, is a well-known example of that genre. The lyrics are widely available in any number of gospel hymnbooks and on the Inter-net. The song has been recorded by many singers, including Elvis Presley, the Byrds, and Dolly Parton, though the canonical version may be that of the Stanley Brothers (reissued on *Precious Memories*, King Records, 2002). In this case, I opt not to play a recording, but, even though my voice is not particularly good, I line the hymn out to the stu-dents so they can sing along. The verse and refrain are essentially identical and the tune is sometimes known to a few students. (An added advantage to singing comes at the end of the lecture.) "Farther Along" resolves the problems of the wicked prospering and the power of death by speaking of a future knowledge which guarantees that human suffer-ing makes sense: "Farther along we'll know all about it/Farther along we'll understand why/Cheer up, my brother, live in the sunshine/We'll understand it all by and by."

The hymn's themes fit nicely with Qoheleth's emphasis on the final-ity of death and his concern for the prosperity of the wicked, so I can refer back to snippets of the hymn as I lecture. Qoheleth, however, can in no way appeal to knowledge to answer his questions, given the instability of all human accomplishments. Despite his rather grim evaluation, Qoheleth refuses to abandon life. In order to help students remember

Qoheleth's perspective, at the end of the lecture, I return to "Farther Along." This time I claim that Qoheleth was kind enough to leave behind a hymn, also published by the Stamps-Baxter Publishing Company. This hymn is comprised of the verses of "Farther Along," which raise the issues of suffering and death, but with a new chorus: "Farther along, we won't know about it/One day you live, the next day you die/Cheer up, my brother, live in the sunshine/There is no way to understand why." Evaluations and anecdotal evidence suggests that the impromptu hymn-sing sticks in students' memories and seems to help them remember the themes of Qoheleth as well.

Donald C. Polaski

151. THE STRUCTURE OF ECCLESIASTES
AND THE VIEWS OF THE TEACHER

In order to help students understand how the epilogue (12:9–14) of Eccle-siastes functions, I use the following exercise. First, I ask students to take out a single sheet of paper and to write the following at the top: "The words of the teacher." Below that they are to list several things that I have said, or suggested, over the course of the term which they found interest-ing, intriguing, or worth considering, but ultimately not quite correct or somehow misguided. Finally, each student must explain briefly why they were not convinced by what was presented in class. Before articulating how this relates to Ecclesiastes, I let them discuss in pairs what they have written. I have found that this part of the exercise—although not directly related to the structure of Ecclesiastes—creates vigorous discussion as students express their dissenting opinions. I then explain how the paper that they have produced mirrors the structure of Ecclesiastes: the pro-logue (1:1) at the top, the body of the book which conveys the views of the Teacher, Qoheleth ("Enjoy life": cf. 2:24; 3:12–13; 8:15; 9:7–9), and the epilogue in which a redactor or author expresses a contrasting perspec-tive ("Fear God and keep his commandments").

To facilitate the discussion of the ideas presented by the Teacher, I play (usually at the beginning of class as students are getting settled) the song "Tripping Billies," by the Dave Matthews Band (1996). The lyrics are not particularly deep or religious, but the chorus—"Eat, drink, and be merry, for tomorrow we die"—clearly echoes Ecclesiastes. (The rest of the song, incidentally, is about getting high and having sex on the beach.) I ask students to compare the chorus of the song with the repeated refrain in Ecclesiastes, which also features the command, essentially, to eat, drink, and be merry. One difference, however, is that the Teacher asserts that his advice is sanctioned by God—that is, God wants one to enjoy the pleasures of eating and drinking (cf. 3:13). Dave Matthews makes no mention of God. From here, one can ask about the "religious" nature of Ecclesiastes, whether or not the Teacher is correct in associating pleasure with God, or whether there is any substantive difference between the views of Dave Matthews and the Teacher.

Finally, the view expressed in Eccl 12:13–14 is similar to the one found generally in Proverbs. I conclude the discussion of Ecclesiastes by posing the following question: Suppose you are parents trying to determine where to put your children in school. Will you send them to "First Proverbs Day School" or "The Teacher's Academy"? This helps students to consider the different worldviews of Proverbs and the Teacher, and it frames the discussion in terms of a contemporary issue. After giving them a few minutes to think about the reasons for their decision, I survey the class to see where they would send their children—usually it is split down the middle. Students then debate the merits of their decision.

Mark Roncace

152. FOOLING AROUND WITH ESTHER

At the end of the class session prior to our study of Esther, I distribute photocopies of the Greek version of Esther to half of the class and photocopies of the Hebrew version to the other half. I do not tell students that I am handing out two different versions. I instruct them to read the text carefully (as always) and to make a number of notes in the margins. I announce that I have photocopied the text precisely so that they could take copious marginal notes which I will collect at the next class period. Although I do not intend to read their notes, it is important to tell them this because students are wondering why I have decided to photocopy Esther, and not any of the other books we have studied. Naturally, requiring them to take notes improves their reading—I think—but the note-taking serves mainly as a decoy. (The Greek version of Esther can be found easily online, but when copying-and-pasting be sure to delete the headings which indicate the additions. You will also likely need to tinker with chapter numbers so that the Greek version does not begin with chapter 11.)

At the next session, I begin the discussion by asking a question that will prompt a different response from each version, such as, "What is the role of God in the story?" Or "What do you make of Mordecai's dream at the beginning?" Usually, after the first student answers, another student quickly asks, "Where do you see that?" or "What are you talking about?" I let the first student respond by pointing to the text, at which time the second student declares that that passage is not in their text, usually followed by a few other students saying it is not in their text either. I like to act confused by the situation and say something along the lines of, "That is strange. I wonder what is going on here. Are you sure those verses are not in your text?" I then ask for a show of hands of those whose version does not have the text in question. Half of the class raises their hand. I then ask those with their hands raised to find someone whose hand is not raise and to pair up and compare their two versions. Alternatively, the Hebrew and Greek versions could be marked ahead of time in an inconspicuous location—the number one on the back of the Greek text, and the number two on the back of the Hebrew version, for example. The teacher would then ask students with a text marked "one" to partner with someone who has a "two."

Each pair of students is to compare carefully the two versions and to outline the differences between them (which can be found in most any introduction to the Greek version, many of which are online). Specifically, they need to identify the added material in the Greek version and then consider the effects of that material on the overall story. After discussing the differences, each pair is to decide which version they prefer or which one they would recommend to be in the Bible, if only one could be chosen. Since I teach at a Baptist institution, I also ask which version they think is, in fact, in their Bible. Many students, not surprisingly, argue that the Greek version is better and thus the one in their Protestant canon. Incidentally, even those students who (think they) know the Hebrew version will rarely realize beforehand that they are reading the Greek.

This exercise encourages students to explore many of the literary features of Esther (both versions), enhances their comparative skills, and opens the door for discussing issues of canon formation.

Mark Roncace

153. CHRONOLOGICAL DISPLACEMENTS IN EZRA-NEHEMIAH

Genres raise expectations in readers. Modern readers invariably bring such expectations of genre with them when reading biblical narratives. Thus, when reading a text such as Ezra-Nehemiah, students will recognize it to resemble what they know as "history." And in our cultural context, the genre of history assumes factual and chronological accuracy. Biblical historical narrative must measure up to what students perceive history to be: a chronologically accurate record. Of course, the fact that the narrative is in the Bible only raises the stakes for many students: an *inspired* text must be accurate. This exercise helps students see the differences between ancient and modern historiography and also provides an opportunity to practice the art of historical criticism despite the fact that they are not (yet) experts on the Bible.

Historical reconstruction of the period of restoration is difficult. One of the thorny questions is, "Who came first, Ezra or Nehemiah?" Students are baffled by the very question, for as one reads the text it is obvious who came first—Ezra appears on stage in Ezra 7 and Nehemiah does not appear on stage until Neh 1, the next book. Why would scholars even ask such a question?

Students are given the task of doing some basic historical reconstruction with respect to the rebuilding of the temple and the arrival of Ezra. They are directed to chronological markers in the narrative, specifically Ezra 1:1; 3:8; 6:15; and 7:1–7. They read these texts and date the following events according to the manner that the narrative dates events. When did the Jewish people begin their return to Judah? The first year of King Cyrus (Ezra 1:1). When did the Jews begin to lay the foundation to rebuild the temple? The second year after they returned, approximately a couple of years after the beginning of Cyrus' reign (Ezra 3:8). When did the Jews complete the temple? The sixth year of King Darius (Ezra 6:15). When did Ezra arrive? The seventh year of King Artaxerxes (Ezra 7:7).

I place on an overhead the dates of the reigns of the respective kings according to modern calendars, so that students can "translate" the dates into more familiar categories. The Jews began their return in 539 B.C.E., they laid the foundation of the temple in 537 B.C.E., they completed the temple in 516 B.C.E. (we deal with the more precise date of 515 later), and Ezra arrived in 458 B.C.E., decades after the completion of the temple. I then ask, "Why did it take so long for the Jewish people to rebuild their temple" (more than 20 years)? I direct them to read Ezra 4:7–24 to answer to my question. Ezra 4:23–24 is quite explicit: a letter from King Artaxerxes compelled the Jews to stop working on their temple "until the second year of the reign of King Darius" (4:24).

My next question is, "What's wrong with this picture?" It does not take long for students to recognize that a letter from Artaxerxes, who did not come to power until 465 B.C.E., decades after the temple was completed, could not have been the reason why the Jews ceased working on the temple ca. 537 B.C.E. I point out that it is not a question of the biblical historian's competence. The historian is well aware that Artaxerxes comes later—he dates the stories of both Ezra and Nehemiah around the reign of this king. But it does raise the question whether chronology is the biblical historian's primary concern. Might some other "-logy," such as theology or ideology, have been what drove his narrative presentation? Those are questions to be addressed later, but, for many students, there is now at least a receptivity to the possibility that the order of events in the literary text does not necessarily match up with the order of events in history.

Consequently, many are more open to give weight to the subtle clues in the narrative that Ezra may, in fact, have come after Nehemiah. Such clues include Ezra's reference to a "wall" (Ezra 9:9), not yet rebuilt, or the reference that Nehemiah was a contemporary of the high priest Eliashib (Neh 3:1, 20), while Ezra was a contemporary of Jehohanan, the "son of Eliashib" (Ezra 10:6). The clues, admittedly, are subtle, but the glaring chronological displacement of Artaxerxes' letter in Ezra 4 at least makes many students recognize that the historian could "rearrange" events if it served his purpose to do so. Subsequent discussion may focus on how or whether such activity is in any sense problematic.

J. Bradley Chance

154. EZRA, NEHEMIAH, AND THE FOREIGN WOMEN

As part of a course on the restoration period in Israel's history, this class will focus on Ezra and Nehemiah and their treatment of the foreign women. Understanding the nature of these postexilic writings is especially important because the Bible can be a dangerous book if used uncritically, particularly in light of the continuing danger of xenophobia in the world.

The class starts with a small-group exercise in which students are asked to read two texts that deal with Ezra's and Nehemiah's treatment of foreign women (Ezra 9:10–10:5; Neh 13:23–27). Most students are not familiar with these texts and are quite shocked by the brutal treatment of these women. Students are then asked to come up with some explanations for Ezra's and Nehemiah's behavior. I provide hints that may help students make sense of these difficult texts, e.g., the nature and significance of Ezra's and Nehemiah's respective tasks (cf. the emphasis on the law in Ezra 7 and Neh 9, and Nehemiah's venture of rebuilding the wall in Neh 6:15–7:4 which symbolizes a renewed fervor for boundaries). I also direct students to a number of texts from Deuteronomy that provide laws dealing with the treatment of foreigners in Israel (e.g., the command to "utterly destroy" the other inhabitants of Israel and the prohibition against intermarriage in Deut 7:1–6; cf. also Deut 23:1–3, where Moabites and Ammonites are prohibited from forming part of the congregation of Israel).

In class discussion, we reflect on these topics, helping students to understand how the writers of Ezra and Nehemiah used and intensified the deuteronomistic legal traditions. We talk about the fear and scape-goating of strangers (and particularly foreign women), which grew out of attempts to find reasons for the exile and the loss of land. The renewed emphasis on the law and the importance of boundaries between us (the people of Israel) and them (the inhabitants of the land) help us to understand why these troubling texts appear in these postexilic writings.

In the next part of the class, we deal with the important hermeneutical question of how the Bible can be dangerous if used uncritically. These problematic texts are in the Bible, and people have used them to detrimental effect in the past. (Ferdinand Deist shows how these troubling texts with regard to foreigners were used in the context of Apartheid South Africa; cf. "The Dangers of Deuteronomy: A Page from the Reception History of the Book," in *Studies in Deuteronomy in Honour of C. J. Labuschagne* [ed. F. Garcia Martinez et. al.; Leiden: Brill, 1994], 13–29.) To understand these dangers is particularly relevant due to the continuing danger of xenophobia. I give students a definition of xenophobia and ask them to come up with instances of xenophobia in the world today—and closer to home, in the United States. In response to this question, students often cite instances of violence against Arabs after 9/11. We also talk about what happened in Nazi Germany, and how the terrible atrocities were preceded by a gradual process of building walls between Germans and German Jews, creating stereotypes, and dehumanizing and demonizing the other.

Toward the end of the class, I introduce the 1895 poem by Thomas Aldrich called "Unguarded Gates" (http://xroads.virginia.edu/~CAP/LIBERTY/aldrichp.html). This poem talks about the fear of foreigners that was present in the U.S. at the end of the ninteenth century. It is a significant teaching moment when students realize that the foreigners, who according to Aldrich have come "to waste the gifts of freedom" and whom he begs Lady Liberty to keep out with hands of steel, are among others from Irish/Italian descent—American citizens who today are considered to be very much at the center of society. This class often generates discussion about popular perceptions of immigrants and how one ought to think about immigrants today.

I end the class with the counter-narrative of Ruth, which comes from the same period as Ezra and Nehemiah. The integration of Ruth, a foreign Moabite woman, into the community of Israel—even becoming part of the royal family—shows how the biblical traditions offer correctives or alternative visions to the very exclusivist texts that we encounter in Ezra and Nehemiah. (For other exercises on women in biblical texts, see §§50, 55, 191, 226, 242, 267.)

L. Juliana M. Claassens

155. ISRAEL'S IDENTITY CRISIS IN THE POSTEXILIC ERA

The objective of this exercise is to understand Ruth, Jonah, and Esther as books addressing the crisis of identity in Persian Period Judah (Yehud), specifically as offering alternatives to the dominant (exclusivist) view of Ezra-Nehemiah. These three books are often difficult for students to incorporate into their understanding of the Old Testament as a whole. Taking advantage of their likely Persian Period origins, this approach links them into a larger interpretive scheme with Ezra-Nehemiah, addressing the burning question of the era: that of the identity of the true Israel.

This session is designed to follow a session that offers historical orientation to the exile and the Persian Period in broad strokes. Specifically, it is assumed that students have been familiarized with the exclusivist perspective on the surrounding peoples embodied in Ezra and Nehemiah, specifically, that foreigners, and especially foreign women, were perceived as a threat to Israel's identity, purity, and orthodoxy, and so should be forcibly excluded from contact with the community as far as possible. When placed alongside Ezra-Nehemiah, the implied perspectives on Yehud's neighbors found in these three books constitute dissenting voices in the canon.

In Ruth, the most important themes include loyalty, even and especially across ethnic/national and religious boundaries, and God's work behind the scenes in the human community. These themes are relevant to the "neighbor question" in that the Moabite Ruth is a vessel and a recipient of Yahweh's blessing, and is even linked to David. Hence, the neighbors have a positive role to play in Yahweh's plans. Discussion could focus on issues relating to intermarriage between cultures and religions, a question that is relevant both to the Persian Period and to the contemporary context of the students.

In Jonah, the most important theme is that God is merciful even when God's people are not. Jonah is a figure for Israel, actively resisting God's call to reach out; held up for ridicule as his halfhearted effort yields incredible results; defiant to the end and resistant to Yahweh's efforts to show care and mercy to Nineveh. Relevance to the question of the neighbors is clear: The neighbors are also proper objects of God's care and mercy, whatever Jonah (Israel!) thinks. The use of satire and humor in Jonah is a fertile source of discussion: What are we to make of a book making fun of its "hero," especially if he is a figure for Israel?

In Esther, the key theme is that God's help for his people is achieved only by those people (Esther and Mordecai in this case) working within the system for Israel's good. Again, this is directly relevant to Yehud's quandary, claiming that the best way for the Jews to survive and thrive is not to withdraw from larger society, but to work within the system and so preserve the ability to affect events that would otherwise be beyond their control. Discussion might consider the impact of Esther's story in a post-Holocaust world.

Concluding discussion may focus on various issues. If the course is more historically oriented, discussion might center on how each of these perspectives relate to the political and historical dynamics of life in the Persian Period. A more theologically oriented class might consider the relevance of this discussion of identity and the "neighbors" for contemporary faith communities. In either case, the current situation(s) in the Middle East offer a great range of discussion possibilities centered around the coexistence of "neighboring" cultures, including Israel. (For exercises on related topics, see §§67, 158.)

D. Matthew Stith

HEBREW BIBLE

Varia

156. COMPARING DIFFERENT PORTRAYALS OF GOD

The first days teaching a survey course on the Hebrew Bible can be especially daunting. Where does one begin? So many introductory issues compete for attention—historical contexts, geographical settings, the diversity of texts and genres, canon formation. And all of these come with the baggage of unfamiliar terminology and foreign concepts, which many students, unfamiliar with critical study of the Bible, find extremely challenging. The situation is particularly fraught since setting the wrong sort of tone at the start of a course can lead to a permanent disengagement on the part of students. For these reasons, on the second day of class, instead of lecturing on, for instance, canon formation or the historical backdrop of the Bible, I move right into an interactive text-based exercise.

The topic is different portrayals of the deity. To prepare for class, students read three texts: Exod 15:1–18; Hos 11:1–9; and Ps 96. All three are poetic, all three have numerous descriptors of the deity, and each of the three comes from one of the three main sections of the Tanak. When students come into class I immediately divide them into small groups. We begin with the Exodus text. I give the students some brief background information (the identity of the speaker, the event being described, approximate date of composition) and explain unfamiliar names (Moab, Edom, Canaan, Philistia). Each group then spends about ten to fifteen minutes coming up with their own answers to the following set of questions: (1) How is God portrayed in this text? Consider names used, actions taken, roles assumed, and so forth; and 2) What was your reaction to this portrayal? What did you like or dislike? What was confusing or strange? Conversely, what was familiar? After the small groups have had time to talk through their responses, the class as a whole discusses and compares their findings. In this discussion, I have the opportunity to introduce such concepts as henotheism, anthropomorphizing the deity, and Divine Warrior mythology. Then we move on to the Hosea text. The same process takes place. In the class discussion that ensues for this passage, besides all the specifics that the students point out, I indicate how

240

the language (especially v. 4) is suggestive of the deity being portrayed as feminine, specifically, as a mother. That, in turn, becomes a major launching point for comparing the Hosea text to that of Exodus, for the differences are striking and quite compelling to the students. As we grapple with some of the reasons for those differences—different time periods, different authors and audiences, different circumstances—students begin to see and accept the immense diversity and complexity of the Bible, and even the challenging possibility that outright contradictions may be found within it.

The discussion is always quite lively on this day (often we do not even have time to consider the Psalm passage). Students may know nothing about the Bible, and yet they have all thought about God. So they all have something to bring to the discussion, they feel confident about participating, and are eager to do so. For me as the instructor, this particular class helps in setting the tone for how teaching and learning will take place throughout the semester: it signals that discussion will be central, small-groups will be utilized frequently, and students will be expected to be active and engaged in their own learning. The class also introduces some key emphases of the course, especially the focus on the many expressions of diversity in the Bible, and the need to attend always to the particularities of any given biblical text. (For other introductory exercises, see §§26–27.)

Karla G. Bohmbach

157. THE CELEBRATION AND COMMEMORATION OF JEWISH HOLIDAYS

In order to show students concretely how the Bible has always belonged to a living community and that it has been enacted, celebrated, and mourned, I ask small groups of students to enact a series of Jewish holidays: Rosh Hashanah, Yom Kippur, Hanukkah, Passover, Shavuoth, Sukkoth, Purim, and Sabbath. These feasts also have the benefit of tangibly illustrating that Jewish scriptures have been modified over the years during holidays such as Purim, during which children nowadays dress up as cowboys and heroines. Similarly, many biblical texts were modified by successive generations (e.g., the Decalogue in Exod 20 and Deut 5; the various poetic versions of prose, as in Exod 14–15 and Judg 4–5; and the Chronicler's adaptations of the Deuteronomistic History).

The greatest challenge of this activity is logistical. I divide the class into small groups. Each group is given a handout that clearly states the required elements of each feast: historical and biblical background; food and drink (lots of it—suitable for that feast); decorations; games and activities; and music for that feast. For resources, I have a few Jewish family feast books on hand and provide a list of websites designed for Jewish children. Because my college is in an urban center (Seattle) I encourage students to visit a local Jewish store and bakery.

It is essential to underscore that the small group which presents is *enacting* the feast rather than reporting upon it. Students who are not Jewish tend readily to adopt descriptive statements such as, "Jewish people celebrate Purim." These are inadmissible. The small group's job is to cause the class to live into the reality of the feasts and fasts of the Jewish calendar.

These mini-holidays last a maximum of thirty minutes, occur typically every Friday, and begin at the start of class. In the past, I ended the class with them, but students had so much to prepare that I shifted these enactments to the beginning rather than the end of class. Very often I am astonished by the level of creativity that has gone into these holidays. Typically the room is decorated, often with simulated tables on the floor with candles and appropriate decorations, with rows of seats in various configurations or with one long runner for the entire class, with a feast spread along it. The food is almost always presented beautifully and amply. Music is invariably playing upon the other students' arrival, and frequently the presenters hand out accoutrements to students as they enter (e.g., coffee filters which they decorate as *yarmulkas*). The scene is nearly always dramatic, and student creativity flourishes. Students enjoy the feasts immensely, the classroom atmosphere lightens and livens, the lesson of a living community that embraces and modifies tradition is learned, and the faculty member has the rare privilege of laughing and lingering with the students and, often enough, dancing with them.

John R. Levison

158. DIASPORA AND IDENTITY

It is commonplace for interpreters and teachers of the Hebrew and Aramaic Scriptures to characterize several biblical texts, including Esther and Dan 1–6, as well as certain books belonging to the so-called Old Testament Apocrypha (including Greek Esther, the Additions to Daniel, Wisdom of Solomon, 3 Maccabees, et al.), as "Diaspora literature." Among other things these texts often attempt to negotiate questions of identity and identity formation for a Jewish audience living outside of the traditional Israelite homeland—questions such as: What does it mean to be a Jew outside of Jerusalem and Judea? How can one be faithful to a community and set of traditions in an environment that may be welcoming, indifferent, or even openly hostile to that community and its traditions?

When studying the Diaspora literature, in order to have students begin actively thinking about how one or more of the biblical texts negotiate these sorts of questions, as well as how such biblical queries and responses might inform our own thinking, I initially ask students to read the first chapter of W. E. B. Du Bois's masterpiece *The Souls of Black Folk* (1903; the text is widely available on the Internet). In this essay entitled "Of Our Spiritual Strivings," Du Bois introduces the rich concept of "double consciousness." Du Bois describes the experience of "double consciousness" as the perennial feeling of "twoness," of being American and also African while existing bodily in the United States replete with its history of slavery and Jim Crow. To this "double consciousness" belongs, Du Bois explains, the desire to merge the "double self into a better and truer self" and the wish for *"neither of the older selves to be lost"* (italics added).

After highlighting in discussion significant features of Du Bois's idea of "double consciousness," I ask students to identify in one or more of the biblical Diaspora texts, such as Esther or Dan 1–6, traces of just such a consciousness. Specifically, I ask them to consider aspects of the characterization of Esther or Daniel (and other textual figures) that illustrate the "twoness" of being Jewish in a Gentile environment. How, or to what extent, do the characters in the text adopt or ignore particular Jewish practices or beliefs? How, or to what extent, do they adopt or reject aspects of the Gentile world of which they are a part? What in the text suggests the Gentile environment is welcoming, indifferent, or hostile to a Jewish presence? In order to have students consider more specifically questions of identity construction I next shift the line of questioning slightly. For instance, I ask if certain things (e.g., adherence to food regulations, avoidance of idols, etc.) are essential to being Jewish for the particular Diaspora text under consideration. Do other Diaspora books answer these questions in the same or different ways? For example, how does Esther offer a different response to Jewish Diaspora existence and identity from that of Daniel? How is it different from the Greek version of Esther (now easily accessible in editions of the NRSV with Apocrypha)? Is one of these texts "more right" than the others? Why or why not?

After broaching and beginning to answer these sorts of questions, I attempt to move the class toward a conversation about how biblical Diaspora texts might inform a range of contemporary questions of identity. I begin either by asking this question explicitly or by returning to aspects of earlier conversations if students have already implicitly alluded to it. Depending on the make-up, concerns, and anxieties of the particular class, this conversation can move in a variety of directions. However, specific kinds of questions such as the following can emerge: What does it mean to be: A Christian in Korea? A person of African descent in the United States? An American with Mexican ancestry? A Jew living in Diaspora in North America? A Christian and a patriot? In guiding this conversation, it is of course important to be careful not to have individual students, or clusters of students, become mouthpieces or essential representatives of whatever communities with which they may, to one degree or another, identify.

The questions can, of course, become even more complicated than the examples just mentioned. The point, however, is that many students possess a deep, but at times inchoate knowledge, of what it means to be a person "between" cultures and commitments. They understand what it means to identify with a community and set of traditions that the dominant culture can embrace, despise, commodify, or co-opt, while at the same time they recognize what it entails to be formed in a meaningful way by that very same culture.

Hence, besides offering a helpful way into the study of certain biblical texts, a class session treating Diaspora literature that begins with something like Du Bois's notion of "double consciousness" can provide much more. It can invite students to begin self-consciously recognizing and articulating their own sense of identity and the practices and processes that continually form that identity. It can highlight as well the tensions that might be inherent in their various self-understandings. The exercise can also help students who associate more strongly with a dominant culture to appreciate and more adequately engage their colleagues whose sense of Diaspora existence may be significantly stronger. In addition, this sort of class session can provide an opportunity for discussion of a central hermeneutical issue, namely, the role of the reader and the reader's context in the process of interpretation. Hence, I sometimes close a class session on Diaspora literature and "double consciousness" by returning to the earlier discussion of the biblical documents. It is often instructive to ask which students were able most easily to recognize in the biblical texts elements of "double consciousness" and the tensions of Diaspora existence. Was it students who themselves live in an analogous Diaspora context? (For exercises on related topics, see §§67, 155.)

Timothy J. Sandoval

159. ANCIENT NEAR EASTERN LITERATURE AND THE BIBLE: THE STELA OF KING MESHA OF MOAB

In this exercise, the stele of King Mesha of Moab is introduced with some brief notes on its discovery, date, and provenance. Students then read an English translation of the text of the stele in groups. A translation is readily available in standard anthologies such as William Hallo, *The Context of Scripture: Volume 2* (New York: Brill, 2000); Victor Matthews and Don Benjamin, *Old Testament Parallels* (rev. ed.; New York: Paulist, 1997); or James Pritchard, *Ancient Near Eastern Texts Relating to the Old Testament* (2nd ed.; Princeton, Princeton University Press, 1955); besides a translation, a very useful discussion is also found in Klaas A. D. Smelik, *Writings From Ancient Israel* (trans. G. I. Davies; Louisville: Westminster/John Knox, 1991). Students are asked to highlight the actions attributed to Kemosh, the god of the Moabites, and to reconstruct, in their groups, the basic theology (or ideology) of the Moabites vis-à-vis their god. In a following plenary, the group reports are used by the instructor to outline the Moabite theology on the blackboard.

The students are then asked to reread the text of the stele, but this time to make the following substitutions: Yahweh or Lord God in place of Kemosh; Israel instead of Moab; Solomon instead of Mesha; Moab instead of Israel; Mesha instead of Ahab. The student groups now discuss whether the text of the stele, thus altered, would fit with the theology (or ideology) of the Hebrew Bible. Biblical passages such as Num 21, Josh 10:28–40, and 1 Sam 15 are read to illustrate the theology in the Hebrew Bible.

In the following plenary, the instructor draws attention to the following similarities between the theology expressed in the Mesha stele and in the Hebrew Bible: defeat in battle is the result of the god's anger; victory is the result of the god's pleasure; in thankfulness for victory, the king builds a temple or "high place" for the god; war has a ritual religious character (it is commanded by the god), plunder is brought to the god in the temple, and the enemy population is ritually slaughtered ("sacrificed" or "put to the ban").

The purpose of this exercise is to demonstrate to students that the various parts of the Hebrew Bible share much the same theology or ideology as the ancient Near Eastern literary and religious context out of which they emerged. Because of this commonality, the study of other ancient Near Eastern texts is indispensable for an understanding of the Hebrew Bible in its original context. (Students at this point could read Morton Smith's old but still relevant article, "The Common Theology of the Ancient Near East," *JBL* 71 [1952]: 135–47.) (For a similar exercise, see §8.)

F. V. Greifenhagen

160. ANCIENT NEAR EASTERN PARALLELS
AND HIP HOP SAMPLING

Students are sometimes troubled (or intrigued) by the use of ancient Near Eastern materials in the Hebrew Bible, especially in the Primeval History, most notably, perhaps, in the creation accounts and their probable dependence on, or at least interaction with, other Near Eastern creation accounts (e.g., *Enuma Elish, Atrahasis,* etc.). One way to approach this phenomenon and student reactions to it is through a comparable interpretive move in popular music, especially in hip hop and rap. The technique is called sampling as it excerpts ("samples") portions of preexisting songs and reuses them in new compositions. The technique caused a big stir in the late 1980s and early 1990s given the widespread use of sampling in rappers like MC Hammer and Vanilla Ice (especially his use of David Bowie's "Under Pressure" in his hit "Ice, Ice, Baby") and the lawsuits that were subsequently filed regarding copyright infringement and fair use. Many artists of many kinds still use sampling extensively now, but with appropriate permissions and credits and usually with time restrictions on the length of the sample.

I usually begin the discussion by playing the newer song long enough to get to the sample. Then I ask the students if they recognize that piece of music. Many will not, but some will; still fewer will be able to place the earlier piece and assign it a name and attribute it to the correct artist. I then play the original song that was sampled from and then, again, the new composition that samples the older piece. The entirety of the songs need not be played; snippets will typically suffice. I ask the students to compare and contrast the two compositions. Students typically enjoy the musical example, especially if the newer song is fairly recent and popular. Past songs that I have used include Puff Daddy's reuse of The Police's "Every Breath You Take" (1983) in his song "I'll Be Missing You" (1997) or the string of samples in Will Smith's popular album *Big Willie Style* (1997).

I also ask students to consider why the new composition sampled the old in the first place. It would seem that samplers, whether intentionally or not, often use the old song in ways that echo the original or that reverse it. Consider Will Smith's use of Sister Sledge's "He's the Greatest Dancer" in his dance song ("Gettin' Jiggy Wit It"). There are other interpretive options beyond these, and students are usually good at identifying them, but, whatever the precise case, the old sample becomes part of a new song when it is set in the new composition. The old is incorporated into a new musical and rhetorical context and lends its voice to the new, even while it continues to hark back to what is best (read: most funky!) about the earlier composition.

The point of this modern musical example is to help students see that there are other ways to "read" an ancient Near Eastern parallel beyond seeing it as a simplistic, unoriginal, and "whole-cloth" borrowing on the part of Israel. In fact, the modern example shows the "commercial" benefits of sampling from preexisting chart-toppers so as to build effectively on what has gone before without having to recreate the wheel (i.e., come up with a new hook). Top ten hits get to the top ten for a reason, and songs that draw on them are hoping for similar success. New compositions that sample the old may also broaden their listener base by appealing to older generations, who knew the originals, as well as newer ones, who do not. So, here too, one finds alternative ways to think about the phenomenon of parallels beyond the older, rather unidirectional, and unhelpful questions of genetic dependence.

Brent A. Strawn

161. ROLE-PLAYING NARRATIVES
FROM THE HEBREW BIBLE

The Hebrew Bible is a very strange text to many students: strange words, strange concepts, strange characters, strange practices. How, then, to span the socio-cultural distance between our own world and that of the Bible? How to get students excited about its stories? How, further, to convey to them the potential relevance of these stories for commenting on, and opening up, some of the truths and realities of their own lives? This exercise attempts to respond to these challenges.

In outline, the plan is quite simple: choose a fairly short narrative from the Hebrew Bible and have students from the class take on the roles of the different characters. (No "acting" is expected; the students are simply to speak their roles.) Narratives that work particularly well include Gen 22, Judg 4 (with reference to Judg 5), Ruth, and 2 Sam 11. Each of these has about eight to ten speaking roles. So, for instance, when we do Gen 22, the roles students take on are that of the narrator, God, Abraham, Isaac, Sarah, angel of the Lord, and two servant-boys; when we do Judg 4, the characters include the narrator, Deborah, Lappidoth (as Deborah's husband), Barak, Sisera, Jabin, Jael, Heber the Kenite, Sisera's mother, and God. (It can be a struggle to create an equal number of male and female speaking roles, though students also often cross genders, with women students taking on male roles, and vice versa.)

In class, then, we simply read through the story, with the students assigned to their roles reading their parts. Upon finishing the story, the remaining students in the class then get to ask questions of the different biblical characters, with the students playing those roles having to stay "in character" as they respond to the questions. This is where the fun really begins, for the students often create rather unusual, not to say provocative, interpretations of the narrative (e.g., Uriah the Hittite was in love with David). Of course, the role-playing students also have to nuance the construction of their character in relation to, and in response to, the characterization constructed by other students for their characters; this is easier for some than for others.

I have also experimented with various overall formats for this exercise. Sometimes we do it only once or twice in the semester; on the days in question, I rather informally ask for student volunteers to fill the roles; they then must construct their characters "on the spot." At other times we have done this exercise enough in the semester so that every student, at some point, has the opportunity to take on a role. In this latter instance, students sign up for roles far ahead of time and must, in addition, to the in-class work, submit a two-page written analysis of their character to me either before or after the classroom role-play occurs.

In the course of the semester, this exercise can really help students hone their close-reading skills of the biblical text. They also come to understand some of the particulars, and the peculiarities, of biblical narrative (e.g., strategic use of repetition; direct discourse utilized for emphasis; thoughts, feelings, and motivations of characters rarely made explicit). Finally, some of the cultural distance between the biblical world and our own is spanned—especially in narratives that touch on domestic or interpersonal relations. The difficulties of Bathsheba—torn between two men and caught up in patriarchal power struggles—can be not so far removed from certain life-situations of women today. Ruth's use of her sexuality, and her manipulation by an older woman to do so, is again something which many students can recognize. And the anguish of Isaac, an almost-sacrifice to his father's god, can resonate very close to the bone of student awareness of child abuse. (For other exercises using role-play, see §§195, 199, 203, 241, 246, 265.)

Karla G. Bohmbach

162. 1 MACCABEES: "THAT ALL SHOULD BE ONE PEOPLE"

One of the fundamental dilemmas addressed in 1 Maccabees is assimilation, an issue many undergraduate students perceive as far removed from their own problems and concerns. This exercise helps to foster some

empathy for those faced with this dilemma in 1 Macc 1–4 by asking them
to consider how reflection on their own experience of otherness facilitates
their reading and discussion of the responses made by various Jewish
groups to Antiochus IV Epiphanes' decree in 1 Macc 1:41–42 "that all
should be one people, and that all should give up their particular customs." (Similar exercises could be designed in connection with texts from
the Deuteronomistic History in which assimilation is a major concern.)

Prior to class each student is asked to write a one-page reflection in
which they identify and evaluate a situation in which they experienced
otherness. Students often turn to an experience in which they were in the
minority category broadly construed (gender, sexual, cultural, ethnic,
religious). Obviously the experiences they elicit will range widely. Many
times such experiences incorporate study, work, or travel abroad, immigrant status, gender or ethnic isolation in an educational setting, or
religious practice. In order to focus their reflection, I give them some
guiding questions: What defines otherness in this situation? What were
the conditions of your otherness (temporary, permanent) and how did
you feel in this situation? How did you think and act as a result of this
status? Are the factors that define(d) you as the other essential to your
identity? If so, how do you appropriate your experience of otherness? On
some campuses this exercise might be expanded or altered to include a
brief interview with someone who has confronted assimilation firsthand.
Interviews might be conducted with immigrant relatives, fellow students,
or campus personnel. In this case, students can be asked to write out their
questions for approval beforehand and to supply in writing interviewee
responses and student assessment. After the students have considered
otherness in either of these ways, they read 1 Maccabees and identify the
Jewish responses to Antiochus's decree in chapters 1–3.

In class, we map these responses on the board: assimilation (1 Macc
1:43–53); resistance and martyrdom of the Jewish women (1 Macc
1:60–63); resistance by not fighting on the Sabbath (1 Macc 2:29–38); and
active resistance of the Maccabees who fight against the king's forces (1
Macc 2:39–43). Students are then divided randomly into small groups.
Each group is given one of these responses for evaluation. How is this
response defined in the narrative? What are the reasons (implicit and
explicit) given for this response? What was sacrificed and what was
gained in this response? How does your own understanding of otherness
affect your assessment of this response? Small groups report a summary
of their evaluations to the class and this, in turn, becomes the basis for a
discussion of these responses in the larger context of the book of 1 Maccabees. Why does the narrative clearly favor one of the responses? Why
might it include the others? What is the purpose of this narrative as apocryphal literature? Many times this discussion extends into the present

HEBREW BIBLE

context and we move to consideration of the risks and gains (personal and social) of instances of assimilation.

Bernadette McNary-Zak

163. THE BOOK OF JUDITH:
TO DECEIVE OR NOT TO DECEIVE?

Undergraduate students often welcome discussion of the book of Judith because its heroine is a complex figure. Her actions emerge from prayerful reflection and forethought and they betray a profound, revered depth of insight about human nature and right relations with God. Students appreciate the opportunity that the book provides to consider operative paradigms for the exercise of loyalty, honor, and faithfulness. Although the following exercise can be adapted to accommodate any of these themes, close reading and assessment of Judith's actions in chapters 8–13 supplies a context particularly suited to a discussion of how deceit functions in a system of values. It is here that Judith gains the blind trust and support of the Israelites in order to effect her plan to slay the opposing Assyrian general, Holofernes, singlehandedly and in secret. She prays for courage and strength: "By the deceit of my lips strike down the slave with the prince and the prince with his servant; crush their arrogance by the hand of a woman" (Jdt 9:10).

The exercise presents a systematic way to think about the meaning of deceit and about the relationship between deceit and one's values. (Similar exercises could be used in connection with other biblical instances of dishonesty; e.g., Abraham, Jacob, Laban, et al.) The students are given two assignments in preparation for class discussion. First, they write a one-page description of two instances in their own life where deceit was a motivating factor for action (one instance must be from the perspective of the deceiver, the other of the deceived) and an evaluation of what they learned about when and why people deceive from these instances. Next, they read the book of Judith in its entirety. Finally, they return for a close reading of chapters 8–13 in which they identify and evaluate Judith's exercise of deceit.

Our class discussion of deceit begins with Judith's intentions and actions. From a literary perspective, what is the role of her deceit in the movement of the story? How does her speech to Uzziah and the other Israelites function to define the broader context of her deceit? From these we move to consideration of the specific nature of her actions. How are her actions deceitful? Whom is she deceiving and why? How does her deceit affect the descriptors that illumine her character, such as her piety? Is her deceit justified? How do the outcomes of her deceit factor into this assessment? Throughout discussion, students are often compelled to return to the narrative in defense of their reading of her actions. When we then read together the Song of Judith in chapter 15 they are challenged further to consider why there is no explicit mention of the deceit that prompted such heroic and saving actions.

It is at this point that I move discussion toward a broader consideration of the nature of deceit in one's system of values. While I do not encourage the students to share the details of the descriptions of deceit that they prepared prior to their reading of Judith, I do ask them to talk in general terms about what they learned regarding when and why people deceive. Under what conditions do we deceive? For what ends? Is deceit ever necessary?

In conclusion, I ask the students to assess the usefulness of the exercise. How did their personal written reflection influence how they read this book? How did it contribute to their understanding of the choice to deceive? Students admit the value of the exercise (in spite of the fact that it asked them to do some additional preparatory work) and leave the class pondering a fairly sophisticated conception of the nature of deceit in the case of Judith and in their own relationships.

Bernadette McNary-Zak

PART 3
NEW TESTAMENT

The Gospels and Acts

164. GOSPEL OR GOSPELS?

After teaching a unit on Jesus and the Gospels, including the move toward a four-gospel canon interpreted harmoniously, I break the class into small groups and ask them to choose one gospel to preserve for themselves and for the church(es). (If they insist, I allow them to choose a private gospel and a church gospel. Their choice may well be a non-canonical gospel.) The exercise encourages students to think about the individual gospels as unique entities and the role of ideology and politics in forming a "canon." As the class is functioning in small groups, each group is, in effect, a canon-forming entity. As a result, the small groups garner first-hand experience with the politics involved in canon formation as individuals lobby in their respective groups for their own preferences.

When the class comes back together, much of the discussion revolves around dissent in the small groups, and this conversation presents an additional opportunity to talk about canon formation and sectarian dissent. As the groups present their preferences, I ask them to explain and to justify their choices. As they do so, they typically highlight distinctive elements of the various gospels. For example, some groups will keep Matthew because of its "ethic" while others will keep John because of its "spirituality." Their explanations also allow discussions about the relative importance of matters like history, theology, and literary merit in the choice of (and make up of) a gospel. Eventually, under prodding, it also becomes clear that the groups' religious and ideological backgrounds played a role in their preferences, as it did in the writing of the gospels and the formation of the canon.

When the class is done with the discussion, I generally ask them if they feel the early church did a good or bad job in assembling the four-gospel canon. This leads to discussion about the relative merit of the *Gospel of Thomas,* Q, and sometimes the infancy gospels. More importantly, it leads the class to reflect on whether there is one "Gospel" or many, and whether unity or diversity is a desideratum in matters religious.

Richard Walsh

165. INDUCTIVE DISCOVERY OF THE SYNOPTIC PROBLEM, OR, CATCHING THE PLAGIARISTS

Years ago I began my teaching of the Synoptic Problem using a traditional deductive method. The problem was introduced in the abstract, the possible solutions were explicated, and then we looked at texts illustrating those solutions. While this worked well enough with students whose theological bent tended toward the liberal end of the spectrum, I always encountered intense resistance from students on the moderate to conservative end. To avoid this I now teach the problem in a purely inductive manner.

The background structure of the course for this assignment is as follows: (1) I no longer use a traditional introductory text. Instead students have a one-volume Bible dictionary—assigned entries provide background and supplement to the primary textbook, the New Testament itself. (2) Textual, interpretive, and historical questions emerge from carefully orchestrated reading of the New Testament. (3) Students are assigned to permanent small groups (reassigned at midterm) and are comfortable working with one another in doing close readings of New Testament texts.

The necessary preparatory work for the Synoptic Problem class session(s) includes the following: (1) Students are intimately familiar with Mark. (2) No assigned readings have referred to the Synoptic Problem in any meaningful fashion. (3) Students know how to isolate a pericope and understand the function of pericopes in the formation of a gospel. (4) The sayings sections of Matthew have been covered, providing an introduction to Matthew's distinctive voice.

For the Synoptic Problem three small-group assignments are given, usually requiring at least two class sessions to complete. In the first I distribute to each small group copies of two (now nameless) student papers I acquired years ago and at a different institution. One of the papers plagiarized the other. They are to determine which one is the "source." In the second, I assign a series of pericopes from the triple tradition. In their groups students are to compare and contrast these passages, looking first for similarities. As they begin to notice extensive overlap in story content and wording I interrupt and ask them to count the number of identical words in specific pericopes and to find the longest phrases which are identical. When this is finished and before discussing any points of significance, they are given the third assignment in which they are asked to outline the sequence of pericopes in Mark 2:1–4:35; Matt 9:1–10:4; 12:1–13:53; and Luke 5:17–6:16; 8:4–18. When the groups have finished we discuss what they have discovered: wording that is often identical and nearly always closely parallel, and stories and sayings in roughly the same order. They are then asked to discuss in groups how (not why) this could happen, and how they might explain what is in front of them. (Often these three steps, plus the following debriefing require more than one class period.)

As the class then debriefs, groups usually report a broad range of possible solutions. These have included: identical inspiration by the Holy Spirit, a commonality based on the idea that they posses the same facts about Jesus' life, common oral traditions, or one or more of the evangelists copying and supplementing the other(s). It is normal that groups lean toward the idea of copying (they have been "set up" for this with the plagiarized papers as a lead in). This usually allows me to interject the question of what disciplinary procedures they would face if they had done this. A standard response is to exhibit great zeal in catching the gospel plagiarist! The completed exercise provides a basis on which I can introduce various solutions proposed by scholars. These are then received not as alien impositions invented by out-of-touch scholars, but rather as sincere efforts to struggle with a real problem with which the texts confront us.

The exercise has also proven useful in providing a base from which to introduce redaction criticism, theological discussion as to how these texts might be understood to be authoritative, and ways in which we might understand "inspiration" to have been an historical process.

Thomas W. Martin

166. WHO'S ON FIRST? TRACKING GOSPEL RELATIONS

Most introductions to the New Testament use some kind of quadrilateral diagram to chart possible source relationships among the four canonical gospels. I adapt the basic geometry to a baseball diamond, which I draw on the board in simple fashion with lines (base paths) and boxes (bases) at the four points of the diamond. Sports illustrations do not work for everyone and baseball may be waning as "America's Pastime," but most American students have played the game at some point in their lives and know the basics. This example works especially well in the fall semester, when it coincides with the World Series.

In the lecture and discussion, I proceed to "load the bases" with gospels and then explore other possible positions on the field.

1. I begin at home plate, where the action starts, and put Mark in the box. This sparks a discussion about "Markan Priority" as a working hypothesis of gospel origins. Why do many scholars think that Mark was the earliest gospel and served as a source for (some of) the others? How and why has this consensus been challenged?

2. Assuming, for argument's sake, the priority of Mark, I then put Matthew on first base and Luke on third base. Since these positions are on direct lines (paths) to Mark on home plate, they illustrate the theory that Matthew and Luke are dependent on Mark for some of their material. Here it is helpful to look at a specific synoptic story (like "Stilling the Storm") in parallel columns to see both the overall similarities among the three accounts (suggesting common tradition) and particular differences (suggesting peculiar redaction). Can we detect evidence that Matthew and Luke have both appropriated and adapted Mark for their own purposes (e.g., Matthew and Luke seem to soften Mark's sharp exchange between Jesus and the disciples during the storm crisis)?

3. Back to the diamond, we have additional lines/paths leading from first (Matthew) and third (Luke) to second base, with no direct connection to home plate (Mark). Second base thus marks the spot for "Q," the hypothetical source accounting for further common material between Matthew and Luke, not shared by Mark. Many questions continue to swirl around Q as a discrete document (and even more about Q as a separate community), but the fact of non-Markan parallels between Matthew and Luke is easily verified by a gospel synopsis. The Lord's Prayer, absent in Mark, and present in Matthew and Luke (albeit in different places and in different versions) is a good case in point.

4. Although seemingly having covered all the bases, I now explain that we still have not accounted for all the gospel tradition. We still have a fourth gospel to deal with, of course, but we are not even through yet with Matthew and Luke. As well as sharing material with Mark and with each other (Q), a substantial chunk of Matthew and Luke is unique to each of these gospels. In fact some of the most familiar and beloved stories appear only in Matthew (wise men, parable of sheep and goats) or in Luke (manger and shepherds, parable of Good Samaritan). What to do on our field with this so-called "special material"? I now draw short horizontal lines off of both first and third bases connected to rectangular boxes representing coaching boxes—which I fill in with the customary designations, "M" (at first, for unique Matthean material) and "L" (at third, for special Lukan creations or adaptations).

5. Finally, what to do with John, the Fourth Gospel? The usual textbook charts have no place for John because of its obvious differences from the three Synoptic Gospels. But everybody gets to play in our game. Assuming that students have some knowledge of John (through prior assigned readings and also popular exposure—many evangelical students will be more familiar with John than any other gospel), this is a good opportunity to discuss some of the distinctive features of this narrative (e.g., "I AM" discourses, unique "signs," "born again" language) and how it fits into the larger gospel picture. After some general discussion about the Fourth Gospel's depiction of Jesus, I ask the students where they might put John on the field, and why. The possibilities range from: (a) Pitcher's mound—because of John's centrality to the gospel message? because this is the highest point on the diamond, apt for John's "high" Christology? (b) Left field—as in "out in left field," that is, off the beaten path, marching to its own beat? (c) Right field—proverbially, where you put your worst player who can do the least damage; few Christians would put John in this category, but some Jews (and Christians concerned about Jewish-Christian dialogue) might be tempted, given this gospel's vitriolic denunciation of "the Jews" in several places. (d) Bullpen—where pitchers wait and warm up in anticipation of coming in and closing the game; as the last gospel in terms of canonical (and possibly chronological) order, how does John "close" the fourfold gospel drama?

Whatever diagrams you draw and strategies you map out, you still have to play the game. And so it is with the gospels: ultimately they are living, dynamic narratives that interface with each other around the preeminent figure of Jesus (where does he fit on the field?) in myriad ways, both comparative and contrastive. Let the interpretive game begin, and expect it to go into extra innings.

F. Scott Spencer

167. THE SYNOPTIC PROBLEM

To introduce the Synoptic Problem, I ask the students to reconstruct from their memories the story of the woman who anointed Jesus (Matt 26:6–13; Mark 14:3–9; Luke 7:36–50; John 12:1–8). This is followed by a collective retelling of the story by the entire class during which I commit each element to the board in unnamed columns. Invariably, most of the students conflate the four gospel stories, which results in various disagreements. Did it happen in Galilee (Luke) or Judea (Matthew, Mark, John)? Did the woman anoint Jesus' head (Matthew and Mark) or feet (Luke and John)? Was she at the house of Simon (Matthew and Mark) or of Lazarus (John)?

Was the host a leper (Matthew and Mark) or a Pharisee (Luke)? The woman inevitably becomes Mary Magdalene, a prostitute, sister of Lazarus and Martha (whom Mary surpasses in Jesus' estimation because Martha attended too closely to housework rather than to the Lord's teaching). Students usually recall Jesus' pronouncement as "he who has been forgiven much loves much." (Luke 7:47 actually reads, "Therefore, I tell you, her sins, which were many, have been forgiven; hence she has shown great love. But the one to whom little is forgiven, loves little.") Rarely, if ever, will a student recall Jesus' declaration found in Matthew and Mark: "Truly I tell you, wherever the good news is proclaimed in the whole world, what she has done will be told in remembrance of her." Judas, betrayer of Jesus, is usually identified as the primary antagonist and described as a thief.

We then read the various accounts in a Gospel synopsis and label the columns on the board. Discussion focuses on our tendency to conflate the story, on the (in)appropriateness of that tendency, and on the hermeneutical presuppositions behind our various answers. Someone will usually suggest that the various accounts are not the same story, but rather different stories, happening at different times (for example, Jesus was anointed in Galilee by the sinful woman and at another time in Judea by Mary). This provides a point of departure for discussion of the relationship not just among the gospels, but between the gospels and the historical Jesus. We then tackle the Synoptic Problem itself. Because the anxiety level of the students during these discussions may be influenced by their religious tradition, it may be helpful to identify the ways in which the Bible was used and presented in the contexts that formed us. (A similar exercise could be used with other passages from the triple tradition, such as Mark 5:21–43 [Jairus' daughter and the hemorrhaging woman]; 6:1–6 [the rejection at Nazareth]; 8:27–33 [the confession at Caesarea Philippi] and parallels.)

The exercise also lends itself to a discussion of gender and the Bible, given the vast differences between the women depicted in the accounts. One can approach this simply by asking, "If you had to play the starring role as the woman in one of these versions, which would you choose and why?" The profound intimacy between Jesus and Mary in the Fourth Gospel is appealing. But in Matthew and Mark, what the woman has done is so important in Jesus' eyes, that it is the only event about which Jesus proclaims, "*Wherever the gospel is preached in the whole world,* what she has done will be told in memory of her" (Matt 26:13; Mark 14: 9). This causes us to ask whether modern Christians attach as much importance to the story as Jesus does, and why this may or may not be so.

Jaime Clark-Soles

168. COMPARING SYNOPTIC TEXTS
USING "JESUS FILM" CLIPS

Whatever their shortcomings, the plethora of Jesus movies, especially now that they are available on DVD, makes it easy and intriguing to introduce students to synoptic parallels and the interpretative character of the gospels through the medium of film. Use of film can also encourage students to engage imaginatively with the written gospel texts. While in some contexts films such as *Jesus of Montreal* or *The Last Temptation of Christ* or *Jesus Christ Superstar* can be used to generate conversation, the somewhat more traditional attempts to render Jesus' life in accordance with the biblical text work well for comparing parallels in the gospels.

Clips from these movies call attention to various aspects of the gospels: (1) what we have in the gospels are accounts, rather than the events themselves, and all accounts interpret the events they report; (2) different gospels tell the same story differently; and (3) all our own readings of the gospels are acts of interpretation, because they supply details and information missing from the pages of the gospels themselves. In fact, films can be useful to show how much a director must supply—characters, costume, scenery, extras—to make a gospel live.

To some extent, this exercise works best with narrative accounts, rather than with clips of Jesus' teaching. One provocative contrast can be found in the differences between the presentation of the temptations of Jesus in *The Greatest Story Ever Told* and in Pasolini's *The Gospel According to St. Matthew*. In Pasolini's stark portrayal we see Jesus in the wilderness, praying with his hands and eyes raised towards heaven. Then we see a figure approaching from the distance, who stops directly in front of Jesus; nothing in particular distinguishes him. This man then says to Jesus, "If you are the Son of God, command these stones to become bread." Jesus answers, "Man does not live by bread alone." (Note: This film is in Italian, and is either dubbed or subtitled.) Then the other two temptations follow, after which the "tempter" simply turns around and walks away. This particular scene shows what it would be like to use the gospel as a literal script for filming: there are no descriptions of character, scene, inner feelings, and so on. Most directors supply some or all of these missing elements.

In *The Greatest Story Ever Told,* directed by George Stevens, the scene of Jesus' temptation is both lengthier and more colorful. Jesus is shown climbing up a hill, where he finds a cave in which an avuncular figure is cooking meat over a fire. After some musing on whether life is hard or easy, he invites Jesus to have some of the roasted meat, saying, "Are you sure you won't have a little?" But Jesus refuses, saying, "I'm fasting."

Jesus goes to stand at the mouth of the cave, and the old man comes to stand beside him and says, "How would you like to be the ruler of all this? All the power and glory of these kingdoms? I can give them to you. If you do me homage, it will all be yours." There follows the third temptation (in Luke's order). Then we return to the first temptation, the command for the stones to be made bread.

This scene stands in stark contrast to Pasolini's version. Students generally recognize that while Pasolini's account reproduces the gospel text more faithfully, Stevens' version in *The Greatest Story Ever Told* seems far more realistic. *The Miracle Maker: The Story of Jesus*—in 3–D clay animation—shows Jesus fainting or passing out in the wilderness, and then the temptations are presented in "cartoon" fashion as either dreams or visions. These various presentations raise questions for discussion: What are the strengths and weaknesses of each film version? What assumptions inform the editorial decisions of each director? What kind of material is this in the gospel? Interpreters have labeled these "historic, dramatized narratives" (R. E. Brown), "story parables" (J. Jeremias), and visionary experiences (M. Borg). Similarly, each of these films presents the temptations quite differently. The graphic depiction of the temptations on film raises the question to what extent the present versions of these accounts in the gospels of Luke and Matthew are stylized accounts to make a point about the identity of Jesus as God's Son. By extension and implication, the differences in such accounts can also serve to highlight differences in the gospels and the extent to which we explicitly and implicitly supply data and details to bring the texts to life.

Marianne Meye Thompson

169. ONE OF THESE THINGS IS NOT LIKE THE OTHERS: INTRODUCING THE FOUR GOSPELS

When introducing students to the academic study of the Gospels, I remind them of the old game on Sesame Street, "One of These Things is Not Like the Others." The television screen would be divided into four squares: one square would have a train, one square would have a truck, one square would have an airplane, and one square would have a duck. One of these things is not like the others! Telling them that John is the duck is one thing; illustrating John's profound dissimilarity requires something more dramatic. Even after giving them the statistics (e.g., ninety percent of John is found nowhere else among the

Synoptic Gospels), students appreciate John's uniqueness best after they go through the following exercise.

Ask the class to brainstorm possible answers to this question: If you wanted to convince someone who was completely unaware of Christianity or the Bible that Jesus was God's unique revelation to humanity, and if you could only take one story from the gospels to try to convince that person, what one story would you choose? As students suggest stories from the texts, write them on the board: feeding the 5000, healing the paralytic, walking on water, turning water into wine, and so forth. Invariably, someone will suggest Jesus' raising of Lazarus. And although the other stories are all excellent representations of Jesus' power and uniqueness, none is more compelling than the story of Jesus and Lazarus. Even though students may already know the story of Jesus' raising of Lazarus, re-tell the story in full detail.

After explaining all the reasons why that story might be the most compelling story of all the stories about Jesus—and after reiterating that the aim of the gospels is to convince their audiences that Jesus is uniquely worthy of their faith and commitment—ask the students why this remarkable story of Jesus' raising of four-days-dead Lazarus is found only in John. Did Matthew, Mark, and Luke not think the story was good enough to make the final cut for their works?

The discussion of John's difference from the Synoptic Gospels now achieves a sharper edge of specificity: Matthew, Mark, and Luke do not include the story of Jesus' raising of Lazarus because they have never heard of the story of Jesus' raising of Lazarus. Then, extend the conversation: Jesus turns water into wine? Matthew, Mark, and Luke have never heard of that story. Jesus visits with Nicodemus? Matthew, Mark, and Luke have never heard of that story. Jesus' conversation with the woman at the well? Matthew, Mark, and Luke have never heard of that story. And so on.

Now, the difference between John and the Synoptic Gospels is not a matter of statistics; it is the reality that some of their favorite stories about Jesus are told by John but no one else seems to know them. Ultimately, this illustration of the distinctiveness of John's gospel helps introduce the larger and more important point that comes a bit later in the course, namely, that the uniqueness of John's gospel moves beyond simple differences of content and raises, instead, more intriguing questions of conceptual differences in John's presentation of Jesus.

Daniel E. Goodman

170. BRINGING THE GOSPELS INTO
CONVERSATION WITH ONE ANOTHER

This exercise encourages students to experience the distinctiveness of the gospels by (a) reading them from beginning to end and (b) articulating the overall impression of Jesus conveyed by those narratives.

At the beginning of the first class session on Mark, the instructor invites students to write three descriptive words in response to the question, "Mark's Jesus is _____ [fill in the blank]." After two to three minutes, the instructor invites students to share one of their responses and records the responses on the class board. With each reply, the instructor repeats the descriptive word and then invites the student to elaborate. For example, I often say something like, "Mark's Jesus is elusive because . . . ," and wait for the student to finish the sentence.

Then, at the beginning of the first class session on Matthew, students repeat this process. They write three descriptive words in response to the question, "Matthew's Jesus is _____ [fill in the blank]." The instructor records student responses on the board. With each reply, the instructor invites the student to elaborate as with Mark (e.g., "Matthew's Jesus is powerful because . . . "). After a few minutes of this process, the instructor invites the class to compare their impressions of Matthew with their earlier conversation about Mark.

This experience typically produces different conversations for Mark than for Matthew. Having read Mark but not Matthew, students often voice surprise at the ways in which Mark's story does not fit conventional images of Jesus. Mark's Jesus often seems angry, aggressive, difficult, mysterious, elusive, hurried, and intense, among other things. He has very little to say by way of direct instruction or moral discourse. Once students read Matthew after Mark, Matthew's more didactic and pastoral material comes through in relief. As time permits, the exercise may be expanded by having students identify specific passages from each gospel which support their characterizations of Jesus. Fruitful discussion may result when students see the evidence (or lack thereof) for a given description.

To gain an appreciation for the variety of distinctive presentations of Jesus in early Christian literature, students may repeat this experience with other canonical and extracanonical gospels.

Greg Carey

171. THE FOUR GOSPELS: SENSING
SIMILARITIES AND DIFFERENCES

Many students who have not previously studied the New Testament in college but have read them in a faith community begin an introductory course assuming that the four gospels are the same and that only the ones not included in the canon are different. To enable these students to feel comfortable making distinctions among the canonical gospels, they need to experience early in the course how texts can be both similar and different and to understand that these differences are not contradictions, but variations in perspective. By comparing the four gospels to four varieties of apples and then sampling the apples, students can affirm simultaneously the similarities and differences among the four gospels and also create new memories of this affirmation. Tasting also requires students to use their tactile and olfactory senses, the latter being the sense most closely related to memory.

Prior to the class period when this exercise will be used, assign your students to read the opening (Matt 1:1–4:25; Mark 1:1–4:41; Luke 1:1–4:44; John 1:1–4:54) and closing (Matt 28:1–20; Mark 16:1–8; Luke 24:1–53; John 20:1–31) sections of the gospels. Tell them to notice the similarities and differences among the texts. For the instructor's preparation, purchase and prepare apples of four varieties. If available, I use Empire (red, semi-sweet, a cross between McIntosh and Jonathan apples), Braeburn (red, semi-sweet, a cross between Lady Hamilton and Granny Smith apples), Jonathan (red, semi-sweet), and Granny Smith (green, tart). This selection makes it possible to talk about the relationships among and sources of the four gospels by discussing the relationships among and origins of the four apple varieties. (The same type of exercise may work with many other fruits as well.)

Distribute the apple slices, displaying what the whole apple looks like and explaining how their different appearance, smell, and taste do not detract from their similarities. Permit them to taste the apples. Then suggest that the differences among the gospels can be understood in a similar fashion. Review the differences and similarities that they found in the assigned reading. Some students may find the differences between the apples more subtle to describe than the differences among the gospels while other students will notice both the differences among the apples and the gospels. Each subject requires special types of observation and a special terminology for articulating what one finds as precisely as possible.

This exercise does not substitute for a traditional discussion of the theological, political, geographical, and sociological reasons for the differences in these chapters, but serves rather as an aid to memory and a catalyst for reflection. The analogy between fruit and written text, of course, has its limits. Student and teacher alike may profit from discussion of the analogy—what it captures as well as what it may miss.

Emily R. Cheney

172. GOSPEL MUSIC

Even for those who strive to be interdisciplinary in their pedagogy, music is difficult to integrate into a biblical studies curriculum. Perhaps because it is so rare to hear music in a course on the New Testament, students respond very positively when I give them a listening quiz in a wrap-up/review session on the Gospels. (The exercise works only if students are familiar with the themes and stylistic tendencies of the four evangelists.) Students who are aural learners especially appreciate the chance to use a different part of the brain in making connections to the material.

The quiz has four questions and four answer choices. The answer choices are Matthew, Mark, Luke, and John. The "questions" are four excerpts from different musical compositions. Before I play the four snippets, I ask the class to think about the themes, the mood, and the tempo of the opening sections of each of the four gospels. With these texts in mind, they listen to the four excerpts and then match each one with the gospel it best fits. For Matthew I use an excerpt from Tchaikovsky's "Marche Slave." The tone of the piece is at once regal and militaristic, which is appropriate for Matthew's birth narrative in light of its christological associations with the Davidic throne and the pivotal role of Herod and the three "kings" from the east. The selection strikes an ominous chord, moreover, as the slaughter of the innocents casts a pall over a story that is supposed to be unmitigated good news. For Mark I play an excerpt from the "William Tell Overture," by Rossini, better known to many students as the "Lone Ranger" theme. Mark bursts out of the starting gate at a full gallop and does not slow down for a long time. There is no boring genealogy (as in Matthew) or a plodding historian's preface (as in Luke). The action begins without delay. John the Baptist appears in the wilderness, Jesus is baptized and spends forty days in the desert being tempted by Satan, angels take care of him, John is arrested, and Jesus begins his public ministry—all in the first fifteen verses. Mark's paratactic style (the repeated use of "and" to join complete sentences) moves the narrative forward at a breathless pace. For Luke I play the choral ode from the fourth movement of Beethoven's Ninth Symphony, the well-known "Ode to Joy." Rejoicing is the dominant mood in Luke's birth narrative, in contrast to Matthew's, and the jubilant melody of Beethoven's chorus nicely accompanies the many hymns recorded in the first two chapters—the Annunciation (1:26–38), the Magnificat (1:46–55), the Gloria in Excelsis (2:13–14), the Nunc Dimittis (2:28–32), and the songs of Elizabeth, Anna, and the angels. Almost every character breaks into song, as if it were a Broadway musical. For John's gospel I play the opening "Fanfare" sequence from Richard Strauss's "Also Sprach Zarathrustra." Many students will recognize it as being from the soundtrack to Stanley Kubrick's *2001: A Space Odyssey*, and even those who do not, as long as they are familiar with the Johannine prologue (1:1–18), will almost instantly intuit that the pacing of the music and the blaring, triumphant horn riffs fit perfectly with the shocking announcements that "the Word was God" and "the Word became flesh." When I give students a few minutes to write down their reasons for their choices, I usually find that they are able to come up with more reasons than those given here.

As musical interpretation is perhaps even more subjective than biblical interpretation, I do not grade these quizzes—which disappoints many students. There is almost always a consensus that my "answers" are the correct ones, but it would not be a bad thing if students wanted to argue that my choices are inappropriate. One aim of the exercise is to alert students to the artistic qualities of the gospels as literary productions. Debates about how or whether joy or gloom, for example, can be translated into a different medium force the class to articulate what they see and hear and feel in the texts. I am not a musician and so there are usually students present with a richer musicological vocabulary who can help describe what is happening in the interplay between the story and the soundtrack. Individual teachers can choose other selections as they seem appropriate. Musical genres other than classical may also work with younger students.

Patrick Gray

173. WRITE YOUR OWN GOSPEL

"Inasmuch as many other students are attempting to put together an account of the material we have been studying in this New Testament class—just as it has been handed on to us by him/her who was from the beginning of the semester a competent and helpful servant of the university—I, too, have decided after reading carefully the course requirements and assigned texts, to write an orderly account for you, O Esteemed Professor _____, so that you may know the truth concerning the things about which you have instructed me." This is a hands-on exercise in redaction criticism, and assumes that students have read a good part of the canonical gospels and at least one non-canonical gospel. It is a good project to assign halfway through a semester, but not earlier. What makes this project work is the tight page limit (students are forced to make tough decisions regarding what to include and exclude in their gospels), and the classroom discussion that follows after students have finished their gospels.

Students are to write their own gospel in no more that five double-spaced pages (12–point Times New Roman font), and in no less than four pages. Each student's "original" gospel must include: at least one saying or story from a non-canonical gospel (e.g., *Gospel of Thomas*); one purely imaginative saying or teaching of Jesus of the student's own inspiration or borrowed from a non-Jesus source; and at least one story or saying from each of the four canonical gospels.

After writing their gospels, students are required to add a two-page summary describing why they wrote their gospel the way they did. To meet the minimum requirement, students must identify by chapter and verse at least five different sources used. The additional page or so demands some critical reflection on the students' part and helps ensure that their gospels do not simply end up being "cut-and-paste jobs" that lack any coherence. However, even a total lack of coherence can lead to provocative discussions. For example, an apparently incoherent collection of Jesus material may lead to a discussion about whether Mark is a coherent narrative or not—or whether the *Gospel of Thomas* is a coherent whole.

A sampling of the gospels can be shared in class in order to explore issues of genre (did someone write an infancy gospel? a passion narrative? a sayings gospel? an "Acts of Jesus"?); theology (high or low Christology?); and ideology (hierarchy? patriarchy? feminism? social class?). The goal of the exercise is to spark critical discussion and insight into the issues that may have affected the formation of the canonical gospels.

Jeffrey L. Staley

174. GOSPEL GENRE

To introduce the topic of genre and the gospels, I have students retell a story from the gospels in their own words. This assignment comes prior to any lecture or readings on the gospels, except the reading of the gospels themselves. Depending on the size of the class, I choose four or five stories, one at least from each canonical gospel, with three to four students assigned to each story. If there are more than four retellings of the same story the students stop listening attentively. The students may use one index card as reference.

There have been varied results with this assignment, ranging from simple retellings occurring behind the podium, to very dramatic presentations in which students have "dressed the part," wearing either full costumes or using props, and acting out their stories in both movement and voice. There have been straightforward re-readings of the story with few modifications to the text, to an eschewing of most of the story in favor of the story's "meaning" or "point." The latter scenario generates great concern for some students ("I thought we were just supposed to tell the story!") who are certain that their grade has been compromised (or direct their frustration at me for not providing them with more explicit instructions). This becomes an excellent segue into what it means to "tell a story." How did the four evangelists tell their stories of Jesus?

We then discuss the similarities and differences between the gospels and their literary contemporaries and examine various genre theories. Quickly, however, we move to the broader issue of narrative by placing the gospel genre in its canonical context. I ask the students to reflect on the importance of narrative, both for the biblical writers, and for their own lives. What is the purpose and impact of story? What does it accomplish for the writers of the gospels compared to another kind of genre? Why is story important for our lives? This conversation also generates a review of the basic elements of narrative (i.e., plot, character, setting.) and how these devices function in the stories the students presented. For example, one student retold the account of the Samaritan woman at the well (John 4) from the perspective of the woman, facilitating a discussion on point of view. What elements are highlighted? Absent? In what ways did the retellings address the narrative elements of the story? In what sense did the narrative features shape the retellings? The aim, in part, is to suggest to the students that *how* a story is told is equally as important as *what* the story is about—that the narrative elements in the story contribute to the meaning of the story as much as the story's content.

By recognizing these narrative elements at both the level of the story and the gospel as a whole, I then suggest to the students the importance of placing their stories in the context of the entire gospel. We talk about the significance of and respect for the narrative context and how a story might be misinterpreted if dislodged from both its immediate and narrative context. To emphasize this point, I ask the students to reflect on the idea of "context" in their own lives, both on a personal level and what they observe on a cultural or societal level. I also use this discussion to place the idea of "context" in a broader perspective, that is, the historical, social, and religious contexts of the gospels and the particular theological context unique to each gospel.

In some cases, at the end of the unit on the gospels, I have the students retell the same story, this time as a written exercise, and ask them to include some reflection on how and why their retelling has changed. The goal is for the students to acknowledge the ways in which the retellings are shaped not only by the many "contexts" of the gospels, but also by the "contexts" the students bring to the story. If the question of genre means more than simply narrative identity, the students begin to understand how their stories interact with the story or stories they encounter in the gospels. This exercise is not only a helpful review but also facilitates a conversation about how stories are retold, thereby considering the ecclesiological, ideological, and cultural function of the gospels in their interpretive communities both past and present. Within this conversation I push the idea of genre even further by having the students compare their oral retellings and their written ones with the intention of helping them recognize the inherent orality of the gospels. We discuss the similarities and differences between oral speech and written texts and the function of each mode of communication. The question of genre and the gospels, therefore, is not only a question of narrative, but also an inquiry into the relationship between the oral kerygma and its narrative culmination.

Karoline Lewis

175. WHITHER HISTORY?
JOHN F. KENNEDY AND THE GOSPELS

Students in introductory New Testament classes often think of the gospels as historical biographies. They have not thought about the gospels as literary creations, nor have they considered the gospels as shaped by theological interests and agendas. This exercise helps demonstrate that while history is certainly part of what comprises the Gospels, it does not account very fully for how or why the gospels present Jesus as they do.

Suggest to students that, as a class project, the class is going to write a historical biography of John F. Kennedy. Have students volunteer ideas about what would be included in a good historical biography of President Kennedy. Write their ideas on the board as they announce them. Soon the building blocks of a good historical biography will be on the board: birth, education, family, formative years, hobbies, values, marriage, children, ideas, successes, failures, physical description, death, and the like.

Working from that list, then, ask the students how many of these "building blocks of a good historical biography" are also building blocks of the gospels' portrayal of Jesus. Usually, about half of the subjects mentioned by the students are also themes of the gospels (e.g., birth [for two of the gospels], parents and siblings, ideas and values) and about half of them are not (e.g., birth [for two of the gospels], formative years, education, marriage, children, physical description). Students now can see and discuss the fact that, if the gospels are attempts at historical biography, they are not very successful attempts. So if they are trying to do something more than history, what is it?

Going back to the board and looking at all the building blocks of a good historical biography, ask the students which of those building blocks all of the gospels seem deeply committed to emphasizing in their testimonies about Jesus. The answer, of course, is his death. Point out, for example, that the Gospel of John devotes about half if its entire presentation of Jesus to the last seven days of his life. John's gospel has no interest in historical biography—John is essentially proclaiming that, while the family or the education or the formative years of Jesus may not distinguish him from other Jews of the time, Jesus' *death* makes him exceptional. At that point, John and the other gospels should be recognized as something other than historical biographies. How, then, do literary and theological interests help shape the presentation of Jesus in the gospels?

Daniel E. Goodman

176. THE GOSPELS AS AURAL
AND SOCIO-POLITICAL DOCUMENTS

How can students who are used to reading biblical texts begin to understand them as aural texts? Experiencing the aural and rhetorical dynamics of a text can help students understand that the gospels were written primarily (1) to be heard by groups of people rather than to be read silently by individuals and (2) to persuade their audiences to respond in specific ways in specific historical contexts rather than primarily to convey objective, historical information or theological beliefs.

By listening to and reading about several arrangements of "The Star Spangled Banner," a song that is in many ways a sacred, foundational document for citizens of the United States (as the gospels are sacred, foundational documents for Christians), and comparing the purposes of the gospels to the purposes of the arrangements of "The Star Spangled Banner," students can experience the gospels as aural, rhetorical, and socio-political documents. The theological themes that most students have already been conditioned to comprehend and explore are intertwined with the political and social themes that most students have not been taught to notice. A secondary objective of the exercise is to teach students that contemporary sacred texts are also socially and politically conditioned. A useful resource for reviewing the sociopolitical context of the arrangements of the "The Star Spangled Banner" is the documentary video titled *An American Anthem* (approx. sixty minutes). This film can provide you as the instructor information about the political and social controversies surrounding its various arrangements, but need not be viewed by the class.

Prior to class, assign the students to research the circumstances for the arrangements of "The Star Spangled Banner" by Igor Stravinsky (1941), Jose Feliciano (1968), Jimi Hendrix (1969), and Bela Fleck (1991). Stravinsky's version performed by the Boston Symphony Orchestra resulted in his brief imprisonment for desecrating the national anthem. Before the fifth game of the World Series and during the Vietnam War, Feliciano performed the first nontraditional version of the national anthem heard by mainstream America and received a fiery response. One of Hendrix's two versions was played and recorded at the Woodstock concert held during the height of the Vietnam War. The version by Bela Fleck and the Flecktones, although upbeat and hopeful, was written as the U.S. went to war with Iraq in January 1991. In their research, students should record the key national and world events that occurred around the time of each arrangement.

After students share their findings in class, play each of the four arrangements. Allow time to consider in small groups and then as a whole class (1) the ways in which the arrangement reflects its historical-cultural context, and (2) the specific response the arrangement attempts to persuade its listeners to make. Next, ask them (in their groups) to consult their notes about the historical and political contexts of Mark and Matthew and decide which arrangement of the national anthem best matches what these authors were urging their audiences to do. What factors influenced their group's reasons for their selection? There is no one right answer, since the purpose is to foster critical reflection on the sociopolitical contexts of the gospels and their rhetorical effects. Have each group report their responses. Keep a poll of how many times each arrangement is matched with Mark and Matthew and their reasons. Concluding discussion may focus on the ways in which reflecting on the different arrangements of "The Star Spangled Banner" helps them better understand these gospels. (For a similar exercise, see §140.)

Emily R. Cheney

177. HOW TO READ A GOSPEL BY VIEWING A MIRACLE STORY IN FILM: AN EXERCISE IN REDACTION/NARRATIVE/FEMINIST CRITICISM

The following scenes from "Jesus films" work well in helping students read the gospels more carefully and in helping them recognize theological, metaphorical, and ideological issues in the gospel stories. Students are usually much more adept at picking up on these abstract issues in film than they are in seeing them in the New Testament itself, so the point of the exercise is to come back after viewing the films and ask more critical, evaluative questions about the canonical gospels.

Begin by having students identify the following elements in the selected story. In small-group discussions students then identify the similarities and differences they find in the stories, based upon the following criteria: (1) What is the plot? Briefly list in order four or five basic plot sequences (e.g., Jesus and his disciples are invited to a wedding, and when the wine runs out Jesus' mother seems to expect him to do something ...). (2) Who are the main characters? Do they have any special traits? For example, is there a difference between Matthew's "ruler" who tells Jesus his daughter is dead, and Mark's Jairus, ruler of a synagogue, who tells Jesus his daughter is ill? (This question also affects the plot of the stories, since in Matthew's rendering, Jesus could stop and take the bleeding woman out to dinner—since the ruler's daughter is not going to get "more dead" if Jesus delays his journey to her.) (3) Where and when does the story take place? (4) What about any "props" (e.g., the six stone water pots at the wedding in Cana appear as two "coffee mugs" in one film version)?

Now watch one or more of the film versions, asking these same questions. Continue with such questions as: Why do you think the movie director has added or subtracted from the gospel accounts? How might these additions or subtractions affect the theological, metaphorical, or ideological issues at play in the films? Then, go back and reread the gospel accounts, asking what theological, metaphorical, or ideological issues might be at play in the canonical stories? With a synoptic story, one can ask further questions: Which gospel is the director following more closely? What evidence can you give to support your choice?

Finally, one may raise gender issues, since most of the film versions of these canonical stories actually either take women out of the scenes or lessen their words and roles, as well as purity concerns and how these do or do not get transferred to film.

What follows is a list of episodes with the information for the corresponding scenes in various film versions:

The Wedding at Cana (John 2:1–11). *The Last Temptation of Christ* (Scorsese); DVD: Chapter 13 ("Casting out devils and working cures" [1:09:13]); VHS: 1.11:30. *Jesus* (2000); DVD: Chapter 12 ("Water into Wine" [52:35]).

The raising of Jairus' daughter (Mark 5:21–34 and parallels). *Jesus of Nazareth* (Zeffirelli); DVD: Disk 1, Chapter 42 ("Healing the Child"); VHS: Tape 2, 37:30. *Jesus* (1979); DVD: Chapter 13 ("Jesus Raises Jairus' Daughter"); VHS (83 min. version): 19:55. *The Miracle Maker*; DVD: Chapter 11 ("Raised from the Dead"). For this pericope, I photocopy an older edition of Throckmorton's *Gospel Parallels* and hand it out, since it uses the RSV, which is a better translation of the Matthean account than is the NRSV. I have students break up into groups of three (each person reading a different gospel account).

The raising of Lazarus (John 11). *The King of Kings* (1927); DVD: Chapter 11 (The Tomb of Lazarus [45:37]), (1928); DVD Chapter 10 (The Tomb of Lazarus [38:09]), VHS: 40:05. *The Greatest Story Ever Told*; DVD: Chapter 21 (*Lazarus Comes Forth* [1:47:40]); VHS: Tape 1, 1:52:00. *The Last Temptation of Christ*; DVD: Chapter 15 ("Lazarus" [1:19:20]); VHS: 1:19:36. *Jesus* (2000); DVD: Chapter 24 ("Resurrection" [1:51:27]).

Jeffrey L. Staley

178. DISTINGUISHING JESUS' RESURRECTION FROM HIS PAROUSIA IN THE SYNOPTIC GOSPELS

Many students in introductory New Testament courses confuse Jesus' *parousia* with his resurrection. This exercise enables students to define *parousia* and "resurrection" more precisely and to associate the terms with texts within each of the Synoptic Gospels. Since the Gospel of John makes little reference to Jesus' return, it is not included in this exercise. Because the so-called "delay of the *parousia*" is such an important concept in New Testament scholarship, familiarizing students with the relevant data will help students to understand the diverse understandings of Jesus in the gospels as well as in the letters of Paul, where the question of Jesus' return is even more pressing.

Prior to class, first assign your students to read and outline the closing sections of the Synoptic Gospels (Mark 16:1–8; Matt 28:1–20; Luke 24:1–53) and to skim the entire text of each gospel, taking note of the references foreshadowing Jesus' resurrection. Second, have them outline the characteristics of the Judgment Day in Mark 13, Matthew 24, and Luke 21, and paraphrase the definition of the title "Son of Man" from a Bible dictionary. Begin the class with a discussion of the major components of Jesus' resurrection (visits to the tomb, Jesus' appearances, etc.) and Jesus' predictions of his resurrection found in each of the three gospels. Emphasize the fact that, from the author's and readers' vantage point, Jesus' resurrection is a past event. Next, move on to discuss their findings about the events surrounding the Judgment Day that refer to Jesus' return/*parousia* and presence, the imagery describing these events, and the use of the title Son of Man. When, in each of the gospels, will Jesus return, and what events will have occurred or will be occurring at the time of his *parousia*?

Students begin to see that in Mark Jesus' *parousia* appears to be immediate, that in Matthew Jesus' *parousia* is soon to occur but not as soon as in Mark, and that in Luke Jesus' *parousia* occurs even further in the future than in Mark or Matthew. Is it possible that the occurrence of the Jewish Wars and Nero's persecution of the Christians, along with the absence of resurrection appearances in Mark, could have influenced Mark's audience to view Jesus' return as immediate? Which parts of Matthew's and Luke's Gospels (e.g., Matt 25:31–46; 28:15–20; Luke 24:47–49) put Jesus' *parousia* later than in Mark's gospel? What might be the theological, social, or ethical consequences of the different conceptions of Jesus' return found in the Synoptic Gospels?

Emily R. Cheney

179. INTRODUCING THE HISTORICAL JESUS

To introduce the controversial topic of "the historical Jesus," I begin class by asking students to choose the one person (either a historical figure or a fictional character) who most reminds them of Jesus and then to spend a few minutes writing a paragraph explaining their choice. After a few minutes I then go around the room asking them to reveal their choices and briefly to explain the reasons for their selection. I at least get all the names and write them on the board, keeping score if any person gets more than one vote.

There is usually lots of laughter as some students try to come up with the most provocative or ingenious answers to the question—for example, Superman, David Koresh, hippie/flower child, and so forth. There are also lots of heads nodding as more conventional names are mentioned—for example, the Buddha, Muhammad, Martin Luther King Jr. Once all the names are on the board and the votes are tallied, I inform the class that, before they started sharing their responses, I had written down my prediction as to whose name would appear the most times. I usually write down, "Gandhi or maybe Mother Teresa," and it is extremely rare that I am wrong. The discussion which follows begins with my ability to read their minds and accurately predict the "winner." Why, I ask, was I able to guess whom they would pick? In the event my prediction is wrong, I can simply omit the mind-reading bit and move the discussion in the same direction by asking why certain names came up and certain others did not. (Even if Gandhi or Mother Teresa are not the clear-cut winners, it is virtually guaranteed that names of similarly humanitarian heroes will far outnumber names like Adolf Hitler and Charles Manson.) Is it really possible that everyone could be right? That is, can it be true that Jesus was Malcolm X, David Koresh, the Buddha, Confucius, Gandhi, and John Lennon all rolled into one? Not likely, even if each of these names gets at some aspect of who he really was.

Scholarly research into the life and personality of the historical Jesus aims at determining which portrait more closely resembles the original. In the way he lived, the things he taught, and how he died, was Jesus more like Gandhi or Muhammad? Was he a wild-eyed prophet who thought the end of the world was near or was he more of a simple Jewish rabbi who roamed the Galilean countryside on donkey-back, speaking in parables? Or is neither of these profiles accurate? How would you know? Is it possible to know? Is the question of interest only to Christians? Or is it in some way important to everyone? Before too long, most classes will hit upon many of the big questions raised by Albert Schweitzer in his seminal work *The Quest of the Historical Jesus* (trans. W. Montgomery; New York: Macmillan, 1961). Schweitzer observed that "each successive epoch of theology found its own thoughts in Jesus," and indeed "each individual created Him in accordance with his own character" (4). Although much had been learned from it, Schweitzer's final judgment was that the quest revealed as much about the questers as it did about Jesus: "There is no historical task which so reveals a man's true self as the writing of a Life of Jesus" (ibid.). As the class begins to see that their choices tend toward persons who embody many of the ideals of contemporary American culture, you can inform them that they have arrived at the same conclusion as one of the greatest biblical scholars of the twentieth century. While it is not necessarily the case that all efforts at reconstructing the historical Jesus will be exercises in projection, it will be easy to illustrate how even supposedly objective scholars tend to produce a Jesus who shares their own values. This is the result of Jesus' peculiar status as the cultural icon *par excellance*. (Teachers with expertise in other areas may be able to describe similar phenomena with respect to the heroes of other cultural traditions—Moses, Confucius, Romulus, etc.)

From here the teacher can move to a lecture on the history of the quest, a recent article about the Jesus Seminar, or a presentation of the scholarly criteria used to determine the authenticity of sayings attributed to Jesus in the gospels. Again, students are usually able to explain the reasoning behind the criteria as well as identify any pitfalls on their own.

Patrick Gray

180. CREATE-A-JESUS: SCHOLARSHIP AND THE SEARCH FOR THE HISTORICAL JESUS

Teaching in the "Bible Belt," I find that many of the students in my New Testament courses have heightened sensitivities to scholarly discussions about "the historical Jesus." The following exercise is one that I use in an effort to bypass their knee-jerk opposition to the idea that reading necessarily involves interpretation, even when we are talking about the Bible.

This class follows a session in which I have provided some historical context on the development of biblical scholarship. Before the students arrive in my class for the following exercise, they should have read an article that describes scholars' search for the historical Jesus (e.g., a chapter from M. Borg, *Jesus in Contemporary Scholarship* [Valley Forge, PA: Trinity Press International, 1994] or P. Fredriksen, "What You See is What You Get: Context and Content in Current Research on the Historical Jesus," *ThTo* 52.1 [1995]: 75–97). This exercise is most successful when the students have already discussed the canonical gospels and have had some introduction to the varieties of Christianity that existed in the centuries immediately following Jesus' death.

To begin the exercise, I break the class into several small groups. I then go around to each group and assign them an identity from the following list: Flower Child/Hippie/Peace Corps; Jewish Historian of Late Antique Judaism; Older White Male "Old-School" Academic/Teacher; Active 1970s Feminist; Communist/Socialist/Marxist. Then the fun begins. I instruct each group to create a picture of a Jesus with whom they (in their assigned identity) could really relate—a Jesus that looks enough like them to be able to speak convincingly to them. I send them searching through the New Testament for passages that they would highlight to support this picture of Jesus. I also remind them to consider non-canonical texts and encourage them to be creative, considering what this Jesus would be like—what would he wear, say, do? Whom would he support or confront?

NEW TESTAMENT

While they are talking, I circulate and offer suggestions. Then I write the categories on the board, which serves the purpose of getting the students interested in the variety, and gives them a glimpse of what the exercise should accomplish. After the groups have had sufficient time to brainstorm, discuss, and find support for their pictures of Jesus, I ask them, one group at a time, to introduce their Jesus. Most groups inevitably come up with wonderfully descriptive caricatures of Jesus and solid proof for their descriptions. This exercise gets everyone laughing but also thinking hard about how to support their own "Jesus."

The ultimate goal of this exercise, of course, is to relate the students' images to the scholars' Jesuses and to use the similarities as a starting point for a conversation about interpretation and relative "truth." Although many different scholars could be used to represent these or other images of Jesus, the five that I use for discussion are J. D. Crossan, G. Vermes, B. Mack, E. Schüssler Fiorenza, and R. Horsley. Recently, I have also talked about the Jesus in Mel Gibson's film, carrying over the idea that anyone presenting the "true" picture of the historical Jesus is necessarily choosing which passages to use and which to dismiss.

Through this exercise, I find that many students who would otherwise write off the possibility of multiple interpretations of the Bible find themselves knee-deep in those multiple interpretations before they realize it. Likewise, by moving from a personal identity to a historical Jesus, the influence of the scholar's context and interests becomes acutely clear, whereas if one were to start with an image of Jesus and claim that it had been culturally influenced, many of these students would stop listening. We discuss what makes some images more convincing than others, but I also try to alert them to the politics of interpretation, and that textual meaning is many things, but one thing it is *not* is "obvious."

Christine Shepardson

181. JESUS AND THE TEMPLE: HELPING STUDENTS TO THINK HISTORICALLY

A perennial challenge in thinking about the Bible confronts students in both college and seminary classrooms: How can we understand important figures and events in the Bible from an historical perspective? This challenge faces especially strong barriers when students are asked to think about Jesus in historical terms. Some students resist thinking about Jesus historically, preferring to envision him purely as he is portrayed in the gospels and in the later confessions of the church; others may find the prospect of historical inquiry promising, yet lack the historical tools necessary for the task.

This activity aims to overcome these frustrating barriers to historical thinking. The goals of this activity are (1) to understand Jesus' own attitude towards the temple through a reading of key passages in the Gospel of Mark; and (2) to place those attitudes in their first-century Judean context through a reading of two passages from Josephus. The activity, thus, encourages students to think historically about one manageable aspect of Jesus' activity: his relationship to the Jerusalem temple, the most prominent political and religious institution of his time; and it equips students with one basic tool for addressing this issue historically: the study of Jesus' contemporaries as described by the ancient historian Josephus. The exercise proceeds through the following stages:

1. Setting the Stage: Students are asked to bring to class a one-page response to the following reading task: Describe Jesus' attitude toward the Jerusalem temple and its leadership based upon the following passages in Mark (1:40–43; 2:23–28; 11:1–12:12; 12:41–44; 13:1–14:2; 14:10–11, 43–50, 53–65; 15:29–32, 38).

Responses need not be sophisticated; but they should orient students to the literary evidence available for addressing this topic. Students discuss their assessments. The instructor's role in this portion of the course is to catalogue and invite an examination of the students' assessments. Instructors may also call attention to how key passages in Mark figure most prominently in this discussion and how students are reading those passages. If students have difficulty stating a firm position on their own, they might select from among the following prompts: (a) Jesus hated the temple and willed its destruction; (b) Jesus revered the temple, yet criticized its leaders; (c) Jesus believed that the temple's time had come; its days were eschatologically numbered.

2. Gaining a Bearing in History: Although we have no direct access to the underlying rationale for Jesus' angst regarding the temple, at least two stories about his contemporaries help us better appreciate the contemporary historical context of Jewish protest and prophecy against the temple. Two passages from Josephus help students recognize that Jesus was not alone in criticizing the practices of the temple and prophesying its destruction. Reading these texts and commenting upon them in class helps students to understand Jesus' actions better in the context of his contemporaries. The instructor's role in these readings is to encourage students to consider their implications for understanding Jesus' actions in the temple.

(a) Mathias and Judas (*War* 1.647–655; cf. *Ant.* 17.149ff.), 4 B.C.E.: According to Josephus, two Jewish teachers staged a provocative protest against the practices of the Jerusalem temple. They removed the image of an eagle from one of the walls of the temple, apparently on grounds that the image transgressed the first commandment. As a result, these teachers and their accomplices were pursued and executed at the order of Herod. This account helps students see Jesus' own actions in the temple as provocative events in a particular political and religious context. Not unlike Mathias and Judas, Jesus attempted to remove something that he believed to be wrong with the temple; not unlike them, he may also have suffered arrest and execution as a direct result.

(b) Jesus son of Ananus (*War* 6.300–309), 63–70 C.E.: The second story is the account of Jesus son of Ananus, a prophet active during the Jewish Revolt who prophesied the destruction of the temple. This prophet also suffered interrogation and physical discipline from the temple authorities. Students comment upon this passage in class; then they address what it might teach us about the original context of Jesus' own prophecies regarding the temple (one may also include reference to Mic 3:12; Jer 7, 26; cf. Ezek 7–10). The study of such contemporary prophetic figures may help students to see Jesus' temple prophecies as actions that were integrally related to a particular setting in history.

3. Forming Conclusions: The class concludes with a discussion of how these texts might help us better understand Jesus' last days historically: In light of the two accounts from Josephus, could Jesus' actions in the temple have led directly to his arrest and crucifixion? By comparing the activity of Jesus and his contemporaries, students may begin to develop an eye for seeing Jesus as an historical figure whose activity was integrally related to the religious and political context of Palestinian Judaism.

For further reading, see J. D. Crossan, *The Historical Jesus: The Life of a Mediterranean Jewish Peasant* (New York: HarperCollins, 1992), 354–60; V. Eppstein, "The Historicity of the Cleansing of the Temple," *ZNW* 55 (1964): 42–58; C. A. Evans, "Jesus' Action in the Temple: Cleansing or Portent of Destruction?" *CBQ* 51 (1989): 237–70; E. P. Sanders, *Jesus and Judaism* (Philadelphia: Fortress, 1985), 61–76.

C. D. Elledge

182. JESUS IN JERUSALEM: VISUALIZING THE SYNOPTIC ACCOUNTS OF JESUS' FINAL WEEK

One of my goals for courses on the Synoptic Gospels is for students to probe the literary coherence of the gospel narratives. This requires, among other things, careful consideration of the narrative and theological relationships between the Passion narratives and the accounts of Jesus' public ministry. I want students to answer the question: "What provokes the Passion, and how does the action against Jesus follow as a consequence of his public ministry?" One approach toward an answer requires giving careful attention to the stories of Jesus in Jerusalem, where the hopes surrounding his arrival eventually yield to the apparent tragedy or injustice of his execution. I use an exercise that introduces these passages (relevant sections of Mark 11:1–15:15; Matt 21:1–27:26; and/or Luke 19:29–23:25) by asking students to consider the gospel narrators' points of view, particularly the imagined contours, scope, and symbolic potential of the scenes.

The chief objective of this simple exercise is to open students' eyes to the importance of perspective and imagination in the interpretation of these and any other narratives. To accomplish this, the exercise asks students to read these familiar texts carefully and visualize the scenes as an ancient person familiar with the settings and political climate might have done. In their reflections on these texts, students typically discover the depth to which their previous exposure to films, images, and liturgies has influenced their own perspectives on these accounts.

Students complete the exercise in small groups. I assign each group one or more significant passages, such as Jesus' entry into Jerusalem (Mark 11:1–10 or par.), his action in the temple (Mark 11:15–19 or par.), occasions of his public teaching (Mark 11:27–12:44 or par.), the Passover meal (Mark 14:12–31 or par.), Jesus' arrest (Mark 14:43–52), and the trials (Mark 14:53–15:15 or par.). Each group must outline a cinematographic plan for filming their scenes by creating a comprehensive inventory of what is required to stage them. The inventory should include a description of the setting and its geographical connections or proximity to the larger cityscape, a list of the major characters present and any necessary props, and an estimate of the number of extras needed to portray the crowds. I may encourage artistic students to sketch storyboards.

Afterward, with the entire class assembled or in clusters of small groups, students discuss the evidence or assumptions that led to the interpretive decisions they made in the process of creating their cinematographic plans, and why these decisions matter for an "appropriate" understanding of the scenes. I am present to pepper their conversations with questions. For example, when talking about staging Jesus' entry into Jerusalem I might ask: What difference does it make if we conclude that twenty or two-hundred people witness Jesus riding the colt? Does it matter that Mark and Luke place this event outside of the city proper, and should we care *how far* away from Jerusalem Jesus is? Can we assume that Roman soldiers are present when people shout royal acclamation about Jesus? As students discuss their plans (especially if I have asked them to conduct research outside of class to complete the project), key historical and textual details usually capture their attention. For example, students discover that the size of the temple complex affects their conception of the extent and visibility of Jesus' actions in Mark 11:15–16, or that the volatile political climate of Jerusalem during Passover week entails consequences for envisaging Jesus' approach to the city and his conduct within it. These reflections thus lay the foundation for the class's subsequent inquiries into the implications that these details pose for an understanding of the gospels' narrative rhetoric and its theological significance. For example, I usually have classes studying Mark reflect on whether Mark 11:15–19 portrays Jesus performing an isolated yet meaningful prophetic demonstration or a massive show of force that demands widespread notice. Together we consider how interpretations of this pericope have implications for grasping a gospel's explanation of the causes and significance of the Passion.

In this introductory exercise my priorities focus on raising questions and examining assumptions, not yet contending for particular interpretations. Nevertheless, I find that this project creates an effective means of exposing the theological and interpretive raw material in these scenes. Although my pedagogical objectives and teaching context lead me to emphasize the symbolic, thematic, or theological effects of the Jerusalem stories from a single gospel, other teachers might effectively adjust the exercise to concentrate on related issues, including the physical locations and historical events that the biblical texts attempt to represent, or the evangelists' redactional activities. (For a similar exercise, see §257.)

Matthew L. Skinner

183. CHRISTOLOGY SLIDESHOW

This exercise is designed to introduce the topic of Christology in the Gospels. I invite the students to imagine that they are constructing a course entitled "Portraits of Jesus in the Gospels." I ask, "When you picture Jesus, what do you see? What color is his skin, his hair, his eyes? Is he tall or short, clean or dusty? Describe his demeanor." I then show the images listed below and ask them to think about which of the slides, if any, best approximates their own image. It is advisable to number the slides and provide a handout with the numbers and titles for purposes of discussion after the viewing.

Upon completion of the slideshow, I ask them to share which images struck them. Which felt familiar and which felt strange or challenging? I ask about what kinds of influences have shaped or continue to shape their image of Jesus and whether other resources might be added. We ponder whether or not one image of Jesus captures everything. We consider art forms as a means of expressing truth. I then suggest that each of our gospel writers, no less than the visual artists, depicts Jesus with different emphases. Our task is to decide which best represents each gospel. Students often relate Mark's Suffering Servant Jesus to images such as Kramskoy's *Christ in the Desert*, da Messina's *Christ at the Pillory*, or Hoffman's *Jesus in the Garden of Gethsemane*. Orozco's *The Modern Migration of the Spirit* echoes Luke's vigorously fatidic Jesus. The *Christ Pantocrator* or *Circular Map of the World* works well for the pre-existent cosmic Christ of the Fourth Gospel. Any image of Jesus as teacher, such as Gebhardt's *The Sermon on the Mount*, fits Matthew well.

Images depicting Jesus as Asian (Ho-Peh), Haitian, female (Sandys), black (McKenzie), or red-headed (Gauguin) raise questions regarding race, ethnicity, and gender in relationship to the historical Jesus as well as the savior Christ. How all of this relates to the Incarnation generates lively discussion.

There are several effective alternatives regarding the placement of this exercise. One can situate it at the beginning of a course on the Gospels and revisit the images after the completion of each gospel, or it can come at the end of the study of all four gospels to decide which images best fit each author's depiction. I have also used it after the Synoptic Gospels and before moving into John. Finally, I have used it in upper level seminars devoted to a single gospel to remind the students about the distinctiveness of each gospel. In each case, I have found that the images serve as a visual note card, shortcut, or anchor for the students; the image emerges from the mind's eye and the student fills in the details of that particular author's Christology.

Images of Jesus, famous and otherwise, are easily accessible on the Internet merely by using a search engine. Some important collections such as the Index of Christian Art at Princeton (http://ica.princeton.edu) require a subscription. I drew many of the images in the list below from Jaroslav Pelikan's *The Illustrated Jesus through the Centuries* (New Haven: Yale University Press, 1997) and Josh Simon's "Who Was Jesus" in the December 1994 issue of *Life* magazine (vol. 17, no. 12). Almost all of the following are available on the Internet:

1. Jose Clemente Orozco, *Modern Migration of the Spirit*, 1934. *Life*, Dec. 1994.
2. Matthias Grunewald, *Resurrection*, 1513–15. Pelikan, 22, 23.
3. Hans Memling, *Christ as Salvator Mundi Amongst Musical Angels*, 1487–90. Pelikan, 46, 47.
4. Unknown artist, *Haitian Jesus. Life*, Dec. 1994.

5. Unknown artist, *African-American Jesus. Life,* Dec. 1994.
6. Edwina Sandys, *Christa,* 1974. On the Internet (edwinasandys.com) and in *Life,* Dec. 1994.
7. Janet McKenzie, *Jesus of the People.* On the Internet (www.bridge-building.com).
8. Marc Chagall, *Yellow Crucifixion,* 1943. Pelikan, 20.
9. Eduard von Gebhardt, *The Sermon on the Mount.* Pelikan, 14.
10. *Circular Map of the World,* ca. 1275. Pelikan, 34.
11. Antonella da Messina, *Christ at the Pillory,* 15th century. Pelikan, 72.
12. Paul Gauguin, *Agony in the Garden,* 1889. *Life,* Dec. 1994.
13. Monika Liu Ho-Peh, *The Stilling of the Tempest,* ca. 1950. Pelikan, 238.
14. Warner Sallman, *Head of Christ,* 1940. Pelikan, 30. This is the image almost every student knows.
15. Ivan Kramskoy, *Christ in the Desert,* 1872–74. Pelikan, 210.
16. Heinrich Hoffman, *Jesus in the Garden of Gethsemane,* 1890. Pelikan, 215.
17. Dante Gabriel Rosetti, *The Passover in the Holy Family,* 1856. Pelikan, 10.
18. *Christ Pantocrator,* apse mosaic, Duomo, Italy. Pelikan, 59.

Jaime Clark-Soles

184. CREATING COMFORT
WITH AMBIGUITY ABOUT JESUS

A general pedagogical problem I encounter with students in my religion classes is that they have a tendency to want me to give them the "right" answers. They often seem to believe that my job is to give them correct information and to clear up any ambiguity. In my New Testament class, particularly since I tend to focus on interpretive questions, my job is rather to create yet more ambiguity as well as a plurality of answers to certain questions. In relation to asking questions about the significance and meaning of Jesus and his ministry, this problem in student expectations is further accentuated by student faith commitments. For those who believe that Jesus is "the Way, the *Truth,* and the Light," the idea of embracing ambiguity and plurality can be very challenging and their instinctual reaction is to seek strategies of resistance. I have found the following assignment helpful in creating student comfort with ambiguity and with a plurality of interpretations of Jesus.

This assignment is the first assignment of the semester, usually given in the second week. Students are given a list of questions and are required to interview two people about their views, ideas, and opinions on Jesus. They are then—and I stress only *after* interviewing others—to answer the interview questions for themselves. The interviews are handed in and I read through them noting unique and interesting answers. We then spend approximately half a class period in discussion of the process and the answers they received. I find students eager and enthusiastic to share their experiences and the ways in which the exercise expanded their appreciation for alternative ways of imagining Jesus. The exercise allows me to preview class sessions on the Gospels and Jesus by saying that just as people today see Jesus in different ways and hold variant views of his significance, so too did the people who experienced his ministry, or those who were responsible for writing the gospels.

The assignment as students receive it is as follows:

This assignment is to interview two people regarding their views about Jesus of Nazareth. *After* doing this you are to fill out the interview for yourself. I will mark it based on the effort apparent in the answers. Please ask your interviewees to take this seriously and to give thought to their responses. It is important that you probe them for detail and specification in their answers. One interviewee may be a fellow student who is not taking this course. The other interviewee is to be someone of approximately your parents' generation (this is to explore generational differences in thinking about Jesus). If you can interview someone of a non-Christian religion (Muslim, Jew, Hindu), that would be very interesting. If your interviewees consent, I would like to know something about their identity (age; major, if a student; occupation; religion; gender; etc.), but they may remain anonymous if you or they prefer. The interviews should be handed in typed. [The specifics of the following questions have evolved and continue to do so, shifting each semester with new insights and changing interests. This is how they currently stand.]

Interview Questions:

Imagine that you must describe the significance of Jesus to someone who knows nothing about him. You must do this in five words or fewer. How would you describe the significance of Jesus?

What was Jesus' physical appearance? Be as specific as possible. Describe his height, weight, hair color, body build, skin tone, eye color, clothing, facial features, etc.

What experiences have influenced you in how you imagine Jesus' physical appearance? Be specific. Have TV, film, paintings been influential? Historical knowledge or reading the Bible?

What was Jesus like as a person? What was his character, his personality like? Again, be as specific as possible, seeking to clearly define his nature as a person. (You may wish to think of descriptors like: cheerful,

NEW TESTAMENT

calm, quick-tempered, sulky, troubled, serious, humorous, a loner, a social person, etc.)

For people who lived at the time of Jesus and encountered him, or heard of him, what were some of the common reactions?

If you had lived during Jesus' lifetime, how do you think you would have reacted to him?

What are some of the ways in which people today react to and/or think about Jesus?

What sources have been most important in shaping your views about who Jesus was and what he did? (For example: family, church, Bible, historical novel, films, etc. Please name specific people, films, books.)

If you have seen it, what was your reaction to Mel Gibson's *The Passion*? Why?

How has your understanding of Jesus developed or changed over time?

If you had one question to ask Jesus, what would it be?

Thomas W. Martin

185. THE GOSPEL TRADITION AND THE MAKING OF MESSIAHS

After teaching a unit on Jesus and the gospels, with some attention to critical theories about the move of tradition from the hypothetical (or, reconstructed) historical Jesus to the gospels, I show a short clip from *Monty Python's Life of Brian*. The clip in question follows Brian's spaceship trip and his pursuit by Roman troops. Brian escapes the troops by posing as one of many prophets haranguing the people. The crowd is completely unresponsive until Brian stops teaching. His silence convinces them that he possesses a "messianic secret" that they need. As they pursue him, they take up those things that he leaves behind (a gourd, a sandal), argue about which one of them is his chief sign and symbol, and form disputing sects. The crowd finally catches Brian after he falls into the hole of a hermit. Brian's abrupt arrival breaks the hermit's years of silence. When the hermit blames Brian for ending his silence, the crowd turns the event into a miracle. As Brian continues to deny that he is the messiah, the crowd considers this proof that he is the messiah. Only the true messiah would deny that he is the messiah. When one of the group dissents from this view, the group unites against the heretic. I usually stop the film at this point because full-frontal nudity follows in the next scene (although the scene with Brian at an upper window imploring the crowds to take responsibility for their lives and the crowd chanting responsively, "we are all individuals," is an even better illustration of the making of a messiah).

I break the class into small groups and ask them to deal with various questions: (1) Who and what makes a messiah? (I usually ask this group to read Mark 1:1–11 and Rom 1:1–4.) How do the New Testament texts and the *Life of Brian* differ? (2) How does the movie suggest that sayings and miracle traditions develop? How do you think the gospel traditions developed? (3) How does the *Life of Brian* suggest that orthodoxy and heresy develop? How did these factions develop in early Christianity? (4) If it is an advanced class, I ask them to relate the movie to Mircea Eliade's and J. Z. Smith's different notions of how religion "begins." While Eliade understands religion as the breaking in upon human experience of a hierophany, Smith understands religion primarily as an interpretative act attempting to relate a religious tradition to present experience.

The point of the exercise is, of course, to reflect upon the role of the supernatural, the individual, the group, and politics in the development of messiahs, tradition, and heresy. In the advanced class, Eliade and Smith make excellent foils as they disagree so completely on these general questions.

Richard Walsh

186. THE DIVERSE WORLD OF JESUS

Monty Python's Life of Brian provides an engaging entrée to the diversity of the Palestinian world which Jesus inhabited. This movie tracks a young man named Brian, who lives in parallel world to Jesus, through his involvement with Zealots. It provides a humorous but instructive glimpse of Jesus' world. My method is basic; I introduce a clip very briefly, show the clip, and ask the students to comment briefly on the ways in which it relates to the New Testament and its context. I begin in apparent seriousness—as if this were going to be a documentary with talking heads and video shots of Qumran—with the very first scene in which the star of Bethlehem appears and the so-called wise men come mistakenly into the stable where Brian is born (minutes from start, precisely where star appears: 0:40–4:40). This scene is just for fun; the others are more instructive:

The Beatitudes (7:00–11:35). This scene provides a superb introduction to the essential point that people from various social classes, ethnic backgrounds, and theological positions interpreted Jesus' teachings differently from one another.

The Zealots who plot blackmail (27:00–29:00). This scene illustrates that there existed a good deal of ambivalence toward Rome, that not all Jews by any means expected a political messiah who would rid the Jews of Roman rule. In this scene, in which the Zealots are plotting in a back room, John Cleese asks, "What have the Romans ever done for us?" His Zealot compatriots, to his chagrin, can think of lots—roads, aqueducts, sanitation, wine, and peace. (For rivalries among Zealot factions, such as we find in Josephus's *Jewish Wars*, see 9:00–34:10.)

Apocalyptic preachers (43:30–44:45). Brian falls from a window and, in an effort to escape from the Romans, feigns preaching (in a very funny, and not particularly irreverent, parody of Jesus' teaching from the Sermon on the Mount about the birds of the air and lilies of the field). The other preachers are various self-styled apocalypticists.

Pontius Pilate (37:30–43:30). Two scenes illustrate that Pontius Pilate was not entirely in touch with his Palestinian constituents. In the first scene, which is vintage sophomoric humor, Pilate fails to recognize that the name Brian adopts for himself, Biggus Dikkus, is a joke. In the second scene, Pilate is mocked by the people when he attempts to release a prisoner. Pilate cannot, it seems, pronounce the letter "r," and so the crowds repeatedly ask for the release of non-existent prisoners whose names contain this letter: Roger, Roderick, and the like. Although the alleged speech impediment may be offensive—it should be shown cautiously—it functions nonetheless to demonstrate how Pilate's Roman dialect differed from the native population of Jews. Both scenes underscore how easily Pilate was alienated and isolated from the Judeans in his charge.

The sandal and the gourd (50:45–55:55). In this scene, Brian's followers (who are increasingly convinced of his significance by his denials of his own importance) choose various aspects of him—a gourd he had purchased, a sandal he lost—and create rival factions. This scene can be used to introduce how difficult it may be to interpret some of Jesus' more ambiguous actions and teachings and how needlessly his alleged followers use these different interpretations to divide and to disagree.

By the time this single class period is over, students have a feel for the diverse sorts of people who populated the world of Jesus, from people of the land to Roman governors. Further, students are able to see a human dimension of the instructor which can perhaps help them to appreciate her or his sense of humor.

John R. Levison

187. JESUS' TEACHING ON DIVORCE AND REMARRIAGE

The notorious "divorce texts" (Mark 10:2–12; Matt 19:3–12) make for lively class discussions, usually because students experience Jesus' stringency as uncharacteristic or even devoid of grace. At the seminary where I teach, probably no students categorically condemn remarriage after divorce, yet most would be uncomfortable with a theological "solution" to these passages that completely cancels them or ignores their implications. Students, therefore, generally express an eagerness to wrestle seriously with these texts, especially since those who plan to serve congregations know that they will have to explain them to others.

These passages present a great opportunity for students to consider the challenges of a theological interpretation of the Bible, particularly the task of navigating the cultural differences between text and reader. What does it mean that the Bible, our ways of reading, and any Christian articulation of the gospel all reflect the social environments and presumptions in which they are situated? These texts press the issue of the Bible's relationship to context, requiring seminarians to consider why the gospels say the things that they do, and to make an argument for how today's churches might live faithfully in light of these words speaking from a distant and alien past.

To surface these issues, and to help students practice crafting interpretations that take seriously the ways these texts reflect the culture and interpretive practices of the first century, I devote a class session to a small-group experience. The exercise has Mark 10:2–12 in view, but it adapts easily to the Matthean parallel. I have developed it for use in a Protestant seminary, but anyone teaching in a different setting could alter the exercise to present different scenarios or opinions while still requiring students to attend to the social assumptions at work in the text and in our interpretive strategies.

After having a student read Mark 10:2–12 aloud, I offer brief comments about how Deut 24:1–4 figured in discourse about divorce during Jesus' time. I divide the class into groups of eight to ten students and distribute the following handout to each student. (Instructors may change the particular elements as they see fit [e.g., How does the equation change if one or more of the divorces were due to "irreconcilable differences"?].)

JESUS' TEACHING ON DIVORCE AND REMARRIAGE

Scenario:

Your friend Mary is forty-two years old; she owns and manages a successful local business. She was married at age twenty-two, about five years before you met her. When she was twenty-four, her husband and another woman had an affair. He left Mary. Their divorce was finalized within months. They had no children. For almost two years now, Mary has been dating Max, who is also divorced. Max divorced his wife eight years ago, after she had a brief affair. Max has sole custody of his two teenaged children from this previous marriage. A month ago, Mary announced to you and other friends from church that she and Max plan to wed in two months.

One day Mary visits you, visibly upset, and says, "I was having dinner with Martha last night." (You also know Martha from church. She and her husband divorced ten years ago, and she has never dated anyone since then, as far as you know.) Mary continues, "We got to talking about me and Max, and Martha asked me if Max and I had worried about what God thinks about our upcoming marriage, since we are both divorced. Then she told me about Mark 10:2–12 and explained that this text convinced her that she shouldn't consider marrying again. I'd never heard this part of the Bible before; it surprises me that Jesus might have said such things. What do you think all this means for me and Max? Did we sin by getting divorces in the past? Would we be committing another sin—and ongoing sins!—if we went through with our plans to marry? These words in Mark 10 just strike me as so *outdated*, but also as very serious stuff! What do you think?"

Exercise:

How would you answer Mary's questions? How do you think Mark 10:2–12 speaks to her and Max's situation? In small groups, explore various perspectives on this issue, *as they pertain to the interpretation of Mark 10:2–12*. In your group's discussion, you must assume the role indicated by the checked box:

❐ Opinion A—You argue that Jesus declares divorce and remarriage as sinful actions, and that no appeals to differences in cultural norms can erase this basic truth. After all, Jesus roots his logic in the fixed design of creation. Churches can allow people like Max and Mary to wed, since no one should cast a first stone at other sinners. But the couple should recognize that they are sinning willingly, and that God would prefer that they not marry but live celibate lives. Your arguments should be based on an interpretation of Mark 10:2–12 and other biblical texts.

❏ Opinion B—You argue that divorce, while often unfortunate, can not be considered sinful. Nor is remarriage wrong. This biblical text reflects an entirely different era and is concerned with the maintenance of entirely different social structures. Mary and Max should claim that remarriage of divorced people is a gift from God, just as any marriage is. There is no adultery here. Your arguments should be based on an interpretation of Mark 10:2–12 and other biblical texts.

❏ Opinion C—You argue that, in a sinful world, disputes about which particular actions are or are not to be called sins is not a helpful approach. You want Mary to see what Jesus attempts to redeem in this text. Jesus is correcting abusive aspects of some people's interpretations of Deut 24:1–4. He is concerned about how marriage ought to reflect God's desire for justice within a sinful world. Connections among marriage, divorce, sin, and justice look different in every cultural context, and Mary and Max should explore these issues in light of the gospel's relevance to our world. Your arguments should be based on an interpretation of Mark 10:2–12 and other biblical texts.

❏ Facilitator—You are not to speak on behalf of any particular opinion but to lead the group discussion and keep a written record of insights and disagreements that surface. Make sure that everyone in your group has opportunities to speak and keep your group on task—focusing more on the interpretive issues than on pastoral-care concerns regarding Mary's personal struggle with this issue.

❏ Assumption Detective—You are to remain silent in your group and listen for the assumptions that undergird the comments and arguments expressed by others. What are people assuming, but not necessarily voicing, about the contexts and meaning of Mark 10:2–12? What are they assuming about the purpose or methods of biblical interpretation? Make notes of your observations.

Every sheet has one of the five boxes checked. One person in each group serves as "facilitator," two are proponents of each of the three general "opinions," and there is at least one "assumption detective." Since assumption detectives must remain silent, I often assign this role to more talkative students. After the groups have taken time to discuss the issue, each of the facilitators reports to the entire class, detailing their observations of the small group's deliberations. Next, each of the assumption detectives gives a brief report, so that the class gets a sense for the array of data and hermeneutical strategies that people employed. The point is to provoke the question: What counts as a valid or convincing argument about this or any text? I may also solicit feedback from students who experienced difficulty in contending for an opinion that they do not personally hold. We conclude with discussion of the assumptions people make (sometimes unconsciously) about the Bible and its contemporary relevance, the theological "authority" of biblical texts, and ways of interpreting this particular passage in light of its historical and literary contexts.

Matthew L. Skinner

188. FORGIVENESS

When discussing the biblical notion of forgiveness (a prominent theme in Matthew and Luke) it is useful to have students read *The Sunflower,* by the famous Nazi hunter Simon Wiesenthal. The first portion of the book is a brief but rich narrative told by a Jewish concentration camp prisoner. The protagonist is summoned to the bedside of a dying Nazi who wants to confess his crimes to a Jew. The Nazi relates a gut-wrenching tale of herding Jews into a house, setting the house on fire, and shooting anyone who tried to escape. The Nazi clearly remembers a certain man who gathered his child into his arms and, along with the mother, jumped to their deaths. The Nazi wants the Jew to forgive him. The story ends with the protagonist asking the reader what he should have done. The second part of the book features responses by fifty-two contributors including Harold Kushner, Abraham Heschel, Dorothy Soelle, Mary Gordon, the Dalai Lama, Desmond Tutu, and Robert Coles.

I require students to read the narrative and at least six of the responses. The six must be varied; they may not choose exclusively Christian or male authors. I then ask students to respond in writing to the narrative itself. Because the book can be emotionally grueling, I think it is necessary to grant some space for the students to express their reac-

tions freely. Then they are to answer the question: "What should the protagonist have done, and why do you think so?" They are also asked to
engage a few of the responding authors. Within two weeks of the date
that the assignment is due (as a posting on the discussion board of the
course web page), students must respond to the postings of at least two
of their classmates.

Questions which regularly emerge include: Can one forgive on behalf
of another person or can only the wronged individual grant forgiveness?
Can one forgive someone who has not repented? Is forgiveness granted
for the benefit of the perpetrator or of the victim? (Many will argue that
the point of forgiveness is to allow the victim the ability to declare the
event "over" so that he or she can move forward rather than being para-
lyzed by bitterness or anger.) Should one urge a victim to forgive? (This is
especially pertinent for those training for the ministry.) If a person asks
for forgiveness, is one required by one's faith to grant it? How would the
various biblical authors we are studying respond to this question? What
elements inform their argument? (If one is investigating Matthew's
stance, for example, one must consider the Hebrew scriptures.)

The discussion easily moves from *The Sunflower* to current affairs—the
Truth and Reconciliation Commission in South Africa, remuneration for
Native Americans, the Comfort Women Project (women used as sex slaves
by the Japanese Imperial Army during WWII)—as well as to stories
regarding parishioners for whom one is pastorally responsible. The exercise works well as a way to broach the subject of "the Bible and Ethics."
How, if at all, might one incorporate the biblical witness into ethical decisions, whether personal, societal, or global? Useful resources on this topic
may be found on the Internet (www.forgiving.org).

Jaime Clark-Soles

189. JESUS, WEALTH, AND WALL STREET

I teach an upper-division course, "Wealth and Poverty in the Bible," in
which we examine a range of biblical texts and themes pertaining to
economic justice and the role of God's people, both individually and
corporately, in the economic sphere of life. It is eye opening for many of
my students when they discover that the Bible contains so much information about money, poverty, material wellbeing, and injustice.
Especially surprising, for many, is the sometimes wide variance
between ancient biblical and modern societal values with regard to economic justice. As we study a variety of biblical passages, from creation

and the Exodus to Amos's prophetic critique of Israel and Jesus' teaching in the gospels, students are encouraged to consider their own approach to the material world, whether or not they identify themselves within the Christian tradition. They readily see that contemporary paradigms guiding economic practice are often quite different from biblical perspectives that champion Sabbath rest for all (even animals!) who labor, gleaning of fields by the poor, and the Jubilee tradition of land redistribution.

One important facet of this course is the opportunity students have to engage the material existentially. At the very outset, I make sure to let the students know that the class is designed for both academic and existential learning. Their grades will not depend on what they think (i.e., economically or politically), but they will be required to reflect carefully and to engage the academic material at a personal level. They must be willing, at least, to deal with some of the "so what?" questions that these texts inspire. In sum, students enter and leave with a range of perspectives, but my hope is that none will have completed the course without some significant individual reflection regarding their own place and role in the public sphere.

To introduce students to the material in the course and to encourage them to reflect upon its relevance for life in contemporary society, on the first day of the semester I ask student volunteers to read Luke 18:18–25 ("Indeed, it is easier for a camel to go through the eye of a needle than for someone who is rich to enter the kingdom of God") and Matt 6:19–21, 24 ("For where your treasure is, there your heart will be also; ... You cannot serve God and wealth"). These passages express in stark terms that money does somehow matter in how one relates to God. The implications of these texts are less clear, and the class will provide ample opportunities to explore such issues. At this point, my pedagogical concern is to persuade students that the overall topic merits their reflection.

In order to suggest that these and other ancient biblical texts may still have some relevance in the modern world, I then show a short clip of the film, *Wall Street,* starring Michael Douglas and Charlie Sheen. In the movie, Sheen plays a young, ambitious Wall Street broker intent on making a fortune. He is soon in danger of turning his back on his blue-collar roots as he is increasingly drawn into the world of blockbuster deals and ruthless financial policy. Gordon Gecko (Douglas), a fabulously wealthy corporate raider, takes the neophyte under his wing. In what may be the most famous moment in the movie, Gecko declares that "greed is good." Soon after, he crows about how wealth and its attendant power allow people like himself to function as gods, creating and destroying at will. The film illustrates in a visually powerful way what it might look like to "serve wealth" in today's society. Even before we begin reading for the course, students can sense that the work of the "gods" in the movie is at odds with "the kingdom of God" (cf. Luke 18:25). The framing of the problem has been established as students can sense the stark contrast between the biblical texts and Gecko's worldview. In fact, "Gordon Gecko" has functioned as a touchstone in class discussions throughout the remainder of the semester.

For those interested in a strong contrast to *Wall Street*, I have found the film *Romero* to be helpful for illustrating biblical concerns (regarding, e.g., land, Jubilee, gleaning, resident aliens, justice for widows and orphans, the preferential option for the poor, human dignity, and prophetic outcry). The film effectively portrays the interpretive dilemmas facing the priests and people as they seek to discern the implications of the gospel. Reflecting on the different choices made by the priests can inspire particularly fruitful classroom discussion.

Michael Barram

190. "WEALTH AND POVERTY" SERMON/STUDY SERIES

One of the most effective assignments in my "Wealth and Poverty in the Bible" course is to have students prepare for a mock sermon or Bible study series. (This exercise could be adapted for nearly any set of biblical or theological topics.) After we complete our readings and discussions of gospel texts pertaining to wealth, poverty, and economic justice, I divide the students into small groups. Their assignment is to pretend they are a group of clergy or lay leaders (many of my students are not at all religious, but they have played along well) who are charged with putting together a series of four sermons or Bible study sessions on wealth, poverty, possessions, and economic justice. The students can choose any four texts (about 4–12 verses in length) from the Gospels pertaining to these topics. As religious leaders, their task is to choose what they believe to be the four most important texts faith communities should wrestle with if they want to be aware of Jesus' perspective on money and material possessions.

First, the groups have to review what they have read over the last few weeks of class. Revisiting the texts helps students remember what they have already encountered and highlights areas where more attention is needed. Second, the groups have to choose what they find to be the four most important texts. To do so, they have to consider a range of issues. What are Jesus' main concerns? Which texts best illustrate these concerns? Third, students are asked to identify the most effective order in which to present the texts (over four sermons or Bible study sessions). Finally, each group is asked to explain to the class its rationale for choosing these four texts and why they would plan to present them in the order they have chosen. The students begin to think about how texts are written and received, consider the variety of topics and themes in various passages, and find themselves considering a range of pastoral issues (e.g., Should we pound the people over the head or should we be subtle? Should there be variations in the "tone" of Jesus' message? If so, how—and why?). Hermeneutical issues (e.g., social location and the reader) become evident without any need for complex theories.

By placing themselves in the "pastoral" role students immediately gain a new appreciation for the power of these texts and the dangers and difficulties inherent in using them. This exercise is therefore particularly useful for illustrating the link between biblical materials and contemporary faith communities.

Michael Barram

191. TEACHING ABOUT WOMEN IN THE GOSPEL STORIES

The status of women in the first century is varied. There is positive and negative evidence about women in Judaism, in the Greco-Roman world, in Paul's letters, and in the Gospels. It is often argued that there is a crescendo of women's voices in the gospel stories, but that the later New Testament writings revert to a misogynist stance. After providing background material on the variety of attitudes toward women in as many first-century cultures as possible, I instruct students to read gospel stories aloud in small groups, purposely positing themselves in an oral culture that listens rather than reads, and to ask the following question: If most first-century cultures are deemed to have been misogynist, does this particular story reflect that same attitude, or might it mirror an attitude of egalitarianism on the part of the authors and/or Jesus? As you read the story, watch for these elements: (1) exploitation of women (or others), (2) marginalization of women, (3) powerlessness of women, (4) cultural imperialism, (5) systemic violence, (6) silencing of women, and (7) vilification and trivialization of women. There are no right or wrong answers in this study, and one must be careful not to posit Jesus as a "feminist" outside of his own culture.

Test cases from the gospel stories may include the following: Mark 5:21–43 (the stories of Jairus' daughter and the hemorrhaging woman);

Matt 15:21–28 (the Canaanite woman); Luke 10:38–42 (Martha and Mary); John 4 (the Samaritan woman; in this pericope, note whose soil Jesus and the woman are on, the time of day [i.e., whose time of day is it to be at the well?], and the relationship between first-century Judeans and Samaritans); Acts 2:14–18 ("women and men shall prophesy"); *Gos.Thom.* 114 ("Mary [of Magdala] shall become a male").

After discussing the individual stories, the following broader discussion questions can be raised: Can one argue that there is a gospel tradition of equality? If so, how did it emerge? If not, what do we do two thousand years later? Why were women often portrayed in the gospels as the ideal disciple, compared to the male disciples who did not understand, according to the evangelists? As an additional activity, students may choose to role play characters in each of the stories in order to see how one might feel in each situation.

If one continues into the Pauline corpus, the following texts are good test cases to see if Paul reflects a misogynist attitude toward women or one of equality: Rom 16; Phil 4:2–3; Gal 3:26–28; 1 Cor 7:1–11; 11:1–16; 14: 33b-36. Suggested questions for discussion include: What roles do women play in these texts? Does Paul contradict himself on the issue of women in leadership? What is the evidence? Pseudonymous texts include 1 Tim 2:8–15 and Col 3:18–4:1. Are these reflective of misogyny or equality? Why do the later New Testament writings and letters adhere to a strict code for the status and role of women? As an additional activity, students may write a letter, in Pauline style, to a female friend, instructing her in regard to her status and role in life. Does your advice fit with her real world? In general, do we read these stories prescriptively or descriptively for today's world? (For other exercises on women in biblical texts, see §§51, 55, 153, 226, 242, 267.)

Glenna S. Jackson

192. THE SOCIAL FUNCTIONS OF PARABLES

The purpose of this exercise is to demonstrate the multivalent nature of New Testament parables. It is often assumed that a parable has a specific social function and, therefore, only one point of comparison. It is, however, a mistake to assume that there is only one central thought or point to a parable with all the details of the parable simply serving to enhance that one point. While parables are definitely rooted in the normalcy of life, real life is complex, multi-dimensional, and multivalent. New Testament parables, therefore, that reflect and address the social realities of everyday life in Galilee are likewise complex, multi-dimensional, and multivalent. To complicate matters even more, the multivalent nature of New Testament parables is heightened by the fact that Jesus' parables, which were often metaphorical explanations of the "Kingdom of God," had to be transmitted and interpreted by the first hearers and final writers at the same time. Therefore, we begin by reading or hearing that which was meant to be multivalent from one of only many possible perspectives.

To illustrate the differing social functions of parables, I divide the class into four groups with different social locations: male peasant day laborers; wives of male peasant day laborers; male vineyard owners; and wives of male vineyard owners. Each student reads Matt 20:1–16 and attempts to answer the following questions from the perspective of his or her assigned social location: (1) What is the message of the teaching? (2) What does the teaching say to you? (3) Do you like what you hear? (4) What questions and comments would you have for Jesus? (5) Do you want to join the community of Jesus' followers? I inform the students that while they are to struggle with their answers to these questions within their group, it is not necessary for each group member to come to the same answer. After working through their answers, each group shares its answers with the rest of the class. After sharing the various answers, we discuss how the parable has similar and dissimilar functions within different social groups and within the same social group (e.g., male peasant day laborers—those who worked all day and those who only worked a couple of hours). We discuss whether the parable should only have one correct meaning or function, and if so, who determines it? We then discuss whether or not there are important elements in the parable that might be overlooked if the perspective of one of the four social groups is omitted. We conclude our conversation by examining how comfortable the students are with the notion that there is not necessarily one central meaning to a parable, but rather multiple meanings. Is the idea of parables being multivalent a strength or a weakness? Why? (If time permits, this question may provide a transition to a discussion of the history of the interpretation of the parables touching on the different approaches of, e.g., Jülicher, Jeremias, Dodd, and Crossan.)

The same exercise could be used for almost any parable in the Synoptic tradition. Different social locations may need to be assigned, depending on the parable chosen for the activity.

This strategy was developed in collaboration with Melanie Johnson-DeBaufre.

Guy D. Nave Jr.

193. PARABLE PROJECT

In the first semester of my "Introduction to the New Testament" course, I require as the major out-of-class assignment a project of the student's own design on one of Jesus' parables from the New Testament gospels. The assignment proceeds in three parts:

1. A two to three page reflection paper, due early in the semester, in which students indicate their choice of parable and reflect on its story, message, and meaning, using no resources except the text (if they can read Greek, language reference works such as lexicons are acceptable). I ask, "Why does this text intrigue you? What is important about it? What significance has it had in your life? What unanswered questions would you like to pursue?"

2. A project proposal reflecting study of and sustained, informed reflection on the parable. The project may take the form of a standard exegesis paper, a review of research, a sermon or set of sermons, or some other form. Artistic projects (painting, music, dramatic script, etc.) are encouraged. In approximately two pages, students describe their project, indicating their focus, their approach, and how the approach is appropriate to their parable and to the issues they have chosen. A working bibliography, indicating sources students expect to be of value for the project, is appended to the proposal.

3. The project, due late in the semester, carries out the plan outlined in the proposal. Projects other than research papers must include an annotated bibliography (for which I provide a model), so that I can see how students' research contributed to their final project.

In several years' experience with this I have received a number of outstanding submissions, such as a dramatic monologue in which Judas identifies Jesus' parables of reversal as the occasion of his turning against Jesus; a quilt depicting the parable of the seeds; and a libretto on the parable of the two sons that was eventually fleshed out, with the help of other students and professional musicians, into a fully staged chamber opera presented in seminary chapel. Since seminary students often arrive with significant creative talents that do not always translate well to classroom assignments, they seem to appreciate this opportunity to integrate their "former selves" with their "student selves." Whether students write a paper, a sermon, a drama, or engage visual or musical arts, I have observed that the assignment leads them to grapple with complexities of the parable that they often did not see in their initial reflection. Frequently, as well, they find that their project resists neat closure—reflecting, I remind them, the surplus of meaning present in the parables themselves.

Sandra Hack Polaski

194. TEACHING THE PARABLES OF JESUS
FROM AN AFRICAN CONTEXT

During the fall of 2000, I taught a course on the parables of Jesus at Africa University in Mutare, Zimbabwe. While there, I discovered that Africans know far more about New Testament contexts than any of us in the Western world. Those insights have provided me with a different way of teaching the parables. Using original parables and stories of students, I have developed the following three-step method for introducing the parables of Jesus. To acclimate them to the oral culture, it is important to arrange students in small groups and always have them read aloud to one another. I also play recordings of African music, such as Ladysmith Black Mambazo, for background context.

Step One: As you read the following original Parable of the Widow by Samuel Dzobo, a Zimbabwean, think about the questions Westerners need to ask and have answered to understand its context and meaning:

"It is like the rains have come and everyone is busy in the fields. Then a widow has her only two oxen get lost in the forest. For two weeks, she has been looking for the two oxen to no avail. She knows she is late with planting. She goes to her deceased husband's brother to ask him to plough her one field, but he refuses because she refused to be inherited. She goes to another and he refuses because he has not finished plowing his last field and his oxen had been tired. The widow then goes to the aunt of her deceased husband to have her son plow her field, but the aunt refuses because her son would want to rest for he had been busy with their own fields. The widow gives up and she knows she cannot plant in her field. Then a friend of her deceased husband comes by and he finds that her field has not been plowed. He brought his own oxen and plows the field and sent his sons to look for the lost oxen. That year the widow had a great harvest, more than anyone else in the village."

What are your questions? They may include: (1) What is "inheritance"? (2) Why are these particular characters included in the story, that is, what is the role of each? After discussion, Dzobo's explanation of the parable is offered:

"In my culture the custom of inheritance is still practiced. A woman who refuses to be inherited after the death of her husband is saying, 'Leave me alone, I can manage my own life.' This woman stays at her home probably because all her daughters are married. The fact that she bore some children makes staying at her home [possible]. Otherwise she would go to her parents if she has no children and refused inheritance. The uncles refused to plow her field because she can do it. For them to plow the field she has to accept inheritance. Her aunt refuses because she is responsible for the inheritance; by refusing the inheritance the widow was disrespecting the aunt. So the widow has no relative in the midst of relatives. Either she accepts inheritance or she has no relative. The other option is that she can go to her parents but she cannot do that because she has children. So the widow is in the midst of nowhere. To lack food would make her depend on the same people by whom she refused to be inherited. But her husband had a friend, *a sahwira*. This is more than a friend. A *sahwira* takes his friend's burdens as his and he can do anything to help a friend like he is doing it to his own family. The friendship is not over because the husband has died. This is what the woman had forgotten—that the *sahwira* was still there. When he comes along, he helped her in her field and having the lost oxen found and she has a great harvest. The Shona proverb which says *usahwira unokunda ukama* (this Agape kind of relationship cannot be compared to family relationship) subverts conventional wisdom of blood is thicker than water which emphasizes the family relationship as more important than any other relationship. Her uncles were ashamed because of the harvest."

(At this point, students are beginning to see that the context of any writing is important and different cultural contexts from our own can be puzzling and mysterious. That is the beauty of parables!)

Step Two: Read aloud the parable of the Good Samaritan in Luke 10:30–35. Write an introduction to this parable from your own experience and cultural context. Share with one another and then read the following introduction, written by Jean Ntahoturi, a Hutu from Burundi, in which a Tutsi Solder is the Good Samaritan:

"In 1995, I was shopping in the suburb of Bujumbma when I heard gunfire nearby. Two soldiers were shot dead. The rebels were around. In a confused situation, I ran away in the hills. I was not alone. When we began to climb the hill, one mother realized that her five-year-old son was not with her. She was so disturbed. She decided to go back to look for him. We [tried to] persuade her not to go back. She refused. 'I have to go to look for my son; if I am to die today, there is no option,' she said. When she was moving around, the child saw his mother in the distance. He was in rebels' hands. He started crying. The rebels suddenly saw the mother and called her to come and take the child. First, she was afraid, but she got courage and she approached them and took the child."

According to Jean, one should identify with the victim rather than with the so-called Good Samaritan because help comes from the most unexpected source, in this case, a soldier from the enemy tribe. How does your introduction compare to Jean's? With which of the characters in the parable of the Good Samaritan do you identify? Who is the one person in the world from whom you would not want to take help?

Step Three: Continue with the reading of other parables of Jesus. Have we been guilty of assigning simple meanings and answers from our own contexts, thus diminishing their impact? Parables are like puzzles; they have the capacity to pull the reader into their world. They are also timeless; they are dynamic means for conveying the meaning of relationships and responsibilities in all cultures.

Glenna S. Jackson

195. EXPERIENCING THE PARABLES

This exercise on the parables seeks to accomplish four objectives: (1) to invite students to encounter the unfamiliar dimensions of some of the narrative parables in the Synoptic Gospels; (2) to bring out multiple interpretive possibilities from the respective characters' points of view; (3) to model the interpretive process by drawing attention to sociocultural dimensions of the parable that call for knowledge of its ancient Mediterranean context; and (4) to reveal ideological textures that lie just beneath the surface of these parables.

The instructor selects a parable that meets two criteria: It has to be a narrative, and it has to include multiple human characters. Promising examples include the Tenants (Mark 12:1–11 and par.), the Prodigal (Luke 15:11–32), the Dishonest Manager (Luke 16:1–13), and the Widow and the Judge (Luke 18:1–8), among several others. Matthew's parable of the Sheep and the Goats poses an intriguing marginal example.

The instructor solicits volunteers to play roles from the parable and asks the rest of the class to develop at least three questions they would like to pose to the "characters." During the three minutes in which the class formulates their questions, the "characters" move to the front of the class. The instructor then facilitates the conversation as students interview the "characters"—and as the characters interact with one another.

When the discussion appears to be winding down, the instructor thanks the volunteer "characters" and invites them to return to their seats. At this point the instructor leads the class in a debriefing session. Fruitful questions for initiating discussion include: Did any of the characters say anything that surprised you? What would you like to know about this parable that none of the "characters" could supply for you? Did you find yourself more sympathetic with one character than with the others? Did your sympathies shift? Did you gain any new insights into this story? What do you think poses the most challenging dimension of this story for a modern audience?

This exercise often produces awkward moments that can foster critical reflection. For example, the "characters" may find themselves stumped by a question of fact (e.g., how did debt work in ancient agrarian societies?). In such cases the instructor may pose the question as a problem for the class: "How would you find out?" Another creative moment may occur when students want to hear from characters that are absent from or on the margins of the parable (e.g., students may ask what a mother or sister might say in the Parable of the Good Samaritan?). Such questions may open the path to ideological investigation of the parable: What points of view does it neglect or overlook? Finally, the instructor should be aware that acting in character can be a very personal experience for some students. (For other exercises involving role-play, see §§72, 161, 199, 203, 241, 246, 265.)

Greg Carey

196. HOW TO WRITE A PARABLE

Parables do not "work" in the same way as other genres. Gordon Fee likens parables to jokes: much in the same way that a joke is ruined if the teller has to explain the punch line, parables are ruined when they are "explained." I ask students to select a narrative parable and retell it so that it has the same "punch" or "catch" today that it had when it was first told (cf. G. D. Fee and D. Stuart, *How to Read the Bible for All Its Worth* [2nd ed.; Grand Rapids: Zondervan, 1993], 139, 147).

Students are to read the biblical parable and answer these questions: Who are the characters? What is the "catch"? Who gets caught? What would they (that is, the characters and the one who gets caught) look like today? Based on successful retellings, I recommend that students use concrete, specific details, limit the retold version to the same length as the original parable, and to feel free to vary the details (for instance, the parable of the ten maidens does not necessarily need to be retold with ten characters).

I offer the following example in class. Once I asked students, "Describe the most popular kid in your high school and the person who was the biggest outcast." I then had them vote on the biggest outcast. Arthur, who described "Larry the Toucher," was the winner. Larry liked to touch other people's hair, massage their shoulders, and give surprise hugs; no one appreciated his frequent attention. I then read the parable of the Good Samaritan with cheerleaders and athletes as the priest and Levite and with Arthur and Larry as the injured man and the Samaritan. When I read, "Larry went to Arthur and bandaged his wounds, pouring on oil and wine," Arthur exclaimed (rather loudly), "I would never let Larry touch me!" I replied, "That's how people thought about Samaritans. That's the person who is our neighbor." The challenge is to recreate the experience that the original hearers would have had. In the next class session, I read and the class discusses their parables.

I have also used this exercise in class with each half of the class working on a retelling of a parable. After about ten minutes of group work, each half retells their parable to the other half of the class, and then we evaluate the effectiveness of the retelling. The goal of this activity is to enable the students to understand how the genre of parable works.

Kenneth L. Cukrowski

197. "EXEGETING" CHRISTMAS

In this exercise in "baby exegesis," students are given a variety of photocopied Christmas carol lyrics and are asked to "exegete" them. Carols are easy to come by, either in carol books that many people have on hand, or downloaded and copied from the Internet (most carols are in the public domain). The assignment works best if students already know what exegesis is, but this exercise can also help to introduce them in a fun and painless way to elementary exegetical techniques and methods.

An instructor might ask students a variety of questions about each carol: Do the lyrics represent a high or low Christology (i.e., is Jesus a sweet little baby in a manger or the Messiah, the Prince of Peace)? Which gospel do carols draw from, predominantly: Matthew or Luke? Why? Which gospel lends itself better to the nativity themes of the carols and why? How many carols rely on gospel harmonization (e.g., are the star and the shepherds both mentioned as present at Jesus' birth)? What elements from the gospel infancy narratives are suppressed, and why might they have been left out (e.g., how many mention Joseph, rather than just Jesus and Mary)? What other texts or themes from the New Testament (or Old Testament) are present in the carols (i.e., Isaiah, Psalms, or Paul)? What themes are extra-canonical (i.e., are the three wise men, the oxen, and other animals present at the manger)? What sort of emphasis is placed on controversial elements of the infancy narratives, like Mary's status as a virgin? How many times is "born from a virgin" mentioned in carols?

Note: A similar exercise works well for Christmas scenes taken from pop culture videos, such as *South Park* Christmas specials (most students will find these hilarious, but be aware of their use of extensive profanity and intentionally provocative satire), *A Charlie Brown Christmas*, the beginning of Monty Python's *Life of Brian*, or even a Christian "life of Jesus" video. All these are readily available at local video stores. Students very much enjoy the opportunity to exercise their critical acumen on biblically-themed "documents" from pop culture.

Nicola Denzey

198. GENEALOGIES AND EXEGESIS

This exercise takes an inductive approach to introducing students to basic elements of biblical exegesis. Precisely because it focuses on a part of the Bible—the genealogies of Jesus—glossed over by many readers, it can be very helpful in one of the first sessions of an introductory course in which students are asked to interpret biblical texts.

Students gather in groups of two or three and compare the two genealogical passages of Matt 1:1–17 and Luke 3:23–38. They read the passages silently to themselves and then each small group compiles a list of all the similarities and differences they notice. After a period of about ten minutes, we gather as a class to compile a larger list. I find that students invariably notice certain things about these texts. For example, they tend to notice that the names in the lists are not the same; that Matthew includes the names of four women; that Matthew's list begins with Abraham and ends with Jesus while Luke's begins with Jesus and ends with God; that Matthew's list is grouped by generations, with an explicit comment to this effect in v. 17; and that the passages occur at different points in the gospel accounts. Students may want to know who some of these people were. Depending on the time allowed for the activity, students can look up certain of the names in the Old Testament, usually with the help of the notes in their study Bibles. They are often especially interested in the women mentioned by Matthew. We also talk briefly about what kind of information it supplies to the reader to know who the named people are. Students can begin to suggest what the inclusion of particular names might contribute to our understanding of the text. The point here is to be suggestive rather than definitive; I want students to see the possible interpretive payoff in their study of the literary shape of the text.

After ample time for all of the observations to be made, I categorize the kinds of observations the students made. They have attended to questions of grammar and vocabulary, to the internal structure of each passage, and to the larger context in which the passage is found. I give a brief overview of what I mean by each of these categories and note examples of each from the students' comments. These are basic questions that we will attend to with each text we read. There are a number of other ways the discussion may go from here, depending on the instructor's goals for the course. For example, attention to these literary categories has also opened up questions for us about the historical background of the writing and of the author's ideological framework, and it may be helpful to highlight these categories as well.

In closing, I identify for students some additional lessons I hope they will take from the class. For example, this introduction to exegesis has the advantage of encouraging students to think that they can actually interpret biblical texts themselves. The ways that we approach biblical texts are not wildly different from other texts that we read. The students' engagement with the text and thoughtful reflection can take them a long way in understanding the meaning and significance of the text. At the same time, because no one person thinks of every difference named, the lesson also points to the importance of listening to the voices of other interpreters. In doing so, we test our assumptions and come to see things we would not otherwise have noticed.

Susan E. Hylen

199. ACTING OUT THE SERMON ON THE MOUNT

Many Jews in the first century longed for a figure like Judas Maccabeus to lead Israel out of oppression by foreign powers. In one way, Jesus fits right into the context of first-century messianic expectation. He too is announcing the inauguration of the decisive moment of history in which God is finally dealing climactically with Roman oppression. But implicit in Jesus' summons is a warning to abandon other visions. If Israel persists in its determination to fight a desperate war against Rome, then Rome will destroy them. This would be seen by many as a sign of God's judgment against his rebellious people. The Sermon on the Mount is Jesus' plan for creating a renewed Israel—for overcoming the kingdoms of Herod and Caesar without using violence and without simply allowing themselves to be dominated. Jesus will himself lead the way in carrying this vision through to fulfillment in surprising and unanticipated ways.

To illustrate Jesus' alternative way between violent revolt and passive acquiescence, I use the work of Walter Wink (*The Powers That Be:*

Theology for a New Millennium [New York: Doubleday, 1999]). I ask for three groups of volunteers to act out or mime Wink's background descriptions of the Sermon on the Mount as I summarize them to the class. The class enjoys the humor and energy which the mime brings as it vividly illustrates Jesus' "third way" of launching the kingdom of heaven on earth. What follows is the synopsis of Wink's analysis, which the students act out while I narrate:

Act One: "Do not resist an evildoer. But if anyone strikes you on the right cheek, turn the other also." The best translation of "do not resist" is "don't react violently against the one who is evil." That is, don't oppose evil on its terms. Don't let evil dictate the methods of opposition.

Don't imagine a blow with your right fist. This is not a fight among equals, but a blow by a superior at an inferior. It is the domination system forcing someone out of line to get back into their place. It is a backhand blow. And if you stand up to it, it's like telling the same joke twice—if it didn't cower you the first time, it simply will not work. Sure, the left cheek would be a target for the right fist, but only equals fight with fists. Last thing master wants to do is establish the underling's equality. You can have the slave beaten, but no longer can you simply make him cower. The point is made: "I am a human being, just like you. I refuse to be treated this way. It's wrong." This is not passivity. It is not saying, "Go ahead, hit me again." It is an assertive, non-violent challenge to the domination system.

Act Two: "If anyone wants to sue you and take your coat, give your cloak as well." The setting is a law court. The biblical context is Deut 4:10–13 which provides that a creditor could take as collateral for a loan a poor person's long outer robe, but it had to be returned each evening so the poor man would have something in which to sleep.

Upon losing one's land, as many had, you sell your labor to an absentee landowner who bought your land. You rent your former land from him, still borrow to pay for food for your family, and thus you can get into the collateral system. They hate this system. Jesus says next time they ask for your outer coat, give them your cloak as well, that is, give them the equivalent of your underwear. This means marching out of the court naked. Nakedness is taboo, and viewing the naked party is a cause of shame for the creditor. So the debtor thus brings shame on the creditor. In effect, the poor man turns the tables, pushing the whole system to its absurd conclusion. He raises a stunning protest against the system that created his debt: "You want my robe? Here, take everything! Now you've got all I have except my body." The entire system by which debtors are oppressed has been publicly unmasked. It is a disgrace. His nakedness lays bare the whole injustice of this oppressive system.

Act Three: "And if anyone forces you to go one mile, go also the second mile." Compulsory labor was a feature of Roman rule. You could be coerced into service by Roman soldiers, but it was relatively civilized in that the basic rule was that they could take you or your oxen for a single mile as a levy on subject people. There is evidence of whole villages fleeing to avoid being forced to carry soldiers' baggage when they are moving camp and the locals get wind of it.

What we overlook here is that carrying the pack a second mile is an infraction of the military code. Now such infractions would be under control of the commander. Such a soldier who breaks this code could be flogged, fined, given short rations, or imprisoned for a week, or perhaps just reprimanded, depending on the seriousness of the offense.

Jesus does not counsel revolt. He does not trick the soldier by pretending to be a friend, and then slit his throat when he's not looking. Carrying a pack a second mile is a strategy for the dominated to recover their dignity and take initiative in a non-violent way. So imagine the soldier's surprise when, at the next mile marker, he reaches for his pack reluctantly and the civilian says, "Oh no, let me carry it another mile." Why? What's he up to? Normally, Romans have to coerce and threaten. But this Jew is cheerfully going another mile? What's going on? An insult to the soldier's manhood and strength? Being kind?

Whereas once the Jew was in a state of servile oppression, he has now seized the initiative. This throws the soldier off balance. Never before has he had this problem. If he previously enjoyed feeling superior, he certainly won't today. Imagine the humor of a Roman infantryman pleading with a Jew to give him back his pack! The humor would not have escaped Jesus' contemporaries. Certainly this could be used in a vindictive way, so we must not forget the sermon also commands us to love the enemy. But for one moment at least, it is no fun to be an oppressor. Of course, this would only work once, and people would probably catch on. So one must improvise new tactics to keep the opponent off balance. Here is a way to resist the powers and principalities without being made over into their likeness.

I have students discuss in groups their response to this re-telling of the story. After some time passes, I put on an overhead the passage from John (18:19) where Jesus is struck on the face and then responds in a way which does not literally turn the other cheek and simply suffer in silence. He stands straight up in a non-violent way and challenges this miscarriage of justice. This is Jesus' subversive battle plan to recreate the heart of Israel from within.

Finally, I ask students to consider how (or whether) Jesus' eschatological message still has relevance today. After discussion of events in the lives of Gandhi and Martin Luther King Jr., its contemporary relevance seems more apparent than before we began our study of the Sermon on the Mount. (For other exercises involving role-play, see §§72, 91, 142, 161, 195, 199, 203, 241, 246, 265.)

Roger Newell

200. JESUS AND THE LAW

Whenever I teach "Introduction to the Bible," about mid-way through the Hebrew Bible, I usually begin to hear one or two students murmuring comments like, "I can't wait until we get done with the Old Testament and all the emphasis on obeying rules and laws. I want to get to the New Testament where Jesus talks about grace and mercy." Many teachers encounter this failure or refusal on the part of students to acknowledge the Jewishness of Jesus and, therefore, the Jewishness of early Christianity. The objective of this particular exercise, therefore, is not so much to make any definitive claims about Jesus' relationship to or understanding of Jewish law. It is simply meant to challenge the simplistic notion that the Old Testament is all about being a slave to "the Law" and Jesus is all about grace and mercy.

Before class each student reads the following passages and answers the following questions: (1) Matt 5:21–24. What does Jesus expect of his followers in this text? Describe how it compares with the teaching in Exod 20:13. (2) Matt 5:27–30. What does Jesus expect of his followers in this text? How does Jesus' advice differ from Exod 20:14, 17 and Deut 5:18? (3) Matt 5:31–32. What rule does Jesus make about divorce? How does it compare with Deut 24:1–4 and 1 Cor 7:10–11? (4) Matt 5:38–43. How does Jesus alter the "law of retribution" (*lex talionis*) found in Lev 24:17–21? How are Jesus' followers supposed to respond to those who harm them or demand things from them? (5) Matt 5:43–48. What does Jesus expect of his followers in this text? Describe how it compares with what is found in Lev 19:17–18; Ps 139:19–22; Prov 25:21–22. (6) Do you think Jesus' teachings in Matthew are more or less demanding than the Torah? Do you think contemporary Christians do, can, or should follow these teachings of Jesus? Give specific reasons for your answers.

In class the students are put into five groups. Students share in group their responses to all of the questions; the group, however, will only have to share with the rest of the class its response to the question that corresponds with its group number. After each group has shared its response, I open the floor for individual reactions and thoughts regarding the last question. Usually during the course of the discussion one or two students will make a comment along the lines that Jesus is concerned with the actions of our heart (i.e., "It's not about murder but about not getting mad," or, "It's not about adultery but about not lusting in our heart"). I will usually use that comment as a transition to my next series of questions: What does Jesus understand his relationship to the law to be? Why does he say what he says in these verses? Does he think the law is too lenient? At an appropriate opportunity, I ask the students to read Matt 5:17–20, which immediately precedes the passages we have just read. I then discuss Jesus' remarks that he is fulfilling the law. I suggest that Jesus understands himself as standing in the tradition of a faithful Torah observer. Jesus suggests that his teachings and actions are consistent with the "true" meaning of the law. I explain that the function of the *lex talionis* was not to promote revenge but rather to limit the extent of the punishment one could inflict. The punishment could not be in excess of the offense. Jesus suggests that the fulfillment of that principle is actually to turn the other cheek. The prohibition against murder is to promote civility and community; and for Jesus the fulfillment of that principle is actually to avoid anger and hatred. Jesus understands himself to be fulfilling the law. By separating Jesus from his Jewish identity, we risk misunderstanding the heart of his teaching.

This strategy was developed in collaboration with Melanie Johnson-DeBaufre.

Guy D. Nave Jr.

201. THE SERMON ON THE MOUNT

When my class studies the Gospel of Matthew, I find that students often have difficulty understanding Matthew's presentation of Jesus and his attitude toward the Mosaic Torah. Matthew's views differ sharply from what we find in other writings of the New Testament, particularly the letters of Paul, but students often—and unconsciously—"harmonize" the two perspectives. This exercise is designed to help students think carefully about the context and content of Jesus' teachings in Matthew's Sermon on the Mount. (Although it works well as an in-class discussion, this exercise can also be framed as a debate: have one side argue that Jesus' statements in Matt 5:21–48 contradict what he says in Matt 5:17–20, and have the other side argue that Jesus' statements in 5:17–20 and 5:21–48 are not contradictory.)

First, I ask the students to read Matt 5:1–7:29 before they come to class. They are to read Matt 5:17–48 at least twice because our discussion will focus on these specific verses. I begin by having a student read aloud Matt 5:17–20. We then talk about the following questions: (1) What are the law and the prophets? (2) What is Jesus' attitude toward the law? What does Jesus mean when he says that he has come not to abolish but to fulfill the law? (3) Jesus says that not a single letter will pass from the law "until heaven and earth pass away" and "until all is accomplished." What point(s) in time does Jesus have in mind? (Have students mention several possibilities. Does this refer to the end of time? To Jesus' death and resurrection? To something else?) (4) What is Jesus' attitude toward those who break the commandments? To those who keep the commandments? What commandments might Jesus have in mind? (5) In Matt 5:20, what does Jesus say is required for entrance into the kingdom of heaven? Does this contradict what he just said in v. 19? Why or why not? (Have students offer arguments in support of both perspectives.) (6) What do these verses tell us about the role of the law in Matthew's community?

Next, I ask a student to read aloud Matt 5:21–30, 43–48, and we discuss several more issues: (1) When Jesus says, "You have heard that it was said to those of ancient times . . . ," to what is he referring? (It may be helpful to have students read Exod 20:14; Deut 5:18; Lev 20:10; and Deut 22:22 at this point.) (2) After each reference to a biblical commandment, Jesus introduces his own interpretation by saying, "But I say to you. . ." What is the relation between Jesus' interpretations and the original commandments? Is Jesus saying that his followers no longer need to obey the commandments? Is Jesus offering a stricter interpretation of the commandments? Is Jesus "spiritualizing" the commandments by suggesting that his followers must adhere to the "spirit" of the law, but not the "letter" of the law? Have students offer reasons for their interpretation. (3) Do Jesus' statements in 5:21–30 contradict what he has already said in 5:17–20? Why or why not? (4) What does Jesus mean when he tells his listeners to "be perfect, therefore, as your heavenly Father is perfect" in 5:48? What, if anything, does this statement reveal about Jesus' attitude toward the law? What does it reveal about the role of the law in Matthew's community?

After we have discussed these questions, I ask students to reflect on whether it is fair to describe Jesus as a "lawgiver" in Matthew's Sermon on the Mount. I also ask them to explain what the Sermon on the Mount tells us about Matthew's understanding of Jesus.

Nicole Kelley

202. MATTHEW'S JESUS AND THE PHARISEES:
THE RHETORIC OF SOCIAL IDENTIFICATION

The forceful language and vivid imagery of Matt 23 lend themselves to a classroom exercise in rhetorical analysis, aiming to heighten students' awareness of the way language functions as persuasive and partisan, urging social identifications and divisions.

To prepare for class, I ask students to read and compare Matt 23 and Josephus's description of the "sects of Jewish philosophy" from *Ant.* 18.1.11–25, particularly focusing on the Pharisees. I then begin the exercise by asking them to list identifying or distinguishing characteristics of the Pharisees according to Josephus and according to Matthew's Jesus. If time allows, this part of the exercise works well as a small-group task, followed by a whole class comparison of findings. Struck by the differences, students will often begin to wonder "who's right?" Josephus's more descriptive, less polemical tone may prompt some students to assume it is he who is providing the "objective" description. I therefore ask them what aspects of Josephus's language in this passage might indicate his interests, his objectives, or his affiliations, then review briefly some of the complexities of Josephus's socio-political circumstance as Jewish historian and apologist to the Flavian emperors, concerned both to recommend to Romans the dignity of Judaism and to urge Jews to acquiesce to Rome.

We then turn to a closer analysis of Matt 23. I ask students to imagine that they are members of the editorial committee for a new study Bible, and that they have been asked to choose a limited number of subheadings for this chapter (at least two, and no more than five). Where would they put the subheadings, what would they be, and how would they justify their choices? Once they have noticed that vv. 1–12 are a teaching addressed to the crowds and disciples, that vv. 13–36 speak harsh denunciation directly to the Pharisees, and that vv. 37–39 form an apostrophe to and lament over Jerusalem, I ask them to offer further descriptive terms for Jesus' tone, stance, and role in each section (perhaps thereby refining their proposed subheadings). We then turn more particularly to the "woes to you scribes and Pharisees." More advanced students can benefit from working carefully through the progression of rhetorical *topoi* and strategies. With introductory classes, I usually ask students to notice features such as: (1) the names Jesus calls his adversaries, (2) the accusations he makes against them, (3) the imperatives he addresses to them, (4) the rhetorical questions he asks of them, and (5) the images that seem most striking, memorable, or disturbing. A few further questions may lead students to describe their own responses to such language. What possibilities and dangers do they see in this kind of sharp polemic? How are their responses affected by the closing tone of lament and the image of the mother bird longing to gather her offspring? How, finally, would they describe the kinds of social identifications and divisions that Matthew's Jesus here urges?

Mixing structured comparative and analytical tasks with open-ended questions about rhetoric and its effects can draw students into a close study of Matt 23, one that may then lead to discussions of other passages (the Sermon on the Mount, Luke's woes to the rich, or denunciations by the Hebrew prophets, for example) or to a broader discussion of the relation of Matthew's community to other forms of Judaism.

B. Diane Wudel

203. TEACHING THROUGH ROLE-PLAY: MATTHEW 23 AS TEST CASE

Upon reading the Gospel of Matthew, many beginning students will remember Jesus' harsh polemic against the Pharisees more than any other scene. It does not surprise me to hear questions like, "Why does Jesus hate the Pharisees?" Since the distinction between "hate" and "intense dislike" hardly resolves the dilemma—much less satisfies students' curiosity—I choose to tackle the issue head-on by contextualizing Matt 23 within a larger narrative purpose. Part of this effort at contextualization involves the standard distinction (which students will have already heard) between the historical Jesus and the Matthean Jesus. Much of Matthew's gospel, I explain, is Matthew's attempt to address questions that Pharisaic Judaism would inevitably ask about the early church: generally speaking, how does your community differ from ours?

Before offering this specific explanation, I present a script for students to read. The script is an imaginary debate between a student and me about a very real topic: the historical accuracy of the gospel narratives. The script is written in such a way as to illustrate how a debate with someone, though often heated and intense, forces us to define ourselves in ways we otherwise might not. My aim is to illustrate, by way of analogy, how Matthew's gospel functions similarly vis-à-vis Pharisaic Judaism.

I distribute a copy of the script to the entire class and then call upon two students to read the script aloud. I pick the two students most capable of reading the script with all the required emotion. Once the exercise is complete, I highlight those exchanges that best illustrate the way debate forces self-definition. For instance:

Student: Prof. Driggers, do you believe the New Testament is historically accurate?

Driggers: I believe that much of it is accurate, but not all of it. For
instance, sometimes gospel writers contradict each other.
Sometimes the events they describe are historically unlikely.

Student: But I thought you were a Christian!

Driggers: I am a Christian.

Student: But how can you be a Christian if you think the Bible isn't true?

Driggers: Who said I didn't believe it was true? I do believe it's true.

Student: No you don't. You just said you didn't think it was true.

Driggers: No I didn't. You asked me if I thought it was historically
accurate, not if it was true.

Student: Huh?

Driggers: You're assuming that the Bible is "true" only if it is "historically accurate."

Student: Hmmm. Yes I am.

For the sake of fairness, I make sure to include exchanges where the
professor is on the defense as well. For example:

Student: Don't you believe that Jesus was crucified and that God
raised him from the dead?

Driggers: Wow. Those are good questions. Yes, I do believe those things.

Student: Then you think the New Testament is historically accurate!

Driggers: Hmmm. Well, those events are obviously crucial to Christianity. And yes, I believe they happened. But the gospels
depict all kinds of other events as well. Some gospels say
Jesus visited Jerusalem only once; others say twice. Some
gospels say Jesus was crucified on Passover, others say the
day before Passover. The gospels also disagree about the
details of Jesus' trial and why he was sentenced to death.

Student: So you believe some of the New Testament is historically
accurate, and some of it isn't?

Driggers: Yes, I guess that's right. But that doesn't mean I'm not a
Christian.

Student: No. It means you're only *partially* Christian!

This exercise (which is only excerpted here) accomplishes two things
simultaneously. With respect to the debate topic, it allows me to reinforce
my view of the gospels' historical accuracy and theological purpose—a
question that most students need addressed more than once. At the same
time, it helps me contextualize the polemic of Matt 23 as part of a larger
theological debate with Pharisaic Judaism.

Once students see the point of the script, I move to the above explanation of Matthew's gospel vis-à-vis Pharisaic Judaism. I then bring in other distinctively Matthean passages to clarify the analogy. Jesus' extended discourse on the law and his relationship to the law (Matt 5:17–48) now make better sense to students (since the law lay at the heart of Pharisaic Judaism), as do passages clarifying the nature of the Matthean community, for example, Matthew's relatively favorable depiction of the disciples (esp. 16:13–20), the nature of discipleship (10:5–42), the practice of forgiveness in the community (18:5–22), and even the Great Commission (28:16–20). When read in the context of a larger debate demanding self-definition, students begin to appreciate—and remember—those passages more than they otherwise would have.

At the end of the day, this approach does not lessen Matthew's harsh anti-Pharisee polemic in chapter 23. It does, however, force students to see that polemic as part of a larger debate—only half of which remains—and perhaps even appreciate the polemic for what it is. When the student of my script cynically concludes that I am only "partially Christian," it is perhaps an unfortunate accusation. But if we keep it in the context of the debate, we understand and appreciate why the student says what she says.

Ira Brent Driggers

204. WHAT DID JESUS THINK HE WAS SAYING? (MATT 26:26)

"Take, eat; this is my body" (Matt 26:26). What did Jesus mean? This deceptively simple question concerning Jesus' deceptively simple statement provides the occasion for broaching a number of topics germane to the task of exegesis such as authorial intent, the role of tradition, the ethics of interpretation, and even Aristotelian logic. Even when the attempt to arrive at a conclusive answer falls short—as it always does—posing this question reminds students that, notwithstanding the difficulty experienced in discovering their intentions and the fact that they are sometimes misinterpreted, most writers and speakers aim to be understood.

So what was Jesus trying to say? Students almost always respond in the same way: Jesus merely meant that the bread represents his body or the life he will soon lay down. When I ask whether there are any other conceivable meanings one could find in Jesus' words, some will grudgingly concede that, grammatically, it is within the realm of possibility that he could have meant that the bread had literally become his flesh in some mysterious way. After all, "is" does on occasion mean "is." My goal at this point is not to introduce the doctrine of transubstantiation, with which most students will already be familiar, if only vaguely. Rather, it is (1) to help them recognize that the text allows either reading and (2) to demonstrate that "it just depends" is an inadequate response when faced with such divergent meanings. Although they hesitate to acknowledge the fact, it hardly seems likely that Jesus could have meant both. Indeed, the principle of non-contradiction precludes the possibility that he intended simultaneously to speak literally and also to utter the phrase "this is my body" within a purely symbolic frame of reference.

While some students suspect a papist plot on my part, others cautiously concede that it has to be one or the other but are quick to add that "it just depends on the reader." Well, yes and no. Different readers undeniably come away from the text having understood it in different ways. And while there are contextual clues pointing in one direction or the other, at such a distance it will perhaps be impossible to settle the question. But that is not the same as saying that "it just depends on the reader." If I am not sure what Bill or Susan are trying to say in their term papers, I ask, how can I resolve the problem? Answer: by asking them to explain. We cannot really do this in the case of Matt 26:26, but by imagining the hypothetical scenario ("Jesus, what were you trying to say, exactly?"), most students are able to see that Jesus probably would not say, "It doesn't really matter what I think. I wasn't really trying to say anything specific. It means whatever you want it to mean." This is essentially what "it just depends" tacitly assumes. This is an excellent moment to distinguish "the world before the text" from "the world behind the text," to borrow Paul Ricoeur's terms, and to explain the difference between exegesis and eisegesis. It also provides a point of departure for discussing the ethical obligations of the interpreter. Are we required to consider what Jesus was trying to say? Or are the gospel texts like potluck dinners to which the author brings the words and the reader brings the meanings? Does it matter whether the author is dead (and thus unable to clear up any ambiguities) or alive? If we consider the distinction, popularized by Krister Stendahl, between "what the text meant" and "what the text means," is it permissible for a text to "mean" what it never "meant" when it was originally written or spoken? Should we operate according to an interpretive Golden Rule: Interpret others as you would have others interpret you?

Scholars will have noted that I have not always distinguished between the intent of the author and the intent of the historical Jesus when he purportedly spoke the words of institution. "The world behind the text" includes the events and sayings reported in the narrative as well as the motivations of the author responsible for the text as we have it, and so many of the same kinds of questions could be asked if, say, a remark of Paul's were under consideration (for instance, Gal 3:28: "There is neither Jew nor Greek, there is neither slave nor free, there is neither male nor female; for you are all one in Christ Jesus"). Matthew is responsible for the inclusion of Jesus' words in his gospel narrative. What did Matthew think Jesus meant, when (according to tradition) he heard him or when he borrowed the scene from Mark? Why did he not explain what he thought Jesus meant in a narrative aside? Did he not think that it required comment? Or did he intentionally leave it ambiguous, perhaps because he himself did not know what Jesus meant? Is there anything about the original language that might shed light on the matter? Could Mattthew have seen significance in these words that somehow escaped Jesus when he originally uttered them?

Wrestling with these questions helps students appreciate a traditional interpretive approach interested primarily in such matters as the historical context and the intentions of the author. Once this is established, it becomes easier to delineate the ways in which this approach differs from those, influenced by the New Criticism, which focus on the autonomy of the text itself as well as those which call attention to the role of the reader in the act of interpretation.

Patrick Gray

205. THE TEXAS TWO-STEP: INTRODUCING MARK'S GOSPEL

Because it is difficult for undergraduates to recognize the literary and theological distinctives of the Synoptic Gospels, I attempt to illustrate the distinctive structure and characteristics of Mark's gospel by teaching them the Texas two-step. The exercise requires music (any popular country group, such as the Dixie Chicks, will do).

The purpose of this dance is to underscore Mark's tendency to utilize a two-step approach, from minor literary details to the theological structure of the gospel as a whole. I begin with small literary features, which he develops in two steps: "When the day ended [step one], when it was sundown [step two]; Jesus came into Capernaum [step one], and went into the synagogue [step two]." In Mark 4, he presents the teaching of Jesus in two steps: the crowds listen and leave (step one), but the disciples and those with them remain in order to hear Jesus' explanation of that teaching in private (step two). In Mark 8, Jesus heals a blind man in two steps in an acted parable of the disciples' need for further clarification, which Jesus gives three times in chapters 8–10: Jesus predicts his suffering (step one) but, due to the disciples' misunderstanding, is compelled to give further teaching to demonstrate that servanthood trumps royalty, that the first shall be last (step two).

This movement from kingship to servanthood is evident in the divine voice that speaks at Jesus' baptism, if it is correct to say that the first part (step one), "You are my son," alludes to a royal psalm (Ps 2:7), while words in the second part (step two), "whom I love," recall the servant figure in Isa 42:1. Finally, it is this shift from kingship to servanthood that characterizes Mark's gospel as a whole. A flurry of miracles occurs in chapters 1–8, *step one* of the gospel, to the point where Peter acknowledges Jesus as the messiah, as royalty, as king; miracles are reduced to a trickle, however, in chapters 9–16, *step two* of the gospel, where they are replaced by the trek to the cross and by Jesus' repeated teaching on servanthood and discipleship. Mark's gospel, in the context of a brief introductory class, can be encapsulated, at least in part, by this two-step feature, which extends from details to the entire structure of the gospel, from the baptism of Jesus to the healing of a blind man. Dancing the Texas two-step functions not only to keep students alert; it also effectively reinforces a pervasive literary and theological dimension of the gospel.

Yet there is a final kick: the second step of the Texas two-step is harder, for only the second step contains a stutter-step, an extra shifting of the feet. In the same way, the second step of Mark's gospel, with its commitment to discipleship, is much harder than the first, in which people flock to Jesus because of his ability to meet their needs by performing miracles. This is the challenge of Mark's gospel: the first step, as winsome and fluid as it is, is a truncation of Mark's message; it is the more demanding and less natural second step, both in the dance and the gospel, that requires a good deal more commitment and practice.

John R. Levison

206. THE COLLABORATIVE COMIC STRIP

Creating a collaborative comic strip is similar to creating a storyboard for a particular text. While it works best with narrative passages, I have also used it with epistolary or poetic passages. As students make decisions about how to divide a text into frames or scenes, how to illustrate a particular panel, what characters to foreground, how to arrange the panels, and where to put the "punch line," they participate in a group exegesis. The discussion leader can encourage debate about how to reflect the text's rhetoric in the structure and illustration of a comic strip. Another beneficial outcome of this exercise is that as students make creative decisions about storyboarding, they become aware of the ways movie, television, and other visual adaptations of Bible stories are *interpretations*, and of the subtle ways in which directors and cinematographers make theological claims.

Begin by dividing the whiteboard into four or five sections, like a comic strip. Using Mark 4:35–41 as our text (The Calming of the Storm), the class undertakes to break the passage into four or five panels. Deciding where to break the text is a major exercise, and we usually have several revisions during the class as we debate the rhetorical goal of the text. It is especially challenging to students (and creates good discussion) if you deliberately begin with a smaller number of frames than "scenes" you can count in the text. This forces them to make choices about where the action changes.

As the class makes decisions about what to include in each frame, we write down narrative elements as captions for each frame. For example:

1. Jesus and the disciples get into the boat.
2. A storm blows up.
3. The disciples panic at Jesus' absence.
4. Jesus rebukes the storm and the disciples.

Deciding where to break the text into panels is a fascinating discussion on its own. A few criteria help students to make those decisions. Advise them to look for transition words such as "and," "but," "therefore," "immediately," and the like. Implicit theological assumptions often come out during the course of the discussion, and we have a chance to examine them critically. Deciding what to leave out (e.g., the "other boats with them"), what to consolidate (e.g., Jesus' rebuking of the wind and the disciples), and what to emphasize (e.g., the placement of Jesus in the center of the last panel) is an exercise that could easily take several class periods.

Prompt students on what kinds of things should be included in each panel. "So what do we draw here? A boat?" Although it may seem simplistic, getting them to visualize the text in this way helps with their interpretation. Do we want a side view? A front view? An aerial view? Reminding them that the boat is often an early symbol for the church may help them with their artistic choices. As we work through the panels, it is helpful to remind students to think of the theological implications for the early church, since they may be used to thinking from a more individualistic point of view.

NEW TESTAMENT

Using this text, when we get to panel three, I ask why they think Jesus is sleeping through this storm. Doesn't it seem strange? Could there be something other than sleep that the author is hinting at here? If so, it may affect the way we draw Jesus. By this time, students are usually already thinking of the implications for the early church, and imagining how to draw "panic" at the perceived death and absence of Jesus lends creative momentum to their storyboarding.

David Barnhart

207. THE ENDING OF THE GOSPEL OF MARK

For this assignment, I ask students to take on the role of textual critics. I explain that we do not have any original copies of New Testament texts; the Greek manuscripts on which our modern New Testament is based are in fact copies several times removed from the originals. Each time a copy is made, scribal errors or deliberate changes to the text become increasingly likely. As textual critics, our job is to try to reconstruct with as much precision as is possible the original text. While textual criticism involves careful study of ancient Greek manuscripts, it also requires that we consider a text's language, style, and content.

In the case of the ending of the Gospel of Mark, we have four main choices for our reconstruction of the original text: (1) Mark 16:8; (2) the "shorter ending"; (3) Mark 16:9–20; (4) a lost ending that would have followed Mark 16:8 but did not survive. It helps to give students a handout that shows all the possibilities side-by-side, which makes the task of comparison much easier.

Have the students divide themselves into four groups, and assign each group one of the four possible endings for the Gospel of Mark. The task of each group is as follows: (1) Assume that your assigned passage is most likely to be original. How will you persuade the other groups that this is the case? What kinds of argument would support a passage's originality, and do they apply to your passage? For example, does your passage fit best with Mark's overall themes and emphases? Does your passage contain problems that later Christian scribes may have wanted to correct? (2) What objections will the other groups make against your passage's originality? Try to anticipate these objections and develop arguments against them. For example, does your passage contain words or ideas that seem different from what we've seen in the rest of Mark? Does your passage sound similar to the ending of Matthew or Luke? (3) Take a few minutes to consider the endings assigned to the other three groups. How will you persuade the other groups that their passages are unlikely to be the original ending of Mark?

Each group should have a spokesperson responsible for recording its findings and speaking for the group in the discussion. Once the students have had time to consider the questions above, ask each group to present their arguments in turn, allowing time for the other groups to respond if they wish. At the end of the discussion, ask students to reflect on which arguments they found most persuasive and why.

This assignment works well as an in-class group discussion, but it can also be an effective assignment for a short essay. For the essay, students should select the ending they believe is most likely to be original, and construct an argument that supports their view. Essays should briefly address each of the other possible endings, explaining why the student believes that they are unlikely to be original. I tell my students that successful papers (1) make a point to relate their argument to larger themes and concerns in the Gospel of Mark and (2) acknowledge problems that later scribes may have wanted to correct. (For a similar exercise, see §93.)

Nicole Kelley

208. FILM AS A RESOURCE FOR THEOLOGICAL REFLECTION ON BIBLICAL TEXTS

Because the cinematic resources for an introduction to the Christian Scriptures are particularly rich, one can effectively incorporate film into even introductory courses on the Bible. (Instructors who want to get up to speed on filmmaking basics and terminology might want to read L. Giannetti, *Understanding Movies* [9th ed.; Englewood Cliffs, N.J.: Prentice Hall, 2001].) I like to have students view Lars von Trier's *Breaking the Waves* (1996) while reading the Gospel of Mark. In the film, a naïve young woman named Bess McNeil (Emily Watson) meets and falls in love with Danish oil-rig worker Jan (Stellan Skarsgaard). Bess and Jan are deeply in love but, when Jan returns to his rig, Bess prays to God that he comes home for good. Jan does return—when his neck is broken in an accident aboard the rig. Because of his condition, Jan and Bess are now unable to enjoy a sexual relationship and Jan urges Bess to take another lover and tell him the details. As Bess becomes more and more deviant in her sexual behavior, the more she comes to believe that her actions are guided by God and are helping Jan recover.

This is an admittedly disturbing film for many viewers and may require some situating to prepare students for the ways in which the film will challenge them. Women may be particularly disturbed by the body of Bess, broken and defiled to save a man's body and soul. More devout students may be troubled and even offended by the mere suggestion that this film has anything to teach us about Christian theology.

In connecting this particular gospel to this film, I am not suggesting that von Trier had Mark in mind when making his film, nor am I suggesting that this is the only gospel that can be mined for provocative connections. Rather, I use this gospel because its tone—which is largely understood as tragic in contrast to the comic trajectory of the other gospels—most closely matches the tone of the film. I like to let students come up with their own connections, hence the questions that are constructed to help them do that (see below), but there are a couple of obvious connections of which instructors might want to be aware. The film's emphasis on profound suffering and unimaginable sacrifice as a means of salvation provides a rich point of entry to discuss the gospel's focus on the suffering messiah. Especially for students who have become "comfortable" with the Christian link between suffering and salvation, juxtaposition of these two texts problematizes such an easy linkage in ways that compel them to think more deeply about the implications of such a theology. Other minor connections students might make include a discussion of the redaction issues that the ending of both the gospel and the film raise. Obviously, in terms of the film, no one came along after von Trier had wrapped up shooting and changed his ending, but as critics have pointed out, the inclusion of bells ringing in the heavens as Bess is buried at sea seems somewhat contrived to put a positive spin on what otherwise calls into question God's motives and mercy. Both of these issues could be addressed in question five below. In connection with question four, students may want to explore the theological implications of a Christ figure embodied as female. Bess's sexualized sacrifice is all the more troubling when one takes into account feminist critiques of patriarchal control of women's bodies. The blurring in this film of God's role with that of Bess's husband is an intriguing area for further theological reflection. For fun, and to add flesh to this question, you might want to play for students the agony in the garden cut (called "Gethsemane") from the Indigo Girls version of *Jesus Christ Superstar* in which Amy Ray sings the part of Jesus. This scene from the rock opera reflects the pathos of the same scene in Mark, whether Andrew Lloyd Webber, its composer, intended as much or not.

The lesson plan requires that students first read Mark, after which we spend a session or two discussing the traditional interpretive issues connected to this book. I then send them home with the assignment to read the chapter on "Formal Structures: How Films Tell Their Stories" in Robert Kolker's *Film, Form, and Culture* (2nd ed.; Boston: McGraw Hill, 2002) and to watch *Breaking the Waves*. I supply them with a list of questions and ask them to write two pages each on three of the questions, one of which must include question five. I include questions about the formal features of film for two reasons: it enriches their overall viewing experience and it helps them understand how form, including literary form, functions to tell stories. I typically divide students into groups of three for this assignment and have them turn in a group assignment.

The entire session is then devoted to student groups presenting their insights. This aspect of the exercise is crucial. Students are required to articulate in their own words complicated theological concepts. In my experience students throw themselves into theological and exegetical reflection much more eagerly with film than with any other medium. In setting up the assignment, I explain that the onlookers are expected to ask questions of the presenters, to challenge or comment on their interpretations. Their own prepared papers should facilitate a dialogic engagement. So successful has been this aspect of the exercise (everyone has an opinion about movies!) that, typically, I am essentially able to absent myself from the conversation. One can also assign just one or two groups to lead the entire session, thus allowing them time to use their creativity to teach their peers. This exercise naturally works best with smaller class sizes, but is still effective for class sizes up to twenty-four. This pedagogical approach can be extended into an entire course. In that case, I use an extended list of questions and each session is run entirely by one group of three students presenting on a particular film. In that case, a class size of no larger than a dozen students is most effective.

I use the following questions for film reports (Note: These questions are purposely somewhat vague so they might be used for a variety of films and biblical texts. Even when dealing with the Gospel of Mark, the instructor may choose to omit the parenthetical examples in questions four and five.)

1. Discuss cinematography—lighting, *mise en scene*, the kind of lens used (close-ups, wide angles, etc.). Angles? Hand-held camera? Scenery? How is the scene framed? What is the cinematographer trying to draw attention to? What kind of emotional response is elicited?

2. Discuss editing. This one is a bit tricky, but try to think about how the scenes work together. Are the cuts smooth? Do scenes follow one another smoothly? Are scenes short or long? Is the final version fast-paced or languorous? Is there any "tricky" editing (i.e., Do you expect to see something in the next scene that you don't? or see something that you didn't expect? Or see it in a way you didn't expect?)? How does the pace compare to the pace of the biblical text?

3. Is this film a reinterpretation or a retelling of a biblical story? Explain in detail what makes it one or the other. Why do you think the director/screenwriter decided to tell the story this way? Is this a pious reading, or a subversive (or challenging) reading? If the latter, what point do you think is trying to be made?

4. How are gender roles depicted? What kind of commentary is such a depiction making on the biblical text? (For instance, what troubling theological issues are raised when the Christ figure is rendered in female form?)

5. What passages from the biblical story are included? What passages are left out? Would you have presented it differently? Why? Why do you think the director/screenwriter chose to leave out certain passages? If the film is not strictly a rendition of a biblical story, then with what biblical themes is the film working? In that case, what theological issues is the filmmaker addressing or problematizing? What fresh theological insights into the biblical story are achieved by the filmmaker? (For instance, you might reconsider the notion of the suffering servant as the author of Mark employs it in light of the ways suffering is used in this film. Or, you might compare the ending of the film with the ending[s] of the Gospel of Mark. What parallels do you find in structure and intent?)

Carleen Mandolfo

209. MARK AND THE MOVIES

Students today are more attuned to visual media (movies, DVDs, and the like) and less inclined to read the New Testament Gospels. This exercise uses the media with which they are familiar and comfortable to familiarize them with the gospels and to introduce them to critical methodologies for reading narratives, in particular source, redaction, and literary criticism.

First, I have students view the movie *It's a Wonderful Life*, paying attention to the film's characters, plot, and settings, and its storytelling techniques. Next they read Mark's Gospel as if it were a screenplay, again being attentive to both content and literary techniques. I ask them specifically to compare the story and storytelling in Mark to *IAWL*. Then we discuss the correspondences between the two dramas. For example, in both a theophany introduces the hero and confirms God's special feeling toward him (Mark 1:10–11). Early in the stories, a precursor—who is a blood relative—foreshadows and announces the hero's career, and shortly thereafter suffers an untimely end which removes him from the story, making room for the hero (Mr. Bailey; Mark 1:2–14; 6:14–29). At the outset of both, lifelong friends are introduced (Mary, Veronica, Marty, Mr. Gower, Bert, Ernie, Uncle Billy; Mark 1:16–20; 3:13–19). The primary antagonist enters the stories early on and conflict with the hero is anticipated (Mr. Potter; Mark 1:22). In the first several scenes, the hero's extraordinary qualities are exhibited (George saves his brother's life and keeps a sick child from being poisoned; Mark 1:23–26, 29–31, 32–34). Both heroes face temptations (Mark 1:12–13). As the dramas unfold, disappointments that at first appear minor are recognized as dark clouds gathering on the hero's horizon. The storm worsens as more serious setbacks cause the hero increasing frustration over his lack of success (Mark 2:1–3:35; 6:1–6; 7:1–13; 8:11–13; 10:2–12; 11:15–19, 27–33; 12:12, 13–44). The climactic sequence begins as the hero is beset by a major reversal for which he is blameless, and upon which his adversary seizes to be rid of the interloper and the changes the hero has sought to bring about by having him arrested (Mark 14:1–2, 10–11, 17–21, 43–50). Facing imminent apprehension and trial, and realizing that he has no one to support him, the hero turns to God in prayer, but God's presence is not apparent and the hero's feelings of loneliness and abandonment become palpable (Mark 14:32–42; see also 14:27–31, 50–51, 66–72; 15:27–34). Finally, both heroes experience death—alone and seemingly total failures—but divinity intercedes. This intervention conquers death and leads to new life for the heroes (Mark 15:21–16:8). This comparison usually leads to a good discussion on the use, redaction, editing, or adaptation of sources (e.g., is Mark the source for *IAWL*?).

In addition to content, we look at stylistic features that the Gospel shares with the screenplay genre, including: (a) terseness of expression; (b) a series of scenes as the primary means of moving the plot forward; (c) conflict as the basis of drama in the story; (d) one main character around whom the plot revolves; (e) the literary techniques of flashback, reversal, montage, transitory action, and sequence (see, for example, R. A. Berman, *Fade In: The Screenwriting Process* [Studio City: Michael Weise, 1988]). Students find it helpful to liken Mark's Gospel to the literary product of a screenwriter who is able to adapt the work of another medium into a dramatic interpretation of the original subject. Viewed through this heuristic lens, students appreciate Mark's artistry in crafting his story of Jesus from "collections of traditional materials" (M. Dibelius, *From Tradition to Gospel* [New York: Charles Scribner's Sons, 1935], 3), and begin to grasp that the keys to understanding Mark's narrative—and so any of the Gospels—are (1) taking seriously its story world, (2) being attentive to how generic tools are applied to fashion a unified drama, and (3) actively engaging the material.

Lastly, I have students write their own gospel screenplay. I supply them with the format, which includes scene number, location (exterior and interior), characters, description of the scene, and dialogue. I also require them to provide a synopsis of their story as if they were going to "pitch" the screenplay to a prospective producer, sketches of the main characters (physical characteristics, sociological profile, psychological make-up), sources from which they draw each scene, and the reasoning for using the scenes they adapt or create. I limit the screenplay to eight scenes and each scene to one single-spaced typed page for the sake of time and to allow them to experience the process of selection for creating their distinctive story. I also require all descriptions and dialogue to be in the students' words (they cannot simply copy from the gospels). This exercise not only forces students to gain familiarity with the gospels, particularly Mark, but also enables them to use their creativity and imagination in fashioning a drama about Jesus for an audience of their choosing. Many students stay within the traditional gospel boundaries, but some will understand the connections between *It's a Wonderful Life* and Mark's Gospel as liberating. For example, one student wrote and illustrated a drama about Omar, an African American electrician from the Brooklyn projects, based on the gospel accounts and her own life.

William Sanger Campbell

210. LUKE'S GOSPEL AND THE PARABLE OF THE GOOD SAMARITAN

This is a discussion-based exercise for small groups that provides an overview of the Parable of the Good Samaritan. One student reads the following script in this present form. It is important that the reader stop at each question mark to allow the other members to respond because the script is designed to have a narrative flow:

The section of Luke from 9:51–19:27, often labeled "the journey toward Jerusalem," includes a large amount of material not found in Matthew and Mark. Thus this section provides insight into distinct Lukan concerns. Luke's parables, in particular, present case studies for sharpening our understanding of Luke's portrayal.

One of the best known parables from the New Testament, the Parable of the Good Samaritan, only appears in Luke's gospel. You have probably heard the phrase "Good Samaritan" many times. When people call someone a good Samaritan, what do they mean? In your responses, you probably focused on the "good" aspect and not much on

"Samaritan." When people use the phrase, do they seem to be references actual Samaritans?

To explore these questions further, read aloud Luke 10:25–37. At the beginning of this passage, a lawyer approaches Jesus. Lawyer jokes aside, how would you characterize this lawyer? Whatever else you might say about him, he certainly appears well versed in Scripture. His response includes citations from both Deut 6:5 and Lev 19:18. The second of these provokes Jesus' parable. The story itself only takes up six verses, but its richness belies its brevity. In these verses, four characters appear. How would you characterize each of these four? With whom do you sympathize?

Some background helps to understand this parable in its original context. The priest and Levite both were Jewish religious figures with duties in the temple. They would have been bound by purity regulations that would have forbidden their contact with dead bodies. This may be why they "passed by on the other side." Judeans typically had antipathy toward Samaritans (from Samaria, north of Judea). The label "Samaritan" would have also implied that the person was sinful. So the story deals not only with kindnesses but also with religious and ethnic differences. If you were to tell the story today, what group would be analogous to Samaritans?

At the end of the story, the question of who counts as neighbor resurfaces. Remember, the lawyer knows he should love his neighbor, but he also wants to know who that neighbor is. According to v. 36, who is the neighbor? What, then, is the conclusion to be drawn from the parable? If the story centers upon loving the neighbor, and if the Samaritan plays the role of neighbor, then how does one go about loving the Samaritan? Usually this story is read as an impetus to go do good works. Is this typical interpretation true to the text?

Finally, we should consider how this story relates to Luke's concerns. In other parts of the gospel (e.g., Luke 4:14–30) the narrative gives some parameters for Jesus' ministry. How does this particular parable illustrate and reinforce Lukan emphases?

Kyle Keefer

211. ENGENDERING THE PRODIGAL SON (LUKE 15:11–32)

In order to illustrate the implications of cultural assumptions (one's own and those of first-century hearers/readers) for one's interpretation of the New Testament, I sometimes invite students to imagine how they might hear a biblical passage differently under different circumstances. For example, how might Luke's gospel "sound" to an impoverished, first-century peasant, compared to an aristocratic religious leader? This exercise highlights the significance of one's cultural assumptions about gender roles and also introduces the idea that that first-century assumptions might not be the same as the assumptions of the students.

I invite a group of students to re-enact the Parable of the Prodigal Son (Luke 15:11–32) as if all the characters were women. I read the parable aloud, substituting "mother" and "daughters" for "father" and "sons," respectively, and changing appropriate pronouns, while the selected students mime the parts. Thus, the story goes, a mother of two daughters divides her inheritance. One of the daughters leaves home to go to a faraway land, spends her money in dissolute living, eventually returns, and is welcomed home by her mother. Meanwhile, the other daughter, who has remained at the homestead, doing all that is asked of her, responds bitterly when her sister is feted by a huge party. The "performance" continues through the conclusion of the parable.

After the performance, the class discusses how (or whether) they "heard" this parable differently from the way in which they have heard it in the past. Student responses vary, of course, depending on their own biases or assumptions, but the following responses are typical in my classes. Some students mention that they expect a mother to welcome her child back home, but they do not necessarily expect a father to do so. Other students may express harsher judgment against a daughter who "runs away from home" than they do against a son. Still others mention that they did not notice that "mother" is absent from the original parable until they realized that "father" was absent from the re-told version. On more than one occasion, male students have noted that they felt excluded by a story that involved only women.

One of the benefits of this exercise is that it does not require a particular answer from the students, since the purpose is simply to raise awareness of gender-role expectations. Students are invited to share their experience of hearing the re-gendered parable and then to reflect together on what differences those experiences might make in their hearing of the original parable. The exercise functions well to introduce a subsequent lecture on cultural assumptions in the ancient world, not only assumptions related to gender, but other sorts of assumptions as well (e.g., honor/shame, inheritance practices, centrality of family, etc.).

Audrey West

212. NARRATIVE CRITICISM:
INTERPRETING THE PARABLE OF THE PRODIGAL SON

One problem with reading the Bible and the task of interpretation is that there are some stories that many think they already know. The parable known as the Prodigal Son (Luke 15:11–32) is a case in point. The purpose of this exercise is two-fold. First, it is an exercise in a kind of narrative criticism where the student is asked to analyze the characters, setting, and plot of the parable. Second, it is a hermeneutical exercise in which the student is alienated from a familiar text in order to reconstruct a story with complex meaning.

This exercise is usually used in a section of a course focused on the gospels. Prior to this class session on parables I have coached the class in the basic elements of narrative criticism. At the opening of the class session I may project Rembrandt's *The Return of the Prodigal Son* on the screen at the front of the room. When the students are settled I divide the class into groups of four. One member of each group is designated the reader and another the reporter for the group. Each member of the class is given a handout with discussion questions. The group session begins with one person reading aloud to the others in the group. The noise level can be distracting but the reason for this approach is to encourage the group to be listeners and not simply readers.

When the reading is finished, the group works together in answering a series of questions. (1) Identify the characters and divide the story into scenes. (2) Define the word "prodigal." (3) Describe the relationship between the father and the younger son. What is an inheritance and how does the younger son shame the father? (4) Is the younger son truly sorry when he returns? (Compare carefully the speech he prepares and the speech he delivers.) Does it make a difference if he is truly sorry or not? (5) Describe the relationship between the older son and the father? How does the older son shame the father? (6) How does the older son know that the younger brother squandered his money on prostitutes? (7) Whose story is it? Is the story properly named? If not, what should the name be (if it is even useful to name stories)? (8) Is there a character to represent God in the story? The groups are given fifteen minutes to discuss the questions among themselves.

One goal of the exercise is to make a familiar story unfamiliar. Students are not permitted to generalize but are pressed to account for the details of the story. One potential goal is that by experiencing alienation from the story the student might be able to reconstruct meaning in a new way. Another potential outcome is that the student realizes that parables can not be reduced to one point or a story with a simple moral such as a fable.

N
E
W

T
E
S
T
A
M
E
N
T

When the groups have finished their smaller discussions, the class is brought back into a plenary session to review and compare results. There are some typical threads to the closing discussion. As it turns out, few in the class typically know the meaning of "prodigal." Similarly, many had previously assumed that the younger son is clearly repentant though the text leaves that ambiguous. To close the discussion the class is asked to suggest names for the parable. At the end I may project the Rembrandt painting again and ask the class what sort of interpretation the artist has given to the text. A homework assignment could involve assigning another familiar parable from Luke, such as the Parable of the Good Samaritan, and asking the students to write a short paper using the techniques learned in class.

Two other resources may inform the instructor on this topic. Marsha Witten, in *All is Forgiven: The Secular Message of American Protestantism* (Princeton: Princeton University Press, 1993), uses this parable as an example of a biblical story which is recontextualized into a secular contemporary setting, reflecting the American cultural appreciation for second-chance stories. Robert Farrar Capon, in *Parables of Grace* (Grand Rapids: Eerdmans, 1988), has called this a misnamed parable, claiming that the traditional title has distorted or short-circuited interpretation. Capon's bold approach to reading parables is a good stimulant for class discussion. (For another exercise on narrative criticism, see §25.)

Philip A. Quanbeck II

213. TEACHING THE UNITY OF "LUKE-ACTS"

How does a teacher introduce the relationship between the Gospel of Luke and the Acts of the Apostles so that students understand and remember the connection between the two works? A traditional answer is to assert the common authorship of Luke and Acts and to list the literary themes and techniques that they appear to share. Another approach is to illustrate their connection through a close reading of a few passages and to relate this connection to the experiences of students in contemporary culture. This second approach has the advantage of providing both a concrete example of the linkage between Luke and Acts, while also engaging the students in a memorable and meaningful literary analysis.

Students are assigned or asked the following question: "How are storylines continued across episodes of a television series or in a movie sequel?" Discussion of the responses should quickly surface common strategies (for example, previewed scenes, replayed scenes, written sum-maries, allusive statements) as well as well-known examples of each (the scrolling narrative at the beginning of the "Star Wars" movies, for example). Storylines, it might also be observed, can persist by the repeated appearance of titles, events, characters, and settings. Two general conclusions are conducive to analysis of the unity of Luke-Acts: (1) connections between stories are often formed by either prospective or retrospective images, and (2) these connective images often indicate significant themes in the two works.

An assigned or in-class analysis of Luke 24:44–53 and Acts 1:1–2:4 will surface connections between these two New Testament writings— connections that are comparable to those observed in contemporary cinema. Students should observe that the narrations of similar events (e.g., Jesus' post-resurrection appearances and ascension), characters (Jesus, apostles, Holy Spirit), and settings (Jerusalem) form links between the two works. Students may also notice the foreshadowing of Pentecost in Luke's Gospel (24:49), as well as the connection back to the Gospel in the opening reference to "Theophilus" and a "first account" at Acts 1:1 (cf. Luke 1:3). In each case, the preceding discussion of cinematic associations finds analogues in the Lukan narratives and highlights the literary and theological artistry at work in their overlap.

This exercise can also introduce major themes in Acts, which are observed in both the closing verses of Luke and the opening verses of Acts: (1) the geographical expansion of the Christian "witness"; (2) the agency of the Holy Spirit in this expansion; (3) the succession of emissaries in this expansion; (4) the suffering of these emissaries; and (5) the fulfillment of God's plan in all these events.

John B. Weaver

214. ACTS 1–8 AND LIFE IN THE EARLY CHURCH

Quite a few Christians hold to the idea that it was somehow easier to be a follower of Christ in the first century. If one had actually met and talked with either Jesus or his immediate followers, surely that experience would have been so overwhelmingly positive that one could not help but convert! This exercise complicates that assumption, while also developing close-reading skills of biblical texts.

The exercise is utilized in my New Testament survey course. Students read Acts 1–8 ahead of time. In class they are then divided into seven groups. Each group is assigned a different, short pericope from Acts 1–8: (1) 2:1–13 (Pentecost, glossolalia); (2) 2:37–47 (communal lifestyle, temple observance); (3) 3:1–10 and 4:1–4 (performance of miracles, imprisonment); (4) 4:32–5:16 (communal lifestyle); (5) 5:17–42 (persecution); (6) 6:1–6, along with 9:2; 24:14; 11:26; 26:28; 24:5; and 12:5 (Hebrew-Hellenist conflicts, various names for the movement); and (7) 7:54–8:8 (first martyr, continued persecution).

I then present three sets of questions that each group is to ask of their passage: (1) What does your text say about what life was like in the early church? Specifically, what did believers both say and do? How did they interact with others? (2) In your group's assessment, what was both positive and negative about this life? (3) In what ways was it unlike life in the present-day church? In what ways was it like life in the present-day church?

After the groups have had time to complete the task, we gather together as a class and tabulate all the responses on the board. At this point a rather free-wheeling discussion can develop, especially around practices that may be either like or unlike present-day church practices. For instance, glossolalia usually receives a lot of attention. Since most of my students are Catholic or come from mainline Protestant denominations, it is an unfamiliar phenomenon to them. But after I gesture towards Pentecostal churches in which speaking in tongues regularly takes place, usually one or two students who are members of such churches describe in some detail either how they themselves practice it or how they have witnessed others do so. In this instance, then, quite a number of students come to realize that some present-day churches continue with worship-practices dating back to the very beginnings of the Christian movement—even practices that they themselves find strange.

And yet, more generally, this exercise brings home to students the cultural distance between many present-day churches and that of ancient Jerusalem. Indeed, when I survey students at the end of the class-period on whether or not they think they would have been attracted to this movement if they had lived in first-century Jerusalem, usually a significant majority responds in the negative. For them, the communal sharing of goods is too off-putting; and even the frequency of miraculous occurrences is not enough to outweigh the risks of persecution, imprisonment, or death.

Karla G. Bohmbach

215. PAUL AND THE AMAZING RACE

Paul's three missionary journeys are incredible travelogues of Asia Minor and southern Europe. The geography of the region, however, is often unfamiliar to students as is the difficulty of travel without all of our modern conveniences. While you cannot take your students to the region and let them loose with nothing but a map and a little cash, you can still manage to help them learn the basics about what it took for Paul to make such trips.

This exercise begins with Acts and some maps. For journey one, we open in Acts 13 and continue through Acts 14. Number two requires a close reading of Acts 15:40–18:17. Number three is detailed in Acts 18:23b–20:38. Students start by identifying each place Paul visits and placing it appropriately on a map of the region. With three maps in hand, the true adventure starts.

Phase two of this exercise generally requires work outside of class. The students must determine the distances between each location and calculate the time it would take to make such a journey on foot (assuming an eighteen minute mile and being allowed to go no longer than seven hours per day) or by boat (I let them web search for a good calculation). In this way, they get the sense of what such a trip might have entailed in ancient times. I also request that they make a list of all the things one would need for such a journey—including where one might stay, what and where one might eat, and other similar considerations. Their work in this phase must also include notations about where each site is found today and what language is spoken in that place so they can think about the language barriers they might face when making such a trip.

Then, the fun really begins. We do a version of the CBS television show *The Amazing Race*. Each team must make all three journeys in the fastest and most cost-efficient manner they can figure out. If it requires a car rental, they need to find a way to do it on the Internet and show the price. If they want to take planes, ferries, and trains, the same demonstration must be made. They can even join a pre-planned tour if that works out best on the budget and moves quickly enough. Every team must price their journey for two people and must add $30 per day for food and water. Hotels or camping or whatever they choose to do also must be shown in their final tally and they must spend nights somewhere (in transit on trains, e.g., is fine, but you cannot have one drive while the others sleep). The team that manages their resources the best in terms of time and price wins this competition.

In class, we share what we learn about the kinds of places Paul visited, the distances he traversed, and the distinctions between modern and ancient travel. This exercise might seem as if it consumes a considerable amount of time and energy, but students quickly grow adept at locating the resources they need and avoiding repetition of certain legs. The testing benefits cannot be overstated; their work with maps improves dramatically and their understanding of the region where Christianity took hold increases exponentially.

Sandie Gravett

216. TRACKING THE PLOT OF ACTS

This classroom experience enables students to appreciate the literary and thematic development of the book of Acts, with special attention to the way in which both progressive and repetitive patterns shape the plot.

In preparation for class, students need to have read Acts in its entirety. Students gather in small groups of three to five. The instructor offers the groups five minutes in which to compile a list of three "turning points" in Acts—moments in which the story changes in a fundamental way, without which later developments in the story could not occur. The instructor then draws a plot line on the class board, from chapter one to chapter twenty-eight, and records the suggested "turning points." (The turning points need not be suggested in narrative sequence.) With each turning point the instructor marks it on the plot line of Acts and asks students to describe (a) why this event is so crucial for the development of Acts' story and (b) what other events in Acts are made possible by this turning point.

When the class momentum begins to wane, the instructor draws back from these detailed observations to lead a discussion concerning the progressive and repetitive dimensions of the students' observations. How many of the "turning points" represent "one of a kind" events necessary for the progress of the entire narrative? Conversely, how many of the "turning points" essentially repeat themes from earlier moments? Examples may include the repeated narration of the visions of Peter and Paul, the repeated evaluation concerning the authenticity of Gentiles' conversion, and so forth.

An optional way to raise the same issue is to follow up with lecture material by laying out the ways in which the plot of Acts relies upon both progression and repetition. For example, Acts 1:8 foreshadows a progressive texture: beginning in Jerusalem, the gospel proceeds to Judea and Samaria, and eventually to Rome. But the elements in Acts 2:17 are repeated in the many visions and prophecies scattered throughout the book. One might also note how the experiences of Peter and Paul fre-

quently parallel one another and echo those of Jesus in Luke's gospel. The
instructor may ask students to reflect upon how progressive and repetitive patterns reinforce one another in Acts.

Students normally respond to this exercise by voicing their own
observations concerning how the story of Acts moves from one set of circumstances to an entirely different state of affairs. The discussion also
opens the path for reflection upon Acts as a narrative construction determined by thematic interests rather than as a journalistic and sequential
report of events in the past.

Greg Carey

217. THE NATURE OF HISTORY IN ACTS OF THE APOSTLES

When studying the Acts of the Apostles, students often suspect that it
must be an accurate account of early Christian events and characters or
an ingeniously constructed literary account of these same events and
characters, but that it cannot be both at the same time. This exercise helps
students to see that the two are not necessarily mutually exclusive. One
approach to the blending of "the chronicle" and "the creative" in Acts is
to ask students to reflect on the means and ends of history in their own
lives, and particularly in the life of their families. The goal of such reflection is to invite students to recognize the complex nature of history in
Acts, both with regard to its sources and its effects on its readers.

This process can begin by asking students to recall an oft-repeated
story about an event, person, or place in the history of their immediate or
extended family. The students are also to identify and assess the significance of this story within their family. These tales will vary in quality and
relevance, but an invitation to share stories in class will hopefully elicit
the most interesting and the most pertinent for comparison to the narratives in Acts. The students should be encouraged to reflect on the reasons
for the reiteration of these stories within their families. The range of stories will hopefully run the gamut from meticulously researched accounts
of family genealogy to romanticized legends of family origins and
exploits. Students should be able to articulate reasons for these traditional
stories and to recognize that even apparently straightforward historical
facts can function to define a group or person in flattering and empowering ways.

From such discussion of family histories one may easily move to a
treatment of the purposeful narrative of Acts. Tales of familial fortitude in
the face of hardship are comparable to the narrative cycles of communal

solidarity and resilience in Acts 2–5 (especially the imprisonments and reconstitutions of the Christian group in Acts 4–5). Tales of the sagacious and principled ancestor are comparable to any number of the narratives involving Paul in the second half of Acts, but especially the farewell discourse to the Ephesian elders in Acts 20:18–35. Other such comparisons are forthcoming (consider especially stories of religious conversion and calls to vocation). As with the stories of family history, students may disagree about the plausibility of the events recorded in Acts, but they will have recognized these narratives as significant and informative elements in the definition of the early Christian community and its leaders.

John B. Weaver

218. ANCIENT HISTORIOGRAPHY AND THE BOOK OF ACTS

Students today will often approach an "historical" text from antiquity with a number of presuppositions about what constitutes "history" and how it should be read. Because modern scholars stress the need for objectivity, students often assume that ancient historiographers were also concerned with objectivity. This exercise comparing the death of Judas Iscariot in Acts 1:15–26 with other death type-scenes in antiquity helps students appreciate the ways in which ancient historiographers presented material to their readers.

I begin the discussion by asking students to compare the descriptions of Judas' death in Matt 27:3–10 and Acts 1:15–26. After we have listed the differences between the two texts, I ask students to offer an explanation of how these two passages can claim to be describing the same death event and yet have so many differences. I will sometimes offer them someone else's attempt at harmonizing the two accounts. (A quick search of the Internet will usually yield one or two examples of harmonization.) Before we come to any definitive conclusions, however, I have them look at several texts which contain death type-scenes and compare them to Acts 1:18. The following is a list where such type scenes can be found: (1) the death of King Joram (2 Chr 21:18–19); (2) the death of Antiochus Epiphanes (2 Macc 9:5–7, 9–10, 28); (3) the suicidal death of Razis (2 Macc 14:37–46); (4) the suicidal death of Cato (Appian, *Civil Wars* 2.14.98–99); (5) the death of Aristobulus (Josephus, *War* 1.70–84); (6) the death of Herod the Great (Josephus, *War* 1.654–665).

During the discussion of these texts it becomes clear to the students that the imagery of bursting bowels was a common literary motif used by ancient historiographers to describe how wicked people died. In four of the six texts, the person who dies is said to be suffering retribution from God because of unrighteous acts they have committed. At the same time, the descriptions of the suicidal deaths of Razis and Cato demonstrate how suicide was sometimes seen as an honorable way to die. This helps set up a contrast between the honorable ways that righteous people die and the death of wicked individuals. To help students understand the function of these death scenes I ask them to list the characteristics of a type of death they would expect the villain to suffer in a modern film. This kind of a comparison helps students to understand that just as modern film viewers expect the villain to act in a particular manner or die in a particular way, so also ancient readers would expect villains to suffer a particularly gruesome death commensurate with their crimes.

The next stage of the discussion gives consideration to what the author of Acts may have been trying to communicate about Judas through the description of his death. Students are usually quick to notice that if Matt 27:3–10 was the only account we possessed, we could conclude that Judas repents and then kills himself in an honorable way. However, when we look at the Acts account there is no hint of repentance, and it is not clear if Judas commits suicide. In fact, Acts is somewhat ambiguous as to how Judas dies. But the description of Judas' bursting bowels seems to suggest that he died the kind of death expected of a villain, or in this case a traitor. I suggest to students that this may be the author's attempt to ensure that Judas is completely discredited. To demonstrate how the Acts account has had more influence than the Matthean, I have students read the description of Judas' death by Papias (cf. T. Africa, "Worms and the Death of Kings: A Cautionary Note on Disease and History," *Classical Antiquity* 1 [1982]: 1–17).

As a final way to emphasize the need to approach ancient historiography with caution, I have students read an article that attempts to identify the illness which killed Herod the Great. (The article can be found via an Internet search for "Jan Hirschmann Herod the Great.") After looking at several death type-scenes, students realize how difficult it would be to diagnose Herod's illness due to the fact that Josephus was using a common literary motif to describe the death of a villain.

The following questions help the class to begin thinking in the right direction:

1. It is not uncommon to hear the suggestion that both accounts of Judas' death are factual and that Judas fell after he hanged himself. Does this sort of reasoning fit with the data? Is it possible to determine which account is more historical? What criteria would we use to determine historicity? Do the similarities preserve an historical core, or perhaps the dissimilarities are so great as to rule out an historical basis?

2. Was there dishonor in or stigma attached to committing suicide in antiquity? What does this passage suggest? Why did the author of Luke choose to describe the death of Judas in this way?

3. Do you think it is possible to make the kind of conclusions presented by the medical experts in the Hirschmann article?

John Byron

219. JUST LIKE MAGIC: THE ACTS OF THE APOSTLES

Although the Bible addresses magic in several places, no other author addresses magic as extensively as does Luke. Acts contains four passages that explicitly treat the relationship between Christians and magic. To approach this issue, I ask students to read the following three items: (1) a chapter from Susan Garrett, *The Demise of the Devil: Magic and the Demonic in Luke's Writings* (Minneapolis: Fortress, 1989), 37–60; (2) the descriptions of magic in Jo-Ann Shelton, *As the Romans Did: A Sourcebook in Roman Social History* (2nd ed.; New York: Oxford University Press, 1998), 423–26); and (3) the four accounts in Acts where Luke refers to magic (Acts 8:4–25; 13:4–12; 16:16–19; 19:11–20). With Garrett's chapter, I want the students to understand Luke's worldview—where magic and demonic activity are integrally connected and where healings and exorcisms are part of an earthly drama that contributes to God's ultimate cosmic victory. The briefly annotated primary sources in Shelton encourage and equip the students to hear biblical accounts about magic with first-century ears and expectations. These sources illustrate how magic was linked to words, objects, and actions.

I then give the following assignment: Based on your reading of Garrett, Shelton, and Acts, describe Luke's teaching about magic in one page. On a second page, consider what might constitute improper contact with magic today? In your response, evaluate at least one of the following: (1) Watching *The Wizard of Oz* with its "good" and "bad" witches; (2) Reading C. S. Lewis' *The Lion, the Witch, and the Wardrobe* with its magical and fantastic aspects; (3) Reading J. K. Rowling's Harry Potter books; (4) Reading or watching fantasy material like J. R. R. Tolkien's *The Lord of the Rings*. You should refer to passages in Luke-Acts to support your claims.

The payoff for this exercise comes in the classroom discussion. In my experience, African students, whose culture (often) takes the spiritual realm very seriously, greatly enrich the discussion. Key concerns that typically arise in discussion include: the intent of the magic—to entertain (e.g., tricks, illusions), to prey (e.g., fortune tellers), to scare, or to change allegiance; the portrayal of magic in a film or book (i.e., fantasy vs. real life); practicing magic versus watching or reading about magic; degree or prevalence of belief in magic in a specific cultural context; individual spiritual strengths and weaknesses; the reading of horoscopes.

I also challenge the class to come up with a definition for magic upon which first-century pagans, Jews, and Christians could have agreed. This exercise gives students an opportunity to explore a recurring theme in Acts and to reflect on important hermeneutical and theological issues.

Kenneth L. Cukrowski

NEW TESTAMENT

Letters

220. READING OTHER PEOPLE'S MAIL

Apart from the Gospels, Acts, and Revelation, reading the New Testament is an exercise in reading other people's mail. Their status as holy writ makes this fact easy to overlook, yet it is important to keep in mind that the letters included in the Bible were not originally written with us in mind. They were written by people about whom we know very little, to people about whom we know even less, and without a date on them. To cultivate the habit of reading the letters not primarily as Scripture but as real letters, I give the students a letter to read in class and we go through an exercise which replicates and makes explicit what scholars do when they interpret these sections of the New Testament.

In the past I have used a letter written by Harry Truman to a female relative a day or two after the bombing of Pearl Harbor. I have also used a letter that a friend wrote to me in college. Almost anything would work so long as the identities of the sender and recipient remain unknown. Interpretation is a process of framing good questions about a text and then trying to answer them. Accordingly, the over-arching question I put on the table as discussion begins is, "What do we need to know in order to make sense of this piece of correspondence?" The class begins to formulate questions, and most of the basic questions covered in commentaries soon appear: Who wrote it? To whom? When? Where is the author? Where is the recipient? What prompted the author to write? Was the letter originally written in English? As we turn to the text of the letter to try to answer questions, it becomes clear that legitimate questions could multiply ad infinitum. Cultural references in the letter alternately clarify or obscure the circumstances prompting the letter. Building on some of the basic questions, I ask students to say everything they know about the author, keeping in mind that this letter is all the evidence we have for his or her culture, nationality, gender, socio-economic status, personality, and so forth. Virtually every line of the letter will provide clues of use in our effort to reconstruct the occasion for the correspondence. I then ask for the same kind of deductions about the recipient of the letter and about the date. Students enjoy the detective work this process involves, and I am able to rely on their creativity in coming up with questions and finding details to support their hypotheses. There are always instances in which another student will construe the evidence in the text to support a very different theory about the letter. This forces us to try to adjudicate between the conflicting interpretations.

After this period of brainstorming ends, I reveal what I know about the letter and we assess how successful we were in forming a picture of the author and the setting for the letter. This de-briefing gives me the chance to explain how, at a very elementary level, this is what scholars have done in writing their textbooks or the annotations in their study Bible. It also reminds us that even the most reasonable readings of these texts can sometimes be mistaken on account of the limited amount of information contained in them and the peculiarities of individual authors. This does not mean that every attempt at reading ancient texts will be a wild goose chase. While many different readings may be possible, as academic interpreters we are prejudiced in favor of probable readings. And even here, our interpretations must remain tentative and open to correction by new evidence and more compelling ways of analyzing the evidence of the text. (For a similar exercise, see §14.)

Bryan Whitfield
Patrick Gray

221. THE LETTERS AND HISTORICAL CONTEXT

Whenever interpreting a New Testament letter, one must first address the issue of the historical context behind the letter. It is important for students to recognize the necessity of understanding why a letter was written and to what situation it responds in order to interpret that letter responsibly. However, it is also important for students to appreciate the ambiguity involved in such endeavors. Typically, one reads a letter for clues to the historical context. From those clues, one reconstructs the historical context and then proceeds to interpret the letter in light of this reconstructed context. This involves a necessary degree of circularity that opens the process to some potential problems. One of the reasons scholars interpret a letter in widely different ways is because they are reading it against different conceptions of the original context. Essentially, if one alters the historical context, one alters the interpretation.

To communicate to students how a change in historical context affects interpretation, I introduce them to a song from U2 called "In A

Little While." This song comes from U2's album titled "All That You Can't Leave Behind" (2000). What makes this an interesting example is that we have direct access to the authorial intent for this song. Bono, the writer of the song and lead singer of U2, has stated that this song was written about a hangover. He writes from the perspective of one who experienced a wild weekend of partying and drinking and now has to contemplate going home to his wife. He is repentant but fearful about what kind of reception awaits him at home. I pass out the lyrics of the song to the students and explain the author's stated intention for the song. After playing the song, I have the students interpret the lyrics from within that historical context. The students see very clearly how this song represents a hangover experience and they recognize how knowing that historical context helps them to make better sense of the lyrics.

Then, I present the students with a different historical context for the song. In April of 2001, Joey Ramone, leader of the punk rock group The Ramones, was dying of cancer. Joey was a big fan of "In A Little While," but he viewed the song in a different light than that under which it was written. As he lay on his death bed, with his family gathered around, he had a CD player by the bed so that he could listen to "In A Little While." Joey had even given instructions to his brother to play the song whenever it seemed like he was close to death. He died just as the song was coming to a close. For Ramone, this was a song not about a man going home to his wife, but about a dying person going home to God. After this event, U2 continued to play "In A Little While" in their concerts, but they did so with a new introduction. Bono announced that Joey Ramone had taken a song about a hangover and turned it into a gospel song. Now, Bono said, whenever they sing it, they do so with that meaning in mind. After providing the students with this new context, I play the song again, only this time I have them listen and interpret the song from this new perspective. They learn that the same words can just as legitimately be read as a gospel song as they can a song about a hangover.

From this assignment, students learn how historical context affects interpretation. It helps them to understand better at least one of the reasons why different people can interpret the same biblical text in very different ways. There are numerous instances in which this could be used to illustrate the complexity of biblical interpretation. For instance, how one identifies the specific heresy in Colossians or how one defines the purpose of Romans or whether one sees Revelation as written to a context of persecution or to one of accommodation greatly affects how one interprets those documents. Also, one could use the assignment to discuss how the church today applies these ancient documents to a modern context. Can we legitimately find new meanings in Scripture (as Joey Ramone does in this song) due to our different historical contexts? Is it the nature of a text that is "living and active" to continue to speak freshly as contexts change?

Gregory Stevenson

222. WILL THE REAL PAUL PLEASE STAND UP?

This exercise works well for an early class session on the Apostle Paul. The purpose is to introduce students to the various ancient sources for studying Paul and to make them aware of the historical problems raised by comparing the various sources. In preparation for the exercise, the professor should take a few minutes at the end of a class to have students count off in fours (i.e., "1,2,3,4; 1,2,3,4") until the entire class has a number. For the next class, "Group 1" is to read the *Acts of Paul* (online: http://gbgm-umc.org/umw/corinthians/thecla.stm); "Group 2" is to read Acts 9, 13–19; "Group 3" is to read the Pastoral Epistles; and "Group 4" is to read Gal 1–2; 1 Cor 1–4, 7; and 2 Cor 11–13.

Students are to address the following questions as they read: (1) Does your text give a description of what Paul looks like? If so, describe. (2) To what places does Paul go? (3) What types of things does Paul do? (4) What types of people does he meet? (5) What does Paul seem to talk about the most? Be specific! (6) What type of responses does Paul seem to "inspire" in his audiences? (7) What does Paul think about himself—what he is doing, and why he is doing it?

For the next class period, one person from each group gets together with three other people (one from each of the other groups). Students then go around their circle of four, sharing the view of Paul they developed from reading their texts and responding to the questions. After about ten minutes sharing in small groups, students gather again with the professor and each group describes their responses to one of the questions. The professor can write the four groups of texts up on the board and the approximate date of composition of each text, and then catalogue student findings. The findings should lead into a discussion about primary and secondary sources for studying Paul and how these sources can be evaluated and weighted.

Jeffrey L. Staley

223. SAINT PAUL?

After teaching a unit on Paul in an introductory class, I show a very short clip from Scorsese's *The Last Temptation of Christ*. The clip comes from the last few minutes of the film, during the fantasy sequence in which Jesus imagines living an ordinary human life rather than dying as the son of God. In the clip, Jesus visits a town in which he hears Paul preaching his gospel to a small crowd. Paul (Harry Dean Stanton) has already appeared in the film as a Zealot and as the murderer of Lazarus. After Paul's preaching, Jesus accosts him and denies the truth of his gospel. Paul—by turns bemused, concerned, angry, and dismissive—follows Jesus and continues the conversation. Ultimately, Paul tells Jesus that his Jesus, the savior of the world, is far more important than the Jesus before him.

I have prepared hard copies of this dialogue beforehand and distribute them to the class after the viewing. I then break the class into small groups and ask them to discuss various questions: (1) What kind of character is Scorsese's Paul? Is he concerned for people? For Jesus? For his own power? Is he villain, hero, saint, or charlatan? (2) Do Scorsese's Paul and his message bear any relation to either the Paul of Acts or the Pauline letters? (3) Is Paul (of Acts, the epistles, or both) concerned at all for the historical Jesus? (4) Is Scorsese's Paul an interpretation of Paul acceptable to the church? To the academy?

After a few minutes, I bring the class back together and invite them to share their thoughts. Invariably, a heated discussion evolves about truth, history, canon, and fiction, among others issues. As I have been trying to bring the class to think about Paul's place in the canon and outside it (in history, interpretation, culture, and fiction), these conversations highlight precisely what I am seeking. Generally, some in the class see Saint Paul, like Scorsese's Paul, as an ideological construct while others remain more solidly entrenched in their religious or non-religious ideology.

If we have covered the topic, I also ask the class to consider whether Scorsese's Jesus bears any resemblance to the Jesus of (any of) the gospels or the Jesuses of historical criticism. In advanced classes, this inevitably raises questions about the relationship between the teaching of Jesus, the stories about Jesus (i.e., the gospels), and Paul's gospel. This conversation leads to discussions about the diversity of early Christianities and to questions about the canon's (dominating) role in interpretation.

Note: If one has more time and inclination, one can do the same type of project in more detail with *The Apostle*. Paul does not appear often in the movies, but Duvall's excellent film offers one of the best "disguised" Pauls in film history. This film offers far more opportunities for comparison to Acts and the epistles. It also offers possibilities for discussions about the difference between, and relative credibility of, Saint Paul or a more human figure like Duvall's title character.

Richard Walsh

224. DEBATING PAULINE THEOLOGY

Toward the end of the semester in a class on the Pauline letters, I set up debate teams and ask students to argue pro or con for these resolutions: (1) The Pauline letters support the full participation of women in ministry. (2) Love is the center of Pauline ethics. (3) Paul is a good role model for missional leaders. This activity can take place in class or online. We hold one debate each week for three weeks. Students participate in two debates and judge a third. When a debate occurs on campus, we allow one hour of class time for it. When it occurs online, short postings are made and replied to by opposing teams over several days.

To prepare for a debate, students complete assigned readings on the topic. As a result of their reading and other prior work in the class, they should be equally ready to argue either side of the question. Students participating in the debate are assigned to groups having four to six members. Outside of class time, the teams brainstorm ideas for arguing each side of the question and decide how to split up the work that the debate will require. The teams do not choose which side they will argue. I assign them pro or con a day or two before the debate begins.

On campus, the debate teams prepare an opening statement and at least one question for their opponents. Pro and con alternate through five short presentations. Each team presents: an opening statement (seven minutes); a reply to the opening statement of opponents (three minutes); a question to opponents (one minute); an answer to opponents' question (four minutes); and a closing statement, summarizing the team's strongest points (five minutes). If carried out in an online class, the debate proceeds in very much the same way, except that a forum or threaded discussion area is the debate space. During the debate, each team posts a single statement that speaks for the whole group each day over a period of days. (Instead of time limits for online presentations, I usually set a 250–word limit.)

After the forty–minute classroom debate or the week-long online debate, those students who were not on a team for the debate act as judges. The judges render their verdict based on how well each team (1) made use of Pauline texts to support their side of the debate; (2) stuck to the topic at hand and the time (or word) limit; (3) honestly acknowledged and addressed objections that could be made to its position; (4) was rhetorically captivating, perhaps using humor, rhetorical questions, quotable quotes, or other devices to engage the audience. The debate format has worked very well to help students move from exegesis of individual texts to engagement of larger questions about Paul's theology and worldview, as well as questions about how his letters are best appropriated by Christians today.

Mary E. Hinkle

225. PAUL'S RELIGIOUS EXPERIENCE: CONVERSION OR CALL?

Most students tend to harmonize Paul's religious experience in the book of Acts and his letter to the Galatians, primarily because they read the two books as purely historical data. Therefore, they need the opportunity to understand the distinctiveness and purpose of Paul's religious experience in each book as well as the specific reasons for these differences. This exercise also enables students to distinguish between first-person and third-person perspectives.

In preparation for class, students should reread Acts and Galatians. Also, divide the class into groups and assign each group to read one of several articles that address whether Paul's religious experience is a call or a conversion (e.g., K. Stendhal, "Call Rather than Conversion," in *Paul Among Jews and Gentiles* [Philadelphia: Fortress, 1976], 7–23; P. Eisenbaum, "Paul as the New Abraham," in *Paul and Politics* [ed. R. Horsley; Harrisburg, PA: Trinity Press International, 2000], 130–45; and A. Segal, "Response: Some Aspects of Conversion and Identity Formation in the Christian Community of Paul's Time," in Horsley, *Paul and Politics,* 184–90). As they read the biblical texts they should reflect upon the way that Paul's religious experience functions in each. As they read the assigned article, they are expected to summarize the scholar's position and the supporting arguments.

Split the students into their groups when class meets and hand out two documents that you have written yourself, one in which a person is explaining why she is the best person for a job and the other in which that same person is described by someone else as being the best person for the job. Have them discuss in what context each document would be the most persuasive and successful in reaching its goals. (One might also distribute editorials endorsing a political candidate along with transcripts of speeches by that same candidate.) Next have them discuss how Paul attempts to persuade the Galatians regarding his authority and how the author of Acts attempts to persuade the reader regarding the authoritative basis of Paul's ministry. After sharing their responses as a class, have the students discuss in their groups the major points in their assigned article. Coming back together as a class, write on the board the two words "call" and "conversion," and ask them under which word they would place the scholar whose article they read and why. Which parts of Galatians and Acts suggest that Paul's experience was a call, and which parts suggest that Paul's experience was a conversion? How might one explain the different emphases? What are the implications of referring to his experience as a call (=connotation of continuity between Christianity and Judaism)? What are the implications of referring to his experience as a conversion (=connotation of discontinuity between Christianity and Judaism and possible anti-Semitism)?

Emily R. Cheney

226. WOMEN'S ORDINATION, THE NEW TESTAMENT, AND THE POLITICS OF INTERPRETATION

Since ordained roles for women in the church remain problematic for a number of Protestant denominations as well as for Roman Catholics and the Orthodox, this exercise is designed to help students see beyond the explicit statements against women in ministry in 1 Corinthians and 1 Timothy to the less obvious passages supporting full inclusion of women in the ministry of the early church. In this light it is a continuation of an historical investigation into the status of women in the earliest church and it serves to explore further the role of politics in interpreting Scripture. It has also succeeded in helping students find empathy with denominational positions with which they disagree. This is a small-group exercise in which students role-play as members of specific denominations, under specific circumstances, and with particular personal histories while debating the role of women in these churches.

Necessary background work for this exercise is that the majority of passages with relevance to the role of women in ministry have been discussed (e.g., Matt 10:1–4; Acts 18:1–4, 18, 26; Rom 16; 1 Cor 11:5, 13; 14:34; Gal 3:28; Phil 4:2–3; Col 4:15; 1 Tim 2:12). For the exercise itself each small group is given "identity papers." These detail what denomination they belong to, what position on women's ordination within that denomination each group member represents, what the denomination's traditions have been regarding women in ministry, necessary theological commitments, and current political pressures within the denomination regarding women's ordination. They are to use the resources provided on the identity papers, plus the biblical passages we have previously discussed in class (and any others they find relevant) to debate women's ordination within the specific circumstances outlined on the "identity papers." When they are finished, they put together a "statement on women in ministry" detailing an argument that they believe will carry weight with other denominational members. (This final step usually requires group members meeting outside of class time.) In the next class session these statements are presented to the rest of the class who are cast as members of that denomination and who decide if they are convinced by the group's argument.

Sample "identity papers":

Catholic. Your group is a study task force to which the bishops of the U.S. have assigned the job of advising them on the possibilities of expanding ordination to women. Your final product will be a statement designed to convince other U.S. Catholics of your solution. You will need to consider the pressures of modern cultural expectations for women's rights, the shortage of priests, the fact that many Protestants ordain women, that there is a strong North American and European demographic in favor of ordaining women, but that the majority of the world's one billion Catholics are opposed to this development.

Catholic background: The Church is officially opposed to women's ordination. The Pope does not support it. Tradition is against it. For centuries Catholics have believed that because Jesus was male and his twelve apostles were male, the priesthood (which is a continuation of their ministry) should be male. For Catholics this is not simply about the Bible, but also about the traditions of the church. However, in theory, women's ordination would only require a Pope willing to make a decision to do so. Perhaps the U.S. bishops could convince the Holy Father.

Biblical issues: The central biblical material supporting Catholic prohibitions against ordaining women is the fact of Jesus' and the apostles' gender. But Catholics believe that all Scripture is important and have a tradition of balancing various biblical voices.

Group members: Two of you are conservative Catholics opposed to change, two of you are liberal Catholics eager for change, while the remaining group members are moderates. Taking the biblical materials, your traditions, and the political situation into account, debate the issue and come to a decision on how to advise the bishops. Frame this advice as a formal statement designed to convince other American Catholics of your position on women's ordination.

Evangelical Lutheran Church in America: The ELCA represents "liberal" Lutheranism; however, some surveys indicate that a sizable percentage of ELCA Lutherans are conservatives. As Lutherans you are proud of being "biblical." You claim to be a Bible-believing church. But your interpretation of the Bible is framed by Lutheran theology. Paul's concept of justification by faith, salvation by grace, and gospel as a free gift requiring nothing are the means by which you interpret Scripture. Many denominational leaders, clergy, and educated laity approach the Bible through a "liberal" interpretation. These Lutherans consider much of the Bible to be culturally bound to its time of writing and not directly applicable to us. The conservative Lutherans would take an opposing view, that all of Scripture is applicable to our situations.

Background: The ELCA has ordained women since the 1970s. Yet the number of women pastors is small and many congregations have never had or been exposed to a woman pastor.

Group members: Your small, conservative, rural church is calling a new pastor. You have never had a female pastor. Some members of your congregation are biblical conservatives and do not believe ordaining women was the right thing to do. Indeed, some are spouting 1 Cor 14:34–36 and 1 Tim 2:8–15. Your group is the call committee. The bishop has put before you a woman candidate. Three of you are older, more conservative members, and the rest of you are more liberal. You must decide if you will accept the woman candidate the bishop is suggesting. If you do, you must make a statement to convince the rest of your church members that this is right; if not, you must convince the bishop. (For other exercises on women and the Bible, see §§50, 55, 154, 191, 242, 267.)

Thomas W. Martin

227. EPISTLE FOR TODAY

My experience in teaching survey courses about Paul's life and thought to undergraduate students reveals a perennial struggle to bridge the expanse of time and culture. Although students recognize that many of the topics addressed in Paul's epistles continue to impinge upon their own world, they inevitably see him as someone "back then" and "over there." To address this cultural-historical distance I have developed an exercise I call the "Epistle for Today." It is normally one of the last assignments in the course and builds upon students' familiarity with Pauline biography, specific epistles, and broader thought trajectories.

I ask each student to submit a paper which, in essence, creates a new Pauline epistle by envisioning what Paul might compose if he were writing today to the community to which they belong. (I have usually used this exercise at a church-affiliated liberal arts college, making the campus the "community.") I stress that the particular content of the project is wide open, although I remind them that Paul always included aspects of his understanding of the gospel of Jesus Christ in all of his epistles. Nevertheless, he also made this message contingent to the specific context he was addressing. Thus, each student is encouraged to wrestle with and articulate the "essence" of Paul's thought and how it pertains to the student in his or her present life situation. While the narrative of all such reports is expected to "retell" Paul's understanding of the gospel in some way, the decisions each student makes concerning presentation, organization, focus, symbol, and vocabulary reflect personal interpretation—and then, of course, their linkage of the message to particular contemporary issues makes the epistle their own.

I announce this assignment at the beginning of the course and encourage students to work on it throughout the semester. As almost all of the canonical epistles are longer than the suggested limits for this project, decisions about what to leave out of such an "epistle" are critical. The project should read as if Paul himself (or his amanuensis) were writing. One exception: they may use an introductory section, short footnotes or endnotes, or a conclusion to justify or discuss key interpretive decisions.

The evaluation of this assignment is more problematic than some, in view of its subjective nature. I look for several key factors: a clear, coherent account of the gospel, analogous to Paul's presentation; a clear contingent focus, again analogous to Paul's positions (although I am willing to consider alternatives if a student offers sound rationale); representation of epistolary structure; representation of Pauline style and vocabulary (although I remind them Paul was intent upon being relevant to his audiences and would have that same concern today, so they are free to use contemporary communication patterns if they can be demonstrated to be analogous to those he utilized in his day); and clear explanation of interpretive decisions.

On some occasions I have offered the sole feedback; on other occasions I have had students post their "Epistles for Today" on a class-restricted webpage and encouraged them to evaluate or offer feedback to each other. This inevitably provokes lively interaction as differing assessments of sexuality, academic honesty, racism, cliques, and other topics emerge. While some students struggle to get beyond "churchy" verbiage and banal pronouncements ("You should be good people and treat each other with love"), many invest themselves in the assignment and use it as a method whereby they might apply Pauline ethics and theology to controversies with which they themselves struggle. This, of course, is one of the broader goals of the exercise. (For a similar exercise, see §104.)

Raymond H. Reimer

228. THE ISSUE OF AUTHENTICITY IN THE PAULINE WRITINGS: 2 THESSALONIANS AS A TEST CASE

The three objectives of this exercise are (1) to introduce students to the question of the (in)authenticity of the letters attributed to Paul, (2) to set forth the criteria that scholars use to adjudicate authenticity, and (3) to offer 2 Thessalonians as a brief test case and invite the students' own critical engagement.

How do scholars adjudicate whether or not a letter attributed to Paul was actually written by him (or, at least, at his dictation)? Scholars have employed three basic criteria when studying the disputed Pauline letters: (1) *Placement*. Can the letter in question be placed within what we know about Paul's career (from the letters and from Acts)? In principle, this is a solid criterion. The problem is that we do not have as much information about Paul's life and ministry as we would like. (2) *Style*. Does the letter in question follow the style of Paul's authentic letters? This criterion presumes that Paul had a discernable style of writing. Scholars look to such things as word choice, sentence structure and length, syntax, mode of argumentation, and the way Scripture is used. (3) *Content*. Does the letter in question deal with themes we would expect from Paul on the basis of his authentic letters? This criterion presupposes that Paul wrote with thematic consistency. Scholars focus, for example, on what is said concerning Jesus (Christology), the church (ecclesiology), expectations concerning the end times (eschatology), and ethics.

Before proceeding to the test case, raise the following questions for students to consider: How do you think the seven undisputed Pauline letters came to be regarded as authentic? (Acknowledge that a degree of circularity is involved.) Given the relatively small number of letters involved, is this a sufficient "database" for determining patterns of style and content? If not, how many more letters would be adequate? How valid is the presupposition that Paul's style and content would not vary (especially when the "occasional" character of his letters is taken into account)? Why even be concerned about authenticity?

Second Thessalonians is a good text to illustrate the process of determining a letter's authenticity. Scholars are almost evenly split on the question, with a slight majority regarding it as deuteropauline. Scholars dispute the authenticity of 2 Thessalonians on two main grounds: (1) it seems to replicate much of the phraseology and the order of presentation of 1 Thessalonians; and (2) it appears to offer a very different scenario of the end time (cf. 2 Thess 2:1–12 with 1 Thess 4:13–5:3). How do scholars apply the three criteria of authenticity to 2 Thessalonians? (Students will need to read both 1 and 2 Thessalonians to appreciate the positions taken by scholars on both sides of the debate.)

(1) *Placement.* We know that shortly after founding the church in Thessalonika, Paul was in Athens. From there, he sent his co-worker Timothy to visit and encourage the fledgling church (1 Thess 3:1–2). This piece of data fits well within the broader description of Paul's initial missionary work in Macedonia and Achaia found in Acts 16:11–18:17. Scholars who argue for the authenticity of 2 Thessalonians believe it was written shortly after 1 Thessalonians (from Corinth?). Paul wrote again to address a new situation that arose in the church at Thessalonika (see below). Scholars who argue for the inauthenticity of 2 Thessalonians believe it was written by someone else in an entirely different context, e.g., one affected by the apocalyptic fervor that arose later in the first century C.E.

(2) *Style.* Both 1 and 2 Thessalonians have simple letter openings followed by a thanksgiving that subtly shifts into the letter body (1 Thess 1:2–2:12; 2 Thess 1:3–2:12). Both letters contain a second thanksgiving (1 Thess 2:13–3:10; 2 Thess 2:13–15) followed by a wish prayer (1 Thess 3:11–13; 2 Thess 2:16–17). Scholars who argue for the authenticity of 2 Thessalonians believe these similarities make sense, given the proximity of time between letters and the fact that Paul was dealing with the same people struggling with the same issues. Scholars who argue for the inauthenticity of 2 Thessalonians believe that these similarities are evidence that someone copied Paul's phraseology and structure in 1 Thessalonians in order to give his work an air of authority. (Note: This use of the criterion of style *differs* from its usual employment to show that a letter differs markedly in style.)

(3) *Content.* While the two letters contain much of the same content (especially about persevering in the midst of suffering), there is one notable exception: 2 Thessalonians offers a much more detailed apocalyptic end time scenario (2:1–12). Scholars who argue for the authenticity of 2 Thessalonians believe Paul learned that his first letter to the Thessalonians had unwittingly contributed to the community's speculation and anxiety about the end time. Thus, he wrote the second letter to calm them down, to assure them that the end has not arrived yet (they will know it when it comes!), and to use the remaining time to grow in holiness. Scholars who argue for the inauthenticity of 2 Thessalonians believe that the different descriptions of the end time show that two different minds are at work (although cf. 1 Cor 15:21–28). In addition, 2 Thessalonians purports to have Paul's personal signature (3:17), which gives it an air of authenticity (cf. 2:2). Scholars interpret this differently. Either Paul is simply doing here what he does elsewhere (1 Cor 16:21–24; Gal 6:1–18; Phlm 19–25; cf. Col 3:18) or it is a forgery by which the author attempts to validate his authority.

Having set forth the evidence and scholarly opinions, discuss the following questions: Based on your reading of 1 and 2 Thessalonians, which is the stronger case—that 2 Thessalonians comes from Paul himself or that it was written by someone else at a later time? Why is the answer to this question important (e.g., historically, theologically, canonically)? What is presupposed or implied about early Christianity if 2 Thessalonians is inauthentic? (For further reading, see L. T. Johnson, *The Writings of the New Testament* [rev. ed.; Minneapolis: Fortress, 1999], 271–73, 287–91).

Thomas D. Stegman

229. LITERARY ANALYSIS AND THE QUESTION OF AUTHORSHIP

Many debates about the authorship of New Testament letters hinge on the comparison of writing style, vocabulary, and grammar between letters in an attempt to determine whether a single author—Paul, for instance—could have written all the documents attributed to him. These types of arguments tend to be highly controversial because of the difficulties inherent in any such analysis. This assignment introduces students to the types of issues involved when analyzing authorship on the basis of literary methods and to the tenuousness of drawing firm conclusions on the basis of such evidence alone.

In 1996, *USA Today* published an article under the heading: "Kaczynski Writings Peculiar to the Letter" (April 24, 1996). The article may be acquired through *USA Today's* archive section on their website (http://pqasb.pqarchiver.com/USAToday/search.html). The article includes photocopies of three short letters sent to the Montana Department of Health and Environmental Sciences by Theodore Kaczynski (a.k.a., the Unabomber). For the assignment, I provide the students with copies of all three letters, having blocked out the author's name. They are told to read and compare all three letters carefully by examining vocabulary, grammar, stylistic features, and content. Then they are to conclude whether all three letters were written by a single person, by three people, or whether one author wrote two of the letters and another the third. They must be prepared to defend their conclusions. Typically the assignment generates much debate among the students as they defend their various positions against each other. Curiously, it is not uncommon for the class to agree that all three letters were not written by one person.

The striking similarities and differences between these letters provide much information for discussion. In all three letters, the author places the date in the upper right corner and includes the address for the Montana Department of Health and Environmental Sciences on the left. Yet, one of the letters leaves out "Montana" while another adds a comma and zip code when the others do not. All three letters begin with "Dear Sirs" and conclude with "Thank you very much for your help." Two of the letters place "Sincerely yours" above the author's name, while the third fails to include it at all. In two of the letters, there is a series of five questions asked. In one the questions are enumerated, while in the other the questions are presented in paragraph form with no enumeration. Also, in one of the letters, Kaczynski uses a contraction (I'm, I've) in every single instance where a contraction is possible. In one of the other letters, he never uses a contraction even though there are several opportunities to do so. (The third letter has no opportunities for contraction.)

These or other comparisons provide interesting fodder for class discussion. Furthermore, the fact that two of the letters were written a day apart while the other was written two years prior illustrates how a person's writing style can vary not only over the course of two years but even over the course of twenty-four hours.

I do not make this a graded assignment, although one could easily use it as the basis for a small essay. Rather I use it to stimulate thinking and class discussion. The goal is for students to learn what kinds of questions are asked when undertaking literary analysis to determine authorship and how to evaluate the answers given to those questions.

Gregory Stevenson

230. AUTHORSHIP AND PSEUDONYMITY

I like to introduce the topics of authorship and pseudonymity, especially as they pertain to the Pauline corpus, by talking about practices of authorship and pseudonymous writing today. Students are frequently concerned about the moral dimensions of pseudonymity, and showing them that various shades of pseudonymous writing are practiced today and considered acceptable helps to ease the tension while still allowing students to make their own judgments. It also problematizes the whole notion of what "pseudonymity" and "authorship" mean, which I find to be a helpful counterbalance to the often simplistic way the issue is presented in textbooks and scholarship.

I give students the following examples of pseudonymity that might occur today and for each ask them (1) whether or in what way they think the idea of "authorship" applies to the situation, and (2) whether they think there are moral problems involved in the situation:

(a) A public relations employee of a business writes a letter for the business. After the president of the company reads and approves the letter, it is sent out with the company president's signature on it.

(b) A public relations employee creates a quote for a press release and attributes it to another employee of the company. After approval by the "cited" employee, the press release is distributed with the "quote."

(c) An author writes a book using a pen name.

(d) An author writes a book using a pen name. The pen name chosen makes it appear that the author is of a different gender, ethnicity, or nationality from what the author actually is.

(e) A politician delivers a speech expressing the politician's views on a topic of public policy. The speech is actually written by an employed speechwriter.

(f) An author dies while writing a book. Another author completes the book. When the book is published, both authors are listed, without any information given as to which author wrote which part of the book.

(g) Same as the previous example, except that only the original author is listed.

(h) A scientist has a stroke and becomes unable to work after having completed the research and analysis of an important experiment. Some students or colleagues of the scientist gather all the data and notes of the scientist, then write up and publish the scientist's findings in the scientist's name.

(i) A preacher delivers a sermon found in a published book of sermons. The preacher makes no statement about the source of the sermon.

(j) A family member writes a Christmas card without help from anyone else in the family, then signs the names of all family members and sends it out.

(k) A church member X is asked to write up an important amendment to be made to the church constitution. Member X thinks member Y would do a better job and asks Y to do it instead. Y agrees, but because of Y's controversial reputation in the church, Y doesn't want Y's name associated with the writing. Therefore X and Y agree that Y will write the document, but X will present it without any indication that Y was involved.

(i) A journalist writes an article for a magazine. The magazine editor makes numerous stylistic changes and cuts much of the content of the article before publishing it in the magazine.

Many other situations could be added, and depending on time constraints only a few might be selected if needed. None of these situations is precisely that suggested in views on the authorship of the Pauline letters—though note that some of them do come close! One of the key things the list shows is the way in which practices of authorship are closely tied to societal standards, and that these standards themselves may be tied to very particular circumstances. Many students express great surprise, for instance, when I tell them that the second item is a very common practice in the field of public relations, and that it is not considered dishonest at all. The other key point is that the idea of "authorship" encompasses a wide range of possible relations between "author" and "text." Once students grasp these points as they pertain to today, it is easier to have a discussion about the variety of options available in interpreting the biblical texts, particularly in talking about whether or not Paul should be seen as the "author" of all the letters attributed to him.

Scott Shauf

231. PSEUDONYMITY AND PSEUDEPIGRAPHY IN THE NEW TESTAMENT

For people living in the twenty-first century it can be difficult to appreciate the practice of pseudepigraphy in late antiquity. Living in a world in which copyright piracy and plagiarism have become such serious issues can cause students to question the validity of ancient documents written by anyone other than the ascribed author. Moreover, the suggestion that such writings might be contained in the New Testament canon can be a challenge for which some students are not prepared. I have discovered, however, that when presented in a non-threatening manner, many students are willing at least to entertain the possibility of pseudepigraphy in the New Testament.

Prior to the class I ask students to do some preparatory reading. For an argument against the presence of pseudepigraphy in the New Testament I assign D. A. Carson, "Pseudonymity and Pseudepigraphy" (in *Dictionary of New Testament Background* [ed. C. A. Evans and S. E. Porter; Downers Grove, IL: InterVarsity Press, 2000], 857–64). For an argument in favor of pseudepigraphy I assign J. D. G. Dunn, "Pauline Legacy and School" and "Pseudepigraphy" (in *Dictionary of the New Testament and Its Developments* [ed. R. P. Martin and P. H. Davids; Downers Grove, IL: InterVarsity Press, 1997], 887–93, 977–84). I ask students to come to class prepared to discuss a definition of pseudepigraphy as well as the strengths and weaknesses of the arguments they have read.

I start the class discussion with a consideration of modern parallels to pseudonymity/pseudepigraphy in antiquity. Most students can identify Samuel Clemens with Mark Twain and then name three or four of his better known works. A few can identify Mary Ann Evans with the nineteenth-century British author who wrote under the pseudonym George Eliot. In order to be published in the nineteenth century, Evans had to write under a male name because writing was regarded as a "male" profession. Far fewer can identify William Sidney Porter as O. Henry, best known for his Christmas story "The Gift of the Magi." Porter had written under his real name, but after a stint in prison for embezzlement he published hundreds of short stories under a pseudonym. Such modern examples help students to understand why authors might be reticent about using their own name.

After this introduction I move to a discussion of pseudonymity and pseudepigraphy in late antiquity. I provide a quotation describing how the Neo-Pythagoreans attributed their own writings to Pythagoras (Iamblichus, *On the Life of Pythagoras* 31.198). I ask the students if, based on this quotation, people living in antiquity may have had a different concept of authorship and literary ownership. I then provide them with a list of Jewish pseudepigrapha. In particular, I want them to be aware of writings such as *1 Enoch, Wisdom of Solomon, 4 Ezra, the Testaments of the Twelve Patriarchs, Testament of Moses,* and any others that are attributed to the Israelite patriarchs or heroes. I may even read aloud a few of the opening lines from some of these works. I then ask students to consider why an author might write under the name of a patriarch or some other famous hero from Israelite history. After some discussion I suggest several possible answers: (1) the author wanted to show respect to the individual; (2) the assertion that it was written by a patriarch might add authority to the document; and (3) if the ascribed author is said to be prophesying about future events, the "fulfillment" of these prophecies during the reader's lifetime would magnify the importance of those events.

After this I provide a list of non-canonical Christian pseudepigrapha, including the *Didache, 3 Corinthians, Protoevangelium of James,* and the *Gospel of Peter.* I ask students to consider whether or not early Christians accepted the practice of pseudepigraphy. Of course, the fact that none of these books appear in the New Testament canon will lead most to conclude that exclusion automatically means rejection of pseudepigraphy. I then ask them to read Jude 14–15 alongside *1 Enoch* 1.9. Once students discover that a canonical book is quoting from an acknowledged pseudepigraphic work, they begin to realize that the categories in which they normally think are not always the most helpful. This allows me to ask more serious questions about particular books in the New Testament. After a few brief statements about the debate over Pauline authorship of the Pastoral Epistles, I hand out a sheet with a passage from the Pastorals which is placed side by side with acknowledged second-century texts. These include: 1 Tim 3:1–13; Ignatius *Magn.* 7.1–2; *Smyrn.* 8.1–2; and *Did.* 15.1. Through this comparison students are able to acknowledge at least the possibility of the Pastorals being later works. Even more importantly, many students are able to comprehend why there is a debate over pseudepigraphy in the New Testament and are not as quick to dismiss it as an attempt to undermine their view of the Bible.

I conclude the class with a discussion of the following questions:

1. Considering the prevalence of pseudepigraphical writings in the ancient world, is it possible that some of the writings in the New Testament are pseudonymously written?

2. What is your reaction to the articles by Carson and Dunn? Be able to articulate both "pros" and "cons" for accepting their positions.

3. Is it important to profess that all writings of the New Testament were in fact written by those to whom they are ascribed?

4. How does the view of Scripture as "inspired" coincide with the practice of pseudepigraphy in the ancient world? Are they able to coincide or are they diametrically opposed? What issues are at stake?

John Byron

232. WRITING TO PAUL

This classroom experience reproduces the contingent and controversial contexts in which Paul composed his letters. It encourages students to imagine how unsettled were the contexts of Paul's epistolary activity and to appreciate the rhetorical, cultural, and religious challenges faced by Paul and his audiences. By exploring rational frameworks for the positions Paul argues against, students may better imagine the multiple perspectives represented in and around these churches.

In preparation for class, students must have read one or more of Paul's letters. In class, the instructor assigns specific passages from 1 or 2 Corinthians in which Paul is responding to events or to reports from the Corinthians themselves. For example, Rom 6:15–23; 1 Cor 7:1–20; 7:21–24; 8:1–13; and 2 Cor 3:1–6 offer promising texts for this sort of reflection. Having chosen or been assigned a specific passage, individual students have ten minutes in which to compose their own letter to Paul. In this letter they must imaginatively reconstruct and argue for one of the positions to which Paul is responding. (E.g., how might Paul's gospel undermine ethical responsibility? Why shouldn't a man touch a woman? Should slaves seek their emancipation? Why is the debate over idol meat important? Why isn't Paul's ministry superior to that of others?)

Having completed their epistles, students gather in groups of three to five according to the passages they have chosen. They share their letters, followed by plenary discussion of the major themes that emerged from the working groups. Some students may resist this assignment by creating superficial or implausible representations of these alternative voices. The group conversation helps toward remediating this situation. Students also come away with an awareness of how difficult it can be to reconstruct the precise historical-cultural circumstances prompting Paul's letters.

Greg Carey

233. WHAT DOES PAUL MEAN BY THE EXPRESSION *PISTIS CHRISTOU?*

The goal of this exercise is to introduce students to an important theological debate concerning the phrase "the faith of Christ" (*pistis Christou*) in Rom 3:21–26 and elsewhere in Paul's letters. The Greek phrase *pistis* + the genitive form of "Christ" (or "Jesus Christ," "Jesus," or "the Son of God") occurs seven times in the undisputed Pauline letters (Rom 3:22, 26; Gal 2:16 [twice], 20; 3:22; Phil 3:9). The context of each instance is the revelation of God's righteousness or how God makes people righteous (i.e., brings them into right relationship with God). The term *pistis* can mean "faith" or "faithfulness." Thus, Paul states that God makes people righteous by means of faith, and this faith is somehow connected with Jesus Christ.

But just what is this connection? For the past twenty-five years, a fierce debate has raged among scholars over what exactly Paul signifies by the expression *pistis Christou*. The name *Christou* is in the genitive case. Most simply put, the genitive case puts a noun in an adjectival relationship with another noun. But the genitive is also very flexible. Thus, the phrase *pistis Christou* can signify the faith that Christ has (in God): this renders the genitive as subjective (Jesus is the subject who has faith and is faithful). Or it can denote the faith that people have in Christ: this renders the genitive as objective (Christ is the object of human faith). These are two very different ideas, especially when one considers Reformation-era debates about the role of faith in God's plan of salvation. Which meaning does Paul use when he says that God makes people righteous through *pistis Christou?* Does he mean "faith in Christ" or "the faith of Christ"? Paul uses this key phrase twice when he explains the essence of his gospel in Rom 3:21–26, a passage which deserves close examination.

The NRSV, like most translations, favors the objective rendering ("faith in Christ") but also acknowledges in a footnote the subjective rendering as a possible translation. In this exercise—whether in a discussion format or in an essay assignment—students should consider each of the passages listed above in which the phrase in question appears, asking whether the objective or the subjective rendering makes the most sense in its literary context. Questions to address include: (1) For each reading ("the faith of Christ" versus "faith in Christ"), what is the implied relationship for Paul between Christology and soteriology, that is, between the role of Christ and God's plan for salvation? (2) What does each reading suggest about the importance for Paul of the humanity and the story of Jesus? (See esp. Rom 5:19, where Paul discusses the importance of Christ's obedience in contrast to Adam's disobedience.) (3) What are the implications of "the faith of Christ" for Christian discipleship? (Cf. Rom 15:1–3, where Paul offers Christ as an example of building up others rather than pleasing himself.)

For further reading, see R. B. Hays, "*Pistis* and Pauline Christology: What Is at Stake?" in *Pauline Theology. Volume IV: Looking Back, Pressing On* (ed. E. E. Johnson and D. M. Hay; Atlanta: Scholars Press, 1997), 35–60. In addition, see J. D. G. Dunn, "Once More, *Pistis Christou*," in the same volume, 61–81. Hays argues for the subjective genitive, Dunn for the objective genitive.

Thomas D. Stegman

234. THE LETTER TO THE ROMANS
AND PAULINE THEOLOGICAL CONCEPTS

Whether it is teaching a Bible survey course to first-year students or an upper division course on the letters and theology of Paul, it is a challenge to help students gain some sense for the thick theological terminology one encounters. Terms such as "justification," "law," "gospel," or "freedom" seem simple but in the interpretive traditions have grown complex and acquired technical definitions. It is helpful to approach these concepts in a way that connects with student experience. To that end I use the film *Ferris Bueller's Day Off* as an introduction to basic Pauline concepts.

The film, directed by John Hughes, was released in 1986. Despite its age, a very high percentage of my students are familiar with the film. Many lines from the film have become embedded in popular culture. When I announce in class that we will use it to explain Paul's letter to the Romans, there is usually some combination of incredulity and interest. In the class period prior to using the film I typically introduce Gal 1–5 or Rom 1–8. This introduction attends to issues such as historical context, rhetorical shape, and the principle arguments of the letters. I use the film on the day in which I plan to address theological issues and content.

On the day I use the film segments I distribute a handout which describes the four key characters: Ed Rooney, the assistant principal; Cameron, the friend of Ferris; Jean, Ferris' sister; and Ferris himself. Rooney represents the Pauline concept of the law which seeks to suppress freedom. At the 14–minute mark in the film, for example, Rooney expresses the need to eradicate Ferris' behavior or else it will infect the whole school. Ferris, consequently, represents the freedom which the law seeks to suppress. It is interesting to note that at the 15–minute mark Grace, Rooney's secretary, terms Ferris a "righteous dude." Ferris' sister Jean represents a kind of self-righteousness which sees freedom as a zero-sum game. She perceives Ferris' freedom as robbing her. Finally Cameron, the friend, represents a person in bondage to some kind of wrathful god. The "car," a Ferarri which figures prominently in the climax, is a sort of idol of that wrathful deity.

With that introduction I usually show a 15–20 minute segment that opens with the swimming pool scene (starting at the 75–minute mark). At the beginning of the excerpt, Cameron is "catatonic" at the edge of the pool after realizing that he has violated his father's command regarding the use of the prize Ferrari and that now he will be found out. Cameron symbolically drowns and is rescued by Ferris. At this point the film weaves the parallel stories of Jean and Cameron.

Jean is in the police station because she has been suspected of a false police call. While waiting for her mother to pick her up, Jean waits with an insightful juvenile delinquent. He unmasks her hatred of her brother and notes her problem lies within her and not outside. Meanwhile, back at the family garage, Cameron and Ferris have the Ferrari on a jack running in reverse hoping to take miles off the odometer. While this is going on Cameron starts kicking the car and shouting, "Who do you love, a car?" Bad becomes worse as the car falls off the jack and roaring in reverse flies out the plate glass wall at the back of the garage and crashes in the ravine below. What seems to be disaster now becomes a point of reversal. Rather than being devastated, Cameron announces that now he will be fine.

The climactic points of the stories of Jean and Cameron both provide experiential examples of concepts of salvation and freedom. I usually prepare a handout for students to make notes on during the film. This handout has questions regarding the relationship between Cameron and his father and between Jean and her brother Ferris. In the discussion which follows the film clip I ask the class to explain the meaning of Cameron's speech while he is smashing the car. I also ask the class to listen carefully to the soundtrack in the pivotal scenes with Jean in the police station and Cameron with the car. In both cases there is no background music until the climax or moment of insight is reached. The intention is to make students aware of the nature of the experience. What does it mean, for example, when Ferris says that Cameron will be okay, for the first time in his life?

Finally, I ask students to describe Ferris' role in the film. Is he the focus of the film or is he the agent of change for others whose stories are the real focus? A concluding question asks students to reflect on why they like the film. I argue that there is a performative character to the film in that it not only tells a story but, like Pauline proclamation, does something to the audience which changes their situation.

Philip A. Quanbeck II

235. TRANSLATION AND INTERPRETATION: SLAVE OR SERVANT IN ROMANS 1:1?

The biblical courses I teach are for a general student audience and must rely on English translation. Few, if any, students have studied classical languages. The problem for the reader, as a consequence, is that the English translation can give a false sense of security, namely, that meaning is easily achieved or recognized. It is also the case that, even though we use an annotated study Bible, students do not necessarily see the purpose of the little translation notes tucked in at the bottom of the page. The purpose of this exercise is to help the class see that it is no simple matter to cross time and culture to render a text in modern English. The exercise also seeks to show that translation might also reflect that which the audience wants to hear.

First, I have the class read aloud from their study Bibles the NRSV translation of Rom 1:1: "Paul a servant of Jesus Christ ..." Then I ask them to find the translation footnote for the word "servant." The note simply reads, "Gk slave." Next I usually distribute a handout which has at the top the phrase "Paul a *doulos* of Jesus Christ." I note on the handout and aloud to the class that the Greek word which is transliterated in the passage can be translated either as "servant" or as "slave." I will also note that the translators show their ambivalence in the way they have printed the text. At this point the class is asked either individually or in pairs to write out their preferred translation. One ground rule: they must choose either "servant" or "slave" but not both. Hedging is not allowed. They are also asked to write out reasons to support their choice of translation. We then take a class vote on the translation. Most in the class will choose "servant." I then ask individuals to give reasons for their choices. Those stated reasons or rationales then provide a way of talking about the historical, theological, and audience-oriented issues of translations.

Typical translation rationales include the following:

1. "Servant sounds better." This of course leads to the questions about why it sounds better to the modern ear and how history and culture shape our hearing. Initially we reflect on how the Pauline audience might have heard the term "slave" in the first century. Then we reflect on what shapes the modern audience's hearing of the term "slave." American history and the tragic experience of slavery certainly shapes the contemporary hearing.

2. "A servant has a choice." This is an example of translation as theological interpretation. This rationale leads to a theological discussion about the Pauline concepts of faith and the freedom of the will, and provides a window into the ways in which theologies and anthropologies interact. American Protestantism, for example, has differing understandings of faith as choice. How, the class is asked, can we support our theologically charged translation on the basis of the Pauline texts as a whole and not simply our personal preferences? This usually leads to an engaging discussion of free will and Pauline concepts of sin as constraining the will.

3. "Do we have to choose? Can't we just leave the text as *doulos?*" This question raises the need for translation and interpretation.

4. "What about slave?" If no one in the class has proposed "slave" for their translation I will make that proposal. The class is then asked to reflect on how the choice shapes their hearing of the text and their response.

Philip A. Quanbeck II

236. ROMANS 13:1–7: CHURCH AND STATE

Church-state issues are constantly in the news in the United States, whether it is the posting of the Ten Commandments in courts or the role

of nativity scenes in public places. With topics such as these as an introduction, the class turns to Rom 13. To get an idea of the background to
the passage, I have students read a passage from Tacitus (*Ann.* 13.50–51).
This text describes the unrest caused by taxation and Nero's subsequent
reform. Nero's decision precedes the writing of Romans by only a year or
two. In other words, there was a problem with taxes at the time of the
writing of Romans.

I then ask students to consider the following scenario in light of Rom
13:1 ("Let every person be subject to the governing authorities. For there
is no authority except from God, and those that exist have been instituted
by God"): "Suppose that you reside in the American colonies in March
1775 (before the battles of Lexington and Concord). The discussion arises
at church whether Christians should overthrow the rule of George III.
What is your advice? What would you do if asked to participate in a revolution against Britain? On what basis, if any, do you think that it is
appropriate for a Christian to participate in the overthrow of a ruler?
Refer to Rom 13:1–7 in your answer."

I have used this exercise in different ways. I have divided the class
into two groups with each group taking a different position. I have also
played devil's advocate against the class. I have also had them write up
their reflections before coming to class. In these discussions, international
students (especially English and Canadian) create a wonderful dynamic
and preclude easy answers to the scenario. Discussion points that typically arise include the implication of a ruler as "God's servant" for
"good" (v. 4), the role of "conscience" (v. 5), and the difference between
first-century Roman rule and democracy.

After discussing the scenario, the students look forward to the
exegetical work on Rom 13. The exercise also works well with discussions
of hermeneutics—how Christians apply Scripture to contemporary
issues. Other hermeneutical issues that often arise include "bearing the
sword" (v. 4) in connection with the death penalty, "being subject to the
governing authorities" and the prevalence of speeding and the use of
radar detectors, and the role of "honor" and jokes about the president.

Kenneth L. Cukrowski

237. "THE RIGHTEOUSNESS OF GOD"
IN PAUL'S LETTER TO THE ROMANS

Righteousness is a central theme in Paul's Letter to the Romans. Indeed, if
a teacher had only one class period in which to present this magisterial

writing, I would recommend tracing what Paul says about "the righteousness of God," which appears in Romans more than in any other Pauline text.

In many streams of Christian tradition, "the righteousness of God" has been understood in anthropological and individualistic terms. It has been interpreted to signify, for example, the righteous standing that God imputes to individuals or the morality and piety that avail a person before God. A recent line of scholarship has challenged this anthropocentric interpretation of the righteousness of God. According to Paul, so goes the argument, "righteousness" belongs primarily to God. First, righteousness is an attribute or quality of God, referring to God's justice and covenant faithfulness. Second, righteousness is an activity of God whereby God intervenes to right the wrongs of a world marked by sin and suffering, and fulfills the covenant made with Abraham to create a new family consisting of Jews and Gentiles. God's righteousness was manifested most dramatically when God sent the Son, Messiah Jesus, whose death on the cross revealed God's love.

The key phrase "the righteousness of God" appears at three pivotal points of Paul's argument in Romans: 1:17 (a verse widely regarded as the "thesis statement" of the letter); 3:21–31 (a restatement and amplification of this thesis statement); and 10:3–4 (in the midst of a larger unit in which Paul discusses God's faithfulness to God's promises [chs. 9–11]).

There are several places in Romans where Paul employs the term "righteousness" as shorthand for what he has said about the revelation of God's righteousness through Messiah Jesus' death and resurrection: 5:21 ("righteousness leading to life"); 6:18 (Christians are "slaves of righteousness"); 8:10 (the indwelling Spirit of Christ gives us life "because of righteousness"); and 14:17 ("the Kingdom of God is not food and drink but righteousness and peace and joy in the Holy Spirit").

After students have read Romans and examined these texts individually or in small groups, discussion may focus on the following questions: (1) What are the implications of placing the emphasis on God's righteousness rather than on human righteousness? (2) What does Jesus reveal about God's righteousness and justice? (3) How do human beings participate in God's ongoing revelation of righteousness? (4) What role does the Spirit play? For further reading, see N. T. Wright, *What Saint Paul Really Said: Was Paul of Tarsus the Real Founder of Christianity?* (Grand Rapids: Eerdmans, 1997), 95–111. The chart on p. 101 is particularly helpful.

Thomas D. Stegman

238. 1 CORINTHIANS 10: CHURCH AND THE CITY

The church at Corinth struggled with the degree to which Christians can be "in the world but not of it." Throughout history, Christian responses to this question have varied from total separation to full involvement, from boycotts to civil disobedience. What, if any, are the limits to Christian participation in society? What principles should Christians use when evaluating their actions?

To help students see that the issues facing the Corinthians are not so different from those facing Christians today, I ask them—either on their own or in groups—to respond to the following scenarios: (1) You are a sculptor asked to sculpt a statue of Venus for a company's lobby. Do you accept the job? What is the rationale for your decision? (2) As a sculptor, you are asked to sculpt a Buddha for a temple. Do you accept the job? What is the rationale for your decision? (3) Is there anything a Christian sculptor should not sculpt? What is the rationale for your decision? (4) You are a landscape designer. Hooters Restaurant, (in)famous for exploiting the female form in its advertising and in the service it provides, asks you to do the landscaping for its new restaurant. Do you take the job? Do you put your company's sign up? What is your rationale? (5) You work for a landscape designer that is putting in the landscaping for Hooters. What do you tell your boss? Issues that the students typically address include the intent of an action, the role of conscience, influence on another person, and support of something sinful.

I vary the examples so as to choose those ones that make the class most uncomfortable. I want the students to consider the warrants for their decisions and to think constructively about how they would respond. Looking at Paul's pastoral considerations (1 Cor 10:23–24; 10:31–11:1), as well as at Paul's "case studies" in 10:25–30, we attempt to extract principles from the text and then compare them to the principles that the students articulated in the above scenarios. Pastoral considerations typically include the following items: the benefit and edification of others (10:24); seeking the good of one's neighbor (10:25); glorifying God (10:31); the salvation of others (10:32–33); and the imitation of Christ (11:1). Paul's case studies in 10:25–30 show remarkable freedom, ranging from our general interaction with society when shopping at the "meat market" (10:25–26) to our personal interaction with a non-Christian at a private meal (10:27). Nevertheless, someone else's "conscience"—likely another Christian's in 10:28—can still play a role in the decision-making process.

Kenneth L. Cukrowski

239. DISCIPLINE IN PAULINE
COMMUNITIES (1 CORINTHIANS 5)

Christians have always misbehaved and will likely continue to do so. This exercise considers the challenges such behaviors present to church communities in connection with Paul's dealings with the Corinthians. As a class, we read 1 Cor 5:1–13, where Paul discusses the case of the man who is sleeping with his father's wife. I then tell the class, "You are an elder [pick your own polity] in an elders' meeting discussing this case. Formulate a response to this case and answer the following questions: What actions do you take? What are the principles that guide you? What are the goals of your actions? What additional information would you like to know?"

We then work through 1 Cor 5 discussing the students' responses. Some students find it difficult to advocate disciplinary action because it would mean "judging others" (5:12); other students think that the man should be immediately removed from the community (5:2) and social contact should be limited or cease (5:9, 11). In terms of guiding principles, two show up most often: (1) sin should prompt Christians "to mourn" (5:2); and (2) discipline is a communal activity (5:4). Regarding goals, the students most often mention "to save the man" (5:5) and "to deal with the man's sin" (5:5). Some students even add "to preserve the identity and purity of the community" (5:6–8).

Finally, when I ask what additional information would be helpful to know, other questions arise: How did this man come to live with his father's wife? What happened to the father? Why doesn't Paul directly address the man? Is the man present when Paul's letter is read? How long had this situation been going on? What role did the church play in this situation? What actions has the church taken to this point? Why does Paul call the church "arrogant" (5:2)? What does it mean "to deliver this man to Satan" (5:5)? What did the church do after reading Paul's letter? How did churches remove someone from the community (5:2)? How did churches treat someone who was expelled (5:11)? What happened to the man in the end? These questions illustrate how specific details may influence the church's response and how our knowledge of the original context can be quite limited.

We also look at other passages that address "church discipline," trying to piece together a fuller picture of Pauline thought and practice: Rom 16:17–19; 1 Cor 16:22; 2 Cor 2:5–11; 13:1–2; Gal 6:1–5; Col 3:13; 2 Thess 3:6–15; 1 Tim 1:18–20; 5:19–22; 2 Tim 3:5; Titus 3:10–11. These individual texts are "snapshots" or individual "frames" of a fragmentary and out-of-sequence movie. The challenge is to "edit" the frames so that we can "re-view the film." Using this movie metaphor, I ask them to place

NEW TESTAMENT

the texts ("frames") in chronological order, reconstructing the procedures that might have taken place from the initial contact to the final action in an extreme case.

Discussion points that typically arise include the following items pertaining to the ancient as well as to contemporary settings: Is it possible to arrive at a description of a process? Were there one or many procedures? Which behaviors merit church discipline? How does one decide when to "draw a line" and when to continue working with someone? How feasible is such a process in our changed cultural context (e.g., the disciplined member can simply go to another congregation)? What is the effect on Christian identity when discipline is not maintained? What are the goals of such a process (punitive versus redemptive)? How is one to re-integrate members into the community once the process is concluded? What is the mechanism for communicating such decisions to other congregations? What are the legal aspects of church discipline in the modern context? Do specific contemporary examples provide fresh insight into the dynamics at play in Corinth? For additional background, see E. Schmidt, "Discipline," in *Dictionary of Paul and His Letters* (ed. G. F. Hawthorne and R. P. Martin; Downers Grove, IL: InterVarsity, 1993), 214–18.

Kenneth L. Cukrowski

240. A THEOLOGY OF SEXUALITY
(1 CORINTHIANS 6:12–20)

In my experience, sexuality is not addressed well, if at all, in churches. For instance, at youth events I often hear the question, "How far can I go?" I tell my students that this is not the most appropriate question, explaining as follows: What if I were to ask my wife, "How much time can I spend with other women, and it will be fine with you?" Or, "How intimate can I be with other women, and it will be fine with you?" What do you think her response would be? Naturally, they see such questions as absurd. Such a conversation would not likely promote a healthy marital relationship; it essentially assumes that "How close can I get to sin?" is an appropriate question for a Christian to ask. This exercise examines 1 Cor 6:12–20 as a first step in recovering a theology of sexuality and the body.

I ask my students to consider the following scenario: A parent sits down to have "the talk" about sex with a son or daughter. What reasons do parents give for remaining chaste? After listing all the reasons, I ask which ones are specifically Christian (often none are). I then ask the class to read 1 Cor 6:12–20 and tell me what theological warrants Paul gives. Key points that typically arise include the following items: the purpose of the body in 6:13; the significance of the body in light of the cross in 6:14; the implications of being in Christ (6:15–17); the use of a command in 6:18; how often commands appear without warrants in Christian discussions of ethics (i.e., merely lists of dos and don'ts); the appeal to Christian identity (i.e., Christians as a temple of the Holy Spirit and redeemed slaves in 6:19–20); the positive call for the use of the body as the climax of Paul's argument in 6:20.

At that point, we discuss Paul's theology of sexuality and the body, looking at his discussion of freedom and the use of the body in 1 Cor 6:12–13. After that discussion, I challenge the class to apply our reflection on the whole passage to other Christian uses of the body, such as dieting, exercise, abortion, sleep deprivation, and obesity. For example, often when Christians discuss any one of these topics, there is nothing specifically Christian about the reflection (Atkins diet versus South Beach diet, the right number of fat grams, the best types of fats, etc.). Furthermore, when there is some kind of specifically Christian appeal, rarely is that appeal a theological one. For instance, perhaps we should ask, "If our bodies are a 'temple of the Holy Spirit' (i.e., not belonging to us and designed to be holy), how should that identity shape our thinking on abortion?" Instead, the language usually centers on "rights"—be it the "right to life" or the right to control "my own body." My conviction is that deliberation that begins with our theological identity and purpose will drastically change, if not transform, Christian ethical reflection and behavior.

Kenneth L. Cukrowski

241. RE-CREATING THE CORINTHIAN COMMUNITY

When students read 1 Corinthians, they sometimes move too quickly toward accepting Paul's perspective as the only one. Involvement in the roles of the members of the Corinthian community enables students to understand and empathize with them so that they can gain a better sense of their conflicts and their perspectives.

In addition to reading 1 Corinthians, prior to class students should gain some familiarity (via lecture or assigned reading from one of the standard commentaries) with the problems of pre-gnosticism and spiritual enthusiasm that, according to many scholars, may have produced the tensions reflected in the letter. In class, put students in separate groups to role-play the problems concerning factions, incest, lawsuits, brothels/temple prostitution, excessive freedom, circumcision, marriage, wearing veils, speaking in tongues, spiritual gifts, eating idol meat, and the resurrection. Because there are multiple factions at Corinth created by lines drawn in different ways in relation to different controversial issues, I usually give cards to each person that specify whether they are educated or uneducated, wealthy or poor, aristocratic or a slave, male or female, Jew or Gentile. After they discuss how they will recreate the assigned controversy on the basis of their assigned "identity," ask each group to perform their short skit and move quickly from group to group, going back later if they have more to add. Moving quickly will help to create the sense of upheaval that the letter conveys.

When the exercise is exhausted, ask students how it might have felt to be a part of this community and in what ways at least some of the Corinthians' theological beliefs differed from Paul's. If the community were to split into two smaller communities, is it possible to predict which sides in which controversies would align themselves? Or are the divisions not so simple? An additional twist to the exercise is to have students write a letter responding to Paul's directives on a given issue, again assuming the perspective of their assigned "identity." (For other exercises involving role-play, see §§91, 142, 161, 199, 203, 246, 265.)

Emily R. Cheney

242. PAUL AND WOMEN (1 CORINTHIANS)

During the opening session in an introductory course on Paul, I invite students to write down one or two things that they "appreciate" about Paul or his letters, as well as one or two things that they find "troubling or confusing." Invariably, a large number of students will list "his attitude toward women" as one of the issues that they find most troubling about the Apostle. Later in the semester, during our discussion of the Corinthian correspondence, we spend some time talking about the roles of women in the Pauline churches. To assist students in their assessment of the evidence, I ask them to complete the following exercise at home and to bring their results to class. During the class session, we discuss what they have discovered, and then I follow up with a short lecture on roles of women in the Pauline churches.

The take-home exercise reads as follows: "Carefully read through 1 Corinthians. Identify all the passages that have to do with women and briefly list them on a sheet of paper (include the gist of what the passage says; i.e., "keep quiet in church"). Do not limit yourself to commands or exhortations about women, but also passages that mention women as characters. Do you note any inconsistencies? Where? What are they? Based on what you have uncovered, what would you say is 'Paul's attitude toward women' reflected in 1 Corinthians?"

The data generated by this exercise serve as the basis for lecture and discussion of the roles of women in the Pauline churches. We cover issues such as (1) the practices in which women are involved in the Pauline churches (e.g., hosting a house church, praying and prophesying, etc.); (2) the inconsistencies regarding what Paul says about women (e.g., 1 Cor 11:3–16 clearly indicates that women pray and prophesy publicly, while 1 Cor 14 suppresses the public role of women in the assembly); and (3) scholarly treatments of these inconsistencies (e.g., noting cultural expectations regarding proper decorum in worship [1 Cor 11:3–16], or the question of interpolation in 1 Cor 14:34–35). (For other exercises on women in biblical texts, see §§50, 55, 154, 191, 226, 267.)

Audrey West

243. SECOND CORINTHIANS AND PARTITION THEORIES

The goal of this exercise is (1) to introduce students to partition theories vis-à-vis 2 Corinthians, (2) to offer a flavor of the questions that scholars raise when investigating this letter, and (3) to provoke critical reflection on the larger significance of what may seem like an arcane academic debate.

Critical investigation of 2 Corinthians has led many scholars to conclude that the canonical text is actually a compilation of two or more letters (or parts of letters). Interpreters have detected several literary "seams" in the text as it now stands, places where the coherence of Paul's presentation seems shaky. For example, at 2 Cor 9:15/10:1, why would Paul, after emphasizing his reconciliation with the Corinthians (7:5–16), and after requesting that they contribute generously to his collection for the church in Jerusalem (8:1–9:15), proceed to harangue and threaten them (10:1)? At 8:24/9:1, why does Paul seem to introduce the collection as a new topic (9:1) when he has just given a long exhortation concerning it (8:1–24)? At 2:13/2:14, why does Paul suddenly interrupt his description of his anxiety over finding Titus (2:12–13) with an exclamation of thanksgiving and a long description of his apostleship (2:14)? At 7:4/7:5, is it not odd that Paul then recounts his joyful reunion with Titus several chapters later, and seemingly from out of the blue (7:5)? At 6:13/6:14 and 7:1/7:2, why does Paul use such unusual phraseology and imagery in 6:14–7:1, a passage that seems to intrude upon two invitations to the Corinthians to open their hearts to him (6:13 and 7:2)?

Scholars have also puzzled over confusing references to Paul and his dealings with the Corinthian church. For instance, Paul tells the Corinthians that he is coming to visit them for the third time (12:14; 13:1). If his first visit was when he founded the church in Corinth, what occasioned the second visit? And what happened during this second visit, which the apostle describes as "painful" (2:1)? How is one to reconcile the change in Paul's travel plans (1:15–17; cf. 1 Cor 16:1–4)? What was the content of the so-called "tearful letter" (2 Cor 2:4; 7:8–12)? Is it no longer extant, or is it embedded within the text of 2 Corinthians? Who was the person who offended Paul (2:5–11; 7:12), and what was the nature of his offense? Was there any relationship between the "offender" and the opposition to Paul to which he alludes in 10:2, 10–11, and 11:13–23? Is this opposition to be identified with or distinguished from a group he derisively calls "the superlative apostles" (11:5; 12:11)? What was the ideology of the opposition? Were they advocates of observing the Jewish Law (3:7–18)? Were they gnostics or pneumatics? How many visits did Titus make to Corinth, and how many co-workers went with him (7:6–16; cf. 8:16–24; 12:17–18)?

To solve these puzzles, scholars have exerted pressure on these seams to break the canonical letter into several pieces (called partitions). Four main partition theories have been proposed. When presenting each, students should comment on which seems the most compelling. With what questions or problems do each of these theories leave us? One might assign a different theory to a different group or conduct the whole discussion as a plenary:

1. 2 Corinthians consists of parts of two original letters: Letter A (written first) = chapters 1–9; and Letter B = chapters 10–13. This theory seeks to explain the change in subject and mood beginning in 10:1. It also claims to account for the references to Titus: what 8:16–24 announces as a future event, 12:17–18 now looks back to as having already happened. The reason Paul wrote Letter B, according to this theory, is that his rivals (either newly arrived, or back on the scene) have turned the Corinthians against him.

2. Letter A = chapters 10–13; and Letter B = chapters 1–9. This theory, like the first, exploits the same literary seam, but proposes the opposite sequence of letters. According to this hypothesis, Letter A, with all its rancor, is (at least part of) the "tearful letter" referred to in 2:4. Paul then wrote Letter B—which is marked by notes of reconciliation—after the Corinthians responded appropriately to his tearful letter.

3. Letter A = 2:14–7:4 (minus 6:14–7:1) + chapters 10–13 + chapters 9; and Letter B = 1:1–2:13 + 7:5–8:24. In this theory, the longer Letter A is the tearful letter, which includes Paul's *apologia* for his apostleship (2:14–7:4), and Letter B is the letter of reconciliation that followed. This hypothesis removes what is considered to be a hiatus in Paul's account of looking for and finding Titus (2:12–13 and 7:5).

4. Letter A = 2:14–7:4 (minus 6:14–7:1); Letter B = chapters 10–13; Letter C = 1:1–2:13 + 7:5–8:24; Letter D = chapter 9. Paul wrote Letter A when he received information that his apostleship was being criticized. After a painful visit, Paul wrote Letter B, which catalyzed reconciliation with the Corinthians and their renewed participation in the collection (Letters C and D).

Once the various partition theories are set forth, discuss the following additional questions: If 2 Corinthians was originally partitioned, how did the text end up in its final (canonical) form? If the text as it now stands was not what Paul intended, was it in any way illegitimate for later editors to produce it? Are the literary and historical "problems" of 2 Corinthians overstated? Can one offer a more plausible explanation for Paul's literary presentation and historical references based on the text as it now stands? How do the editors of the Bible we are reading deal with these "seams" (e.g., in their typesetting of the text or the addition of section headings)? In what ways, if any, is it important to solve these interpretive problems? Is the matter of significance only for scholars, or might there be important implications for contemporary Christian communities as well?

Thomas D. Stegman

244. PAUL'S LETTER TO THE PHILIPPIANS: A LESSON IN CITIZENSHIP

Even in a course devoted to Paul, there is not adequate time to delve into the intricacies of his theology or fully to cover his approach to ministry. Focusing on one metaphor or concept in a single letter, however, gives students a manageable platform from which to examine Paul's theology, ethics, and rhetorical style. This exercise focuses on Paul's use of citizenship in Philippians.

The class period before the exercise, I hand out the four chapters of Philippians on photocopied pages and ask the students to find Phil 1:27. I read this verse aloud and translate the Greek literally: "*be worthy citizens of the gospel of Christ.*" Then I read Phil 3:20, where Paul reminds the

Philippians that their "citizenship (or commonwealth) is in heaven." Paul is using the metaphor of "citizenship" to teach the Philippians how they should live. For homework, students are to read carefully the photocopied letter and highlight all the characteristics of "a worthy citizen." Then they read a second time and circle all groups or individuals who are either worthy citizens or enemies of the "heavenly" commonwealth.

When class meets again, I give a brief introduction to the letter that covers Paul's situation and the historical background of Philippi. Paul is writing from prison (Phil 1:12–14) and thanks the Philippians for their financial support in his humble situation. They keep in contact by exchanging letters and delegates (Timothy and Epaphroditus). The legacy of their city includes the honor of Roman citizenship (granted in 42 B.C.E.) and a civic life modeled on Rome's constitution. In other words, although the recipients of Paul's letter live in Macedonia, they are technically citizens of Rome and follow its laws. This background is important because the situation of the Philippians' Roman citizenship parallels the situation of their "heavenly" citizenship and constitution.

To open up the concepts of citizenship, constitution, and nation-state, the class brainstorms characteristics of the ideal U.S. citizen (one who defends the constitution, obeys the laws, pays taxes, votes, respects all people, speaks out for freedom and justice, etc.). I ask about the function of laws, the role of the constitution, how citizens relate to one another and to their enemies, and how one learns to be a citizen. I may also ask the class to name a historical figure that fits the ideal, or how they would characterize an enemy of the state.

Next, working in groups of four, the students construct a profile of *Paul's* ideal citizen using their highlighted photocopies of the letter. Their profiles should include: citizens stand united, love others, put other people first, humble themselves, think the same way, give gifts, pray for each other, visit one another, obey, and do not argue or cling to disagreements. After constructing a profile, each group selects one figure from the letter who exemplifies the ideal citizen, and one figure (or group) who does not.

Once students have made their profile and chosen an ideal figure, discussion may pursue a number of issues:

Structure of the letter. Paul writes Philippians as a series of ethical examples leading up to, and following from, Christ's paradigmatic example in 2:6–11. One way to show students this structure is to ask them to write on the board the ideal citizen and "enemy" they chose from the letter. The ideals may include the loving brothers (1:15–18), Timothy (2:19–24), Epaphroditus (2:25–30), Paul (1:9–11, 21–26; 2:17–18; 3:7–16), and the Philippians themselves (1:19; 4.10–18). The enemies include the antagonistic brothers (1:15–18), those who oppose (1:28), the enemies of the cross (3:18–21), and possibly Euodia and Syntyche (4:2). By setting the examples in their order of appearance, it becomes clear that Christ's example is the centerpiece of the letter, and the examples radiate out from him. It also becomes clear that Paul alternates positive and negative examples throughout the letter, but focuses more attention on the positive. Finally, all of the examples lead up to the corrections to behavior Paul makes in chapter 4.

Christology. A constitution defines how citizens are to order their lives together. What does Paul present as the constitution for the heavenly citizens? This idea is less obvious, but if students have identified Christ as the centerpiece of the examples in the letter, connecting Christ to the idea of a constitution follows. Paul uses the same phrases for Christ in 2:5–11 to describe the human examples in the letter (Epaphroditus: 2:30; cf. 2:8; Paul and Timothy: 1:1; cf. 2:7; the Philippians: 2:12; cf. 2:8). Paul does not apply all of the language ("until death," humility, obedience) from 2:6–11 to any one person. But the whole community together constitutes the "body" of Christ—the body politic. This raises the point that Paul's focus was corporate, rather than individual. The ruler of the political body is the "Savior," Christ (2:10; 3:20), who is the pattern that citizens follow. In other words, what the Philippians believe about Christ (Christology) determines the ethics of the community (ecclesiology).

Ethics and Politics. To address the political tensions in the letter, I ask: Where do the Philippians practice their citizenship? They are citizens of Rome, but Paul tells them they are citizens "of heaven." What kinds of tensions arise when someone has dual citizenship, or is a resident with a green card sending money to family in another homeland? What kinds of pressures might arise for the community (particularly with their "enemies") as they try to live as citizens of heaven in the world of Empire? One can move from this discussion into political tensions for churches today.

Soteriology. The other side of political tension is soteriological tension. Paul presents salvation as a present reality that is both "now and not yet." What does Paul means by "salvation" (1:19, 28; 2:12–13; 3:20)? What does salvation have to do with citizenship (1:27–28)? On the one hand, salvation means belonging to a "heavenly" commonwealth where Christ reigns as "Savior," the ultimate "head of state." On the other hand, the Philippians are to "be worthy citizens" in the present. The ethical life of the community manifests their salvation (1:28; 2:13–14) on earth. But salvation is only fully realized in a future time and place. The soteriological tension is spatial (earth/heaven), just like the Philippians' political citizenship in Rome, and is also temporal—lived out in the present but consummated in the future. Students may also note the way that political language, theological language, and ethical language are hopelessly intertwined, much like the "dual" citizenships being lived out in the U.S. today.

One might conduct a similar exercise using "friendship." Although Paul never uses the term "friend," when students first construct a description of an "ideal friend," they quickly recognize the ancient phrases that characterize friendship among the Philippians.

Julia Lambert Fogg

245. THE THANKSGIVING AS EPISTOLARY PREVIEW (PHILEMON)

Early in their study of the Pauline corpus, it is helpful for students to be able to recognize the formal structure of Paul's letters and to discern the function of each structural element in the overall rhetoric of a particular letter. The goal of this exercise is to demonstrate the general principle that the greeting/thanksgiving introduces or previews themes that will be addressed in the rest of the letter. Students literally "draw" the connections between words and ideas found in the thanksgiving and similar words and ideas found in the rest of the letter. The resulting map provides a visual overview of significant themes as well as the interconnections between the thanksgiving and the rest of the letter. This exercise is especially helpful for students who tend to be visual learners.

After offering a mini-lecture on epistolary form (e.g., Greeting, Thanksgiving, Body/Exhortation, Conclusion), I provide the students with a one-page copy of the text of Philemon. This exercise would work with any of the Pauline epistles (with the exception of Galatians), but Philemon is particularly useful because it is so short and the text can fit on one page. It is important for the text to fit on the front of one page, in order that the whole of the letter is visible at a glance.

I invite students to work in groups of two or three. Their task is to circle key words or ideas in the greeting and thanksgiving (vv. 1–7), and then to note where (and whether) those words or ideas occur again in the rest of the letter. I ask them to draw a line from the first occurrence of the word or theme to each subsequent occurrence, with the end result looking something like a spider-web of connections.

For example, readers of the NRSV translation might note the following: terms of fictive kinship (brother or sister: vv. 1, 2, 7, 16, 20; father: vv. 3, 10); love (vv. 5, 7, 9); "good" (vv. 6, 14); prisoner/imprisonment (vv. 1, 9, 10, 13); "heart" (vv. 7, 12, 20); "my prayers" (v. 4); "your prayers" (v. 22). Students using a Greek translation will be able to notice additional repetitions, e.g., *syn-* compounds (vv. 1, 2, 23); words with the root *koin-* (vv. 6, 17); and so forth.

Once students have completed the exercise, we discuss as a class how the repetition of words and phrases "works" in the letter to help persuade Philemon to do what Paul wants him to do. By witnessing the careful construction of even so short a letter, students come away with a greater appreciation for the way scholars pay close attention to literally every word Paul writes.

Audrey West

246. READING PHILEMON

For many people, understandings of slavery in the United States have informed assumptions about slavery in antiquity. Much of the scholarly literature on Philemon asserts that Onesimus was a runaway slave, even though the text says nothing of the sort. The objective of this exercise is to demonstrate how cultural assumptions and social location are an implicit part of the interpretive process.

Before class the students read Philemon and answer the following questions: (1) Who is Onesimus? (2) How did Onesimus meet Paul? (3) What type of relationship develops between Paul and Onesimus? (4) What type of relationship does Paul desire to have with Onesimus? (5) What is Paul's advice to Philemon? (6) What is Paul's position on slavery?

In class the students are divided into four groups: (1) Philemon and his family, (2) Onesimus and his family, (3) slave-holding members of the Christian community, and (4) slaves within the Christian community. Members of each group pretend they have just heard Paul's letter to Philemon read. As a group, they have to prepare a collective response to the advice in the letter. As each group attempts to prepare its collective response, students quickly realize they do not all interpret the text the same way. Members within each group end up having to negotiate their differences in order to come up with a collective response. After preparing responses, each group delivers its response to the rest of the class. Each group usually ends up interpreting the advice in a way that promotes the interest of that particular group. We discuss how it is that each group came to different conclusions about the meaning of the same text, and what that suggests about the motivations and ideologies at work within the interpretive process.

After our discussion, students are asked to move to the group that gave a presentation closest to their own personal interpretation of Paul's letter to Philemon. I then ask one question of the students who changed groups and one question of every student. The question to those who changed groups is: "Why did you advocate for an interpretation different from the one you believed?" Usually some students respond that they advocated for what they thought was in the best interest of the group to which they belonged, even though it went against what they believe the text means. This helps highlight the influence of social location in general on the interpretive process. The question I ask to everyone is: "How did your current social location affect which group interpretation you most agreed with?" This question helps students recognize the impact of their own social location on their interpretive process.

We conclude by doing a close reading of the text to see if we can come to any agreement regarding the six questions they each answered before class. I challenge the depiction of Onesimus as a runaway slave by asking, "Why would a runaway slave who had allegedly stolen money from his master go visit a known friend of his master in jail?" I then present an alternative to the dominant construal. I point out that slaves in antiquity often held positions of responsibility within households such as managing property and finances. In Luke 16:1–13 we find an account of a slave, who—possibly like Onesimus—had mismanaged his master's assets. I then point out that it was common practice for slaves to seek the intervention of a third party to plead their case. I propose that Onesimus, knowing that Paul was a friend of Philemon, sought out Paul to speak on his behalf to Philemon. While visiting Paul, Onesimus became a believer. Paul writes Philemon asking that Philemon treat Onesimus as a brother rather than a slave. He also suggests that Philemon give Onesimus to Paul (vv. 13–14), which challenges the idea that Paul was asking for Onesimus's freedom (how does one give a "free" person to someone else?). While many Christians would like to believe that Paul wanted Philemon to free his slave, the institution of slavery was taken for granted as fundamental to the social, economic, and political structures of Roman society. There is nothing in the text to suggest that Paul was speaking out against the institution of slavery. (For other exercises involving role-play, see §§91, 142, 161, 199, 203, 241, 265.)

Guy D. Nave Jr.

247. PAUL'S RHETORIC IN PHILEMON

In discussing scholarly interpretations of Paul's letter to Philemon, the dynamics of ancient slavery, and the rhetoric of the letter, some students do not understand why Paul may have been indirect in his request to Philemon that he take back his slave Onesimus without punishment. This exercise helps students distinguish between the propriety of indirect requests and the impropriety of direct requests, as well as the social-cultural conventions underlying Paul's approach.

After forming small groups, students consider the following scenario: A first-year college student, while working in the audiovisual room, has borrowed (stolen?) an expensive camcorder and broken it, is afraid of the consequences, and quits going to work. Instead, the student goes to an English professor whom she admires and explains the seriousness of the situation. Because the English professor knows that the supervisor could submit a complaint and require the student to withdraw from college, the English professor does not want to antagonize the student's supervisor. The English professor, sick with the flu and unable to visit the supervisor, can only write a note on the student's behalf to the supervisor. Ask each group to assume the role of the English professor and draft a letter on behalf of the student that will be addressed to the student's supervisor. Each group is to consider what would convince the supervisor to have a change of heart and what cautions the English professor must take. (Many students have recalled their own experiences where they could not openly voice their opinions and had to make it appear that those in power had had the idea first. In other situations, a mediator had to be careful not to make matters worse for the person with less power. How might these cases be similar to or different from that of Onesimus's situation?)

Because it is not always possible to anticipate how the recipient will respond to a letter, the exercise may be continued by having the groups exchange letters and assess the likelihood that they will prove successful. For an excellent discussion—and accessible to undergraduates—of the dynamics at play in the case of Onesimus, see J. M. G. Barclay, "Paul, Philemon and the Dilemma of Christian Slave-Ownership," *NTS* 37 (1991): 161–86.

Emily R. Cheney

248. THE PASTORAL EPISTLES

In part because most scholars agree that Paul did not write the Pastoral Epistles (1–2 Timothy and Titus), these letters are frequently omitted from introductory New Testament courses. Nonetheless, these letters are some of the most important letters in the New Testament because they reveal the *modus operandi* of the proto-orthodox church. The Pastorals exhibit, in very early forms, three elements that helped proto-orthodoxy gain supremacy. First, they show the development of clergy: they are addressed to leaders of communities and not to the communities themselves. Second, they refer to "the teaching," a creed or body of knowledge held as authoritative by all Christians. Third, these letters show the movement toward developing a specifically Christian Scripture. Although Christians did not claim a particular group of books as authoritative until the end of the second century, the words of Jesus and the apostles were deemed authoritative much earlier.

When I teach the Pastorals, I have several goals in mind. First, I want students to think about the issue of pseudepigraphy. Second, I want students to attempt to place these letters in a particular theological milieu. Third, I want students to understand the role of these epistles in the battle between "heresy" and "orthodoxy."

I typically begin the discussion by asking students about ancient forgeries: do they think the New Testament could contain pseudepigraphical writings? Students are often hesitant to suggest that a book in the Bible might be a forgery. It can be helpful, therefore, to point out that we have evidence that Christians did indeed forge writings. Tertullian exposes the *Acts of Thecla* as a presbyter's forgery done "for the love of Paul" (*Bapt.* 17). The New Testament itself alludes to forgeries: in 2 Thess 2:1–2, "Paul" warns against letters that claim to be from him, and 2 Thess 3:17 suggests that Christians needed a way to determine the authenticity of Pauline letters. Another question to pose to students is "Why might a person forge a document?" Students may respond by suggesting that a person could receive financial or personal gain—thus, the forgery may be attributed to greed. Forgeries could also be produced out of respect for the supposed author. Or, an author might claim his work to have been the product of a famous person in order to have his opinions receive greater respect or authority. Finally, you might ask students to reflect for a moment on how they feel about the possibility that forgeries could exist in the New Testament.

Rather than simply asserting scholarly views of authorship, I try to show students why most scholars doubt the authenticity of these epistles. An inductive writing assignment to prepare for this topic is to have them read 1 Timothy and comment on the ways the letter sounds like Paul and the ways it does not. Since most students will not know Greek, I ask my students to concentrate on some of the theological and ecclesiological differences. For example, does the false teaching described in 1 Tim 1:4–7 sound at all like Christian teachings that Paul combats elsewhere (in particular, Galatians and 1 Corinthians)? Do "myths and endless genealogies" sound like mid-first-century heresies? Or is this more reminiscent of the second-century Gnostic heresy (though perhaps an early form)? How do students reconcile 1 Tim 2 with Paul's other teachings about women in the church (e.g., 1 Cor 11)? Would the same author condone women praying and prophesying in church *and* condemn their participation in church (1 Tim 2:8–15)? In the undisputed letters, does Paul ever mention clerical positions? Isn't it Paul himself who is in charge of his churches (cf. the greetings of Paul's undisputed letters versus the greetings in the Pastoral Epistles)? Do the requirements for the office of bishop (3:1), deacon (3:8), and presbyter ("elder": 5:17 sound like Pauline injunctions?

At this point a number of post-canonical writings can be of use to students who are trying to understand the place of the Pastorals in Christian history. Having just observed the lack of clerical hierarchy in the undisputed Pauline writings, have students turn to the letters of Ignatius (available widely on the Internet). In particular, Ignatius' letters *To the Philadelphians* 1–8; *To the Ephesians* 2–6; *To the Magnesians* 4, 6–7, 13; *To the Trallians* 1–3, 7; and *To the Smyrnaeans* 8–9 reveal mid-second-century orthodox concerns over apostolic succession (these excerpts are short enough to have students read in class as you discuss the issue). Here Ignatius asserts the special role of the bishop in Christian hierarchy and his importance in establishing the rule of faith. If we fit the Pastoral Epistles somewhere in between Paul and Ignatius, how do they reflect the rise of church offices? After Paul's death, why might clerical hierarchies be an important safeguard to orthodoxy?

Through this textual analysis, I strive to show students how we can read Christian history in the text of the New Testament. In addition, I hope that students will see that the significance of the Pastorals does not reside solely in its claims to Pauline authorship.

L. Stephanie Cobb

249. GUIDE TO A HAPPY HOME

To prepare for a study of early Christian household codes, I give students the following assignment: Read carefully the following New Testament "household codes": Col 3:18–4:1; Eph 5:21–33; 1 Tim 2:8–15; and 1 Pet 2:18–3:8. Think about the three key pairings that are repeated in such codes—husbands and wives; parents (or specifically mother or father) and children; masters and slaves. For each of the passages listed above, trace which of the pairings receives the most emphasis, which of the parties receives the lengthiest instruction, where (if anywhere) the advice seems unexpected or unconventional. Be prepared to share the results of your examination with your classmates.

When students arrive in class, however, we begin, not with one of the New Testament passages, but with a provocative excerpt from a women's magazine from the 1950s. In a column titled "The good wife's guide" from *Housekeeping Monthly* (13 May 1955), wives were offered advice about how to treat their husbands' return from work in the evening. The following points are representative:

✦ Greet him with a warm smile and show sincerity in your desire to please him.

✦ Listen to him. You may have a dozen important things to tell him, but the moment of his arrival is not the time. Let him talk first—remember, his topics of conversation are more important than yours.

✦ Make the evening his. Never complain if he comes home late or goes out to dinner or other places of entertainment without you. Instead, try to understand his world of strain and pressure and his very real need to be at home and relax.

✦ Your goal: Try to make sure your home is a place of peace, order, and tranquility where your husband can renew himself in body and spirit.

✦ Don't ask him questions about his actions or question his judgment or integrity. Remember, he is the master of the house and as such will always exercise his will with fairness and truthfulness. You have no right to question him.

✦ A good wife always knows her place.

These points can prompt a lively small-group writing exercise. I provide a copy of this excerpt from "The good wife's guide" to students and then give them a choice of two tasks to undertake in a group of three to five people. The group must either (1) compose six corresponding points for a "good husband's guide"; or (2) compose a six-point "Guide" for contemporary members of households to describe behaviors and attitudes that would contribute to worthwhile goals for a home. The "guides" may be humorous or even indignant, but must also show thought and care. I set clear time limits for the exercise so that it stays fast-paced and engaging. How fully the small groups can share their efforts with the entire class depends on the class size and the time available, but hearing some sample is important. In the discussion that follows, I mention that the point of the exercise is not to trivialize the efforts people have made to think through issues of marriage and household in times and places removed from ours, but to analyze difference, acknowledging that fifty years hence, our efforts to articulate roles, behaviors, and goals for members of a household will likely also seem outmoded and marked by transparent investments in power and privilege. The opening exercise then sets the stage for examining several of the New Testament "household codes," attentive to differences among them, and to the cultural conventions that they variously enforce or resist.

B. Diane Wudel

250. EXPLORING INTERTEXTURE
IN THE LETTER TO THE HEBREWS

An essential aspect of exegesis involves the study of how a biblical passage uses older traditions and texts in the invention of a new word to communities of faith. New Testament authors often explicitly quote a text from the Jewish Scriptures, or more subtly introduce the language of identifiable passages from those Scriptures and other extra-canonical Jewish texts, or refer to traditions and conversations carried on within Jewish or Greco-Roman streams of culture. In these cases, the older text (whether a literary or epigraphic text, an oral tradition, or some piece of culturally transmitted knowledge) contributes meaning to the new text, while the new text guides the hearers' or readers' understanding of the older text.

I regularly use the following exercise in order to teach students the basic skills of analyzing intertexture, introduce them to the complexities of the text types of the Jewish Scriptural tradition, encourage them to wrestle with the questions that arise as they uncover the differences between New Testament "quotation" and Jewish scriptural "original," and direct them to keep asking the rhetorical-critical questions about the "payoff" that the author believes interaction with these traditions will yield for the new situation to which it is applied.

In this exercise, students are divided into working groups of three or four around a passage. Hebrews 10:1–10 and 10:26–39 are extremely rich texts for this exercise since they open up many of the issues named above. The passage can be divided up (e.g., Heb 10:26–27, 28–31, 35–39 [10:32–34 is devoid of overt intertexture with Jewish Scripture]) and parceled out among the groups. It is frequently helpful to have several small groups working at the same time on each block of text to enhance conversation when the full class is reconvened. Instruct each group to address the following questions to their passage (Note: It would be helpful for each group to have access to the Septuagint version or to an English translation of the Septuagint of the First Testament texts invoked by the author of Hebrews):

N
E
W

T
E
S
T
A
M
E
N
T

1. Relying on the notes in a good study Bible or the margins of the Nestle-Aland Greek New Testament, what Jewish Scriptural resources does the author appeal to overtly or weave in more subtly in the invention of the passage?

2. How are those Scriptures introduced into the text? Are they explicitly quoted or merely woven in? Do they involve importing actual words from another text or referring to some story or information that can be found in another text?

3. At what points does a quotation or recontextualized string of words differ from the original text as represented in the Masoretic Text tradition (the Hebrew text underlying virtually all English translations)? How can you account for the differences (an accident of translation? reliance on a different text tradition, like the Septuagint? the author's alteration of the text for purposes of his or her own?)?

4. What do these Jewish scriptural resources contribute to the content of the author's argument and to the hearers' experience of the new text? (Another way to get at this would be to ask what would be lost if the author did not quote or refer to that older tradition.) How does the author use (and shape) these resources to advance specific goals?

An "answer key" for this exercise can be found in D. A. deSilva, *An Introduction to the New Testament: Contexts, Methods & Ministry Formation* (Downers Grove, IL: InterVarsity, 2004), 802–6. If you want to give your students extra practice exploring the use of resources from the Jewish Scriptures in the New Testament, consider assigning a short paper in which they pose the four sets of questions above to Heb 1:1–13; 4:1–11; or 10:1–10.

For the purposes of the exercise, students are looking only at the First Testament, since most if not all will have brought a Bible to class. Repeating the exercise in another session with Jude or 2 Peter would provide an opportunity to explore how extracanonical Jewish texts and traditions inform the New Testament authors, always yielding fruitful conversations about the implications for canon and inspiration. Vernon K. Robbins (*The Tapestry of Early Christian Discourse* [London: Routledge, 1996], 232–35) extends an important challenge not to neglect Greco-Roman intertextual resources when studying the New Testament. Repeating the exercise with the birth narrative in Luke or with a number of passages in Revelation widens the circle admirably to include intertextual interaction between the New Testament and Greco-Roman "texts" available to readers of literary texts, inscriptions, coins, and monuments expressing Roman imperial ideology.

David A. deSilva

251. THE GREAT CLOUD OF WITNESSES IN HEBREWS 11

Although teaching survey courses that cover the entire Bible can be challenging for both students and professors, one of the benefits of such courses is the ability to make connections between the Old and New Testaments. It can be especially gratifying when students begin to realize how much the New Testament builds upon and presupposes a level of familiarity with the Old Testament. Close and careful readings of the New Testament may lead students to discover, however, that the ways the New Testament uses the Old Testament are not always what we might expect. At this point, it becomes natural for the professor to introduce conversations about intertextuality and canonical readings of the Bible. Richard Hays' *Echoes of Scripture in the Letters of Paul* (New Haven: Yale University Press, 1989) provides a thorough discussion of the creative and sometimes puzzling ways Paul takes up certain Old Testament passages.

A focused exercise to illustrate one way the New Testament uses the Old Testament involves working through the list of the "great cloud of witnesses" in Heb 11. I ask students to take the characters mentioned by name (or by description) in this chapter and evaluate two things: first, what was said about that individual; and second, the author's choice of that individual. Finally, I ask them to write their own version of a list which names examples of faith.

The first evaluative task is a good opportunity for students to review the Old Testament chapters where the individual characters were introduced. I encourage them to notice what is highlighted about the character in Hebrews and what is left out. I also ask them to pay attention to explanatory clauses and any editorializing. A particularly interesting description of Moses' faith is found in manuscripts which add to 11:23 that Moses killed the Egyptian by faith because he observed the humiliation of the Israelites. I invite students to respond to that claim, asking them if they understand Moses' murder in Exod 2:11–12 as an act of faith.

The second evaluative task is interested in asking why certain characters are included in Heb 11. Some of the individuals are not obvious candidates for models of faith, especially when their whole story is reviewed. For example, although Abraham's story is marked by his faith and belief (Gen 12:4; 15:6; 22:12), it also includes moments of weakness and doubt, as when he fears for his life and tells his wife to pretend she is his sister (Gen 12:11–13; 20:11–13), or when he wonders about God's promise (Gen 15:2–3, 8; 17:17–18). In my experience, students have frequently protested at the inclusion of Jephthah as an example of faith (Heb 11:32). Why not his daughter instead? At this point, with the superficial reading of the characters' stories in question, students can discover one of the Old Testament's powerful theological affirmations: God's ability to

N E W   T E S T A M E N T

work through and within and despite human frailty. Moreover, Heb 11 ends by asserting that even though these characters were commended for their faith, they do not receive the promise. As the author explains, "God had provided something better so that they would not, apart from us, be made perfect" (Heb 11:40). In their humanness and doubt, these examples of faith become witnesses not to their own faith, but to the one who is "the pioneer and perfecter of the faith" (Heb 12:2).

In the final part of this exercise, I ask students to write their own personal version of Heb 11. Which biblical characters inspire them? Which Old Testament stories do they think exemplify faith? If a student sees Jephthah's daughter as a better example of faith than Jephthah, then that student would substitute the daughter for the father. As they list their own great cloud of witnesses, they are asked to explain which biblical characters they would choose, and what they would say about each character. One student affirmed Delilah as an example of persistence and faithfulness to her people. Modifications to this exercise could include asking students to write a list that has the same number of women named as Hebrews has for men, or asking them to write a list that would include extrabiblical characters.

Sara Koenig

252. ANTICHRISTS AND LITTLE CHILDREN: IMAGINING THE JOHANNINE EPISTLES

The Johannine epistles provide an opportunity to introduce students to the different and sometimes competing interpretive traditions within early Christianity. By having students participate in an exercise in which they read the epistles alongside of the prologue to the Gospel of John and selections from the *Acts of John,* students imagine these later letters as a response to a docetic reading of the Gospel within the Johannine faith community. This class allows students to see how the epistles present only one side of the issue at hand, as well as to experience, through imagination, some of the difficulties early Christians must have faced as the tradition solidified.

This teaching strategy builds upon two basic assumptions. First, I assume that there existed something of a "Johannine Community" or at least a strand of early Christianity that privileged the traditions associated with the Beloved Disciple, the author of the Gospel of John. Second, this strategy assumes that a leader within this community wrote the Johannine epistles sometime after the Gospel was written.

In preparation for class students read 1, 2, and 3 John and perhaps a short secondary source. To guide their reading, I instruct the students to imagine why the author feels compelled to write these letters and to pay special attention to how the letters, especially 2 John, employ the term "antichrist." I also ask them to make note of any "echoes" of the Gospel in 1 John.

I start class by asking the students to characterize the beliefs of the "antichrist," according to the epistles. Students should note the description of antichrist in 2 John, which reads, "...those who do not confess that Jesus Christ has come in the flesh; any such person is the deceiver and the antichrist!" (v. 7 NRSV). This verse provides our entry point into imagining the scenario that the epistles address. Students are then asked to describe how the epistles echo the Gospel. Students should note, among other things, the allusions to the Johannine prologue in 1 John 1:1: "We declare to you what was from *the beginning*." This observation serves as a starting point for the class activity, since the students will formulate two very different interpretations of the prologue.

After this opening I break the class into small groups and give each group a copy of the Johannine prologue and excerpts from the *Acts of John* (in J. K. Elliot, ed., *The Apocryphal New Testament* [Oxford: Clarendon], 303–47). I give the students portions of the *Acts of John* that describe the "polymorphous" Christ (87–93) and recount Christ's explanation of his crucifixion (97, 99–100). The latter excerpt describes Jesus coming to John while his body hangs on the cross in order to console John and to explain to him the significance of the cross. The excerpts essentially reflect the viewpoint which 2 John claims to be characteristic of an "antichrist." Before having the groups read these, I explain that the *Acts of John* is a late second-century writing, although it presents itself as being written by John.

The groups are instructed to read the texts together and then to imagine themselves as part of the Johannine Community. The members of one group are instructed to imagine themselves as those individuals being characterized negatively in the epistles—the "antichrists." Their task is to develop a reasonable case for interpreting the prologue of John in a way that is consistent with the *Acts of John*. How might an interpretation of the prologue lead to the view of Jesus articulated in this apocryphal writing? This group prepares to explain and defend the position that the epistles appear to redress. The members of the other group are asked to be the "little children" described in 1 John (2:1). Having heard from the author of 1 John, they are asked to offer an interpretation of the Johannine prologue consistent with the views presented in the epistles. This second group is also asked to use the epistles to decide whether or not it will allow the members of the other group to remain within the community.

In other words, this group is asked to resolve 1 John's polemical language (e.g., 2:18–25; 3:15–17) with its assertion that "God is love" (4:8).

When the groups reconvene, the "antichrists" present their understanding of the Johannine prologue first. I encourage them to use the first person to inhabit their roles. Following this, the second group offers its perspective on the prologue. This group also presents and explains its decision about whether or not the others, the antichrists, should be allowed to remain in the community. I give the members of the antichrist group an opportunity to respond.

After the groups present their positions, I ask the class to consider what they have learned through this exercise. What does this exercise teach you about the Johannine epistles? What does this exercise teach you about early Christianity? What does this exercise teach you about the process of interpreting biblical texts? Ideally, students begin to see the complexity of early Christianity and begin to wonder about the "antichrists" whose perspectives are only hinted at within the canon.

Lynn R. Huber

Revelation

253. THE SYMBOLISM OF THE APOCALYPSE THROUGH POLITICAL CARTOONS

When I teach the book of Revelation, I use a variety of political cartoons to illustrate the different sorts of symbolism and caricature found in the book, as well as to suggest that our understanding of and sympathy for Revelation may be hampered without a knowledge of the circumstances that lie behind it. To those ends, I use a series of political cartoons to suggest how the symbolism of the Apocalypse works. These cartoons have been gathered from the local newspaper, as well as from national magazines. There are also published collections and histories of political cartoons that provide useful historical examples such as R. Fischer, *Those Damned Pictures: Explorations in American Political Cartoon Art* (North Haven, Conn.: Archon, 1996), as well as archives available on the Internet (e.g., http://www.cagle.com/; http://www.politicalcartoons.com/).

First, I use some cartoons in which familiar "stock" symbols appear, such as Uncle Sam for the United States or the donkey and elephant for political parties. I also have some cartoons that use symbols with which my students are not likely to be familiar. Such cartoons can be found in foreign newspapers or journals. A second sort of cartoon that I find useful is one in which a figure is portrayed with certain features greatly exaggerated. So, if a national leader has a particularly large nose or ears, distinctive hair, or other noteworthy features, these are typically exaggerated by artists. For example, the national deficit is sometimes portrayed as a bloated glutton, gorging himself on ever more food. Together these cartoons illustrate the way in which artists use well known cultural symbols, or caricature what they see, in order to score a particular point.

A third set of useful cartoons consists of cartoons which make an editorial comment on recent current events. Particularly useful are cartoons that portray a current event in terms of another well known story, person, or event. In 1967, for example, *Time* magazine nominated for its (then) "Man of the Year" award President Lyndon Johnson as King Lear. In order to understand the "cartoon," one has to know the tragic story of Lear—and how he evoked the plummeting popularity of Johnson during the years of the Vietnam War. It is, therefore, also these cartoons that most typically evoke our own response, "I don't get it," when we are unfamiliar with one aspect of the cartoon, or with the events or persons being portrayed in the cartoon.

I start by trying to use some fairly recent cartoons that students are likely to grasp immediately (at least if they are at all up on current events!). Then I gradually move into events in the more distant past, of which they may or may not have some memory. Then I use some cartoons from foreign papers that illustrate events with which they are likely to be completely unfamiliar. My aim is to have them see that the symbolism of Revelation may seem opaque today, but that it was not designed to be so to its original readers. The purpose of the symbolism is not to conceal, but to reveal, and to do so with a particular slant on things—and, as I note as well, a particular slant on a *political* situation.

One cartoon I use portrays a skull and crossbones, and the caption reads, "May God have mercy on our souls." In order to understand this cartoon, it helps to know three things: (1) that the skull and crossbones symbolize death; (2) that the prayer repeated here reflects the traditional words of a judge to a condemned prisoner, "May God have mercy on your soul"; (3) the occasion that evoked the cartoon (the lifting of the ban on the death penalty in 1976). Students may know some of the symbolism and the reference to events; but the more they know, the more the cartoon makes sense—whether or not they agree with the sentiments of the cartoonist. One particularly apropos cartoon is that of a large dragon swallowing up a city. I ask students to guess what this is about before showing them the caption, "Today, Hong Kong ... " The cartoon depicts China, symbolized by the dragon, "swallowing up" Hong Kong as it reverted to Chinese governance in 1997. The caption underscores the cartoonist's foreboding about China's possible designs on accumulating territory and power.

It is useful to have some cartoons that the students are likely to "get" immediately—hence, these need to be kept updated—as well as some with which they are likely to have little or no familiarity. This emphasizes the point that Revelation may have been understood by its first readers in a way it cannot be grasped by later generations. One can also note, of course, that political cartoons are not "neutral"; they make decided and emphatic judgments, using hyperbole and symbolism—exactly the way in which the book of Revelation delivers its warnings about the Roman Empire and the burgeoning imperial cult in the Asian provinces. Students may not necessarily like or agree with the cartoons, but they begin to understand how the apocalyptic symbolism of Revelation might convey its multifaceted message.

Marianne Meye Thompson

254. SYMBOLISM IN REVELATION

As is well known, the symbolism in Revelation challenges the most skilled interpreter. To illustrate the point that symbols can and have been understood in a myriad of ways, I turn to the most famous of symbols, 666 (13:18), and declare to the class that what they have suspected all semester is, in fact, true: I am the beast. I then write on the board a variety of information about myself: my full name, birth date, telephone number, driver's license number, anniversary date, number and names of children, and so forth. and I ask students to do some "creative math" to "prove" that I am 666, the beast. They perform operations similar to those of interpreters throughout the centuries—counting the letters in names, taking the sum of this number and dividing by that number, taking nines and turning them upside down. Students enjoy the opportunity to demonstrate that the teacher is the personification of evil! More importantly, they see that the interpretation of symbols is limited only by the reader's imagination and creativity. This exercise can be followed by offering examples of how 666 has been understood, from Nero to Ronald Wilson Reagan (six letters in each of his names). Encouraging students to do their own creative readings helps them to understand the implications of prophetic readings of Revelation.

To extend the exercise, I ask students to read the description of the beast in 13:11–17 and indicate how it applies to me, since, if I am 666, then I should also fit these other details. Students have proven quite creative here (I may be more susceptible since, as is often pointed out, it is called the *Mark* of the Beast), but the task is much harder. This aspect of the exercise helps students to appreciate the tricky and complicated nature of the process, namely, how difficult it is to be consistent. Interpreters regularly select only that information which seems to apply to their desired reading, ignoring the descriptions that do not correspond as well.

Although the exercise challenges a prophetic reading of Revelation's symbols, I do not dismiss this approach altogether. Specifically, I conclude the discussion by asking students to compare Matthew's fulfillment quotations (studied in some detail earlier) with prophetic interpretations of Revelation. I ask them to consider the implications of the fact that other New Testament writers have (re)appropriated ancient scriptures for their contemporary Christian context.

Mark Roncace

255. ANCIENT APOCALYPTIC
AND ITS CONTEMPORARY EXPRESSIONS

For this exercise on apocalyptic and its contemporary expressions, I start with the well-known definition of apocalyptic proposed by the Apocalypse Group of the Society of Biblical Literature's Genre Project: "'Apocalypse' is a genre of revelatory literature with a narrative framework, in which a revelation is mediated by an otherworldly being to a human recipient, disclosing a transcendent reality which is both temporal, insofar as it envisages eschatological salvation, and spatial insofar as it involves another, supernatural world" (quoted in M. G. Reddish, ed., *Apocalyptic Literatures: A Reader* [Nashville: Abingdon, 1990], 20). Students are assigned to search the Internet to find a non-Christian or nonreligious apocalyptic website. In a class presentation of no more than ten minutes, each student describes (1) the Internet search strategy that came up with the site; (2) whether the site is religious (if so, what religious tradition does it purport to represent) or nonreligious (if nonreligious, is it scientific, science fiction, political, or some other type); and (3) using the definition given above, why the site is apocalyptic in nature.

Student presentations should address the following issues related to website evaluation: (1) Who wrote the page and can you contact him or her? (2) What is the purpose of the website and why was it produced? (3) What qualifications does the website producer have? (4) What is the domain of the website (e.g., "edu" or "com")? (5) What institution or community (if any) publishes this document? (6) When was the site produced? When was it last updated? Are there any dead links? (7) Does the author provide e-mail or other contact information? (8) What goals or objectives does this page meet? (9) How detailed is the information? (10) Could the page or site be ironic (a satire or a spoof)?

The goal of this exercise is three-fold: (1) to have students experience the wide variety of apocalyptic traditions on the World Wide Web today; (2) to be able to identify apocalyptic motifs when they see them—even if they are outside of an explicitly Christian tradition; and (3) to be able to critically evaluate a website.

A valuable portal that can take students in many different directions in connection with apocalyptic is at http://www.geocities.com/ athens/ oracle/9941/.

Jeffrey L. Staley

256. APOCALYPTIC LITERATURE
AND TESTIMONIES OF SUFFERING

While most colleges offer Daniel or Revelation as separate classes, the books share common themes which makes studying them together very valuable. First, since Daniel is not part of the Prophets but the Writings, the book can be discussed as a story of wisdom or heroic characters. Revelation is also not just a prophetic book, but one that involves heroic characters. In both books the ones who resist their "Babylons" and remain faithful, even at the threat of death, engage in a spiritual battle between good and evil. Both books also treat the themes of endurance and suffering with hope of redemption, justice, and vindication (Dan 12:2–4; Rev 20:4).

Both Daniel and Revelation, of course, also belong in the category of apocalyptic literature. According to John J. Collins (*The Apocalyptic Imagination: An Introduction to Jewish Apocalyptic Literature* [2nd ed.; Grand Rapids: Eerdmans, 1998], 5), this style of writing has three basic concerns: (1) a crisis experienced by the community; (2) comfort and hope provided by the text or author; and (3) a reminder that there is divine authority. While I am able to illustrate to students the crises of the early communities I have found that there can be little connection between student and text as long as they are emotionally removed from this crisis. Finding comfort in the text therefore becomes a form of mental gymnastics. The class is also further distanced if they do not struggle with the issue that God saved the faithful from death in one book (Daniel) but not always in the other (Revelation).

I have found that the introduction of testimonies from those who experience emotional pain has been a powerful tool for involving the students in the search to find comfort in the text. The students are given chances to empathize with suffering by reading written testimonies and listening to personal testimonies of people who have experienced the loss of a child to a disease, abuse or molestation by a family member, suffering and struggle in their own recoveries, debilitating accidents themselves or in their family, and other tragic events. These individuals also share their feelings about their faith, God, and their faith communities. In many of the printed stories I respect the privacy of these women and make changes to names, cities, and schools. I also use taped presentations of abuse survivors. The Faith Trust Institute in Seattle has produced video programs which include stories from abuse survivors (www.faithtrustinstitute.org). Their videos *Broken Vows* and *Wings Like a Dove* provide excellent stories from women who are survivors of spousal abuse. (Similar television programs may also be used.) After the students read or watch these testimonies, I spend a class period in which we put the stories into conversation with the biblical text. I find that students empathize with those sharing the stories and also discuss their own questions and uncertainties about faith and God. Those who wish to use this practice in their teachings can find the best resources by contacting domestic violence and abuse agencies, counselors, or social workers in their area. Survivors who are willing to talk with the class can provide the most powerful testimonies. This connection makes many students more attentive to the ways texts like Daniel and Revelation provide comfort and answers to question posed by those in crisis.

As we proceed through Daniel and Revelation I refer back to these testimonies and encourage the students to articulate the ways in which comfort and hope are offered in these writings. Students who have heard these stories have expressed anger, grief, and doubts about God, Satan, and their outlook on life. In many ways they approach Revelation as did its first readers: they are people seeking comfort and hope in a world that faces crisis, pain, suffering, and fear.

The students also come to understand the apocalyptic perspective that God is in control whether individuals suffer or not. The issue has never been whether or not we enjoy life, but, rather, what does a suffering messiah say to his followers? In both books the students read that endurance, faithfulness, and an end to suffering are the messages of comfort (Dan 3:17–18; 12:12; Rev 2:7, 10; 6:9–11; 13:10). In surveys the students indicate that they are motivated through these testimonies to seek comfort from the text and help others find the same comfort in Daniel and Revelation. I find that the students have learned how to apply concepts in seemingly esoteric apocalyptic texts to those suffering today, with a desire to provide comfort and hope to those facing their modern "Babylons."

Ron Clark

257. TEACHING THE BOOK OF REVELATION AS A SCREEN PLAY

The goal of this small-group assignment is to help students grapple with the visionary aspects of apocalyptic imagery; that is, that the Revelation is not so much to be "read" as it is to be "seen." It is also designed to move students from literal appropriation of the extreme images of Revelation toward viewing the visions as extravagant metaphors for much more mundane aspects of normal human living. The preparation for this assignment includes a lecture on the generic features of apocalyptic literature and an initial exploration of uses of extreme images as metaphors which shock us out of complacency with familiar, yet problematic, aspects of living.

Each small group is constituted as a production team making a short film from one (or part of one) of the self-contained visions (e.g., the six seals of 6:1–17 or the scarlet woman of 17:1–15). In phase one of the assignment they can imagine their film with unlimited special effects. They produce storyboards, grappling with pictorial representation of what they see, and sketch out plot and action, scene changes, use of flashbacks and any other film techniques they would wish to incorporate. It becomes quickly apparent to them that these visions cannot be taken literally. Most groups come to understand that a special effects film of the revelatory visions would have to be classified as a fantasy film, not a film dealing with real life.

In phase two the production teams must struggle with shooting a more conventional film. Taking the images as metaphors of something more common, they are charged with producing a film about "real life." They now operate on a limited budget and special effects are mostly out of reach. The content of the visions must be conveyed using live actors portraying believable people in real world settings. Working storyboards, plot, and action for this is more difficult, and I usually have to work with the groups helping them to "see" in different ways. But groups have come up with very interesting portrayals. One group decided to film the shopping frenzies in American malls at Christmas, with cut away shots to starving or disease-ridden children in impoverished third world countries. This was their rendition of the "fornication" of the nations with Babylon in Rev 18:1–20 and its trade in "human lives." (At the other end of the spectrum there once was a group I had to move away from doing an X-rated version of the fornication/harlot themes.) The various visions of seven plagues are often conveyed by students as environmental disasters, genetic engineering of viruses or microbes gone awry, or the effects of prolonged warfare and arms races on humanity.

Debriefing the assignment allows the class to begin more serious attempts to understand what the extravagance of the visions might have conveyed for John and his church. It also opens lively discussion of the various ways in which the images have been appropriated by the church across the centuries and ways in which we might "envision" meaning in them for ourselves. (For a similar exercise, see §182.)

Thomas W. Martin

258. REVELATION AND POP CULTURE

As much as any book in the New Testament, the book of Revelation has worked its way into American popular culture. From horror films to "goth" music to grassroots religion to role-playing games, apocalyptic imagery has spread throughout almost every form of art and entertainment.

Students' familiarity with apocalypticism provides an entrée into the Apocalypse of John. For a class on Revelation, I begin by asking the students to name any cultural allusions to Revelation—songs, books, movies, social movements—that they have encountered. Usually the list will include items such as the movie *Armageddon*, the Branch Davidians, the *Left Behind* book series, and Marilyn Manson. After listing these on the board, I will then ask the students to explain the popularity of one or more of these phenomena. Responses will vary depending on the list, but usually the students will talk about the thrill of horror, the desire to know secrets, the fascination with evil, the paranoia of certain religious groups, and the urge for good to triumph over evil.

The class discussion then moves to Revelation itself, and I ask the students to think of it in terms of the cultural phenomena they have just explained. To bridge the gap between pop culture and the Bible, I highlight how Revelation works as an exciting drama in which the reader vicariously experiences the triumph of good over evil by learning secrets about the future. I ask the students to compare the social function of, for instance, apocalyptic movies to the social function of Revelation. One might also try a thought experiment in which students imagine the character of a religious group taking one of these contemporary texts as scripture.

If the students can first see Revelation alongside contemporary cultural works, they are more receptive to seeing it within the categories used by scholars. Any discussion of ancient apocalyptic literature will inevitably include a treatment of dualism. Certainly many passages in Revelation point to dualistic thinking (2:19–29; 14:1–13), and students generally do not have difficulty grasping this concept. The implications of dualistic thinking, however, gain a greater force if students think about a group such as the Branch Davidians. Similarly students understand readily that Revelation includes the triumph of good over evil. But Revelation's particular method of describing this battle becomes sharper if it is compared to a movie such as *The Omen*. The battle scenes of Rev 12 and 19 depict a swift and decisive victory for God's forces without much resistance from the armies of the beast and dragon. In most horror movies, forces of evil tend to have the upper hand, and if good does triumph, it does so only barely.

Many topics besides dualism and the battle of good versus evil also work well in a comparative discussion of Revelation and popular culture.

(The social setting of persecuted peoples and the accompanying crisis of meaning come to mind.) This inductive approach to the traditional scholarly concerns is frequently more effective than a simple lecture detailing the characteristics of the apocalyptic genre.

Kyle Keefer

259. PASCAL ON READING REVELATION

Some students love the Book of Revelation, some hate it, but most approach it with the mindset described by Pascal:

> We never keep to the present ... [W]e dream of times that are not and blindly flee the only one that is. The fact is that the present usually hurts. We thrust it out of sight because it distresses us .... We try to give it the support of the future, and think how we are going to arrange things over which we have no control for a time we can never be sure of reaching. Let each of us examine his thoughts; he will find them wholly concerned with the past or the future .... Thus we never actually live, but hope to live, and since we are always planning how to be happy, it is inevitable that we should never be so. (*Pensées* [trans. A. J. Krailsheimer; Harmondsworth: Penguin, 1995], 43)

To help students gain a better appreciation for the medium of Revelation and its message, I have them discuss in groups the ways in which Pascal's words apply to their own personal experience of reading the book.

A key theme that emerges is the tendency to use the book to feel some sense of control over our futures by providing a map for coming events. Recent best-sellers like the *Left Behind* novels tend to value Revelation chiefly as a source of detailed knowledge of the future, communicated through a secret code of symbols that only the correct interpretive scheme can unlock. Borrowing Pascal's language, reading Revelation in this way may keep us "always planning how we shall one day be in Christ's presence sometime in the future," but not actually being in God's presence in the present moment.

I offer three different strategies to help students avoid a futuristic fixation when they read Revelation. (1) Have students read through the book as a whole. This will make it more difficult to pick out a few symbols and speculate obsessively on their "true" meaning. If time permits, one may read aloud the entire book in class, without pausing for rest or for discussion. This perhaps recreates the way the original auditors experienced the seer's work. An alternative is to have students stage their own similar reading outside class or to listen to a "books on tape" version of Revelation. In either case, an interesting follow-up exercise is to assign a short paper describing the student's response to this experience of the work. (2) Assign a simple research paper in which students choose one or more symbols and report to the class on the many different ways in which the symbol(s) have been interpreted. Especially with the resources available in the Internet, there should be no shortage of interesting material. The fact that most of it will be outlandish is not a problem. (An additional resource is the brief history of interpretation in D. Guthrie, *The Relevance of John's Apocalypse* [Grand Rapids: Eerdmans, 1987].) When students see for themselves that throughout history there have been literally dozens of calculations for the date of the second coming and interpretations of the real identity of "the whore of Babylon" or "the beast," and that it is impossible for all of these interpretations to be correct, many see the possibility that none of them are correct. In this way, they become more wary and are less likely to believe that the latest deciphering (unlike all the mistaken interpretations of the past centuries) is finally "the" correct one. (3) Have students re-read the text, this time imagining themselves as first-century believers undergoing persecution by the Romans. A short paper might have them consider the value of Revelation in such a context and how they might respond to the various symbols.

After reviewing their findings and a survey of historical trends in interpreting Revelation, I ask the class to reflect on the difference between the elaborate schemes and debates of dispensational theology and the simple affirmation that the future is in God's hands, not ours, as found in such texts as Acts 1:7 ("It is not for you to know the times and the seasons"), the Apostles' Creed ("I believe in ... the resurrection of the body, and the life everlasting. Amen."), and the Nicene Creed ("And we look for the resurrection of the dead, and the life of the world to come. Amen.").

Roger Newell

260. INTRODUCING REVELATION THROUGH THE VISUAL ARTS

The various artistic representations of John receiving his "apocalypse" provide a unique opportunity for introducing students to the book of Revelation. Viewing a variety of these images in class, along with a close reading of Rev 1:1–11, serves as a creative way to initiate student thinking about Revelation's authorship, setting, and function. The use of visual arts to teach Revelation underscores the visual nature of this book, which John describes as an account of "all that he saw" (1:2), as well as highlighting the ways that a reader's social location shapes her interpretation. While this type of exercise demands ample preparation and flexibility on the instructor's part, I find that it engages students and inspires them to begin thinking about important interpretive issues.

Preparing for a class that employs the visual arts requires a good deal of forethought. The process of gathering a sufficient number of images, anywhere from five to fifteen, and preparing them to view in class may take over a week, depending upon whether one shows images with a computer and data projector or with a conventional slide projector. Locating images to show also requires a fair amount of time, although numerous images are available on the Internet (see especially the web site constructed by Felix Just at http://myweb.lmu.edu/fjust/Revelation-Art.htm). Useful print resources include Nancy Grubb's *Revelations: Art of the Apocalypse* (New York: Abbeville, 1997) and Frances Carey's *Apocalypse and the Shape of Things to Come* (London: British Museum, 1999). It is important to include citations for all works. I typically include the work's title, artist, medium, date, provenance, and current location (on the slide and on the list I compile for students).

A variety of different images allows students think about the different ways Revelation's authorship and setting can be understood. Some images that I have found fruitful for discussion include Hans Memling's *St. John's Altarpiece* (available in Grubb, *Revelations*), Titian's *Saint John the Evangelist on Patmos* (www.nga.gov), the chain of communication illustrated in the medieval commentary Beatus la Seu d'Urgell (http://casal.upc.es/~ramon25/beatus/pictures.htm), and Myrtice West's painting *Who Dare Record the Word of God* (Myrtice West et. al., *Wonders to Behold: The Visionary Art of Myrtice West* [Memphis: Mustang, 1999).

One resource for images of Revelation is the medieval apocalypse "cycles," manuscripts that include anywhere from fifteen to almost one hundred illustrations of the text. Albrecht Dürer's woodcuts of Revelation, likely the most famous apocalypse cycle, include an illustration of John being boiled in oil by the Emperor Domitian (http://camel.conncoll.edu/visual/Durer-prints/index.html). A number of the medieval cycles include similar images, reflecting a tradition about the Apostle John recounted by Tertullian. These images, which identify John the Seer with the apostle, provide a way to introduce students to the issue of Revelation's authorship. Likewise, these images raise the important issue of whether or not Revelation assumes a context of oppression at the hands of the Roman Empire. Other apocalypse cycles that are generally available include the *Cloister's Apocalypse* (select folios available for classroom use at http://myweb.lmu.edu/fjust/CloistersApocalypse.htm) and the different versions of Beatus's commentary on the Apocalypse.

NEW TESTAMENT

Students prepare for this class by reading the first chapter of Revelation and a secondary source about the book's authorship and provenance. In class I ask a student to read Rev 1:1–11 aloud before we view the images. I encourage the students to envision the events of the text as they hear it being read aloud. After this, I show the slides two times. The first time I show the slides, I ask the students to withhold their comments, but to think about how the different images resonate with their initial thoughts about the events of Rev 1:1–11. I encourage the students to make notations about their favorite images on their handouts. The second time I show the slides, I invite students to comment upon the relationship between the images and the text of Revelation. As we view the images, I use questions to prompt the students to articulate how the images "read" Revelation. How do the images interpret the character of John? How do the images represent John's experience? Is it a vision, a dream, an altered state, or an otherworldly experience? What does this suggest about the nature of the apocalypse? Does the artwork represent the text of the Apocalypse, perhaps as a book or a scroll that Christ or an angel hands to John? Or does John himself write the events he witnesses? What does this suggest about John's role in crafting Revelation? As students answer these questions in relation to the artwork, I offer key points about these issues.

Using visual art to introduce Revelation also encourages students to start thinking about how the text employs vision language as a tool for persuasion. As John describes what he "saw," the audience is encouraged to envision the events he describes. John literally tries to capture his audience's imagination and thereby persuade his audience to see reality from his perspective. In spite of John's efforts, the artistic renderings allow students to see and begin to understand how different interpreters imagine Revelation in different ways.

Lynn R. Huber

261. THE BOOK OF REVELATION: A BOARD GAME?

In this assignment, students are asked to develop a board game based on the book of Revelation. Although this exercise initially strikes students as easy and entertaining, it actually challenges their creativity, ingenuity, and understanding of the text. They quickly learn that to create a board game, their knowledge of the text has to be substantial, and that to integrate material from the Apocalypse, they must read the text many times, think about it, organize its themes and symbols, and then translate these into a dynamic, well-executed game—not so easy! In my experience, Revelation works well for this assignment because it is so rich in imagery, symbolism, and repetition. It can also be an intimidating text, and this exercise ensures that students will read the book thoroughly. That much having been said, many books from both the Hebrew Bible and the New Testament can be substituted for the book of Revelation. I have seen wonderful student games based on Genesis, Exodus, and Job.

Whatever book you choose as a base for this assignment, students are free to generate any type of game they wish: a trivia game like *Trivial Pursuit,* a pursuit or chance game like *Chutes and Ladders,* a strategy game (*Risk, Monopoly*), a role playing game (*Dungeons and Dragons*), or a board-based card game (*Magic: The Gathering*). Students may model the game on a better-known game (students have submitted games to me like "Hellopoly" and "Chutes and Lazarus"), but they must create their own boards and cards. Bear in mind that some types of games require less skill to create than others. Trivia games, most notably, generate simple, "trivial" questions based on the book ("How many candlesticks?" "How many horsemen?"). Although these trivia questions require the least amount of critical analysis of text, at least students must make their way through the text and read it well enough to pose and answer their own questions.

In order to head off some problems in advance, I suggest that the instructor distribute with this assignment a grading rubric. Since, for instance, trivia games are the simplest to create, these might not receive grades as high as a complex strategy game; it is best to be clear about your expectations in advance. Bear in mind, too, that students can sometime create a very attractive game which nevertheless lacks solid content, or which reflects poor or ill-considered treatments of the biblical book on which it is based. These students can be disappointed if they receive a low grade, since they are proud of how attractive their game looks; thus the rubric should reflect which percentage of the grade is devoted to aesthetics and which portion to content, analysis, or interpretation of the Bible. A clear grading rubric can help remind the students to use their ingenuity and critical judgment along with the sense of humor. Other categories for evaluation should be its playability, originality, effective use of text, and understanding of the complexity of the text. All games must also work properly and logically.

Students must submit with their games a set of instructions and a written rationale to explain the relationship between the text and the game. The instructions ensure that you (and others) will know how to play the game, which will be necessary to evaluate it properly. It also requires the student to test it out in advance and to think through the mechanics of gaming.

It can be fun to have each student present his or her game to the class, and to break students into groups to play the games for the final class of the semester. Part of the assignment might also be a peer review in which students play the games together in small groups and then evaluate them. Finally, at the end of the semester, the instructor might consider donating the games—or the best of them—to a local church for their Sunday School activities.

Nicola Denzey

262. ALL THE SENSES OF REVELATION 8: EXPERIENCING FIRST-CENTURY RHETORICAL STRATEGIES

We live in a commercial world where media advertising urges, cajoles, and convinces consumers to buy more. This advertising uses powerful rhetorical tools to change human behavior. Biblical writings also use powerful rhetorical tools to change human behavior. Students, however, often miss the power of a written text when the Bible sits "passively" on their desk. To bring the rhetorical power of a biblical writing to life, this exercise invites students to enact the multi-sensory language of Rev 8 in a participatory reading.

I begin the class with a brief introduction to the historical context, the literary structure, and the symbolic world of the book of Revelation. Then I divide the students into seven groups and assign each group a church from chapters 2–3. Working together, their first task is to develop a profile of their "church" identity. We return to this profile at the end of the exercise, but beginning this way frames the exercise in the context of a first-century Asia Minor "church."

The next few steps are preparation for the participatory reading. The class turns to Rev 8, a chapter that engages all five senses, and everyone takes out a sheet of paper. I ask all the students to read chapter 8 and to write down any language that appeals to the first sense: sight. This is a rather long list. (To speed up the process, you could have some students responsible for reading 8:1–5, others for 8:6–9, and others for 8:10–13. The point is not reading comprehension, but to compile a cumulative list of the sensory language.) The students then pass their papers to their left, (and receive one from their right), and write down all the language that appeals to the second sense: hearing. This is another long list. They pass the papers again and record the language appealing to smell; pass the papers and record the language of touch; pass the papers and record the language of taste. Now every student has in front of them a list that contains the notes of four colleagues and herself. After the simple act of passing the papers, I remind the class that interpretation is a collective enterprise, building on and contributing to the observations of others.

I now divide the students into five groups. Each group is responsible for creating some of the experiences pertaining to one sense. For example, those who have "sight" flash the classroom lights to "make" lightning for Rev 8:5; those who have "hearing" imitate a trumpet (8:7). You may want to bring two props to class: incense (Rev 8:3–5) and something bitter to eat (Rev 8:11), such as coffee beans or bitter chocolate. Students responsible for the taste of wormwood can pass out the bitter coffee or chocolate. Because the tasks are uneven and class sizes differ, you may want to experiment with distributing the tasks.

The class is now ready to stage a participatory reading of the passage. I remind the students that first-century texts were written to be read aloud, and that the early Christians listening to the Seer's Revelation may have been about the size of our class (fifteen to thirty people) gathered together in one house. To imitate the shape of a first-century floor-plan, we arrange the desks to form a triclinium and central hallway, with the students sitting close together. One student takes the role of the Seer, or scribe of the house church, and reads the text aloud while the other students enact the sensory images of Rev 8. The act of reading becomes a bit like a *Rocky Horror* film skit, where all the listeners participate in the reading by creating the sounds, sights, smells, taste, and feel of the language as it happens. And this is precisely the point: the Seer uses language to create a multi-sensory experience that involves the listeners in a revelation as it unfolds in "real time."

After reading the text once with the multi-sensory prompts from students, we discuss the experience. We have now seen, heard, smelled, tasted, and touched the richness of this passage. What images stand out? What is the over-all effect of the sensory language on the hearer (to confuse, excite, repel, invite, confront, over-stimulate)? Does the experience change their understanding of Revelation?

Finally, I ask the students to relate our experience of the sensory language to the Seer's rhetorical strategy for the seven churches. The students reconvene in their original seven (church) groups and recall their profiles: some churches are suffering; others are losing faith; others are actively collaborating with the Empire. Now, imagining they are members of their church in Asia Minor, they listen (eyes closed) while I read a scene of heavenly worship (e.g., Rev 4:1–11). They are to pay attention to the Seer's sensory language, images, and tone, and to think about how the language addresses the situation of their first-century church. What does the Seer want them to do? How will they respond? How might a full sensory experience of heavenly worship (Rev 14:1–5; 19; 21) or beastly worship (Rev

13:1–18) support, challenge, or re-shape their church identity? Is the Seer combating the power of the Roman Empire by creating an alternative experience? If so, how? If there is time, the students share their observations with the class. We note the different ways the Seer's language speaks to the churches and discuss his goal for each group.

By evoking the sensory experience of Rev 8, students can connect the rhetorical and imaginative power of the spoken word to the effect of that word on community behavior. The book of Revelation aims to (re)shape communities by creating an experience that involves all of the senses and by creating a vision of the world that is more compelling than that of the Roman Empire. A broader discussion of rhetorical power might include the PBS documentary *Merchants of Cool,* which presents today's advertising "empire" as a modern equivalent to the political, economic, and social power of Rome.

Julia Lambert Fogg

263. READING REVELATION 14 AND 19: TRAMPLING OUT THE VINTAGE

The book of Revelation gets a lot of play in popular religious culture. As a result many students have preconceptions as to how the book is to be read, while the literary prejudice of others may result in a desire to avoid the book altogether. An exercise for teaching Revelation that I have found useful involves showing how its apocalyptic language has engaged American history. I have come to use Julia Ward Howe's "Battle Hymn of the Republic" as an example of using a text from Revelation to interpret a particular period of history, in this case the Civil War. Howe is said to have written the hymn in 1861 after visiting a Union Army camp near Washington, D.C. The text of the hymn is readily available and can be accessed on the web (www.cyberhymnal.org).

The class period begins with a recording of the "Battle Hymn of the Republic" playing as students enter. It is also possible to use clips from Ken Burns' PBS series *The Civil War* or another Civil War film. I begin the exercise itself by distributing handouts with the text of the hymn. I may also project the text of the hymn in front of the class. The students then work in pairs. First they read Rev 14:14–20 and 19:11–16. The working groups are asked to summarize each of the passages and then identify similarities between those sections of chapters 14 and 19. Both passages use the wine press as a metaphor for the wrath of God. Chapter 14 pictures an angel of judgment harvesting grapes as a judgment image.

After identifying the images and symbols in the Revelation texts, the class is then asked to look at the first stanza of the hymn and find similarities in language with the biblical texts. It is relatively easy to identify the source of phrases like "trampling out the vintage" or "terrible swift sword." Less obvious is the phrase "grapes of wrath." Howe is constructing a new phrase from the biblical text.

So, I ask, what is Julia Ward Howe talking about? When her poem is given historical context, it seems evident that she is talking about the Union Army. Howe furthermore uses language from Revelation to describe what she believes to be the Union Army's significance. The reader might conclude that Howe regards the Union Army as an agent of God's judgment much as the divine army described in Rev 19. Discussion questions might include the following: Is Howe understanding her own time and experience in apocalyptic terms or does she see the words of Revelation being fulfilled in her own time? What happens when we see a direct correspondence between the words of Revelation and the times in which we live?

As a counterpoint to the "Battle Hymn of the Republic," it is interesting to contrast the biblical imagery and reflection on divine judgment in Lincoln's second inaugural delivered on March 4, 1865. Howe wrote with an apocalyptic zeal at the start of the conflict knowing which army was God's army. Lincoln, writing near the end is less certain about whose side God was on. Lincoln does draw a connection between the events of the war and God's judgment using such biblical texts as Matt 18:7: "Woe unto the world because of offences" (KJV). Lincoln, however, sees all, both North and South, as being under God's righteous judgment (Ps 19:9). Unlike an interpreter of apocalyptic who claims to know God's intentions and judgments, Lincoln regards God's ultimate intentions as unknowable.

This exercise illumines how a particular biblical text was read at a particular time and place. By analyzing that situation, perhaps it is possible to gain a perspective on similar contemporary readings of apocalyptic texts. A final aside: I sometimes prod the class into actually singing the hymn.

Philip A. Quanbeck II

Varia

264. THE NEW TESTAMENT CANON
(UNITY AND DIVERSITY)

Theology students often assume that the New Testament canons of various Christian traditions are identical. This assumption seems to be based on their observation of whatever happens to be between the two covers of their own Bible. The problem, however, is that many of my students' comprehension of canon is predicated on a western Protestant understanding. This exercise aims not to address the formation of the New Testament canon but rather to increase their appreciation for the diversity of canons within the Christian tradition.

I begin the discussion by giving students a comparison sheet of different canonical collections that existed in the fourth century C.E. This sheet contains lists from Vaticanus, Sinaiticus, Alexandrinus, and the Peshitta (G. M. Hahneman, *The Muratorian Fragment and the Development of Canon* [Oxford: Clarendon, 1992], 164). The value of this portion of the exercise is to demonstrate that there was not always consensus on what constituted an authoritative set of Christian writings in antiquity. I follow this with another comparison sheet listing three canons: Protestant, Roman Catholic, and the Ethiopic (narrow). With the exception of the apocrypha, students will be able to see the close similarities between the Protestant and Roman lists. The Ethiopic list with its 87 books helps to demonstrate the diversity among Christian traditions today. I ask students to begin to formulate in their minds what kind of criteria they would use to determine which canon is more authentic or authoritative than the others.

The second step is to introduce them to some facts about canon in other traditions. For instance, the Syrian Orthodox tradition continues to reject 2 Peter, 2 and 3 John, Jude, and Revelation. For the Syrian Church and for all Eastern Churches connected with the Syrian, the Peshitta holds the same authority as the Septuagint and is honored with far more authority than the Hebrew original. In the Greek Orthodox Church, the Bible comprises all of the books accepted by the Roman Catholic Church,

406

plus 1 Esdras, the Prayer of Manasseh, Psalm 151, and 3 Maccabees. Also important to note is that in the Orthodox faith it is the Septuagint (Greek) rather than the Masoretic Text (Hebrew) which comprises the Old Testament canon. A simple comparison of Isa 7:13–17 reveals just one of the numerous differences that exist between these two textual traditions. This provides an opportunity to point out that most of the Old Testament quotations in the New Testament are from some form of the Septuagint and not a Hebrew text. I then ask students to consider how Protestants should respond to such a conundrum, namely, that our understanding of Old Testament passages fulfilled in the New Testament are not drawn from the textual tradition we claim to be authoritative, that is, the Hebrew text.

The third step is to ask students whether we should now consider reopening the canon in response to the diversity that exists, and to the fact that new books have been discovered that are not in our canon. At this point I provide them with a portion from the *Gospel of Thomas*. I find that sayings 1, 2, 12, 13, 20, 54, 104, and 114 are the most helpful. Having read these sections I ask students if we should add *Thomas* to the New Testament canon, especially since it contains some sayings that are very similar to those found in the Synoptic Gospels. Usually there is universal rejection of this suggestion due to the late discovery of *Thomas* and its original exclusion. However, I counter their argument by pointing out that John 7:53–8:11 does not appear in any of our manuscripts prior to the tenth century and that it has not always been located in John, but has also been found after Luke 21:38 (B. M. Metzger, *A Textual Commentary on the New Testament* [London: United Bible Society, 2002], 187–89). I ask students why it is we want to exclude *Thomas* if we are willing to include this passage in John? Are we being consistent?

A consensus is rarely reached and it is probably better that one not be attempted. This is not an issue that can be sorted out in a half-hour discussion. The major accomplishment of the exercise is to help students to begin thinking in new ways about what constitutes canon and how their own tradition can relate to the variety of other traditions that exist. (For another exercise on canon, see §35.)

John Byron

265. JOURNALING IN CHARACTER

Many students in introductory courses do not appreciate the significance that an awareness of the Greco-Roman and Jewish environments in which the New Testament writings were produced has for understanding and interpreting the texts. Indeed, students tend to ignore dissimilarities between the first- and twenty-first-century contexts and between ancient readers and themselves. Journaling in character is one way to overcome students' reluctance to engage issues of historical context and to help them grasp the "otherness" of the first-century world and its inhabitants. Journaling challenges students to imagine how they might have read and reacted to the New Testament literature had they lived during that time. In addition to broadening their perspectives by attempting to view the New Testament through other lenses, the insights that students gain from this exercise enhance classroom discussions in valuable ways beyond the usual lecture on historical backgrounds.

To begin, each student develops a written character study that profiles the personality of an (imaginary) unhistorical figure from the New Testament era, for example, a Galilean woman, a Zealot, a Roman soldier, or a wealthy Judean landowner. This task involves learning as much as possible about the person's geographical, ethnic, and social locations, values, life issues, and typical experiences, and then describing the character in a short paper. To assist students in gathering information about the political, social, cultural, religious, philosophical, and literary environment in which their fictitious character lived as well as about private life in general in the first century, we assign as background reading Paul Veyne's *A History of Private Life: From Pagan Rome to Byzantium* (ed. P. Veyne; trans. A. Goldhammer; vol. 1 of *A History of Private Life*, ed. P. Ariès and G. Duby; Cambridge, Mass.: Belknap, 1987).

Students then keep a journal as they read the New Testament, responding to the texts as if they were the person they have described. From their location within the household, for example, how might such ordinary people have understood, reflected on, and reacted to a given writing? After that, students compare their speculations about the texts' impact on and implications for their character with its effects on them as twenty-first-century readers. When we discuss historical issues relating to each New Testament text, the results of the journaling exercise not only become an important part of the conversation, but also bring the historical context alive for students in ways that simply reading secondary sources cannot. It is not unusual, however, for students to conflate the personal lives and experiences of the characters they have constructed with their own. Although this is impossible to avoid entirely, it is helpful to remind students throughout the project not to ignore the disparity between their historical experience and that of their first-century alter egos as they read, reflect, and journal. For each major block of material (i.e., Gospels and Acts, Paul's letters, deuteropauline letters and Pastoral Epistles, General Epistles, Revelation), we have the students summarize their journals, which we collect and review. (For other exercises involving role-play, see §§91, 142, 161, 199, 203, 241, 246.)

Stanley P. Saunders
William Sanger Campbell

266. ONE-SOURCE SOCIAL HISTORY

The move from reading a text to reconstructing a community is a perilous journey. It is, however, a project that students are eager to undertake. People want to know: What were early Christians like? What did they do? What did these folk believe? Who would join an early church? Too often, however, the way students answer such questions is to project their own experiences into the past. It is as though Pauline Christians attended the First Baptist Church of Corinth. As a way to help counter millennia worth of assumptions and simultaneously to illustrate how critical scholarship can help recover social history, I devised the following project for my introductory courses.

I have students read a fairly short passage from a first- or second-century text. My favorite for this exercise is the letter from the Roman governor Pliny to the Emperor Trajan regarding Pliny's encounters with early Christians. Canonical texts such as selections from 1 Thessalonians or Acts could also work. After students read the text in question, I ask them to pretend that this is the first time they have ever heard the word "Christian" and that the text they just read is the only extant source describing this group. Using only this one text, how could we reconstruct what these people might have been like?

At first, I have students simply list different places where the text could help us understand who was part of this community, what they did, and what they believed. Then we examine passages where we may have accidentally projected our own assumptions into the text (e.g., when the text mentioned "Jesus" we assumed we knew exactly which Jesus—it was a common name—the document was talking about). Next, we discuss the author's own agenda and how this might affect the accuracy of any given data point. Finally, after having identified some of our own biases and those of the author, we categorize our evidence by probability. Given only the data from this document, what do we feel fairly confident saying about this group, what do we think is likely but we are not sure about, what do we have little support for one way or another?

Our conclusions help us better understand early Christianity. I think, however, that more important than the end product is the method. My goal is to illustrate (albeit in a simplified fashion) how scholars go about reconstructing social history and to invite students to participate in this process.

Michael Philip Penn

267. WOMEN AND EARLY CHRISTIANITY

After having examined Paul's letters, the Gospels, Acts, the deuteropauline letters, the Pastoral Epistles, the *Acts of Paul and Thecla,* and the *Passion of Perpetua and Felicitas,* I assign this exercise on women in early Christianity. It is important to have already discussed the patriarchal framework that existed within Judaism and throughout Greco-Roman society. The objective of the exercise is to consider the various factors that might have contributed to the conflicting portrayals of the status and role of women found in the New Testament. We conclude by reflecting on what, if anything, we can say about the ongoing tension regarding the status and role of women within Christianity.

I distribute the following list of questions the class session before we discuss them:

1. According to the Gospels, it appears that women were actively involved in every aspect and phase of Jesus' life and ministry. Read Mark 14:3–9; 15:40–41; Matt 27:55–56; 28:1–10; Luke 2:21–24, 36–38; 8:1–3; 10:38–42; 24:1–12; John 4:39–42; 20:11–18; Acts 1:12–14; 9:36–37. What do these verses suggest about the involvement of women in the ministry of Jesus?

2. Read Luke 2:21–24, 36–38, as well as Matt 28:1–8; Luke 24:10–12; John 20:11–18. Who were the first ones to preach about Jesus and to announce his resurrection?

3. The earliest Christian churches met in houses. Read Acts 12:6–17; 16:11–40. As you read, pay attention to the two leading female figures in these passages. Why is it that Peter, as well as Paul and Silas, go to the homes of these two women when they are released from prison? I ask the students to express what role they think these women had in the "house churches" that were meeting in their homes.

4. Read Rom 16:1–15. How many female names are listed? What are the roles of the women listed (Note: Prisca in vv. 3–5 is the same person as Priscilla in Acts 18:18, 24–26)? What do these verses suggest about the involvement of women in the Pauline ministry?

5. Read Phil 4:2–3; 1 Cor 1:11; 16:19; Phlm 2. Do these verses suggest anything about the involvement of women in the Pauline ministry?

6. What does 1 Cor 11:2–5 (cf. Acts 21:7–9) suggest about the involvement of women within the worship service?

7. How do the depictions of women in the "household codes" (i.e., Col 3:18–4:1; Eph 5:21–6:9; 1 Pet 2:18–3:7) and the Pastoral Epistles (esp. 1 Tim 2:8–15; Tit 2:3–5) compare to the depiction of women in the other verses we have studied? How does 1 Cor 14:33–36 compare to 1 Cor 11:5? How do we determine which of these views and practices should be followed today?

I exhort the students to be mindful of the fact that the depictions of women in the verses they are reading have been written by men. I ask them to consider what impact that might have on the depictions and also to consider how the events in those depictions would have fit within the patriarchal framework of the society at that time. In class, I put the students in small groups to discuss their answers. After about fifteen to twenty minutes, I ask the groups to share their responses with the class. In relation to Jesus, two issues frequently arise: (1) What do the texts mean when they say the women "served" and "provided for" Jesus? (2) While it appears women may have been involved in Jesus' ministry, he never selected women as members of his "inner circle." Regarding the first question, I point out that the word translated "served" and "provided for" (*diakonēs*) is the same word that is used in Jesus' statement, "the Son of Man came not to be served but to serve" (Matt 20:28). I also mention that the word is from the same root as the words translated "servant/minister" (*diakonos*) and "ministry" (*diakonia*). With regard to the second comment, I respond by challenging the notion that there were no female members of Jesus' "inner circle." I point out the reference in Acts 2:14, which mentions the presence of women when the apostles gathered to select a replacement for Judas. If time permits, one may also refer to passages from the *Gospel of Mary* (6.1–3; 10.3–4, 7–10) that challenge common conceptions about the role of women in the ministry of Jesus.

When we turn to the passages from Paul, I point out that the list in Rom 16 makes reference to ten women (Phoebe, Prisca, Mary, Junia, Tryphaena, Tryphosa, Persis, the mother of Rufus, Julia, and the sister of Nereus) and that the word translated "deacon" for Phoebe is usually translated "servant/minister" when used for men. Why might modern translators choose to translate it as "deacon" for Phoebe? I then mention how later manuscripts of Romans changed the spelling of "Junia" to "Junias." We conclude by placing the "household codes" in conversation with the other passages we have considered. I ask them to speculate on why there would have been a need to give these types of instructions. What relationship might have existed between these documents and the *Acts of Paul and Thecla* and the *Passion of Perpetua and Felicitas*? We end by discussing possible implications for our understanding the role of women in the church today. (For other exercises on women in biblical texts, see §§50, 55, 154, 191, 226, 242.)

Guy D. Nave Jr.

268. THE IMPORTANCE OF THE SEPTUAGINT

A concrete way to emphasize the importance of the Septuagint (LXX) for understanding the New Testament is to have students examine Paul's scripture citations in Rom 15:7–21. The biggest point to be made is that Paul's use of Scripture is very much dependent on the particular version of the passages found in the LXX—Paul's use of the passages would make little sense if the Hebrew texts were used. The exercise may also be used with texts from virtually every book in the New Testament as well as to discuss the basic importance of the translation of Hebrew texts into Greek, general issues of translating ancient languages into contemporary ones, problems that arise from the scribal transmission of texts, and the importance of literary context in interpretation and translation.

I have done the following exercise both by dividing the class into small groups to work on it and by walking the class through it as a whole. First, I have the students read Rom 15:7–21 and summarize Paul's main point in the passage, especially in vv. 7–13 and 20–21 (where the LXX citations occur). This is usually pretty easy for them: Paul's point has to do with the inclusion of the Gentiles. I then ask them why Paul quotes Scripture as a part of this argument. This is also pretty easy: All the passages that Paul quotes refer to the inclusion of the Gentiles; it is thus important for Paul's mission to the Gentiles that he finds the inclusion of the Gentiles foretold in Scripture.

I then provide the students with a handout that covers each of the five scripture passages quoted by Paul in Rom 15:7–21. For each passage I print English translations of: (1) the text as Paul has quoted it, (2) the text as translated from the Hebrew version, and (3) the text as translated from the LXX. (For the LXX, I usually use the Brenton translation.) I ask students to compare Paul's citation with the Hebrew and Greek versions in order to see how close his citation is to each. I then ask them for each passage whether or not Paul's use of the passage would work if he were using a different version of the quoted passage (in particular whether the Hebrew version would work). Of the five passages, Rom 15:10 (=Deut 32:43) jumps out; here the Greek and Hebrew traditions are completely different, and the Hebrew contains nothing of the passage as cited by

Paul. Perceptive students may note that also in Rom 15:12 (=Isa 11:10) and 15:21 (=Isa 52:15b), Paul's use of the text would make much less sense if the Hebrew tradition were used. For the remaining two passages, Romans 15:9b (=Ps 18:49) and 15:11 (=Ps 117:1), the Hebrew and Greek are similar. Having seen these differences, the importance of the LXX generally becomes quite clear to students.

Students invariably notice additional differences, however, and these provide the opportunity to discuss other issues. Always noticed is the fact that the translations of Paul's texts and the LXX texts say "Gentiles" (the latter in Brenton, at least), whereas the translations of the Hebrew texts say "nations" (in the NRSV and most other English translations). Since this will strike students as being just like the other issues related to the differences between the Hebrew and Greek texts, it is worth pointing out that, while the Hebrew *gôyim* and Greek *ethnē* do have some different nuances, this is really an issue of English translation. The translation of "Gentiles" instead of "nations" in Romans results from the context in which Paul has set his scripture citations. Students may also note such differences as "LORD" versus "Lord" or more subtle differences in translations (e.g., "understand" versus "contemplate" versus "consider" in Rom 15:21/Isa 52:15) that may bring up issues of Hebrew/Greek/English translation. Finally, students may also note places where Paul's text differs from both the Hebrew and Greek (e.g., Rom 15:9b), and this may be used to discuss issues of manuscript traditions and text criticism, as well as the possibility that Paul may have intentionally altered his sources.

Scott Shauf

269. GREEK ATHLETES AND ATHLETIC ANALOGIES IN THE NEW TESTAMENT

Many students feel that the ideas and images used by the biblical writers are too foreign to be understood by or relevant to contemporary readers. Because so many students are involved in or at least familiar with sports, it can therefore be profitable to alert them to the ways in which New Testament writers make frequent use of athletic analogies and metaphors in their discussion of religious subject matter. While there is much in common between athletic metaphors used in ancient Greece and those now in use, there are also many differences. Representations of athletes in art tell us about the specific images which may be been evoked in the minds of Hellenistic audiences by allusions to contests or training. Collections of images may be found in M. B. Poliakoff, *Combat Sports in the Ancient World: Compe-*

tition, Violence, and Culture (New Haven: Yale University Press, 1987). Images can also be found by searching the word "athlete" in the sculpture and vase catalogs at the Perseus Digital Library (www.perseus.tufts.edu /cache/perscoll_Greco-Roman.html). The firsthand witness of activities in stadia and gymnasia would certainly have reinforced these images. The objection may be raised that Jews and Jewish-Christians would have avoided these social and cultural arenas because of the nudity of athletes and the association of "sacred games" with pagan deities, as 1 and 2 Maccabees attest. However, the polemic of the Maccabean histories in effect testifies to the popularity of the games among Jews.

The athletic analogies in the New Testament are of two types: those which allude to "contests" where athletes compete for prizes and those which allude to athletic training. For example, Paul evokes the image of a footrace when describing his own pursuit of perfection (Phil 3:14) and his apostolic mission (Gal 2:2; Phil 2:16). The writer of 1 Timothy exhorts the reader to "train" for attaining piety, comparing it to the "training" of the body; for toil and "struggle" are involved in both (4:7–10). Such allusions evoke general images that presume only a superficial understanding of athletic competition and training. Moreover, such allusions are commonplaces in the self-descriptions and exhortations of Hellenistic moralists. Therefore, allusions to athletic training or competition may function as figures of speech rather than metaphors that involve visualization. However, there are instances where such allusions are genuine metaphors and have a significant rhetorical function.

In 1 Cor 9:24–27, for example, Paul draws on his audience's direct knowledge of athletic competition—the biennial Isthmian games—as he evokes the image of runners in a stadium. He exhorts them to exercise "complete self-control," as they seek to attain an "imperishable crown." Then he likens himself to a runner who does not run "aimlessly" and a boxer who "does not beat the air." The latter image likely refers to "shadow boxing," a form of training that allowed boxers to avoid injury, but did not make them fit for grueling competition. Paul proceeds to say that he "pummels and subdues" his body, lest he be proven "unfit." Paul's self-description evokes images of athletes in combat sports, such as boxing, wrestling, and the *pankration*. Renowned athletes were regularly depicted in sculptures with scarred faces, disfigured noses, and cauliflower ears. Just as such visible features testify to an athlete's endurance of grueling training and fitness for competition, Paul suggests that his endurance of hardship, which the Corinthians have witnessed (1 Cor 9:12), makes him fit to be an apostle. In this manner, he presents himself as a fitting model of self-control.

Another New Testament text that evokes more than a superficial knowledge of athletic competition in the Hellenistic world is Hebrews

12:1–4. Here the writer exhorts the readers to run the "contest" set before them with perseverance. After presenting Christ as "forerunner and perfecter of faith" through his suffering on the cross, the writer admonishes some in the community for not resisting to the point of blood in their "struggle" against sin. If Christ is the supreme example of struggling and resisting sin "to point of blood," then Christ, who ascended to sit at the right hand of God, is a model of inspiration much in the same way as the Greek athlete, Arrichion. Philostratus's description of Arrichion's death in a *pankration* contest is based on a vase painting (*Imag.* 2.6). After dying in competition, Arrichion is crowned victor and his dusty body is lifted to the land of the Blessed, inspiring some spectators to begin wrestling each another. Unlike later Roman gladiatorial games, Greek combat sports were not intended to be decided by death. However, the brutal nature of the competition, especially in the *pankration*, meant athletes did occasionally die. Thomas Scanlon (*Eros and Greek Athletics* [Oxford: Oxford University Press, 2002]) argues that in many societies those who struggle to the point of death are regarded as leaders. Such people are honored in a manner that inspires others to emulate them. There is reason to believe athletes enjoyed this status in the Hellenistic world, making an analogy between Christ and an athlete quite apt in the context of the Hebrews passage.

Another common type of vase scene depicting athletes helps us to see a connection between Heb 12:1–4 and remarks about divine discipline that follow. We are told that God disciplines like a father (12:7–8) and that those who have been "trained" by enduring pain reap benefits. The reference to weakened limbs regaining their power (12:11–13) might well be taken as an analogy to athletic training. Athletes in the combat sports are often depicted being observed by a clothed figure holding a staff, representing either a game official who would strike a competitor for breaking a rule or a trainer who would strike an athlete to make him more aggressive. Epictetus likens God to an athletic trainer in this regard (*Diatr.* 1. 24.1–2). Picturing God as an athletic trainer in Heb 12:5–13 coheres with the preceding presentation of Christ as the perfecter of faith through his endurance of suffering.

Fruitful discussion may include consideration of the ways in which athletic activity is similar to as well as different from the spiritual endeavors described by the biblical writers. A creative exercise may require students to consider whether the same arguments or exhortations could be written using modern sports analogies (basketball? football? hockey?) without losing the specific point made in the original texts.

Russell B. Sisson

270. NOTIONS OF "THE MESSIAH"
WITHIN FIRST-CENTURY JUDAISM

While the issue of messianic undercurrents and hopes during the Second Temple period arises most naturally in a course on Judaism or as a component of surveying the historical context of the New Testament, I address it early when I teach the gospels and their functions as Christian proclamation. As students consider the contexts to which the gospels were written and what kind of literature the gospels are, I want them to understand that any expectations of what kind of figure the Messiah would be and what he would do varied and did not match the life Jesus lives in the gospels. By familiarizing students with some of the few contemporary Jewish texts that speak of the Messiah, I aim to illustrate that early Christians, when they proclaimed Jesus as Christ, were not appropriating a universally recognized (or perhaps even recognizable at all) image of the Messiah. The points of disconnect between traditions about an expected Messiah and the Christology of the New Testament stimulates students to consider the purposes of the gospels, especially the particular kerygmatic tasks the evangelists were taking up when they announced Jesus to be the Christ. Another pedagogical aim of this exercise is to shine light on the confusion, secrecy, and volatility that surround Jesus and the title Christ in the gospel narratives.

To get a sense of the kinds of messianic expectations that some of Jesus' Jewish contemporaries had, I give students selections from the Old Testament Pseudepigrapha and Qumran literature, texts that usually none of them have seen previously. (Of course, this exercise also provides a good opportunity to address introductory students concerning the nature and functions of apocalyptic, and the community that left the Dead Sea Scrolls.) After offering prefatory comments about Old Testament texts that sparked or fueled hopes for a Davidic or anointed deliverer, I divide students into small groups. Each group is assigned one or more of the following texts: (1) *Psalm of Solomon* 17.21–34; (2) *Psalm of Solomon* 18.5–9; (3) *4 Ezra* 7:26–35; (4) *4 Ezra* 12:31–34; (5) *2 Baruch* 39.3–40.3; (6) *2 Baruch* 72.2–73.4; (7) 1QS 9.9b–11; (8) 1QSa 2.11–22; (9) CD 19.9b–20:1a.

I instruct the groups to read their assigned text(s) and look for places that speak of the "Messiah" or "Anointed One." Each group must come up with answers to these questions:

Who is the deliverer described in the text(s)? How many deliverers are there? What events accompany the coming of this deliverer? What is the deliverer's role? What does he do? How, or by what means, does he accomplish his task(s)? What kinds of people would these images comfort? Of what movies do the scenes in your text(s) remind you? If you were filming these scenes, what music would you choose for a soundtrack?

Once I reconvene the entire class, each group summarizes its text(s) and shares its answers. As the groups report, I interject comments to explain where these writings came from and to frame similarities and contrasts among them. I usually underscore the fact that the texts offer divergent expectations concerning the deliverer's relationship to militancy, Jerusalem, the Gentiles, the Davidic line, and other salient details. We take note that the Qumran literature reflects an expectation of two messiahs, and that no extant pre-Christian texts speak explicitly of "the Messiah" as a healer, teacher of parables, or crucified "suffering servant." All this suggests that the New Testament authors faced a significant challenge in explaining to Jewish audiences how Jesus could possibly be the Christ, and what it could mean that *this particular person* was God's Anointed. When students imagine the additional problem of explaining this title to Gentiles, they see that merely calling Jesus "the Christ" was hardly the sum of early Christian proclamation. The New Testament documents attempt many kerygmatic tasks that require utilizing and reshaping traditions from the theological and cultural repertoires of their audiences.

Matthew L. Skinner

271. USE OF A LEXICON AND THE *ANCHOR BIBLE DICTIONARY*

In order to understand what a word "means" for a particular writer, one must consider a number of things, including the following three elements: (1) lexical definitions, that is, a range of possible meanings for the word in question; (2) cultural milieu, that is, how the word was used or understood in its ancient context; and (3) the word's context within the writing of which it is a part, within other works by the same author, or within the New Testament as a whole. For example, we can expect that Paul and the Gospel of John do not necessarily mean the same thing when they use the word *logos*. The purpose of this homework exercise is to focus on the first two elements with reference to the prologue of the Gospel of John.

Lexical Meaning. Have students look up the word *logos* in these two Greek-English lexicons and list ten to fifteen possible translations of the word: Bauer, Danker, Arndt, and Gingrich, *Greek-English Lexicon of the New Testament and Other Early Christian Literature*, 3rd ed. (Chicago: University of Chicago Press, 2000); and Lidell and Scott, *Intermediate Greek-English Lexicon*, 7th ed. (Oxford: Oxford University Press, 1959).

Contextual meaning (within the cultural milieu). Have students look up the entry for *logos* in the *Anchor Bible Dictionary* and skim through the information found there. They should write down two or three things they learn about the non-biblical uses of the term. It is not necessary to be exhaustive—the purpose of the exercise is to gain an appreciation of the richness of the word and its varieties of meaning within different cultural settings.

What difference does it make? Have students read John 1:1–11 in English. As they read, they should replace "Word" with one of the other definitions or meanings learned from their lexical and contextual study. For class discussion, they are to write a paragraph answering the following question: How would this different definition of *logos* affect your understanding of the prologue to the Gospel of John?

The same exercise could be used with other polyvalent terms (e.g., *deisidaimonia* in Acts 17:22; *eulabeia* in Heb 5:7; *pistis* throughout Paul's letters).

Audrey West

272. NON-CANONICAL WRITINGS

Since the earliest list of the twenty-seven canonical books in the New Testament dates to 367 C.E., students should know that "orthodox" Christianity developed within a widely divergent Christian movement. In particular, exposing students to other early Christian Gospels, Acts, and Apocalypses can help students understand better these genres and their functions in the Christian movement. In addition, orthodox Christian theology was often established in the midst of debates with rival Christian groups. Thus, recognizing the varieties of early Christianity helps us to understand more fully the books of the New Testament: knowing what an author is *not* saying is often as important as what an author is saying.

Gospels. A particularly useful gospel is the Coptic *Gospel of Thomas.* This is a list of 114 sayings attributed to Jesus. The instructor might briefly discuss the main theological, christological, and soteriological claims of Gnosticism before asking students to read *Thomas* carefully. Two approaches to the text can help students' reading comprehension: (a) Do any of these sayings resemble sayings in the canonical gospels? (b) Pick several sayings and try to understand them based on your understanding of Gnosticism. You may use students' responses to these questions to introduce a discussion of diversity in early Christianity. For example, many of Thomas's sayings are similar to those found in the New Testament. How might students explain this? Interestingly, students often suggest that some of Thomas's sayings seem particularly harsh (e.g., logion 55) and are surprised to learn that they have canonical parallels (Luke 14:26). This can lead to an interesting discussion of how students' theological expectations differ when reading canonical rather than noncanonical texts. As a way to apply their understanding of Gnosticism to *Thomas*, students might attempt to interpret some of the sayings of Jesus (e.g., logia 1, 3, 18, 29, 42, 70, 112, 113–114).

When asked what is different about this gospel compared to the canonical gospels, students may point out that there is no birth story, no miracles, no trial, death, or resurrection story. These elements are central to Christianity today—but they are not a part of Thomas's "good news." What is Jesus' function in the Gnostic worldview? If his death and resurrection do not bring salvation (as Paul vehemently argues), what does? The fact that this work contains only sayings may suggest that Jesus' teachings—that which brings knowledge or gnosis—are themselves salvific.

Finally, *Thomas* provides scholars with an example of a sayings source (like Q is believed to have been). Before its discovery one of the principal objections to the Four-Source Hypothesis as a solution to the Synoptic Problem was the idea that Christians might have produced a gospel comprised only of sayings. Thus, *Thomas* provides evidence that some Christians, at least, found a gospel of sayings to be useful.

Apocryphal Acts. The Apocryphal Acts provide a helpful comparison to the Acts of the Apostles. Students may notice that, in spite of its title, the Acts of the Apostles is not about all the apostles; it is about Peter in the first half and Paul in the second. Thus the existence of Acts that focus on one apostle should not be surprising. I find the Apocryphal Acts most helpful in discussing the role of women in early Christianity. An instructor might distribute copies of the *Acts of Thecla* (a major portion of the *Acts of Paul*) to students before class. Ask students to read 1 Corinthians, 1 Timothy, and the *Acts of Thecla*. How do the views of women differ in each of these texts? In particular, how do these authors envision appropriate roles for women in the church? Another topic on which the Apocryphal Acts sheds light is the role of the family in early Christianity. Again, have students turn to 1 Corinthians, 1 Timothy, and the *Acts of Thecla*. What do these authors teach about marriage and family? What relationships are Christians to have to others? Have students discuss why Christian groups might teach such different things about the earthly family.

Many scholars have suggested that the Apocryphal Acts and the Pastoral Epistles are records of conversations among Christian groups in the post-Pauline period. The author of the *Acts of Paul* and the author of the Pastoral Epistles are staking claim to Paul's teachings on women, marriage, and family, but with extraordinarily different results. You might ask students to write a paper in which they try to account for the ways Paul is appropriated by Christianities of different stripes. Do they find one of the streams of tradition more authentically Pauline than the other? Why? (One particularly helpful resource for this topic is D. R. MacDonald, *The Legend and the Apostle* [Philadelphia: Westminster, 1983].)

Apocalypses. Perhaps more than with Gospels and Acts, introducing students to other apocalypses helps them understand this difficult—and foreign—genre. Students often find Revelation to be inaccessible or even unsettling. Once they see that this was an established genre, both in Judaism and Christianity, they may be able to move away from concerns about mapping the events leading to the end of the world and to concentrate instead on the function of the genre within a historically situated community. Particularly interesting to students is the *Apocalypse of Peter.* An instructor might ask students to read the *Apocalypse of John* and the *Apocalypse of Peter* carefully and try to identify generic elements. What, in other words, do these apocalypses have in common? What is different? Even more importantly, why would this kind of writing be produced? What community would write and read this?

Students may be resistant to the suggestion that Revelation is not a timetable of the coming of the Son of Man. If this is the case, you might ask students to read the book carefully and map out the sequence of events. Can they do this? Can Revelation, in fact, be read linearly? Is it a chronologically-ordered text or is it chaotic? Might an author wish to disorient his reader through an enacted element of the genre—that is, perhaps the community is living in a chaotic time and, thus, the text reflects that instability? In addition, like other Christian texts, these books were written to specific communities at specific times in history. If these apocalypses are predictions of things that are to happen at some point in the distant future, what role did they play in their original communities? Why, in other words, would this kind of literature be produced?

The apocalyptic genre has also been popular in Hollywood of late. Students may enjoy taking their knowledge of this type of literature and analyzing its use in modern films such as *The Matrix, Twelve Monkeys,* or most any of the natural disaster movies, such as *Deep Impact.* Students should pay attention to the movie's use of generic elements.

L. Stephanie Cobb

273. THE ORIGIN AND SOURCE OF SCRIPTURE

The issue of biblical authority often revolves around the question of the "origin" of Scripture. Many students have strong convictions regarding the origin or source of Scripture. The purpose of this exercise is to examine what the authors of Scripture have to say about the origins of their writings. In so doing I hope to provoke the students to consider how their own conception of the origin of Scripture compares with what these authors have to say, as well as to consider why it is important for them to believe what they believe about the origin of Scripture.

I begin the class with the question, "What do you think it means to call the Bible the 'Word of God'?" I summarize on the board as many of the responses as possible and encourage the students to comment on each other's responses. After getting a number of responses on the board, I ask, "Is there a title other than 'Word of God' that you think accurately reflects what the Bible is?" Again, I summarize on the board as many of the responses as possible. I select one title from this list of alternative titles (usually "the word of men" or a similar phrase) and ask what does it mean to call the Bible that alternative title? Again, I summarize the responses on the board.

I then divide the class into three groups. Each group is responsible for a particular text: (1) Luke 1:1–4; (2) 1 Cor 7:10–13; (3) Heb 2:1–4. Each group is to discuss what that particular author says about the *origin* of his information (i.e., how did he get his information? what was the *source* of his knowledge?). After they have discussed what the author says about the origin of his information, they should ask, "If what the authors says about the source of his information is true, does that change the meaning of what he says? Does it change for me the importance of what he says?"

After each group reports its findings, we then read 2 Tim 3:16–17 together. I ask them what they think the author means by "scripture." I point out that the author was not referring to the sixty-six books of the Protestant Bible. I then ask what it means to say Scripture is "inspired" by God. We also discuss what it means to say someone "inspires" us. How might that concept of inspiration affect our understanding of the Scriptures being inspired by God? Does the passage suggest that the author of 2 Timothy is primarily concerned with the "origin" of Scripture or the "function" of Scripture? We conclude by discussing what these four passages together suggest about the origin, meaning, and function of Scripture. Does Scripture itself suggests that origin, meaning, or function is most important? I finish by asking the class which of the three they consider to be most important.

Guy D. Nave Jr.

Index of Biblical Texts

OLD TESTAMENT/HEBREW BIBLE

APOCRYPHA/DEUTEROCANONICAL BOOKS

NEW TESTAMENT

Art Index

Music Index

Film Index

FILM INDEX

Literature Index